Marriage,

Politics,

and Betrayal

Among the

New York Intellectuals

DAVID LASKIN

PARTISANS

SIMON & SCHUSTER
NEW YORK LONDON SYDNEY SINGAPORE

SIMON & SCHUSTER
Rockefeller Center
1230 Avenue of the Americas
New York, NY 10020
Copyright © 2000 by David Laskin
All rights reserved, including the right of reproduction in whole or in part in any form.
SIMON & SCHUSTER *and colophon are registered trademarks of Simon & Schuster, Inc.*

Permissions acknowledgments appear on page 320.

Designed by Karolina Harris
Manufactured in the United States of America

1 3 5 7 9 10 8 6 4 2

Library of Congress Cataloging-in-Publication Data
Laskin, David, date.
Partisans / David Laskin.
p. cm.
Includes bibliographical references (p.   ) and index.
1. American literature—New York (State)—New York—History and criticism. 2. Women
authors, American—New York (State)—New York Biography. 3. Politics and literature—
United States—History—20th century. 4. American literature—Women authors—History
and criticism. 5. American literature—20th century—History and criticism. 6. Intellectu-
als—New York (State)—New York Biography. 7. Partisan Review (New York, N.Y. :
1934)—History. 8. New York (N.Y.)—Intellectual life—20th century. 9. Women intellectu-
als—United States Biography. 10. Authors, American—20th century—Biography. 11. New
York review of books.   I. Title.
PS255.N5L37   2000
810.9'97471'0904—dc21   99-41977   CIP
ISBN 0-684-81565-6

Acknowledgments

I'D LIKE to thank the late Diane Cleaver, my literary agent for several marvelous years, who was in on this book from before the beginning and believed in it absolutely. Bob Bender, my editor at Simon & Schuster, helped me find my true subject and provided valuable commentary, advice, and suggestions at every stage. I want to thank Heide Lange, who succeeded Diane Cleaver as my agent, for attending to all the details and for her infectious enthusiasm.

Many have written about the New York intellectuals before me, and I learned a great deal from their books and articles, as well as from the biographies of the figures in my book. For background, "color," political views, anecdotes, and accounts of old scores to settle, I relied on the memoirs, essays, and reminiscences by members of the circle and their friends. Most valuable to me were the essays of Philip Rahv, the three volumes of Mary McCarthy's memoirs, the correspondence between Mary McCarthy and Hannah Arendt collected and edited by Carol Brightman in the volume *Between Friends; The Beginning of the Journey,* by Diana Trilling; Elizabeth Hardwick's *A View of My Own* and

Seduction and Betrayal; Poets in Their Youth, by Eileen Simpson; *The Truants,* by William Barrett; *Near the Magician,* by Rosalind Wilson; *A Partisan View,* by William Phillips; and *The Intellectual Follies,* by Lionel Abel.

I am especially grateful to all those who shared their memories, thoughts, insights, opinions, and gossip in personal interviews and letters: Daniel Aaron, Lionel Abel, William Alfred, Robert Berueffy, Philip Booth, Carol Brightman, Blair Clark, Lewis Dabney, Barbara Epstein, Jason Epstein, Elizabeth Hardwick, James Robert Hightower, Ann Hulbert, Alfred Kazin, Lotte Kohler, Jerome Kohn, Ruth Schorer Loran, Michael Macdonald, Paul Mariani, Mary Meigs, Frank Parker, William Phillips, Patrick F. Quinn, Jonathan Raban, Arthur Schlesinger, Jr., Eileen Simpson, Cecile Starr, Diana Trilling, Margo Viscusi, Ann Waldron, James West, Reuel Wilson, Marcella Winslow, Dennis Wrong, and Elisabeth Young-Bruehl.

Librarians and staff members at a number of university libraries provided much-appreciated help with archival research. In particular, I'd like to thank Kris McCusker at the Norlin Library, University of Colorado at Boulder; Nancy MacKechnie at the Vassar College Library Special Collections; Dr. Thomas F. Staley, Cathy Henderson, and the staff of the Harry Ransom Humanities Research Center at the University of Texas at Austin; the staff of the Houghton Library at Harvard University; the staff at the Department of Rare Books and Special Collections at the Princeton University Libraries; the staff at the Jean and Alexander Heard Library, Special Collections, Vanderbilt University. I want to thank Nancy Tate Wood for granting me permission to read her parents' letters at the McFarlin Library, University of Tulsa.

The "Centennial Reflections" conference on Edmund Wilson, held at Princeton University on November 17 and 18, 1995, was illuminating in many ways. Of particular use to me were the papers delivered by Paul Berman, Daniel Aaron, and David Remnick.

Many thanks to friends and relatives who put me up and put up with me during my research and interviewing jaunts: my in-laws Kathleen and Lawrence O'Neill, Joyce Hartsfield, Regis Obijiski, Gail Hochman and Michael Levi, Susannah and Wiley Wood, Karen Pennar and Fred Wiegold, and Ann Waldron. I want to thank my parents, Meyer and Leona Laskin, for every kind of support. I'm grateful to my friends Phil Patton, Jack Litewka, Joëlle Delbourgo, Erik Larson, and the late Linda Corrente for listening, commenting, debating, or laughing with me during the long haul of writing this book. Johanna Li at Simon & Schuster did a wonderful job of shepherding the book through the editorial process.

And finally I want to express my love and gratitude to my wife, Kate O'Neill, who heard it all and lived through most of it.

To Kate
my partisan

Contents

Introduction

A career of candor and dissent is not an easy one for a woman; the license is jarring and the dare often forbidding. Such a person needs more confidence and indignation. A great measure of personal attractiveness and a high degree of romantic singularity are necessary to step free of the mundane, the governessy, the threat of earnestness and dryness.

—Elizabeth Hardwick, "Mary McCarthy"
(essay published in *A View of My Own*)

THEY WERE the last generation before feminism. The American women writers and intellectuals who came of age in the strident Depression years before World War II rose to prominence on the strength of work published primarily in *Partisan Review* starting in the 1940s and exercised an enormous if largely unacknowledged cultural authority from the late 1940s to the early 1960s. Our immediate past, our teachers and mentors, they were the writers whose words taught us what we were thinking, the critics and opinion makers whose opinions mattered—mattered to us who came after but most of all to each other: Mary McCarthy, Elizabeth Hardwick, Jean Stafford, Hannah Arendt, Diana Trilling; the women of the so-called New York intellectuals, each one married to a prominent male writer or thinker, yet each attaining considerable prominence in her own right. They were wives and they were writers, and the order in which they arranged these terms for themselves was crucial. For in these final decades before feminism, being a writer and the wife of a writer required terrific powers of concentration, control, denial, silence, subterfuge, sacrifice, and self-punishment. As a generation, these women had unprecedented opportunities—to write, to publish and edit, to stand up as public figures, to marry multiple times and have love affairs as they desired. They were well educated in the liberal arts, as their mothers for the most part had not been. They were professionals, assuming they would work for pay after college, at least until domestic demands became too onerous. And when they began to publish, they were lucky enough to encounter a generation of men who were interested in their minds as well as their bodies and as eager for their work as their love. With men such as Philip Rahv, Robert Lowell, Edmund Wilson, Allen Tate, Lionel Trilling, Randall Jarrell as their editors, partners, critics, advisers, collaborators, lovers, and husbands, these women produced some of the most brilliant, distinctive works of the midcentury: Mary McCarthy's *The Company She Keeps,* Jean Stafford's *The Mountain Lion,* Hannah Arendt's *The Origins of Totalitarianism.* America had known women writers of genius in previous eras—Emily Dickinson, Edith Wharton, and Willa Cather come at once to mind—but they were isolated exceptions who swam against the currents of their time, while these women of the 1940s were truly a literary *generation* who came up together in more or less the same circumstances, who knew one another, sometimes intimately, and who wrote with intense awareness of one another.

This last generation of women before feminism had more power, access, success, and recognition than any group of women had enjoyed before. They were ambitious and, for the most part, skilled at turning their ambitions to their advantage. They lived boldly, winning acclaim by writing better than anyone else, loving freely if not always wisely or happily, shouting down literary and political opponents in a time and place renowned for noisy argument. Consider the twenty-five-year-old Mary McCarthy breaking off an affair with Philip Rahv to marry Edmund Wilson and then satirizing both of them scathingly, scandalously in novels. Consider Jean Stafford publishing a best-selling novel while her ambitious husband, Robert Lowell, had to submit to a small private printing of his first book of poetry or Elizabeth Hardwick exposing the shriveled inanities of Boston in a lacerating essay written while she was presiding over its preeminent literary household. In their accomplishments and nerve, they were the very model of what used to be called "liberated women." Yet they were emphatically not liberated in the way they conducted their private lives, in their assumptions, in their relationships with men, particularly the men they married. At home with their brilliant husbands, they were wives in the old way their mothers had been and proud of it. "Men writers write, that's all they do," Hardwick told an interviewer in 1979, "somehow men have to make it clear, even to themselves, that they can say, 'I am a writer.' Men don't make dinner and keep house as well, so men have more consistency in their writing. . . . I think men are more ambitious than women, don't you?" This is not complaining. This is just the way things were for Hardwick and the women of her generation. Far from resenting their double roles, these women gloried in their domestic control, their superb outlay of energy on several fronts at once, the richness of their experience. They refused to see that they were exceptions. And because they were successful, at least by their own lights, they refused to see the point of feminism. Gender had been no impediment in their own careers, every one of them insisted at various times in her life. So why make such a fuss about it? The consensus of both sexes was that women such as Mary McCarthy, Elizabeth Hardwick, and Hannah Arendt didn't *need* "liberation"—they were liberated enough already. It was precisely this attitude that bound them together, that defined them as a generation—and that eventually doomed them to retreat from the center to the margins of our culture, that "placed" them as targets for those who came after.

My book is about this extraordinary generation of intellectual women and the paths they traveled together—their interconnected lives and careers; their marriages, love affairs, and friendships; their engagement with the culture, with one another, and with the leading male writers and thinkers of their day; their place in American intellectual history; their sense of themselves as women, wives, and writers; their sense of belonging to a generation.

"The nineteenth century came to an end in America only in the 1960s," Janet Malcolm declared in *The Silent Woman,* her book about Sylvia Plath and Ted Hughes. What brought the old regime to an end was feminism. The women's movement was, we can now see looking back, the great social revolution of the late twentieth century, the only revolution (with the possible exception of the civil rights movement) that has brought a tangible, enduring difference to the way we live our lives. The fact that this generation was the last to come of age before the change makes their lives, and especially their marriages, extraordinarily interesting. "Feminism had not emerged," Arthur Schlesinger Jr. told me when I questioned him about how his friend Mary McCarthy managed the conflicting demands of her life and work. "You were used to women who combined involvement in the arts with a love of cooking and being affectionate to men. It did not seem incompatible." The change that feminism ushered in baffled them, the women as much as the men. McCarthy, Stafford, Arendt, and Hardwick all ridiculed "women's lib," as they called it, at various times in their lives. Liberation from what? was their attitude. *They* weren't victims, at least in their own minds. Indeed, they considered themselves comfortable and happy in their relationships with men. Talk to them today, the few who survive, and a shade of peevishness comes into their voices when you ask about feminism, as if the women's movement had spoiled a perfectly sound state of affairs by making men and women ornery and self-conscious about the most elemental things. Why burden these ancient, adequate arrangements with politics? "Mary McCarthy led a life of attaching herself to men, loving them, but she was also a woman of strong convictions," *New York Review of Books* editor Barbara Epstein responded when I asked her whether she considered Mary McCarthy a feminist by example if not by conviction. "Feminism was less an issue with strong women. Mary admitted she learned a hell of a lot from Edmund Wilson. I hope that women are still learning a lot from men without being ashamed of it."

These women all indulged in a kind of willed blindness, a stubborn clinging to old forms that worked or seemed to work for them. "Are women 'the equal' of men?" Hardwick asked rhetorically in a memorable review of Simone de Beauvoir's *The Second Sex*. "This is an embarrassing subject." Embarrassing: unseemly, shaming, inconvenient, unworthy of serious attention, the last refuge of fools and weaklings. And so, rather than risk embarrassment, they avoided or denied the subject as long as they possibly could. Or they dismissed the whole business as just an excuse for shrill, second-rate, disappointed, vindictive women to insist on recognition they didn't deserve. "People with a real gift for writing find the time; people with no talent complain about time," Hardwick told me when I asked her if being a wife had interfered with her writing. The men certainly agreed. "We didn't need feminists, especially radical feminists," *Partisan Review* editor William Phillips insisted when I talked to him. "There was no real discrimination [against women]. With women who wrote, there was no emphasis on the fact that they were women." Editor and publisher Jason Epstein had a slightly earthier take on the position of women in the *Partisan Review* circle: "With women in that crowd, the first thing you thought about was whether they were good-looking and if you could sleep with them. But if a woman could write like a man, that was good enough. You wanted a piece, a piece of writing—you'd forget everything else for a good piece. There was no need to be a feminist in that group. Why would they bother?"

She writes like a man: it was the ultimate compliment you could pay a woman. It meant she belonged, she was one of you, and you could forgive and forget everything else—unless, of course, you were married to her. These women were male-identified, as we say now, with a vengeance. It was an identification purchased at a very high price, for beneath the seeming complacency, the chumminess, the unself-consciousness of relations between the sexes there was often violence, rage, wild frustration, despair, and self-destruction. So many of their marriages ended in divorce. So many of the women (and the men) became alcoholics. So many were beaten, abused, deceived, betrayed, bested, and debased by the men they were involved with. So many dreamed of—or went ahead and took—revenge, both in word and in deed, and especially in word written for publication.

And still they failed or refused to "get" it. Yet "liberation" came anyway, willy-nilly, in a rising, crashing wave that left them stranded. It is no coincidence that the preeminence and authority of this crowd waned during the late 1960s. The Vietnam War, the New Left, and Black Power cut their politics to shreds; the women's movement undermined their social and sexual arrangements. Assumptions that had worked for decades— since the nineteenth century—suddenly looked dated, "placed" in history. Rahv might dismiss celebrants of the "counterculture" as "swingers," just as McCarthy wrote off feminists as a bunch of lesbians and slobs, but what they didn't perceive was that the terms of the debate had changed: attitude was more important than polemic, and no matter how eloquently or vituperatively they argued, they had lost. In fact, they had lost most decisively because their opponents weren't listening and didn't care who they were or what they knew. *Their* culture was no longer *the* culture. Many members of this generation survived into the 1970s and in a few cases beyond, but their cultural moment was over. They were the generation before feminism, the generation that didn't need feminism—and now another generation had moved to the fore, a generation that didn't need *them,* their stern Cold War ideology, their complex, boastful, contradictory attitudes toward sex, their peculiar tribal mores that for so long had seemed normal and natural and now suddenly appeared ungainly, archaic, vicious, a touch absurd.

Nothing was more archaic than marriage. Of all their peculiar tribal customs—the bruising cocktail parties, the publicly aired adulteries, the ever-burning cigarettes, the vicious political infighting, the all-but-compulsory psychoanalysis—their marriages were the most peculiar. Marriage was their mode, their stage, their fallback position, their default option. They were marriers, these women and men of the 1930s and '40s. They married swiftly, frequently, and sometimes heedlessly, often without much love or desire. And for all their brains and creativity, many of them married exceptionally foolishly. McCarthy craved reliability, emotional respect, and stability—and in Wilson she married the man least likely to furnish them. Stafford spent all her money on the beautiful old house she had always dreamed of owning, a shrine to her marriage, and the paint was barely dry when Lowell left her. Lowell, in the turmoil of insanity, repeatedly fled Hardwick to start life anew with some younger, freer, more worshipful woman—but "cured," he always returned, eating coffee grounds of remorse. And Hardwick, though she agonized about it, always took him back. Nobody, least of all the actors themselves, can explain the reasons for their actions: their need to be in a marriage, to conceive of themselves in terms of the rules and trappings of the married state, lay deeper than reason. They were deeply serious about marriage. As wives and husbands they were most fully and unconsciously themselves, playing parts they had known by heart all their lives. And they had many opportunities. When a relationship had reached a certain temperature, it never occurred to them *not* to marry. "Dear Cal—I find *no* advantage in not being married, not one," Jean Stafford wrote Robert Lowell (Cal was a prep school nickname that stuck) after their unhappy marriage was over. "I think it is infinitely *more* complicated besides being the most miserably lonely nightmare I've ever known." "She'd been married every day of her life," Elizabeth Hardwick told me, laughing, about her friend Mary McCarthy. "She never could spend a night outside." In a sense this was true for all of them. The men as much as the women couldn't bear to be without a lawfully wedded other. Love affairs and mistresses were just not good enough; they had to be *married*. Edmund Wilson had four wives, of whom McCarthy, to whom he was married from 1938 to 1945, was the third. Robert Lowell married Jean Stafford when he was still in college, replaced her with Hardwick just about as soon as the divorce went through, and went right from Hardwick to his third wife, Lady Caroline Blackwood, without a break. McCarthy, like Wilson, had four spouses—one before Wilson and two after him. Caroline Gordon and Allen Tate married each other twice, divorcing briefly in 1945, then remarrying only to divorce again. And so on.

But it's more than their tireless, if unsteady, devotion to marriage as an institution that looks so odd today. The marriages these intellectuals embarked on so enthusiastically embodied, each in its own way, a contradiction. The men and women were intellectual peers and companions, but socially, professionally, and emotionally, the men came first. The husbands wrote; the wives did everything else—the housekeeping, child rearing, entertaining, nursing, gardening—and then wrote. And it never struck any of them to arrange things differently. Caroline Gordon, who was a generation older than McCarthy and Hardwick but moved in the same circles and knew everyone, explained the rules of the game to the younger wives: first you got the housework done, then you did your writing. "Gordon was extremely scornful of any woman who did not run her own household and prepare meals," one of these younger wives told me. "She thought it was nonsense that a woman couldn't do both." Both sides collaborated in this division of labor; both took for granted that this was what marriage entailed. The women fully expected the domestic front to fall to them, and they prided themselves on the brilliance of their household campaigns, campaigns carried out in the crevices between deadlines or, more often, at the expense of composition. The men needed women who could comprehend their conversation and comment intelligently on what they wrote, and they truly loved the "shimmering of intelligence" (Lowell's phrase about Hardwick) that their wives brought them; but they also expected that these brilliant women would run interference with the world while they thought and wrote and talked to one another.

It wasn't just who cooked the dinner and washed the dishes that mattered. What it really came down to was status: who held higher rank, whose work took priority, whose needs dominated. As Edmund Wilson's friend and drinking partner Dawn Powell confided to her journal, "In order for a genius to be a genius, he must have a selfless slave between him and the world so that he may select what tidbits he chooses from it and not have his brains swallowed up in chaff. For women this protection is impossible." Another friend of Wilson's, the painter Mary Meigs, wrote much the same thing in her autobiography as she mused on the lot of "the wife of a great man": "Finally, she is less in his light than in his shadow. Great men—with nothing to prevent them from soaring as high as they can, all those qualities of greatness (the selfishness, the iron will, the discipline that sets hours and refuses to be disturbed) coddled and encouraged and excused by the women around them, for every great man needs his slaves, even if one of them, his wife, is a great woman. She, with the same qualities perhaps, running into the stone wall of Him." What's striking about this group is that the "selfless slaves" were also brilliant, accomplished writers, "great women"—and that the men married them precisely because of their brilliance and accomplishments. The men wanted slaves *and* peers, and the women did their damnedest to be smashing in both roles, even if it killed them.

Which it very nearly did. Stafford suffered a serious mental breakdown when her marriage with Lowell failed; a heavy drinker before the marriage, she slipped into alcoholism during her years with Lowell and never mastered her addiction. Mary McCarthy had a breakdown four months into her marriage with Wilson, possibly as a result of being punched and kicked by him while she was pregnant. After the marriage ended, she spoke—and wrote—obsessively of his tyranny, his abuse, his emotional oppression (although by most accounts she gave back as good as she got). Hardwick, though blessed with a strong, resilient temperament, nearly cracked under the strain of dealing with Lowell during his yearly bouts of insanity and all but stopped writing during long stretches of their marriage. Diana Trilling wrote that it never occurred to her to place her career on the same level as that of her husband, Lionel, or to expect any sympathy or acknowledgment from him for her "expenditure of double energies"; yet she railed at how members of her generation, women as well as men, insisted on pegging her as "Trilling's wife" and dismissed her as a "marital appendage." Today, in the age of traumatic memoir and talk-show confession, we feel we have a special claim on domestic horror, but these marriages were as fraught with physical and emotional abuse, violence, madness, drunkenness, sexual deception, brutality, contempt, and revenge as any 1990s tell-all autobiography. As Delmore Schwartz, who was certainly in a position to know, wrote with biting humor: "All poets' wives have rotten lives, / Their husbands look at them like knives . . . / Exactitude their livelihood / And rhyme their only gratitude." When the poets' wives were themselves poets of some sort, their lives became "rotten" in truly strange and fascinating ways. It is these lives, and the extraordinary times that shaped them, that I examine in the pages that follow.

It was not that their lives or marriages were "rotten" all the way through; far from it. The women, like the men, were figures of stupendous intellectual energy, passion, and engagement, forever debating and defending ideas, tastes, politics, art, and personalities. And their marriages, though the partners often put each other through hell, were in many ways good ones, inspiring and rewarding relationships. Even when things went sour, the women had worlds in common with their husbands: friends, publishers, books, music. They bickered, but they also shared outrageous jokes (usually about other members of the group), a tremendous store of literary and social allusion, a commitment to freedom of expression in literature and politics. They discovered Europe and European writers together; they worshiped together at the shrine of modernism; they were mostly left-wing radicals or outright Marxists in their youth, and most of them migrated to the right as they aged, with an unsteady lurch leftward in the late 1960s; they drank hard liquor, smoked cigarettes, threw parties, and had a good time in a way we seem to have forgotten how to. And they had a lot of sex, both in and outside marriage, and analyzed it compulsively when they weren't doing it. "We talked incessantly about sex, sex, and more sex, with particular emphasis on adultery," Diana Trilling recalled in her memoir of her marriage. "[S]ex took up as much conversational space as in later years we would give to politics." Everybody in that circle seemed to have multiple love affairs ("people were shocked if the husband did *not* have affairs," *PR* writer Lionel Abel told me) and to know all about everyone else's affairs. Insisting on privacy was proof that you were hiding something *really* bad. Their adulteries and divorces were breathtaking, even by our standards and certainly by the starchy standards of their day, but they drew the line at "deviation": homosexuality was a subject of nearly universal private ridicule in that proudly promiscuous heterosexual circle.

What's remarkable about this literary generation is how many of the women were just as promiscuous as the men—and just as proud of it. This was perhaps the first generation in which the women *assumed* they would have sexual adventures. No one had more adventures—or swaggered more about them—than Mary McCarthy. As she boasts in her *Intellectual Memoirs,* at some point after her first marriage ended she "stopped counting" the number of men she slept with in the studio bed of her Greenwich Village apartment: "[T]here were a lot. . . . [O]ne morning I was in bed with somebody while over his head I talked on the telephone with somebody else. Though slightly scared by what things were coming to, I did not *feel* promiscuous. Maybe no one does." McCarthy is clearly having a good time shocking her "gentle reader" here, and she probably did, as Diana Trilling insisted, go further than any of her peers, but there is a sense in which she spoke for her generation. Freedom, curiosity, daring, and the desire for experience impelled them to experiment in a way that intellectual women had not done before, at least not as a group (though there had been isolated exceptions such as George Sand and Katherine Anne Porter). And of course sex was always intimately bound up with what they could get from men by sleeping with them. Rahv comes immediately to mind, for both McCarthy and Hardwick got a lot by sleeping with him. We think of the so-called sexual revolution as breaking out with the advent of the birth control pill in the 1960s, but clearly these women writers of the 1930s and '40s were in the vanguard. Hardwick reported in an essay she wrote about McCarthy in the early 1960s that she had once heard a young woman claim McCarthy's "The Man in the Brooks Brothers Shirt" as "my Bible." The casually graphic Pullman car sexual encounter between a corpulent middle-aged businessman and McCarthy's fierce young alter ego, Meg Sargent, was, the author freely admitted, drawn from experience. McCarthy was indeed a prophet of sorts, both in what she did and in how she wrote about it. She certainly gave her friends and lovers a lot to talk about.

Circle, gang, coterie, crowd, clique: I haven't found quite the right term for the connections that bound these women, and they didn't know what to call themselves either. They were certainly a loose-knit, far-flung group. Their lives and works intersected, but often obliquely, obscurely, at one remove. All of them at various times in the 1930s and '40s published in *Partisan Review,* moved in the *PR* social orbit, and adopted the *PR* style (described by one critic as "wide-ranging, cutting, self-assured"), and later most of them shifted over to *The New York Review of Books* (which Hardwick and Lowell helped found); all subscribed to more or less the same brand of liberal anticommunism; they were each other's allies and rivals, supporters and confidantes, the subjects of each other's poems, essays, reviews, and letters. They shared lovers and editors. They were aware of one another's thoughts, views, feelings, and words, sometimes to the point of obsession. When they published, it was the approval of the others that counted most.

McCarthy met Hardwick through *Partisan Review* founder and editor Philip Rahv, and they labored side by side, though often on different continents, for decades, glancing over their shoulder at the other, smiling at each other's foibles, occasionally turning on each other. Lowell and McCarthy had a close friendship of their own that ran parallel to the friendship between the two women. Lowell admired McCarthy's verve tremendously ("our Diana, rash to awkwardness," he wrote of her), and McCarthy thought Lowell an exasperating genius, but a genius nonetheless—a rank she would never have accorded Hardwick (or vice versa). Though Stafford removed herself to the fringes of the scene after she divorced Lowell and began placing her work in the lucrative, and then rather lightweight *New Yorker* rather than the somber, strapped *Partisan Review,* she had been very much in the thick of the action during the 1940s, winning high praise from Rahv for her first and second novels, attending *PR* cocktail parties, and drinking with Delmore Schwartz (and possibly having an affair with him). Stafford and Lowell furnished an important, if somewhat fragile, link between the New York intellectuals and the Southern poets and writers who called themselves the Agrarians, especially Allen Tate and Caroline Gordon, who became surrogate parents of the younger couple during the stormy first years of their marriage. The Jewish, Marxist immigrants and children of immigrants who staffed *PR* and the heirs of the old Confederacy who banded together as Agrarians were on the opposite sides of most political and literary issues of the day, but Lowell and Stafford managed to straddle the two camps and entertain both sides with tales and gossip of the others. Tate and Edmund Wilson were friends as well, and there was a memorable encounter between the Tates and the Wilsons during the early months of the Wilson-McCarthy marriage.

During the war—and as a result of it—Hannah Arendt joined the circle. A Jewish woman of immense intellectual authority, strong convictions, and deep learning, Arendt left her native Germany when Adolf Hitler came to power, emigrated to New York in 1941 with her political philosopher husband, Heinrich Blücher, and began publishing in *Partisan Review* in 1944. Arendt and McCarthy met through their *PR* contacts, and after an initial misunderstanding they became close friends, indeed best friends in many ways. Arendt brought an Old World rigor and abstraction to the group—Lowell, who met her through McCarthy, called her "the strongest theoretical writer of her age," but he was quick to point out that her "theory is always applied to action," a quality he found "rare and courageous in a thinker." Arendt never ceased to be fundamentally German in her outlook, but she profoundly influenced the thinking of her American friends, particularly McCarthy, and she shared with McCarthy and Hardwick a fierce outspokenness on the social and political issues of the day.

The affinity among McCarthy, Arendt, and Hardwick is at the heart of my book. Emotionally, temperamentally, and intellectually, they were on the same wavelength. Perhaps it was the quality of their scorn that bound them together. Not exactly comrades in arms and far too proud to think of themselves as an intellectual sorority, they enjoyed the same ambiguous status as women who had made it in a man's world, and they knew it. Diana Trilling derisively lumped them together as the *PR* "girls" (the magazine's male editors were commonly known as "the boys") and felt, with some justification, that they despised her and excluded her. "They crossed the line and were accepted among the boys," she told me when I interviewed her shortly before her death. "They were power women. All of them were very sexually promiscuous. Hannah Arendt was Mary McCarthy's heroine—they deserved each other. Hardwick was Lowell's willing accomplice—she believed she was married to the most important poet of his generation and she reveled in this. They thought life was literature—they confused the two. Their lives were lived under the aspect of literature in a way my life was not. Mine was lived under the aspect of life." Beneath the bitterness, there is something to this. The Trillings, though they moved in the same circle, published in the same journals, and carried on a fascinating and complicated literary marriage, lived their lives under a different "aspect." Diana never became "one of the boys" (or the girls) in the way that Hardwick, McCarthy, Arendt, and even Stafford did. Perhaps sexual promiscuity had something to do with it (although Arendt's close friends deny that she was promiscuous after her marriage to Blücher). Or maybe it was the predictability and cautiousness of what Philip Rahv called "middleclassicism à la Trilling." The Trillings were staid in a way that Lowell, Stafford, Hardwick, and McCarthy were not. The Trillings were compromisers and self-appointed arbiters, while the others were extremists—emotionally, aesthetically, and morally, if not always politically.

The Trillings appear as minor figures in my narrative, as do a number of other literary figures of the period: Allen Tate and Caroline Gordon, John Berryman and Eileen Simpson, Randall Jarrell, Peter and Eleanor Taylor, Alfred Kazin, Dwight Macdonald, Delmore Schwartz and Gertrude Buckman. My "major figures"—McCarthy, Stafford, Hardwick, and Arendt and their writer husbands and lovers, Wilson, Rahv, and

Lowell—dominate my stage because they fit together both personally and professionally. As career writers and wives of prominent intellectuals, they faced the same dilemmas and crises, and they did so with an acute, sometimes bitter awareness of one another. They knew one another and knew about one another; they read and reviewed one another; they measured with the exactness of peers and rivals one another's reputations, successes or failures in the marketplace, standing within the narrow yet tremendously significant world they shared. Other brilliant women moved and wrote in the same milieu and grappled with some of the same issues—Lillian Hellman, Gertrude Himmelfarb, and Midge Decter, to name three—but I've left them out of the narrative because I find their lives, works, and interactions less compelling and less meaningfully intertwined. Hellman, by reason of her steadfast Stalinism, was not welcome in the *PR* crowd, though she was a friend of Edmund Wilson and Robert Lowell for many years and a bitter enemy of Mary McCarthy at the end of her life; Himmelfarb, the wife of neoconservative pundit Irving Kristol, was close to Diana Trilling, but the Kristols became too conservative too early on to suit the *Partisan Review* liberals; Decter was not as visible or prominent in the crowd as her much admired, then much reviled husband Norman Podhoretz.

I freely admit that my own tastes, preferences, and judgments guided my choices to some extent (perhaps to a large extent). I was seduced by what they wrote—both for publication and privately in letters and discarded drafts full of candid revelations, often about one another. I found myself awestruck by the breadth of their authority: sharp, informed, utterly self-assured pronouncements on everything from the Moscow trials of the 1930s to the birth-control practices of Depression-era Vassar graduates to the hideous logistics of slaughter practiced by the Nazis in Europe to the place of violence in the "youth culture" of the 1960s—all of which they lived through together and talked about every day as if their lives depended on it. Above all I was struck by their intimate, immediate awareness of one another, even when living far part: McCarthy feeling Arendt peering dubiously over her shoulder as she composes a juicy, humiliating sex scene for one of her novels; Stafford keeping tabs on how Hardwick was managing as the second Mrs. Lowell; Hardwick marveling at McCarthy's ability to make a handsome living from her writing; McCarthy and Arendt speculating about Hardwick's future after Lowell left her for another woman in the early 1970s. Somewhat arbitrarily, perhaps, I have narrowed the field to the most telling incidents, most colorful characters, deepest friendships, fiercest fights, keenest affinities. I dwell on the events, both public and private, these people experienced together and in common: the political and literary upheavals of the Great Depression; the emergence of *Partisan Review* as the premier journal of the New York intellectuals; the vagaries of Mary McCarthy's love life; Lowell's conversion to Catholicism and its impact on his marriage to Stafford and his poetry; the violent and almost simultaneous dissolution of the Stafford-Lowell marriage and the McCarthy-Wilson marriage at the end of World War II; the Cold War; the public outcry that greeted the publication of Arendt's *Eichmann in Jerusalem* in 1963; the founding of *The New York Review of Books* and its impact on the New York intellectual scene during the 1960s; the social and political revolutions of the late 1960s; Lowell's break with Hardwick and the controversial volume of poetry he wrote about it. My players at times jostle one another roughly off the stage and summon one another back at odd moments. But I hope I make it clear that a common thread runs through these parallel lives.

It is a thread that begins and ends in custom. Though most members of the group have been dead for only twenty years or so, their habits, rituals, personal styles, tastes, and prejudices have already taken on the blurring patina of the old-fashioned. How strange they look to us today with their cigarettes and highball glasses, their hats and stockings and shirtwaist dresses; how cavernous their apartments; how prodigious their literary output; how ferocious their politics. In her foreword to Mary McCarthy's *Intellectual Memoirs*, Elizabeth Hardwick writes with some amusement of being asked by a younger woman writer, "Just what is a Trotskyite?" "Trotskyite and Stalinist—" Hardwick tosses off with a laugh, "part of one's descriptive vocabulary, like blue-eyed." It was a vocabulary always broadcast back then at maximum volume, for this was a group famous for loud argument and notorious for rudeness and harshness of manner. "We were not gentlemen—or ladies," *PR* editor William Phillips told me with a touch of regret. "We had strong egos." He mulled over the same theme in his memoirs: "[O]ur little world was deficient in friendship and loyalty," he writes, and their self-proclaimed objectivity was often "a mask for competitiveness, malice, and polemical zeal—for banal evils." *Banal evils:* a deliberate—and provocative—echo of the phrase that Hannah Arendt used so provocatively in her book about the Eichmann trial. "They were not easy companions, these intellectuals," writes Diana Trilling in her memoirs. "They were overbearing and arrogant, excessively competitive; they lacked magnanimity and often they lacked common courtesy. Ours was a cruelly judgmental society, often malicious and riddled with envy." It was also an obsessively self-reflective society, riddled with gossip, back stabbing, and power struggles. Alfred Kazin nails this group compulsion to keep tabs in his volume *Starting Out in the Thirties*: "The *Partisan Review* group were interested in the people around them to the point of ecstasy; in this world nothing interested them so much as the personalities of their friends. The ability to analyze a friend, a trend, a shift in the politico-personal balance of power, was for them the greatest possible sign of intellectual power."

In solitude they wielded such power as they possessed by writing; in company, especially at their never-ending cocktail parties, they brandished their power by gossiping. All close-knit, self-aware communities gossip—but this crowd raised it to an art form, "a sub-literary genre," as Rahv, a grandmaster, wrote Mary McCarthy, "of which fancy is only a small ingredient garnishing a piece of truth." In her brilliant, despairing story "Children Are Bored on Sunday," Stafford anatomizes the *PR* cocktail-party gossip ritual with almost anthropological detachment: "These cocktail parties were a modus vivendi in themselves for which a new philosophy, a new ethic, and a new etiquette had had to be devised. They were neither work nor play, and yet they were not at all beside the point but were, on the contrary, quite indispensable to the spiritual life of the artists who went to them. . . . The gossip was different, for one thing, because it was stylized, creative (integrating the whole of the garrotted, absent friend), and all its details were precise and all its conceits were Jamesian, and all its practitioners sorrowfully saw themselves in the role of Pontius Pilate, that hero of the untoward circumstance." Stafford herself was an adept at this "stylized, creative" gossip, but she couldn't stand the hothouse atmosphere and the glare of exposure. And whenever she was around the New York crowd, she drank too much. They all drank too much in those days. "[O]ur generation bred to drink the ocean / in the all-possible before Repeal," Lowell wrote in one of the poems in his *Notebook*. Wilson was famous for downing trays of martinis and quarts of whiskey and rising fresh as a daisy the next morning; Lowell was forever going on the wagon and falling off with a bang; Stafford, a heavy drinker since college and a wildly out-of-control drunk in the last months of her marriage to Lowell, was hospitalized repeatedly to dry out, but she always went back to drinking; Rahv's death may have resulted from a combination of sleeping pills and alcohol; and on and on.

Drinking fueled the gossip; the gossip made many of them turn to drink for consolation or courage. Diana Trilling recalls fortifying herself with two or three stiff drinks before she could even face a hard-drinking *PR* cocktail party. All the wives did. Their lives were intense, sometimes to the point of frenzy, and often brief. Lowell died at sixty, Stafford at sixty-four, Rahv at sixty-five, Arendt at sixty-nine. Wilson and McCarthy, made of stronger stuff, both made it to seventy-seven.

Most of them are dead today, but their battles live on. I was amazed, reading the memoirs these people wrote and talking with the survivors, how fresh the old wounds remain, how sharp their judgments, how fierce and unforgiving their opinions of one another. "She was never taken seriously as a writer," one woman snapped at me about a recently deceased rival seconds after our interview began. "What she published in her last years was a grotesque enlargement of the self in old age." "Mary McCarthy!" an elder statesman of the New York literary world all but spat the name out over the phone. "She began by making fun of Hannah Arendt's refugee accent and ended up being her slave." Who was a Trotskyite and who was a Stalinist; how hard or soft you were on communism during the 1950s; who "turned" (i.e., became a neoconservative) and who didn't: these things mattered to this crowd, mattered more than anything, years or even decades later. This is astonishing to a generation like mine, in which most of us can't even remember our *own* political views twenty years back, let alone anyone else's, in which SDSers became stockbrokers, hippies traded in their beads for microchips, and the antigovernment rhetoric of the radical New Left now streams from fanatics on the far Right. Perhaps politics was a more serious, more urgently personal matter back then because the world was a darker place. God knows it's dark enough now, but consider the times these people lived through: Wilson fought in the First World War; McCarthy, Hardwick, Lowell, and Stafford went to college during the Depression and graduated into the tense, uncertain period before World War II; Blücher and Arendt escaped Hitler's Germany during the first wave of crackdowns on Jews and Communists and were among the fortunate few to find asylum in the United States. Totalitarianism in Germany and the Soviet Union, genocide in Europe, political purges in the Soviet Union and the Eastern Bloc, world war followed by cold war, and then the threat of all-out nuclear Armageddon: calamity shadowed these lives relentlessly, and as a result, politics pervaded every aspect of existence, even the most intimate.

It was an embattled, scarred generation, and looking back, we—and they—tend to see only the fights, the follies, the extreme positions: the flirtation with—or outright marriage to—communism during the 1930s; the blindness to what was happening to Jews in Nazi Germany and Nazi-occupied Europe; the opposition to America's entry into World War II; the apologies for McCarthyism in the early 1950s; the savage attacks on Arendt's *Eichmann in Jerusalem;* the fear and ridicule of African-American political and cultural activists in the 1960s; the hysteria over the Vietnam War; the disdainful rejection of "women's lib"; the sacking of liberalism. All of this happened, and a lot of it happened in ugly, vicious, vengeful ways. There are many blots on the record of this generation of intellectuals. They stumbled often. They meddled in affairs of which they had small knowledge and little expertise. As one younger member of the group told me, "Thank heaven their political influence is gone—what little they had. They didn't know any more about politics than anyone else. What they knew from reading books did not equip them to deal with large public questions. Having read Keats carefully doesn't qualify you for anything." Yes, they erred through arrogance and overreaching; they shot themselves in the foot and stabbed one another in the back; they were given to grand gestures, panic, paranoia, and overcharged rhetoric. But they also had a zeal and idealism and originality that have all but vanished from the American political scene or migrated to its fanatical fringes. As one critic wrote in a recent review of a biography of *PR* art critic Clement Greenberg, "Their generalizing, overbearing manner and their frantic competition were the underside to their impassioned, beautifully complex and independent minds." Alongside the rancor were fire and commitment; their fiercely debated ideologies sharpened their mind; beneath the pomposity and self-importance they had a sense of public responsibility, an urgent concern for something greater than their own backyards and tax liability. They believed that their discourse mattered; they assumed they spoke the same language as their audience. They lived the "life of significant contention," in Diana Trilling's rather high-toned phrase, and they lived it together.

They lived it most passionately, most tellingly in their marriages. Like their politics, their marriages in retrospect look like a series of disasters: bad choices, wrong turns, betrayals, lies, drunken shouting matches, slapped faces, hideous divorces. Yet they also, at times, had marvelous lives together. As Hardwick said of Lowell, "He was not crazy all the time. Most of my time with him was wonderful." They were all, in their way, crazy at times, mad in every sense—but when they were sane they were extraordinarily brilliant, often charming people, most charming of all when they were with each other. In telling the stories of these women and the men they were involved with, their lives and works, friendships and marriages, I have tried to illuminate some of the finest minds our culture has produced; and beyond this, to capture the ardor and shimmering intelligence of an age that is fast slipping away into the fabulous past.

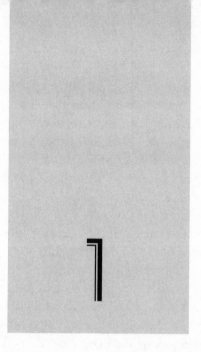

Partisan Review *Reborn*

EVEN MARY MCCARTHY, a demon for uncovering hidden motives, is a little uncertain about how or why she was included on the masthead of the *Partisan Review*—the sole woman in a company of ambitious, combative young men—when the magazine was reborn in December 1937. "None of the histories I've looked at tells how I happened to be on the magazine," she wrote five decades later in her memoir of the period. "I am not sure myself, but I suspect that Philip imposed me on the others. And they were not altogether pleased." Philip Rahv, a Jewish immigrant from the Ukraine with whom McCarthy was then living, was *PR*'s coeditor. Being Rahv's "girl," as they said back then, gave McCarthy standing—but only so much. "[T]he boys . . . made me the theatre critic," she wrote, "not trusting my critical skills in other fields." McCarthy was twenty-five years old, four years out of Vassar, recently divorced, soon to marry Edmund Wilson, and on the threshold of a brilliant literary career that took her far beyond the confines of theater reviewing. *Partisan Review* also stood on the threshold of brilliance: for the next twenty-five years it would reign as New York's most influential intellectual journal, making (and in some cases breaking) the reputations of a generation of American writers: male writers primarily—men such as Delmore Schwartz, Meyer Schapiro, Clement Greenberg, Robert Lowell, Randall Jarrell, Lionel Trilling, Lionel Abel, and James Agee—but also some exceptional women, including McCarthy, Hannah Arendt, Elizabeth Hardwick, and, to a lesser extent, Jean Stafford, Eleanor Clark, and Elizabeth Bishop. For a long stretch, in literary New York, winning favor with the *PR* "boys" was the surest way to make yourself heard.

PR's rebirth coincided with—and was in part caused by—the Depression, which had been going on for eight grim years, long enough that it no longer felt like a departure from prosperity but like a dark hole that the world had fallen into. Among writers and intellectuals, the Depression precipitated what one social observer called a "spiritual and intellectual migration . . . to the left." Marxist politics of some stripe became practically de rigueur among the intellectual elite. The pitched battles of the day were fought not between left wing and right wing, but within the Left itself: Stalinists versus Trotskyites, Communist Party members versus those who did not or would not join, mild socialists versus fanatical hard-liners who took their cues directly from Moscow. As Elizabeth Hardwick recalled several decades afterward, "In that circle, the Soviet Union, the Civil War in Spain, Hitler and Mussolini, were what you might call real life."

It was in this heated Red atmosphere that the original *Partisan Review* was launched in 1934 as an organ of the Communist John Reed Clubs. "We shall combat not only the decadent culture of the exploiting classes," the editors declared aggressively in the first issue, "but also the debilitating liberalism which at times seeps into our writers through the pressure of class-alien forces." That was the literary tone of the day. The magazine folded without funds two years later, when the Party abruptly dissolved the John Reed Clubs as a result of a sudden political shift in Moscow. Then, in 1937, Philip Rahv and William Phillips, having secured financing from a well-heeled abstract painter named George L. K. Morris, brought *PR* back to life in a new, radically independent guise: Marxist but anti-Stalinist, and dedicated to the cause of literary modernism. "We think that the cause of revolutionary literature is best served by a policy of no commitments to any political party," ran the "Editorial Statement" in the first independent issue, dated December 1937. "The *Partisan Review* aspires to represent a new and dissident generation in American letters." An all-star lineup turned out for the opening issue:

Delmore Schwartz (whose memorable story "In Dreams Begin Responsibilities" ran as the lead piece), Edmund Wilson writing on Flaubert's politics, Wallace Stevens, Lionel Abel, James Agee, Dwight Macdonald (who wrote an essay slamming the *New Yorker* magazine for interposing "a decent veil" between "reality and its readers," for overindulging in whimsy and trivia, and for remaining "ostentatiously neutral" in "the class war"), and Mary McCarthy on theater. The marriage of Marxism and modernism was not always a happy one (after all, Eliot, Pound, and Yeats—ranking deities within the modernist pantheon—were notorious for their right-wing politics), but the magazine seemed to thrive on controversy, tension, upheaval, and dissent. High-toned, fiercely contentious, merciless, brilliant, rough, competitive, and exclusive, *PR* was a world unto itself, both socially and intellectually. After Philip Rahv died in 1973, *The New York Times Book Review* stated flatly that *PR* had held sway for thirty years as the "best literary magazine in America": "It would be hard to overestimate the cultural importance of Rahv's and Phillips's decision to break with Stalinism without abandoning the social and political ideals (and analytic technique) of the Marxist tradition."

But it wasn't all high-minded analysis and embattled idealism down at the seedy little *PR* office near Union Square. There was also plenty of gossip, intrigue, and back stabbing, as well as off-hours boozing and competitive sex. It was a milieu that fit McCarthy perfectly. She and Rahv were a striking couple—McCarthy with her bohemian unshaven legs and drab clothing (she would soon abandon this look for more elegant attire and grooming), loose hair, brightly fixed smile, scrubbed Irish complexion; Rahv with his dark, hooded appearance, liquid bedroom eyes, gruff accent, and bulky, big-shouldered, pugnacious style. McCarthy was "not quite beautiful, and too good-looking to be called pretty," *PR* editor William Barrett wrote of his first impression of seeing McCarthy with Rahv at the magazine's office. There was something "wayward and even *gamine* about her. . . . Nobody seeing her for the first time would have surmised that this striking and vivid girl would prove to be one of the most brilliant women and formidable intellectuals of her time." Dwight Macdonald, another crony from the early days at *PR* and a close friend then and after, made a memorable wisecrack about the ferocity of this "vivid girl": "Mary's smile is very famous. It's not what it seems at all. It's a rather sharkish smile. When most pretty girls smile at you, you feel terrific. When Mary smiles at you, you look to see if your fly is open." "Bloody Mary" became one of her nicknames. "She would say devastating things to people," a friend told one of her biographers, "and because she was totally honest and never pulled any punches, people were terrified of her. People are afraid of extreme cleverness and a sharp tongue and pen." As Arthur Schlesinger Jr., who liked and admired her very much, wrote, "She thoroughly believed in offending people. She believed in provocation as incitement to thought, to reform, to life itself."

Rahv was just as formidable and intimidating, though more guarded in his provocations. Only twenty-nine when he and McCarthy met, he was already a major player in literary/socialist New York—an opinion maker, a heated debater, a brilliant editor, often a bully, who, by force of will and grit, ambition and political savvy, made *PR* very much "his" magazine (even their initials were the same). Rahv was too bearish and shambling to be handsome—"He would lurch across the room," recalled Irving Howe, "weighty, unnerving, like a capsized ship"; but he had a sexual magnetism—"primitive, even animal-like," Diana Trilling wrote with a little frisson—that attracted women. And he was never one to restrain himself sexually. Yet for all his smolder and swagger there was something of the tense, insecure arriviste about Rahv. Howe described him as "a somewhat timid man" and noted that though his magazine had "a polemical air," Rahv himself "was not really much of a fighter, for he shared both the uneasiness of the immigrant (you had to watch your step in this land of the goyim) and the anxieties of the ex-Communist." "In a certain way Rahv was not presentable," as a younger colleague puts it. Lionel Abel found him "sharp, crude and outspoken. And full of clichés. He was always careful and cautious because he had no college training. Everything he knew he picked up by himself." He was a schemer, a deflater of reputations, and, when it suited him, a back stabber. Abel recalls him growling on one occasion, "Don't give me that crap called friendship." Delmore Schwartz, master of the sly put-down, once said, "Philip does have scruples, but he never lets them stand in his way." But although he blustered and barked in debate, Rahv shrank from physical violence (Barrett recounts the elaborate measures Rahv took to avoid a confrontation with the art critic Clement Greenberg, who had a reputation, albeit exaggerated, for socking his adversaries). Jason Epstein says that despite his "big bluster" Rahv was really like Ferdinand the Bull—he just wanted to sit under a tree and smell the flowers. For all his intellectual energy, there was a slothful, luxury-loving side to Rahv. "[H]e loved Henry James and every kind of rich, shimmery, soft texture in literature and in the stuff of experience," McCarthy wrote of him in a fond memorial essay published in *The New York Times Book Review*. Alongside his masculine persona, which she identified with politics and aggressiveness, there existed a feminine side—artistic and dreamy—that the world rarely saw. An avowed Marxist and advocate of revolution, Rahv nonetheless gazed longingly through the shiny plate glass of social prestige, rootedness, and *standing* on the American scene. He had a penchant for rich women—"a tropism for money not of his earning," as Diana Trilling put it—and married twice into considerable wealth, the first time to McCarthy's Social Register Vassar classmate Nathalie Swan, an architect. Breeding and class status preyed on his mind: he was always telling people that Robert Lowell was not a *real* Lowell (in fact he was, though not an especially rich one).

McCarthy and Rahv met in 1936 at one of the Sunday open-house parties that leftist novelist James T. Farrell hosted at his Greenwich Village apartment, and they connected again when McCarthy, who was then working as a reader for Covici-Friede publishers, asked Rahv to look over a German text (the son of Ukrainian Zionists, Rahv had emigrated to Israel with his parents as a youth before settling in America in 1922, acquiring a knowledge of Russian, German, Hebrew, and some French along the way). "We talked a little in the waiting-room," McCarthy recalled. "He had a shy, soft voice (when he was not shouting), big, dark, lustrous eyes, which he rolled with great expression, and the look of a bambino in an Italian sacred painting. I liked him. Soon he was taking me out to dinner in the Village, holding my elbow as we walked, and soon we were lovers."

McCarthy had been out of college and living in New York for only four years, but already she had acquired a practiced, worldly nonchalance about her love affairs. Born in Seattle in 1912 to charming, attractive, well-to-do parents, she was orphaned at the age of six, when the great influenza epidemic of 1918–1919 killed her mother and father within days of each other. She spent five grim years in Minneapolis as the ward of her shabby, abusive, stupid aunt and uncle—a trauma she reconstructed in gory detail in her *Memories of a Catholic Girlhood*. Eventually, her wealthy Seattle grandparents "rescued" her (leaving behind her three brothers), brought her back to their plush home overlooking Lake Washington, and sent her to boarding school and then on to Vassar College. But the nightmare in Minneapolis marked Mary for life (in her memoir, written nearly three decades later, she still burns with angry resentment over the beatings, the inane, rigidly enforced rules, the tape applied to mouths each night before bed to stifle mouth breathing, the shabby clothes, the paucity of books and toys, the suffocating atmosphere of deceit and deprivation). At Vassar, she cast a cold, curious eye on the customs and habits of the rich eastern girls. Occasionally she was invited to their Manhattan town houses and Hudson Valley country estates, but she never really belonged "in society." In a funny way, she never belonged anywhere, except in the theater of her imagination. "She had a defective sense of reality," says Random House editor Jason Epstein, who saw a good deal of her in the 1950s and '60s and clearly never cared for her very much. "She was always performing. She invented herself—her best theatrical work was her self—the brilliant, sexy ex-Catholic." The poet Elizabeth Bishop, who knew McCarthy at Vassar and maintained a wary friendship with her from then on, made a similar observation in a letter to a friend: "Oh poor girl, really. You know, I think she's never felt very real, and that's been her trouble. She's always pretending to be something-or-other and never quite convincing herself or other people." That eternal pretense turned out to be beside the point; McCarthy would succeed in her performance even without fully believing in her character.

She set about the task of self-creation in the brisk, rather calculating fashion of one of Balzac's heroes. At Vassar, she'd been "seeing" an actor and struggling playwright named Harold Johnsrud, and as soon as she graduated in the spring of 1933, she married him (she rechristened him Harald Petersen in *The Group* but changed little else about him aside from the name). It's far from clear that Mary loved John, as she called him, or even cared very much for him. But being married was essential to her persona, and John was a willing mate and promising enough prospect. They moved into a sublet apartment in the East Fifties and together faced down the grim, strident New York of the early Depression. The marriage ended three years later.

McCarthy covered a terrific amount of ground in her first few years in New York—swiftly launching a career as a book and theater reviewer, carrying on multiple love affairs of varying degrees of intensity and duration once she'd discarded Johnsrud, toying briefly with marrying again, and drifting into and out of interlocking social and political circles, all more or less left-wing, hard-drinking, and bohemian. Back in those days, reviewing books for one of the intellectual journals was the way to make a name for yourself with the people who mattered. McCarthy distinguished herself almost immediately for the hard, sharp, metallic gleam of her style and for her precocious assumption of authority. "She had such tremendous confidence so young," recalls Elizabeth Hardwick, "it was as if she came out of the head of Zeus. I remember reading a piece of hers in *The New Republic,* a review of Christina Stead's *The Man Who Loved Children.* I violently disagreed with what she said, but I still found it brilliantly written. I was struck by the confidence and gracefulness of her prose and how she had it from the beginning." Diana Trilling, though she had almost nothing good to say about McCarthy as a person, couldn't help admiring her literary style, as she wrote grudgingly in her memoirs: "There was a shine on everything she wrote, and whatever she wrote was always a statement of her sense of her own power." Alfred Kazin also remarked on the high gloss of her prose—"the crispness, hardness, shininess of her performance," as he put it—but he saw it not as the gleam of acuity but rather as the glint of sharpened steel: "She had, I thought, a wholly destructive critical mind, shown in her unerring ability to spot the hidden weakness or inconsistency in any literary effort and every person. To this weakness she instinctively leaped with cries of pleasure—surprised that her victim, as he lay torn and bleeding, did not applaud her perspicacity."

McCarthy consolidated her power and her reputation when she published a searing five-part series of articles in *The Nation* called "Our Critics, Right or Wrong" in which she "took on" as she put it "the entire critical establishment." Though *Nation* editor Margaret Marshall was technically her collaborator and was billed in the magazine as her coauthor, McCarthy claimed later that she had actually done almost all the writing herself. The series was "an immense succès de scandale," according to McCarthy—just the kind of "succès" she relished most. She was only twenty-three years old, and already she was weighing in as an intellectual contender.

Rahv, four years McCarthy's senior, looked, acted, and came across as a considerably older man—a man of authority, strong opinions, and emphatically blunt expression (he was famous for his way of barking out "dis" and "dat"). Rahv was the quintessential immigrant intellectual. Instead of Harvard or Yale or even City College of New York, where many of New York's smart immigrant kids went in the 1930s and 1940s, he got his education standing on breadlines, sleeping on park benches, and immersing himself in books in the great high-ceilinged reading room of the New York Public Library. He came by both his politics and his passion for English and American literature straight from the source, without of-

ficial sanction or professorial mediation. As an editor, Rahv took seriously Trotsky's dictum that "Art can become a strong ally of revolution
only in so far as it remains faithful to itself." It was *quality* that mattered
to him above all, even more than dogma, and Rahv had a nose for it—
for the new, the original, the pulse-quickening, the controversial. Rahv
was *PR*'s catalyst and prime mover, a born editor who trusted his gut and
wrung the best prose out of those who wrote for him. Rahv, the pen
name he invented for himself, means "rabbi" in Hebrew (he was born
Greenberg), and that was the role he played: the one who first read and
interpreted text, who set the tone, led the debate, and silenced, when he
could, dissenters. So what if *PR*'s Marxism gradually withered away as
aesthetics muscled out revolution? Rahv published what he liked because he liked it, and for a run of two and a half decades what he liked
was by general consent what thinking people felt they had to read. Rahv,
who was not an especially brilliant writer or commanding theoretician
himself, had influence. And for McCarthy, as for many other smart, ambitious young women, this was surely part of his sex appeal.

Though he could be overbearing and demanding, Rahv seems to have
given McCarthy her freedom during their love affair and to have enjoyed
seeing what she did with it. "Mary McCarthy was the 'bright light' of the
Partisan Review," Alfred Kazin recalled with a snarl. "Why? Because she
frightened all those timorous Jews." Frightened or not, Rahv was very
much taken with her in every way—and she with him—and they
promptly moved in together. Not that they didn't argue. "Sex and arguing," McCarthy wrote later, were "the only pleasures that were considered 'serious' " during the "sectarian thirties." She and Rahv had plenty of
both in the improbably swanky Beekman Place apartment ("severely elegant modern furnishings, all glass, steel, and chrome on thick beige
rugs") that Mary borrowed from rich friends. The plebeian (his own
word) Rahv felt "compromised by that apartment," according to Mc-
Carthy, and embarrassed to receive his socialist comrades there; while
McCarthy, secretly reveling in the tony address, clung to her bourgeois
pleasures. "We polarized each other," she wrote in *Intellectual Memoirs:*

> That was perhaps why we quarreled so much that summer, although
> we were greatly in love. It was a class war we fought, or so he defined
> it. I defended my antecedents, and he his. He boasted of Jewish supe-
> riority in every field of endeavor, drawing up crushing lists of Jewish
> musicians and scientists and thinkers . . . with which no Gentile list

could compare. . . . He was a partisan of what he called "plebeian" values—he loved that word. I stuck up for patrician values, incarnate, as I imagined, in the professional class I issued from, exemplified by my grandfather. . . . Anyway we argued amid the glass and the chromium. Philip brought an enormous zest to the exercise. Dispute was his art form. In some part of his quite complex mind, it entertained him to hear us go at it.

In a way, their relationship itself was an argument—against convention, for "free unions" (McCarthy's term). The fact that they were living together, and in Beekman Place yet, was shocking even to their radical downtown friends. In 1937, it simply wasn't done. Delmore Schwartz, irked by their public displays of affection, began referring to her as "the whore." Lionel Abel recalls that what the other male contributors noticed was not her prose style but her legs. McCarthy didn't care. She was getting published and talked about, and she was having a wonderful time with Rahv, even with all their brawls over religion, art, and interior decoration. McCarthy was living the ultimate fantasy of the ambitious, "artistic" Vassar girl: reaping the pleasures and rewards of the "liberated" woman without embracing the dreary, dowdy rhetoric of women's rights. For McCarthy, the affair with Rahv was an idyll, a final patch of warm, youthful, erotic Eden before the fall—before Wilson.

It pleased McCarthy in 1937, and it would still please her fifty years later, to shine in the eyes of her old Vassar classmates, to dazzle and shock them. They were an extraordinarily gifted and privileged group, these women with whom she had lived for four years on the college's stately green Hudson Valley campus. Poets Elizabeth Bishop and Muriel Rukeyser, writer Eleanor Clark (later married to Robert Penn Warren) and her sister Eunice (married for a time to the magazine editor and critic Selden Rodman), the painter Margaret Miller, the architect Nathalie Swan (who became Philip Rahv's second wife), and musicologist Frani Blough were all at Vassar at the same time as McCarthy, and all were to remain in her life in some fashion from then on, if not as friends then as colleagues, competitors, and judges, the people she played to, the audience whose smiles and envy she most wanted to elicit. This was not "the group" of the notorious novel—those rich, wide-eyed, self-deceived, sexually eager but inexperienced future suburban matrons she satirized so gleefully—but rather the circle of aesthetes with whom McCarthy started a short-lived, anonymously written magazine called *Con Spirito*. These girls were at Vassar not to acquire social poise and polish, which most of them didn't need, but to steep themselves in the best and brightest minds of Western culture, to learn how to argue, dissect, and synthesize, to recognize and praise the deserving and decry the inferior—in short, to prepare themselves to be Mary McCarthys. And Vassar was the place to do it. Though it was still the college of choice for society girls, it also offered intellectual women a rigorous, stimulating, challenging curriculum; thus it was elite in both senses. As McCarthy later wrote wryly, she expected Vassar to be a "Forest of Arden and a Fifth Avenue department store combined." Without being explicitly or dogmatically feminist, Vassar encouraged its women to take themselves seriously and to play as equals on the same field as men. McCarthy, the outlander orphan from Seattle, never quite fit in with her confident, discreet East Coast classmates—"I was not ill-bred but untrained and 'wild' . . . very outspoken and extreme in all my enthusiasms and dislikes," she told an interviewer after *The Group* appeared in 1963—but she came to embody the Vassar ideal. The fame and success she achieved carried the Vassar stamp of approval.

Though McCarthy was the only one who made it to the *PR* inner circle, several other Vassar women were affiliated with the magazine back in the late 1930s and early 1940s: Elizabeth Bishop and Eleanor Clark published some of their first work in *PR;* Nancy Rodman Macdonald, a graduate of the class of 1932 and *PR* editor Dwight Macdonald's wife, worked as business manager; and Nathalie Swan entered the *PR* orbit when she married Rahv soon after McCarthy left him. Their appearance in the pages of *PR* was a sign of the magazine's prestige and the women's ambition. As Diana Trilling, who aspired to publish in *PR* alongside her husband, Lionel, put it, "In those days, for anybody with intellectual ambition, to publish in *PR* was to have made it." Neither Diana Trilling, who had gone to Radcliffe, nor the vivid young Vassar graduates of the 1930s challenged the fact that only men made the decisions that counted.

McCarthy was seeing a lot of her college friends during these first few years in New York, and she was being talked about by everyone who saw her. She flourished on indiscretion. In college she had a reputation for knowing and doing more sexually than anyone else, and in New York she capitalized on this. But knowing and doing more sexually wasn't enough; everyone else had to know what she was doing too. For

McCarthy, sex was something of a spectator sport, even if the onlookers were only imaginary (recall Dottie Renfrew in *The Group* engaging in a prolonged mental dialogue with her Vassar friends and mother when she loses her virginity to the sexy, dissolute Dick Brown). Graphic, anatomically explicit couplings were a trademark of McCarthy's fiction and memoirs, and she could be astonishingly frank in person too. Mary set herself up as a fearless sexual adventurer, but there was a competitive, compulsory cast to her erotic exploits, as if the sex didn't "count" unless it got toted up, analyzed, broadcast, and preserved for posterity. How else to account for the joyless, malodorous Pullman car quickie in "The Man in the Brooks Brothers Shirt" or a revelation like this from her posthumous *Intellectual Memoirs:*

> It was getting rather alarming. I realized one day that in twenty-four hours I had slept with three different men. . . . I was able to compare the sexual equipment of the various men I made love with, and there were amazing differences, in both length and massiveness. One handsome married man, who used to arrive with two Danishes from a very good bakery, had a penis about the size and shape of a lead pencil; he shall remain nameless. In my experience, there was usually a relation to height, as both Philip Rahv and Bill Mangold, both tall men, bore out. . . . None of my partners, the reader will be relieved to hear, had a venereal disease.

Though she pretends to be blasé ("rather alarming," "in my experience," "the reader will be relieved to hear"), McCarthy is clearly swaggering. Curiously, most of the sex in McCarthy's fiction is awkward and degrading for both partners: either the man is a rapist or arrogant or impotent or his "equipment" is the wrong size or shape; the woman can't enjoy herself because she's worried about what it means or how she'll look in the eyes of the world or whether it will lead to anything "serious." As Elizabeth Hardwick wrote acutely in a 1961 (pre–*The Group*) essay on McCarthy, "In her fiction, shame and curiosity are nearly always found together and in the same strange union we find self-condemnation and the determined pursuit of experience; introspective irony and flat, daring action. . . . The heroine, in these encounters, feels a sense of piercing degradation, but it does not destroy her mind's freedom to speculate; her rather baffling surrenders do not vanquish her sense of her conqueror's weaknesses and absurdities." For McCarthy, sex was not a path to liberation or self-fulfillment but a test, a trap, a status symbol like matching luggage or an embarrassing defect like bad teeth. A shaming "should" trails behind McCarthy's sex scenes: it should have been better, more frequent, more passionate, consummated with someone else. McCarthy's women are as sexually free as her men, but their freedom yields only disappointment. It's as if sex were a contest that every woman is doomed to lose—except the author herself.

Most of the literary women of McCarthy's generation were also sexual adventurers—Hardwick, Hellman, Bishop, and to a lesser extent Stafford—racking up many more partners and spouses than their mothers did. In a sense, sexual adventurism was the badge of their generation, the thing they had in common and that distinguished them from previous generations. Sex was their favorite topic of gossip and speculation, a contest they carried on with an intense awareness of one another. Of the women in this group, no one was as driven, self-conscious, or frank about sex as Mary. From Vassar on, she prided herself on her well-publicized promiscuity.

McCarthy did not stay on the *PR* editorial board for very long, as Diana Trilling noted in her memoirs, but she remained, in Trilling's words, "one of its most valued contributors." Mary may have entered the *PR* orbit as Rahv's girlfriend, but she soon became one of the boys—accepted and respected as Trilling never would be. "To enter a man's world and to hold one's own there—intellectually and sexually!" *PR* editor William Barrett marveled in his memoirs. "Mary McCarthy certainly did that intellectually, and from what one would gather from her writings, as well as from other reports, sexually too. So much so indeed, that she rather struck terror into some male bosoms." In fact, Elizabeth Hardwick and to a lesser degree Hannah Arendt were the only women who ever rivaled McCarthy's standing on the magazine. "Mary was talented and beautiful and hard-working—and there were fewer talented women back then," Lionel Abel says today, trying to account for her unique position. "Yes, she could be malicious, but even her maliciousness had a kind of elegance about it. At the parties, people came with their wives, but she was a writer. She was with the boys." Nobody, including McCarthy herself, thought to remark the oddness of this: it was just how things were. For McCarthy, the real distinction was not gender but politics and what we would call "lifestyle": "I remained, as the *Partisan Review* boys said, absolutely bourgeois throughout," she told an interviewer. "They always said to me very sternly, 'You're really a throwback. You're really a twenties figure.' . . . I was wounded. I was a sort of gay, goodtime girl from their point of view. And they were men of the Thirties. Very serious. That's why my position was so . . . lowly." Lowly or not, McCarthy was in her element on *PR;* it was her natural habitat, and the friends she made in these heady months of the magazine's rebirth—Dwight Macdonald, a rumpled Yale-educated radical who shaped and shared her political views; William Phillips, Rahv's moderate, cautious coeditor (and increasingly, as years went by, his bête noire); critic Fred Dupee; and of course Rahv himself—would remain her comrades and allies for decades.

McCarthy's rivalry with Diana Trilling dates back to this period or shortly afterward, when Trilling began publishing book reviews in *The Nation.* Diana's husband, Lionel Trilling—a rising star of the Columbia University English Department, one of the first Jews to get tenure at Columbia, a lucid prose stylist, an appealingly modest man whom many women found extremely attractive—was writing regularly for the revitalized *PR,* and Mary and Diana inevitably encountered each other at the never-ending *PR* cocktail parties. The two women had met, McCarthy recalled, at a downtown Trotskyite meeting, and Mary was struck by Diana's beauty: "[W]ith her dark eyes and flaring nostrils, she looked like Katherine Cornell. Among Stalinist males, I heard, the Trotskyists were believed to have a monopoly of 'all the beautiful girls.' " But once she married Lionel, Diana ceased to register with McCarthy as either a beauty or a Trotskyite and devolved into a mere *wife.* This may have been the root of the problem between them. For in the *PR* world wives were invisible, negligible—except when they were sleeping with you—and in Mary's mind Diana would always remain a wife even after she began to publish. In her memoirs, Trilling writes sardonically of her remarkable metamorphosis from "marital appendage" to serious player after she began to write for *The Nation:* "Now at *Partisan Review* parties it was as if I had all at once acquired new power of mind or a new endowment of personal charm; the other writers could talk to me without the fear that they were squandering time." But McCarthy steadfastly refused to recognize Trilling's new and improved status: in her mind, Trilling would always be something of an upstart, a grasping ambitious *wife* who had clawed her way to prominence on the power of her husband's name. (Trilling recounts in her memoirs how she agonized over whether to sign her reviews with her maiden or married name: the *PR* boys "were united in the

the eyes of McCarthy and company; being *almost* one of them was worse than being nothing at all.

McCarthy was the marrying kind, and so was Rahv, but there never seemed to be any question of marriage between them. Living together, even on swanky, decidedly non-Marxist Beekman Place, suited both of them better. Rahv, as it turned out, was already married but couldn't (or wouldn't) divorce his wife just then. And McCarthy, despite her protestations years later of being "greatly in love," was still looking around. She adored Rahv, but in some unfathomable, inexpressible way she didn't quite respect him. Her snobbish side—the part of her brain that supplied her satirical fiction with damning data on how people dressed, ate, traveled, furnished their homes, voted, and conducted their adulterous affairs—sized Rahv up and found him wanting. As Delmore Schwartz wrote in an unfinished short story based on their liaison, "She soon found that there was a roughness about Stanislaus [the Rahv character] and a rudeness and a habit of being too serious in conversation which she did not like in the least." Rahv was uncouth, and that bothered McCarthy. He was too Slavic, too Marxist, too Jewish, too un-American to suit her. In the fiction she wrote soon after the affair ended, McCarthy vented (and probably amplified) the disdain she felt for Rahv and the other New York Marxist intellectual men she was running around with in the late 1930s. In the shocking (for its time) and deservedly famous story "The Man in the Brooks Brothers Shirt," McCarthy sets her protagonist and alter ego, Meg Sargent, on a westbound train, makes her succumb to a one-night stand with a paunchy middle-aged, Middle American businessman, and then has her reflect bitterly on the men she had left behind in the city:

> [I]f she had felt safe with the different men who had been in love with her it was because—she saw it now—in one way or another they were all of them lame ducks. The handsome ones, like her fiancé, were good-for-nothing, the reliable ones, like her husband, were peculiar-looking, the well-to-do ones were short and wore lifts in their shoes or fat with glasses, the clever ones were alcoholic or slightly homosexual, the serious ones were foreigners or else wore beards or black shirts or were desperately poor and had no table manners. Somehow each of them was handicapped for American life and therefore humble in love.

Meg, taking severe stock of her recent past, wonders whether she really belongs with "this fraternity of cripples." Had she "been spending her life in self-imposed exile, a princess among the trolls?" For all his brains and power, Rahv was one of the trolls in McCarthy's eyes. Her success with the *PR* crowd had come too effortlessly. Rahv and the boys overvalued her because they didn't know any better. "The men she had known during these last four years had been, when you faced it, too easily pleased: her success had been gratifying but hollow," McCarthy writes of Meg in the story. "It was not difficult, after all, to be the prettiest girl at a party for the sharecroppers. At bottom, she was contemptuous of the men who had believed her perfect, for she knew that in a bathing suit at Southampton she would never have passed muster." This may well be an example of the way she "proclaimed the endless treacheries of the human heart—" as Kazin wrote irritably, "proclaimed it with a discipline of style, a show of classical severity and subtler manners than their [the *PR* crowd's] own, that pointed up her *right* to take such a very large bite of her victim." But she was onto something. She had wowed Rahv and the *PR* boys not because she was such hot stuff but because they lacked "breeding," manners, an innate sense of fine distinctions. They didn't know from Southampton, these immigrants and sons of immigrants. They knew Henry James, but Henry James would never have condescended to know *them*. Their American experience came from books, and their judgments were sharp, shrill, and rough around the edges. They were stars in New York, but they faltered when they stood on native ground.

Things were altogether different with Edmund Wilson, the commanding, difficult, massive man of letters who entered McCarthy's life shortly after she started living with Rahv. Wilson, whatever else was wrong with him, radiated perfect confidence in his judgment—whether of books or of women in bathing suits. The power to discriminate and assign proper value was his by birth. And McCarthy was highly susceptible to this power. Actually, the *PR* boys were too. It was their idea, not hers, to woo Wilson and get him to contribute to the magazine. Sometime during the autumn of 1937, they invited Wilson to lunch in Union Square, bringing McCarthy along as bait (she remembers wearing her "best clothes—a black silk dress with tiers of fagoting and, hung from my neck, a long, large silver fox fur"). Everyone, including McCarthy, was worried that she would make a fool of herself—and disgrace the magazine—in front of the great man. But as it turned out, Wilson, in the flesh, was not all that imposing. "He bustled into our office," McCarthy wrote later in her memoirs, "short, stout, middle-aged, breathy—born May 8, 1895; we others were in our twenties—with popping reddish-brown eyes and fresh pink skin, which looked as though he had just bathed. Perhaps it was this suggestion of baths—the tepidarium—and his fine straight nose that gave him a Roman air."

Wilson, at forty-two years of age, had already left his mark on two decades of American literature. He had published widely and deeply on everything from symbolist poetry to the Scottsboro trial; he had written an influential novel of the 1920s, *I Thought of Daisy,* along with plays, poetry, reviews, and social criticism. He knew just about everyone on the literary scene—F. Scott Fitzgerald, John Dos Passos, Louise Bogan, Dawn Powell, and Edna St. Vincent Millay were among his intimates— and he even had a cordially combative relationship with conservative Southern poet Allen Tate. Wilson, like most of his fellow American writers and intellectuals, had taken a sharp turn leftward during the 1930s, and by the end of the decade his politics were more or less aligned with those of *PR,* though he had arrived at his brand of independent-minded Marxism along a rather different path from the one Rahv and his cronies had traveled down. The learned, respected, left-leaning Wilson would be a big catch for the resuscitated magazine, and the editors did everything they could to land him. Rahv, in particular, was obsessed with Wilson: obsessed with publishing him, but perhaps even more obsessed with puncturing the Wilson balloon. "Wilson is a good writer, but he has no ideas," Rahv went around telling the boys (poverty of ideas being the unforgivable sin in Rahv's book). *PR* editor William Barrett wrote in his memoirs that Wilson became "like a boil on the brain" to Rahv. Rahv would later show the same obsessive ambivalence toward Robert Lowell and Hannah Arendt, formidable intellectuals he picked apart viciously in private while printing their new work in the magazine. With Rahv, it wasn't so much jealousy as a street fighter's instinct to catch the other guy, the big guy, off-guard.

So McCarthy, Rahv, Fred Dupee, and Dwight Macdonald took Wilson to lunch. And Wilson promised to send along something for the new magazine. But before he did, he had McCarthy out to dinner and then, unknown to Rahv, into his bed.

Rahv's "boil on the brain" grew more inflamed when McCarthy broke the news, a few short months later, that she was leaving him to marry Wilson.

2

The Southern Branch

■ IN HER *Intellectual Memoirs* of New York in the 1930s, Mary McCarthy recalls that when she first looked into *Partisan Review*—the original Communist Party *PR*—she was baffled by its contents: "I found that it was over my head. It was devoted to an onslaught on the American Humanists . . . with a few rancorous sideswipes at the Southern Agrarians—Allen Tate and John Crowe Ransom." It's revealing that McCarthy singled out the Southern Agrarians, and Tate and Ransom in particular, from the welter of people and ideas that *PR* was sideswiping back then. For in a sense the Agrarians and the *PR* intellectuals were two distant branches of an extended, quarrelsome literary family; not related by blood, certainly, for the southerners, whose ranks also included Robert Penn Warren, Donald Davidson, and Andrew Lytle, were mostly WASPs (or Catholic converts) from "good" "old" families, while the New Yorkers, with a few notable exceptions, were immigrants or the children of immigrants from the Jewish ghettos of eastern Europe, but connected by their shared devotion to literary modernism, by the intense cultural moment they were living in and interpreting together, and perhaps most of all by their cranky, obsessive *awareness* of each other. The two groups could be counted on to take almost exactly opposite positions on the major social and political issues of the day—the issues that had provoked them both into print in the first place: the southerners were conservative, even reactionary, whereas the New Yorkers were progressive; the southerners were infatuated with rural, aristocratic values—land, family lineage, religion, honor—whereas the New Yorkers were urban, atheist, and proletarian in their sympathies; in literary criticism, the Agrarians and their New Critical heirs were bent on severing texts from historical and biographical context, while the New Yorkers were just as determined to view fiction and verse through a Marxist and/or Freudian scrim. Feuding cousins, they fired volley after volley at each other from their opposite sides of the Mason-Dixon Line, calling a cease-fire only when Eliot, Yeats, or James Joyce loomed over the battlefield.

And yet, this being the American republic of letters, ideological differences did not preclude a certain amount of fraternizing, hobnobbing, and curious gossipmongering. Of the emissaries who ran back and forth between the two camps, none was more active, sought-after, and listened-to than Kentucky-born poet Allen Tate and his prolific Southern novelist wife, Caroline Gordon. The Tates had in fact lived in New York for several buzzing years in the mid-1920s, moving in loose-living, hard-drinking, left-wing bohemian circles and consorting with the likes of Hart Crane, Maxwell Perkins, Katherine Anne Porter, Louise Bogan, and Edmund Wilson. Though by the 1930s they had elected to keep their distance from the city and to scoff at the fashionable Marxist politics of the day as a "ruse to maintain the New York supremacy," both maintained close ties to northern intellectuals. In the years ahead, both were to be important influences on the rising generation of American writers. Younger poets such as Randall Jarrell, Robert Lowell, William Meredith, and John Berryman learned from Tate that "poetry must be burly, must be courteous, must be tinkered with and recast until one's eyes pop out of one's head," as Lowell wrote in a fondly teasing tribute, and Tate helped them publish their verse and get them teaching jobs; while Gordon dispensed stern, sometimes unwanted, and often voluminous advice to Jean Stafford, Flannery O'Connor, Walker Percy, Ellen Glasgow, and Eudora Welty, among others. As a successful, if beleaguered, literary wife of many years' standing, Gordon viewed herself as an authority on coping with the demands of art and life, especially married life—an authority one crossed at one's peril. For the younger literary wives who entered her orbit, Gordon became a strong, though not altogether uplifting, model.

Tate and Gordon's marriage was in many ways a kind of living symbol, almost a test case of the Agrarian ideals they both espoused. Certainly their mutual attraction was bound up with a fantasy of the Old South—that sacred, silvery, lost-cause nostalgia that led Yankee critics (and some southerners as well) to ridicule the Agrarians as "neo-Confederates." In Tate's case the fantasy was at least partly fabricated or heavily embellished, for though his fierce, delusional mother did indeed hail from patrician Tidewater stock, John Orley Allen Tate, as he was christened in 1899, was born not in Fairfax County, Virginia, as his mother had told him, but in the east Kentucky hill country, where his father had a lumber business. Tate, a small, slim child with a large, bulbous head, endured the humiliation of family financial decline, and by the time he was a teenager his father had lost both his business and what was left of his fortune. The family managed to scrape together the money to send Tate to Vanderbilt University in Nashville, and it was here that he dedicated himself to poetry and became involved with the Fugitives, a group of young poets and teachers who tried to resuscitate the South as an important subject of and occasion for verse. The Agrarian movement of the early 1930s was essentially a continuation and extension of the Fugitives' bull sessions at Vanderbilt, only now, with the nation sunk in depression, the Tennessee poets widened their focus from verse to social, economic, and religious issues (in his rather cryptic contribution to the seminal Agrarian collection *I'll Take My Stand,* Tate argued that Catholicism was, or should have been, the true religion of the Old South—an early sign of the Catholic piety that was to color his life and his marriage). Tate, with his beautiful manners, irascible, volatile temperament, and wildly reactionary politics, naturally took his place at the center of Agrarian debate and controversy. One acquaintance described him as "a rabid Southerner of the old school who thought it was a crime that lynching had been abolished." Alfred Kazin, in *New York Jew,* recalled the way Tate "furiously began every conversation as if I personified the liberal New York Jewish enemy. . . . When half seas over, he was insulting enough to satisfy his longing for strength." Tate's other defining characteristics were a lofty, uncompromising dedication to the life of letters, a taste for alcohol, and an insatiable desire to seduce new women, with whom he had amazing success given his ungainly appearance. (Malcolm Cowley, an acquaintance from New York in the 1920s, wrote that Tate's "enormous head" gave him the "look of a greedy child," and another male friend remarked that "his expression when it was not hawklike was impudent." Kazin thought his nose and eyes looked like candles planted in a cake and gave him an "oddly pitiable but still aggressive" expression. But perhaps men simply did not understand what women saw in him.)

Gordon seems to have surrendered instantly and totally when they met in the summer of 1924. Four years older than Tate, she had been born and raised in southern Kentucky in the kind of Old South rural grandeur that Tate's mother always claimed as her own family's heritage—the "Southern Myth," Tate called it. On her mother's side, Gordon was a member of the Meriwether clan, holders of immense tracts of fertile black tobacco-growing soil and inheritors of a wonderfully shabby old plantation house called Merry Mount that was staffed by former slaves. Gordon grew up not rich, for not even the landed gentry in the South had much money back then, but proud and privileged—and she held on to this family pride all her life, along with a relish of the pig-headed eccentricities of her Meriwether kin and especially her grandmother Miss Carrie Meriwether, the family matriarch. But Gordon was also something of a rebel, determined to escape the stifling, moth-eaten provincialism of southwest Kentucky. Passionate about literature, she got a job after college as a reporter for *The Chattanooga News* (in which she published an effusive appreciation of the Fugitive poets in 1923 under the headline "US Best Poets Here in Tennessee"), and in her spare time she worked on a novel. Then, in the summer of 1924, one of these best poets turned up in the neighborhood on a protracted visit to Robert Penn Warren, who was recovering from depression and a suicide attempt at his family's home in nearby Guthrie. Warren brought Gordon and Tate together, and the romance kindled. "She was the prettiest girl I ever saw," Tate supposedly said long afterward of his first glimpse of the slight, small, dark-haired, dark-eyed, luminously pale Gordon, "and I pissed in my pants." According to Tate, they consummated their love that summer in the Guthrie churchyard. At summer's end, they agreed to rendezvous in New York, where Tate had spent a few happy months earlier in the year.

By the time they connected in Greenwich Village in November, the romance seems to have cooled, at least on Tate's side. But soon it was impossible for him to back out because Gordon informed him she was pregnant. They married sullenly and against Tate's wishes the following

May. Tate entered into the union only on the condition that they divorce right after the baby was born.

The Tates stayed married for nearly three decades (with a pause for a brief divorce), but emotional tumult would always be their element. Their baby, a girl they named Nancy, was only days old when Gordon's mother came up from Kentucky, took one look at the bare, primitive Greenwich Village apartment, and insisted on removing the child and raising her in Kentucky. Caroline, uncharacteristically, submitted passively—in fact, she was probably relieved not to have an infant interrupting her work and dragging on her marriage. That was in September 1925. By early December, the Tates decided they'd had enough of city living. They arranged to rent an unheated, plumbingless house in upstate New York and invited Hart Crane to join them. The rustic ménage was not a success. Though Tate and Crane admired each other's work and had been blissful drinking companions in the city, they were disastrous as housemates. And Gordon discovered that as a "mere" journalist and struggling novelist she had no claim on the respect of poets, particularly male poets. She was the *poet's wife,* which meant that she cooked and cleaned house and wrote at the kitchen table (to be fair, Crane and Tate did help with the dishes). By winter's end the three of them were numb, half crazed with the cold, and furious at one another. In April, as the weather began to thaw, Tate and Gordon both wrote poisonous letters to Crane insisting that he leave. The friendship, miraculously, survived, though they never lived together again.

Makeshift communal arrangements ending in acrimony proved to be an enduring feature of the Tate-Gordon marriage. No matter where they were living—and they were on the move incessantly, from upstate New York to the city and then to Paris in 1928, then back to New York briefly in 1930 before decamping for Tennessee and then Europe once again—they housed a steady stream of visitors, often Allen's Fugitive "brethren," who descended for weeks or even months at a time. And when the stream ran dry, the Tates invited friends or other couples to share their houses, most memorably Robert Lowell and Jean Stafford during the winter of 1942–1943. It was strange that they let go of their own baby daughter for a couple of years, since they were always taking in strays and making them surrogate children. Perhaps they enjoyed having a buffer between them and, in Tate's case, a cover for his myriad infidelities. Then too, when the housemates became annoying or vicious, the Tates pulled together in excoriating them. Excoriation of intimates was a passion they shared with New York adepts such as Rahv and Delmore Schwartz.

Out of necessity, Gordon became a brilliant, if sometimes furious, domestic strategist, able to feed many mouths on a pittance, find beds for picky gentlemen poets, and somehow squeeze in time for her own writing (she published nine novels and two short-story collections between 1931 and 1972). She "had some saintly qualities," recalls Vanderbilt English professor Walter Sullivan, who knew the Tates well. "She was strong, and she was as single-minded, as purposeful as any person I have ever known. Even for a novelist, she seemed deeply immersed in her work." Sullivan adds that "one of Caroline's talents was to be minimally inconvenienced by her guests." This was a talent she acquired through many years of practice. But once she had it down pat, Gordon had no sympathy for less nimble literary wives. As Eileen Simpson, who was married to the poet John Berryman for several years, remembers, "Caroline had little patience with married feminist writers who 'whined' about having domestic chores to do. Her practice had been to organize the house first thing in the morning, then go to the typewriter." And once she was at the typewriter, she wouldn't budge until her work was done. Writing was her creed and her religion, and if she had to send her daughter away or leave her behind to finish a novel, she did it. The writing came first, and the fact that she also took care of the housework was a tribute to her energy and determination. Gordon prided herself on how well she managed and couldn't imagine why other women had trouble following her example.

Despite her domestic adroitness, Gordon was never one of those mousy, dutiful wives dedicated to the comfort and pleasure of their husbands—but she did put Tate and his work first. No matter how obstinate and argumentative she was with others—and a formidable tenacity, especially in literary debate, was one of her outstanding characteristics—she almost always deferred to him. According to Simpson, "He was probably the only person capable of making Caroline docile. It was one of the things she loved about him." The docility was rooted in her absolute faith in Tate's superiority as a writer. In her eyes, he was The Poet. Gordon believed her husband was miles ahead of her when they married, and she was convinced she would never catch up, even though she outearned him as a writer—not only that she *wouldn't* but that she *shouldn't*. She needed Tate to be her literary conscience, hero, and master, and there were times in her career when she showed him everything she was writing and took his suggestions to heart. He was her first, her most important, and often her most severe critic. And she was always grateful to him for including her in his world of books and writers, for taking her seriously as a writer herself. Gordon was so sensitive to Tate's stature as an artist that she even blamed herself for the long creative dry spell that afflicted him during the 1930s and early 1940s. As she told Katherine Anne Porter, "When one is married to a poet one always feels a little guilty when he isn't writing poetry, the supposition being that he might be writing if he were married to someone else." It was this kind of thinking that would make Gordon such a destructive influence on younger literary wives, especially Jean Stafford.

The one arena in which Gordon held sway over Tate was the garden. Gordon had grown up loving the soil, and no matter where she lived as an adult she always planted vegetables and flowers and learned the names of all the wildflowers and trees and mushrooms (a passion of hers). Early in the marriage, during that first summer in upstate New York after Hart Crane had decamped, Caroline learned that her husband was hopeless around plants—he was too distracted to pay much attention, too much the dandy to get down in the dirt—and she gave up trying to interest him in the garden. The irony, of course, was that while Tate was espousing the great Agrarian ideal as the salvation of the South, he barely knew a hoe from a hatchet. None of the Agrarians did, with the exception of Andrew Lytle, who owned a farm and worked it (and to a lesser extent John Crowe Ransom, who raised geometrically perfect beds of annuals). As Gordon's biographer Ann Waldron puts it, "Allen *talked* Agrarian, but Caroline *was* Agrarian." Indeed she carried the Agrarian flame longer and higher than the menfolk, both in her gardens and in her fiction, which may explain why her writing seems rather dated today. Elizabeth Hardwick feels that Gordon ended up taking Agrarianism "almost too seriously" and that as a novelist "she got trapped in it" and never emerged.

The Tates' field for both entertaining and gardening widened considerably in 1930, when they bought a lofty, pillared, sagging old house on a hill overlooking the Cumberland River near Clarksville, Tennessee. They christened the property Benfolly after Tate's rich businessman brother Ben, who loaned them $10,000 (interest free) to buy the place and fix it up, and over the next few years they spent as much time there as they could (which for Gordon was disappointingly little: she was always complaining that they moved away—to Europe, to Memphis, to Greensboro—before she could enjoy the fruits of the garden). It was here that they hosted Edmund Wilson, a friend and sparring partner from Allen's early New York sojourns, on a memorable occasion in the winter of 1931. The story goes that Wilson, a fresh convert to Marxism, no sooner dropped his suitcase on Benfolly's peeling porch than he demanded of Tate and Gordon, "Now, where are the sharecroppers?" Gordon fomented a bit of down-home mischief when she urged Wilson to "nibble the tiniest tip of a leaf" of tobacco and then watched while he "went into a slight convulsion." Perhaps in revenge, Wilson soon afterward published an essay entitled "The Tennessee Agrarians" in which he took the group to task for their tendency "to marry girls at home, to renovate family mansions, to do some farming with the aid of a sharecropper, to write books about the Civil War. . . . As lacking in a religion or a common ideal as their compatriots of New York or Paris, they try to find one in ancestor-worship." Tate, predictably, was outraged: "Can you really with such unblushing glibness reduce our position to *ancestor-worship?* . . . You like to think that we are wistful boys mooning over the past." Relations between Wilson and the Tates were a good deal chillier from then on, although the Southern couple did turn up at Wilson's Connecticut home a few years later to witness an especially ugly episode in his marriage to Mary McCarthy (see Chapter 3).

Benfolly reached its apogee of fame and anecdote during the summer of 1937, when the house was full to bursting with literary lions, cubs, and consorts. The Tates had been away for two years, and characteristically, when they returned, they invited friends to join them for a prolonged stay—in this case the English novelist and critic Ford Madox Ford, who had once employed Gordon as his secretary in New York and ended up coaching her through her first novel and championing the work with a rave review, along with his young wife, Janice Biala, a painter, and her sister-in-law Wally Tworkov. The Ford party arrived with the hot weather in early May, and a small herd followed hard on their heels: at various times during that long, sweltering, festive summer, New Critic Cleanth Brooks and his wife, Tinkum, Katherine Anne Porter, and *Southern Review* editor Albert Erskine were in residence, most of them (including Tate and Gordon) attempting to write. Tate was toiling over his lone novel, *The Fathers,* while Gordon plugged away at her fourth novel, *The Garden of Adonis*. "I've had to develop a brand new technique for writing—" Gordon told a friend, "one hand on the kitchen stove and one on the typewriter. It works to my surprise—I do my five or six pages most days. Rotten they are, too." Years later she was still bragging to Eileen Simpson, "When I think of the cooking I did at 'Benfolly'! We never had less than ten at the table." "It was a situation perversely planned by fate to expose human weakness," Tate wrote in *The New York Review of Books* in 1963. He marveled that there had been no "scenes."

One of the hungry ten was an uninvited but extremely persistent college student by the name of Robert Traill Spence Lowell IV. How and why the twenty-year-old Lowell wound up in Clarksville, Tennessee, that summer is a curious tale of sexual infatuation, familial rage, grand ambition, hero worship, and an almost religious devotion to the art of poetry—all the obsessions that were to propel him through the rest of his life. A scion of two old, distinguished New England families (his mother's people, the Winslows, had arrived on the *Mayflower;* his father was one of *the* Lowells, albeit from one of the lesser and poorer branches), Robert Lowell, nicknamed "Cal" in prep school for Caligula and/or Caliban, was a formidably odd young man—movie-star handsome in a sort of smoldering, glowering Olivier-Heathcliffe fashion, yet also habitually dirty, slovenly, uncombed, sloppy beyond belief, trailing clouds of chaos and lost objects. He was sufficiently convinced of his literary promise to seek out Robert Frost and solicit his opinion of his youthful verse, yet so shy that he spoke in a diffident whisper. He was fated from birth to go to Harvard—his kinsman A. Lawrence Lowell was the university's president from 1909 to 1933, and eminent Boston poets James Russell and Amy Lowell hung heavy on the family tree—but his year and a half at the college was disastrously unhappy, mostly because of the looming proximity of his oppressive parents, the dull former naval officer Bob and the icy, controlling Charlotte. There was also the disaster of his rash engagement to Anne Dick, an older woman (she was all of twenty-four when they met, he nineteen), to whom he proposed at the end of his freshman year after a few months' acquaintance. Lowell was a "marrier," as a cousin of his put it, always hell-bent on getting, though not necessarily staying, married. The elder Lowells vehemently opposed the match (as their son knew they would) and made their opposition embarrassingly public in a letter to Anne Dick's father. At the height of the family fracas that erupted over the affair, the hotheaded young Lowell stormed over to his parents' house on Marlborough Street and knocked his father down—"torpedoed my Father to the floor," as he put it in one of the many, many verse versions of the event. Boston psychiatrist Merrill Moore—a Vanderbilt graduate and member of the Fugitive circle, the author of a never-ending sonnet cycle and almost certainly Charlotte Lowell's lover—was summoned, and Moore recommended sending "Bobby" down South to rusticate with the Agrarians (Charlotte leaned more toward interring her son in an insane asylum, but Moore prevailed).

And so in the spring of 1937 Cal Lowell hit the road for Tennessee, literally "crash[ing] the civilization of the South," as he wrote years later, when his car plowed into the Tates' "frail agrarian mailbox post." (Jean Stafford would suffer far more seriously from Lowell's hazardous driving.) According to Gordon, Lowell added insult to injury by promptly turning his back to "answer a call of nature." But once they learned the young man's name and ancestry, they were delighted: here was literary New England incarnate come to sit at the feet of the great Southern sage. What a coup for their side! Lowell, for his part, was only too pleased to be held hostage by the likes of Allen Tate. Tate could be peevish, cantankerous, absurdly old-fashioned, and ferociously partisan, but, as Lowell wrote in his memoir of the visit, he had "all the English classics, and some of the Greeks and Latins . . . at [his] elbow" and he "maneuvered through them, coolly blasting, rehabilitating, now and then reciting key lines in an austere, vibrant voice." Lowell was equally enthralled with the Tates' brand of devastating gossip: "regional anecdotes, Greenwich Village reminiscences, polemics on personalities."

Without consulting his hosts, the young poet made up his mind to return to Benfolly that summer and install himself as disciple. By summer, of course, the house was already packed to capacity, "groan[ing]," as Lowell wrote, "with the fatigued valor of Southern hospitality." Gordon told the Yankee wayfarer, as a joke apparently, that if he wanted to stay he'd have to pitch a tent in the yard. Deaf to the brush-off, Lowell took himself to the nearest Sears, Roebuck, acquired a tent, and returned to camp out among the wandering farm animals for the better part of three months—and, of course, to write poetry: "Every other day, I turned out grimly unromantic poems—organized, hard, and classical as a cabinet." This was pure Lowell—heedless, endearing, impossible, inconvenient, headlong, grandly egotistic. Another youth would have taken the hint and departed or stayed in a hotel or hung sheepishly around the periphery of the charmed circle of the published great. But Lowell instinctively went for the fierce, attention-grabbing gesture, even at the risk of making himself a nuisance. Nuisance or not, he was one of *the* Lowells, and the assembled Southern literati forgave him his awkwardness in their delight at having captured such a prize Yankee (Ford was not so taken and supposedly refused to address Lowell or acknowledge his existence until Gordon kicked up a fuss, whereupon he began referring to him as "Young Man"). Katherine Anne Porter spoke fondly of having "this solitary, strange, gifted child . . . among us." The waspish Gordon, impressed with Lowell despite her resentment at having another mouth to feed, wrote to a friend that he was "the handiest boy I ever knew" (this must have been the only time in his life that the notoriously clumsy Lowell won praise for helping around the house). Tate decided he was "the real thing" and encouraged him to pursue his studies under John Crowe Ransom, who was in the process of moving from Vanderbilt University to Kenyon College in Ohio.

Benfolly emptied out for a few weeks at midsummer, when those assembled dispersed to attend writers' conferences. The Tates and the Fords planned to attend a July conference at Olivet College in Michigan, and when they set off from Benfolly in the Tates' shuddering car, they took Lowell with them like a beloved, difficult pet. After Olivet, the Tates returned to Benfolly via Virginia with Katherine Anne Porter in tow, while Ford, accompanied by the unshakable Lowell, proceeded westward to another conference at Boulder, Colorado. It was here, in the august presence of Sherwood Anderson, Ransom, and John Peale Bishop that Lowell met the woman who was to become his first wife: Jean Stafford.

A fresh-faced, funny, strikingly pretty, fast-talking, aspiring novelist of twenty-two, Stafford at a single glance seems to have driven all thoughts of Anne Dick clean out of Lowell's mind. Stafford smoked, drank, wisecracked, held an audience spellbound with her racy stories, laughed deep in her throat. She had studied abroad. Her writing won high marks from Lowell's literary gods of the moment. He was smitten. Love at first sight is far too tame a phrase for the hungry, obsessive claim that he made on Stafford's life. His wooing, which began innocently enough with an exchange of letters, escalated rapidly into something approaching a stalking. Lowell was indeed a marrier, and once he made up his mind he was going to marry Stafford, there was little she could do about it.

On paper, anyway, the match had everything going for it: brilliance, beauty, shared ambitions, a zest for what Stafford called "stylized, creative" gossip, dedication to the written word, convergent religious leanings. But in practice the two proved to be spectacularly unsuited to each other. Lowell and Stafford married figments of their imaginations and then spent six years finding out the painful, often humiliating truth about each other. Stafford was not really the sophisticated, tough-minded, iconoclastic woman of the world Lowell had taken her for. As a husband, Lowell proved to be far less the Boston Brahmin of his pedigree and far more the wild-eyed, obsessive, fire-breathing poet fanatic of Stafford's nightmares. Success, which came to Stafford fairly early in the marriage and to Lowell near its end, drove them in different directions—Stafford to a compulsive artful domesticity, Lowell to the task of managing and magnifying his public image. They had no children, and by some accounts they had no sex, at least with each other, for much of the marriage. They drank too much, though seldom at the same time and usually with snide disapproval of the other's excess. Their fights turned violent on several occasions, enough for Stafford to require hospitalization. Yet the marriage might have survived all this. What was fatal, finally, was knowledge. Lowell and Stafford discovered, to their horror, how remote the other was from the person they thought they had married. The truth was shattering, at least to Stafford. Lowell, by the time the marriage ended, had already left its truths and falsehoods far behind.

For Stafford, the Boulder conference was a homecoming of sorts, for she had lived in Boulder for several years during her later childhood and attended the University of Colorado there from 1932 to 1936. Born in 1915, she had spent her first years on an idyllic ten-acre walnut farm that her father, John Richard Stafford, had planted in the southern California town of Covina (now part of the Los Angeles sprawl). The walnut farm, acquired with money that John Stafford inherited from his rich cattle rancher father, turned out to be yet another abandoned experiment in a long life of botches and disappointments. A moody, unsteady, downwardly mobile man, he thought of himself primarily as a writer; he was the author of a slew of Westerns (*When Cattle Kingdom Fell,* among others) and angry diatribes on assorted topics. Though he published some of his work, he failed to command either money or many readers, and he proved equally inept at handling his business affairs. A decade before the Depression, he managed to lose all his inherited money in the stock market and bring his family to the brink of poverty. (In 1940, Jean stumbled upon some documents that revealed that her father's fortune in

1920 had been "something short of 300,000"—a discovery that "will keep me awake the rest of my life," as she wrote a friend.)

In 1921, the Staffords sold the walnut farm and moved to Colorado, settling in 1925 in Boulder, where Jean's prudent, long-suffering, devotedly bourgeois mother made ends meet by taking in female college student boarders, to the everlasting humiliation of her sensitive daughter (the humiliation burns hot in short stories such as "The Tea Time of Stouthearted Ladies" and "In the Zoo"). The images of her mother toiling away at the thankless, penny-pinching tasks of running a boardinghouse while her father banged out yet another unprofitable piece of prose left painful marks on Jean's adolescent imagination. "Mother said she did not understand how I could write, having witnessed Dad's thirty-year miscarriage," Stafford wrote a friend in 1938, after one of her brief, unhappy family visits. On another occasion she summed up the family dynamic tersely: "[M]y mother spared [my father's] feelings; we believed he was an artist." The family paid a ruinous price to spare those artistic feelings.

Paul and Dorothy Thompson, dear friends of Stafford's from her college days until her death, have written of the difficulty of fathoming or encompassing the "real" Jean Stafford: "Much of her life we knew nothing of: for example, her Catholic tutelage by Father Agatho, although it was going on during the time when we were seeing her regularly. . . . Hers was a complex, multi-faceted personality. No friend or, we suspect, relative or husband knew her entirely. All were up for surprises, sometimes troubling ones. Yet she had a remarkable talent for durable friendships." Like the diction in her stories, Stafford was by turns fastidious and down-home, wickedly satirical and exquisitely refined. She loved to talk at great length, and to dramatize herself and the events of her life, and at parties or with friends she was famous for her comically embellished anecdotes—"always far more interesting than the actual event," as one friend remarked. Yet, with high-powered literary folk, she took refuge in the role of the outsider—the "rube," as she puts it in her famous story "Children Are Bored on Sunday."

"She played the role of the cowgirl," says Harvard sinologist James Robert Hightower, a fellow Coloradan who loved her and wanted to marry her before Lowell came into the picture. "She was a comedian—she could take on the coloring of any society she found herself in." Lowell's close friend Blair Clark, an editor, writer, and television news director who knew her well both during and after the marriage to Lowell, was evidently taken in by the cowgirl act, for he now says of the young Stafford, "The sophisticated European patina was a millimeter thick. She was a sort of flat-heeled country girl in New York–Boston terms. She was a bluestocking, wide-eyed before the great world of society and intellect." A natural performer, she loved watching her own act reflected in the eyes of her audience—but when the show was over, she sometimes felt a little lost. This was particularly true when the people watching were high-powered New York intellectuals, the people whose approval and power Lowell most craved. As Ann Hulbert, the most acute of Stafford's biographers, puts it, "She wanted to be connected with the most famous and important literary figures, and yet when she was in their midst she always felt exiled to the periphery." She never quite believed that she made the grade with the New York crowd, even though she had each of their numbers and could hilariously mimic their verbal tics and eccentricities of taste and manner. She never quite believed that making the grade was *worth it*. Mary McCarthy gave her the creeps; Rahv made her tense; Delmore Schwartz amused her (they were rumored to have had an affair), though she soon wearied of his paranoid antics. Yet many brainy, well-connected New Yorkers were highly impressed with her—her savoir faire, her wide range of acquaintances, her haute-bohemian interiors. "Miss Stafford is a constantly surprising person," writes New York attorney and author Louis Auchincloss, who knew her well. "It would be natural to assume that a woman of such intense sensitivity and intellectual awareness might be vague and otherworldly, or that a woman as dogged by illness as she has been might be deficient in physical vitality. But she is sharply practical as a housekeeper, as a cook, in all the minutiae of life; she can summon a taxi out of air and find a telephone booth in a block where one *knows* there was not one before; and one is constantly amazed at the breadth of her travels and acquaintance. For all the exoticism of her studies and interests, however, she remains firmly rooted in the western soil where she grew up."

"She was always trouble," says Hightower, still admiring, still wondering all these years later. "Wherever she was, things happened. She had a way of getting to know people, of making contacts wherever she went. But she was always getting herself in a mess. There was a core someplace, although she played a lot of roles with a lot of different people. Jean was self-created. She invented herself and imposed the inventions on other people. She made a character of herself."

"Self-destructive" is a word that always comes up in conversations about Stafford. There was the drinking, which was already a problem by the time she met Lowell, got much, much worse in the course of their marriage, and remained pretty bad for the rest of her life. There was the self-loathing—the compulsion to anatomize her failings, to blurt out the most embarrassing details about herself. Like her alter ego, Molly Fawcett, in *The Mountain Lion,* she saw *everybody's* faults too clearly, but her own most clearly of all. Intimate knowledge gave her power, the child's power of hoarded secrets, but she knew too much for her own good. Her Jamesian appreciation of motive and appearance, her unshockable skepticism left her passive and vulnerable. She would walk into traps with open eyes—willingly, resolutely, with chin up and never a glance behind. Lowell may have been the biggest trap of her life. But he was also in over his head with her before he knew it.

When they crossed paths at Boulder, Lowell, despite his impressive name and high-profile connections, was still a student, an *undergraduate* about to resume his derailed college education at Kenyon, while Stafford was a *woman,* a woman in the process of establishing herself as a *writer.* This was the real trigger of Lowell's fixation: he *had* to marry a writer, he always would. After graduating from the University of Colorado in 1936, Stafford had spent a year in Heidelberg, where she dabbled at studying philology, acquired shockingly little German, became mesmerized by the Nazis' irresistible rise to power, and decided that she was not meant to be an academician at all but rather a novelist. Actually, this was not so much a decision as a resignation to the inevitable. Stafford had been writing since the age of twelve, according to Hightower, and inside she had always known she would be a writer, just like her father. "It never occurs to her that she will not be a writer," Stafford says blithely of an alter ego in an unpublished novel, "and only occasionally does it occur to her, depressingly, that she is going to grow into a woman, not a man." Or, as Peter Taylor writes of a character modeled closely on Stafford in his fond nostalgic story "1939," "Ever since she was a little girl on a dairy farm . . . she had dreamed of becoming a writer and going to live in New York City. She had not merely dreamed of it. She had worked toward it every waking hour of her life."

By the time she came back from Germany in the spring of 1937, Stafford was well along in the manuscript of a novel and brooding over other ambitious literary projects. She was also seriously ill, possibly with venereal disease, although this has been a subject of dispute and indignation among her friends. Stafford's health in general was something of an issue for much of her adult life: she was sick a lot, but it wasn't always

clear with what. The endless series of diseases and conditions she contracted became part of her self-invention and self-destruction, an escape
from pain into suffering, so that it's often difficult to sort out illness and
metaphor. "Jean was a hypochondriac—to put it mildly," according to
Eileen Simpson. In any case, whether or not she had gonorrhea or
syphilis, she languished for some time that spring in a Brooklyn, New
York, hospital. She was "miserable," she wrote a friend, at being back in
the States. She was also very much at loose ends—a novelist in her own
mind but with no published work and no clear prospects. She knew, or
at least suspected, that she was good; the essential thing now was to
make the right people recognize how good she was. A lot was riding on
the Boulder conference.

To Stafford's surprise and pleasure, the conference leaders singled her
out right away. She reported breathlessly to Hightower that the critic
John Peale Bishop (a college chum of Edmund Wilson's) "Said I was
best." And Evelyn Scott, an older female writer who took Stafford under
her wing, "said I was the most unusual for age had ever seen. Have not
embellished. Am not embarrassed. Know for sure I'm good—like hell.
Will doubtless spend life writing novels." Ransom was also impressed
with her and later reported in a letter to Tate, "The sanest and most
charming and at the same time most promising girl at the Boulder Writers' Conference last summer was Jean Stafford. Her best work is fiction."

Less enthralling was the swift recognition Stafford received from the
young poet everyone called Cal, whom she encountered at the house of
her former teacher and mentor Edward Davison. Though diffident
around people he didn't know, Lowell had a way of zeroing in on attractive, articulate women. And Stafford, despite the frumpy oxford shoes
and dirndl skirts she had adopted in Heidelberg, was a beauty with luminous skin, straight, clear features, and what a contemporary described
as "a model's figure." Stafford didn't know what to make of her new admirer. On the one hand, there was the Lowell name, with its rich New
England literary resonance. On the other hand, there was this strange,
large, dirty, hollow-eyed youth before her. Lowell tried to repeat his Tennessee stunt of camping out uninvited in someone's yard, but this time
the homeowners asked him to leave since, as Stafford told a friend, he
was "shitting" on their property. The poet and editor Peter Davison, the
son of Stafford's teacher, recalls that "Lowell kept presenting himself for
every social occasion, though uninvited, and with manic heedlessness
paid few of the appropriate courtesies to his hostess." Finally Mrs. Davi-

son turned him away, saying, "I'm sorry, Mr. Lowell. You can't come in. I don't like your manners." There was something very animal-like about the young Lowell. He was a slob, a fanatic, a bull, and a bully, but also incredibly magnetic and, when he wanted to be, charming. "Cal had this imperative to change people's lives," says Blair Clark, a close friend since prep school days. "Later on this was clinical, but we did not know it at the time. He had an evangelistic notion of human behavior with himself as the evangel." Clark thought there was something "sickly" about Lowell's intensity and self-obsession in his early twenties: "I would never use the word lovable about him. Never." He had a violent physical and sexual energy with an enormous intellectual current surging through it. The terrible tension between mind and body made him seem dangerous, tortured, impulsive. His will was formidable. He was the kind of young man who would devise a program for himself—lose his virginity by such an age; read all of the Elizabethan playwrights by summer's end; publish by a self-imposed deadline—and then carry it out methodically, ruthlessly. After the Boulder conference ended, he had a new goal on his program: to marry Jean Stafford.

Lowell, whose own father was by most accounts vague, weak, boring, and remote, spent his young manhood looking for literary "fathers" who could guide and inspire him. Robert Frost and Ford Madox Ford declined the honor, but in Tate Lowell struck gold. Tate enjoyed having disciples, as long as they were bright and appreciative, and Lowell had the added attractions of a famous Yankee name and a grounding in classical antiquity. Though two decades later he would fondly mock the Tates for their "stately yet bohemian" ways, at twenty he was only too pleased to be adopted by them—adopted and, in an enduring way, altered. "Like a torn cat, I was taken in when I needed help," he wrote in "Visiting the Tates," "and in a sense I have never left." What began for him as a kind of desperate, recuperative exile turned out to be an important juncture in his career. Lowell acquired more than a faint Southern accent and courtly manner from his alliance with the Agrarians. Through Tate and through Ransom at Kenyon, he met the writers who were to become some of his closest friends through life: Peter Taylor, Randall Jarrell, Robert Penn Warren, Southerners all. During the 1940s, when Lowell established himself for a time in New York, he would become a kind of emissary connecting the Southern group with the *Partisan Review* crowd. Lowell, a terror during his periodic descents into madness, had a gift when sane for staying on good terms with disparate, warring factions. He managed to be close to both Rahv and Ransom, Delmore Schwartz (until they fell out) and Jarrell, Mary McCarthy and Edmund Wilson (after their divorce), Lillian Hellman and Flannery O'Connor. Most of them despised one another, but they all got along with Lowell and through him enjoyed an endless stream of irresistible gossip about all the rest. He was a natural, if often mischievous, literary ambassador.

Stafford also loved being around smart, funny, gossipy writers, and in company she could be the smartest and funniest of them all; but unlike Lowell she needed to keep an ironical distance between herself and any literary crowd. Too much exposure wilted her. Gordon and Tate, especially Gordon, could be especially wearing. The Lowells and the Tates were together a lot in the 1940s, and the parallels between the couples were obvious: the husbands writing poetry, the wives writing novels and short stories, both pairs flitting around the outskirts of universities, landing temporary appointments, moving frequently. Yet Stafford resisted apprenticing herself to Gordon as Lowell had done so enthusiastically with Tate. Gordon was too harsh, too demanding a "mother." She delivered broadsides and ultimata; she was too frank and free in her criticism of Stafford's work; she brooked no rivalry in the kitchen. When crossed or confronted, she exploded. Her temper tantrums were notorious; her self-assurance unyielding. After years of practice, she had worked out her own way of being a writer and the wife of a writer, and though she often went through her routine "with clenched teeth and curses," as she wrote Stafford, she assumed that what worked for her should work for everyone else. Stafford fell in with it for a while during the winter of 1942, when the two couples shared a house in the Tennessee mountains; but eventually she quailed under Gordon's rigorous regime.

It wasn't that Stafford was a budding feminist who would fight to free herself from the burdens of wifeliness altogether or insist that her art came before everything else—in fact, just the opposite. As her marriage with Lowell grew increasingly strained, she wanted to be more of a wife, not less—or at least said she did. The idea of becoming Caroline Gordon—"one hand on the kitchen stove and one on the typewriter"—filled her with panic. It didn't help that Gordon was in the habit of composing lengthy unsolicited letters pointing out where Stafford's prose went astray in diction, tone, credibility, point of view. "What I am trying to say," she wrote in one particularly stinging passage, "is that I don't think you observe things closely enough, or perhaps it's that you don't observe them passionately enough to render them the way I like to see them rendered"—passion being precisely the aspect of her life and work that Stafford felt most insecure about.

Of all the prominent women writers of her generation, Stafford was the least equipped temperamentally to deal with the conflicts between her life and her work, her marriage and her fiction, her need to have a lovely, loved home and her desire to be the best—"like hell." It's possible that Stafford would have self-destructed no matter what the circumstances. But it didn't help that just when she was coming into her own artistically she had Robert Lowell as a husband and Caroline Gordon as a mentor.

3

Seven Years of Hell

"SHE WAS trouble," recalls New York editor Jason Epstein, who knew Mary McCarthy well and never liked her much. "You could see it a mile away." Edmund Wilson didn't. What he saw in McCarthy when they met in the fall of 1937—just around the time Robert Lowell began writing letters to Jean Stafford—was a bright, witty, attractive, neurotic young woman. Just his type, in fact. "He had always had a weakness for intelligent women," McCarthy wrote of the Wilson character in her lightly fictionalized novel *A Charmed Life,* "though he knew them to be bad for him, like drink or certain kinds of food. They disagreed with him, in both senses of the word." As Gore Vidal put it, "Wilson was a man of the previous century and the idea of a brilliant woman as an equal was always intriguing (he married one, after all, McCarthy, and duly suffered) but somehow against nature." Intriguing but unnatural: maybe Wilson *did* suspect that McCarthy would be trouble, but he went ahead and pursued her anyway. He always had tremendous confidence in his ability to handle difficult people. And of course he was famously difficult himself.

Strikingly, even to some eyes grotesquely, different as they were in age and appearance (Wilson was forty-two years old, two hundred pounds, and easily winded when they met; McCarthy twenty-five, slim, and robust), the two of them had enough in common to sustain them through their first awkward encounters. They knew some of the same people and valued many of the same books. Their politics were congruent if not identical, their tastes in art harmonious and welling from the same source. The distance between Princeton before World War I and Vassar of the 1930s was not very great. They both knew and valued good, clean American prose when they saw it—and they both wrote it. They were both more interested in words and people than in the abstractions of politics, certainly less interested in politics than most of their fellow intellectuals. And they were both sexually promiscuous and willing, even eager, to be frank about their sex lives on paper, as if writing their adventures down made them more real and important. All of which sounds like the basis for a lively, if somewhat rocky, marriage. Yet in defiance of reason, Wilson and McCarthy proved to be a spectacularly ill-suited couple. Wilson, at some level not very far beneath the surface, expected his wives (there were to be four in all) to be his slaves—to apply a considerable part of their talent and charm to catering to him, making him happy, keeping the world at bay while he worked. And McCarthy, by temperament, by psychology, by the circumstances of her life was simply not cut out for slavery, no matter how generous or compelling the master. Their age difference—nearly seventeen years—was of course a factor, but not a major one. Nor was the trouble a simple matter of a brilliant woman burning with resentment at being under the thumb of a brilliant man. McCarthy *wanted* to succeed at being Wilson's wife, wanted it just as much, and in much the same way, as she wanted to succeed at being a writer. "There were many things Mary didn't believe in," recalls Elizabeth Hardwick, "but she certainly believed in marriage, or rather in being married." "She was in many ways a traditional wife," according to her friend and literary executor Margo Viscusi.

She wanted the marriage with Wilson to "work," yet she hated almost everything about it from the start. She wanted to be a good wife, but she found that it was hopeless. "It's unfortunate that you should have chosen to marry exactly the kind of man who would make you feel most enslaved and helpless," murmurs the exasperating psychiatrist in her story "Ghostly Father, I Confess" (thinly disguised autobiography, like nearly all her fiction). McCarthy couldn't help it. She had a penchant for throwing herself headlong into impossible roles and situations and refusing to admit defeat.

Ultimately, it came down to a marital power struggle, a battle of wills: his insistence against her defiance. Wilson roared and bellowed, threatened, slammed the door and refused to open it (on one occasion raising McCarthy's ire to such a pitch that she shoved a stack of burning papers under the door of his study). He withdrew from her for days on end, physically and emotionally. It's possible (definite, some say) that he beat her (it's also possible that she beat him). And finally he refused to let her go—his ability to keep her being the ultimate expression of his power over her. She may have been a bitch and a hellcat of a wife, but he wanted her. Indeed, he liked being married just as much as she did, though for somewhat different reasons. He liked the security of having a wife in the house, even with all the Sturm und Drang that went with it. He may even have *liked* the Sturm und Drang—certainly he took it in stride better than McCarthy did. He liked being married to a young, attractive woman. He admired her intellect and encouraged and promoted her writing. He liked having someone to run the house, cook the meals, and entertain his friends, with however much anxious overkill (McCarthy was famous for her exquisite, elaborate, labor-intensive dinner parties and holiday celebrations). He liked having an intellectual sparring and gossiping partner there beside him. He wanted a stand-in mother for his teenage daughter from his first marriage, Rosalind. He enjoyed the regular sex—as did McCarthy, apparently, although she insisted over and over again in print that she found the fat, wheezy, tight-lipped, red-faced Wilson repellent.

And so the marriage from hell endured for seven difficult years. "Mary and my father could be very amusing," recalls Rosalind in her rather arch memoir, "but cozy and tranquil were never words you'd apply to their household."

But why ever did they get married in the first place? "I was *dragooned* into this damn thing," McCarthy told an interviewer years later. That's *her* version, anyway, or one of her versions. The courtship was rather brutal and short. After that first, fraught *PR* lunch in company with Rahv and Dwight Macdonald, there was a very drunken dinner in the city, another drunken dinner up at Wilson's house in Stamford, Connecticut, and then the inevitable drunken seduction on the couch of Wilson's study. "He had me wrong: I only wanted to talk to him," McCarthy protested long after it ceased to matter. Little did she know that *talk* was Wilson's prime stratagem of seduction: when a friend asked him how he got so many "dames" into bed, he replied with the nonchalance of the practiced seducer, "I talk them into it, of course." The power of the word: their common ground and battleground from the start. Having slept with him a couple of times, however unenthusiastically, however drunkenly, McCarthy felt that she had incurred some kind of debt to him (at least she *said* she felt this later on, when she came to write about the courtship and marriage). And then Wilson, ever shrewd at intuiting the deep desires and vulnerabilities of the women around him, began haranguing her about marriage. "He started bulldozing her into marriage before she really knew him," Martha Sinnott, McCarthy's heroine and alter ego in *A Charmed Life*, muses bitterly after the Wilson-like marriage has ended. "It was what she needed, he reassured her, appraising her with his jellied green eyes when she woke up, for the second time, in bed with him, after a lot of drinks. . . . And yet he must be right; even her teachers would think so. She would never, surely, have yielded to his embraces, shrinking, as she did, from his swollen belly and big, crooked nose, if some deep urge in herself, which *he* seemed to understand, had not decreed it." (Of course, *A Charmed Life* cannot and should not be read as a direct transcript of what happened between them, even though McCarthy herself cites it in her memoirs to explain her motives. As Wilson and others have tiresomely pointed out, there are more differences than similarities between him and the character Miles Murphy: his eyes were not "jellied green," he was not Irish as Murphy is, he did not have red hair or a crooked nose, and so on. One must adjust for the broad, satirizing brush with which McCarthy painted. Even so, the novel cuts close to the bone; and the closer it cuts, the funnier it is.)

Marriage may not, in truth, have been what the young, divorced Mary McCarthy needed ("No, I did not want to marry him," she confided later in her memoirs. "As a radical, I was against marriage"); but it was certainly, in 1937, what *Wilson* needed. When he wooed her, he had been single for five years, his second wife, Margaret Canby, having died after falling down a flight of stone steps in California, his first wife, the actress Mary Blair, whom he had married in 1923 and separated from two years later, having died of tuberculosis. The 1930s had been a rough, bruising, knockabout decade for Wilson, as for everyone. Although initially the Depression and the Marxist reaction in the intellectual world excited and inspired him, by 1937 he was disillusioned with politics and depressed by his disillusionment. He had been rattling around literary New York for the better part of two decades, starting off after World War I at *Vanity Fair* and moving on to a reviewing slot at *The New Republic*. He had "done" literary modernism in his pioneering 1931 critical study, *Axel's Castle,* and he had written brilliant, vivid dispatches chronicling America's social and economic unraveling in *The American Jitters: A Year of the Slump* (1932). But now he found himself at loose ends, chronically short on cash, exhausted both intellectually and emotionally. He was lonely and drinking too much; he had grown sick of moving from one shabby apartment or country house to another, sick of chasing and losing women, sick of living a bachelor's life with only his devoted housekeeper, Hattie, to look after him and put food on the table. Wilson's daughter, Rosalind, recalls that in the months before he married McCarthy, her father had taken to calling up his "lady friends" and proposing to them over the phone. "He needed a wife 'the worst way,' to use one of his expressions," wrote McCarthy in her memoirs, "[but] the women he had been having affairs with were either unwilling to marry him or unsuited to the job or both. When I met him, he must have been desperate." McCarthy looked like the answer to all his (godless) prayers: young and pretty, bright and recently divorced, she was perfect for "the job."

As for McCarthy, she seems to have staggered into the marriage like a sleepwalker or a dazed hostage. What was she thinking? Long after it ended, she mulled over this question repeatedly, almost compulsively, in fiction, memoir, and memory. The overriding impression she conveys in her various accounts is that she wandered, an unwitting victim, into Wilson's lair, and when she woke up and realized where she was and what she had done, she married him out of guilt and shame. According to *A Charmed Life,* the marriage was "a punishment for the sin of having slept with him when she did not love him, when she loved, she still felt, someone else." From a 1985 interview: "I felt that I had to pay for the fact of having slept with him when I was tight." Pay, punishment, sin: this is the vocabulary of Mary's Catholic girlhood—the religious drilling that engendered what Elizabeth Hardwick called the "Jesuitical aspect to her moral life which for me was part of her originality and one of the outstanding charms of her presence." Charming or not, this confession doesn't quite hold water. McCarthy had slept tipsily with scores of other men she didn't love. So why surrender to Wilson?

Part of it, unquestionably, had to do with his stature as an American man of letters and as an American man—and with her yen to boost her own stature. She valued him for his prestige. It was literary social climbing. Unlike most of the men McCarthy was meeting in those days, Wilson carried the stamp of unassailable social and literary authenticity: a descendant on his mother's side of a cousin of Cotton Mather, "an Enlightenment polymath like Goethe, Dr. Johnson or Voltaire," as one friend put it, he belonged by right of birth to the great tradition of American letters, and he had long been accustomed to taking his privileges and his authority for granted. "Our last great man of letters (he thought so himself)," wrote Alfred Kazin. Distant kinship with Cotton Mather may strike some as a dubious distinction, but as critic Paul Berman insists, it was "no small point" in literary New York in the late 1930s: "The great American critics in the twentieth century, quite a number of them, have had immigrant sensibilities and have wanted to embrace what was not theirs by ancestry, and have made outsider enthusiasm into their gift and insight; but this thing that they wanted to embrace, that arouses their love and enthusiasm—this thing is what Wilson already has." He was rooted to American history and American literature in a way that McCarthy never could be with her brazenly Irish name, her outlander childhood in Seattle and Minneapolis, her mongrel pedigree (Irish Catholic on her father's side, half Protestant and half Jewish on her mother's side—Elizabeth Bishop used to call her an Irish Jew).

At the time of their marriage, Wilson, though not yet the great man of American letters that he was to become, was already a powerhouse of long-established reputation and considerable intellectual heft. Part of his authority derived from his uniqueness: no one else commanded his breadth of knowledge, the range of subjects he undertook, the sheer volume of output. He was a one-man literary factory. The pieces he "worked up" through massive reading and research projects were first published in magazines, then refined and collected in books, and in some cases recycled through several different books: no waste, maximum output. He refused to specialize: he published literary and social criticism, poetry, plays, fiction, travel books, and political history, all the while keeping a frank and detailed journal of his travels, dalliances, friendships, and impressions of people and nature (published posthumously, these may turn out to be his greatest work of all). Wilson's *Axel's Castle* was one of the first and remains one of the most influential studies of the great masters of literary modernism: Joyce, Yeats, Proust, Eliot, and Valéry. Other important critical volumes include *The Triple Thinkers*, *The Wound and the Bow*, and *Patriotic Gore*, his magisterial study of American literature written during the Civil War. Wilson is difficult to type as a critic—he belonged to no school, adhered to no single, overarching theory, had no particular ax to grind. "I never think of myself . . . as a literary critic," he insisted in an interview; "I think of myself simply as a writer and a journalist." It's true that his literary pieces read more like journalistic profiles than like academic exegeses. He was as interested in writers' lives—their circumstances, intimate relationships, motives, and emotional deportment—as in their ideas: he was always trying to delve down to the core of what made an influential artist or thinker tick. Wilson was restless, tireless, and endlessly curious, forever making intellectual conquests, working up a new set of writers, mastering another foreign language, annexing a fresh discipline (Native Americans, the Dead Sea Scrolls, Haiti). He succeeded by refusing to be daunted. A true workhorse, he was satisfied ("happy" was not in his lexicon) only when he was in the traces.

Supposedly Delmore Schwartz (or, in some tellings, Harold Rosenberg) spread it around literary New York that McCarthy had left Rahv for Wilson because Wilson had a better prose style. It was a nasty little wisecrack, but not without a hard nut of truth. Wilson had not only a better style than Rahv but more authority, an easier command of the culture, a finer pedigree, more "class": "Wilson, relatively speaking, was upper class," as McCarthy put it. "That was all there was to it." But of course there was a good deal more. For McCarthy, Wilson represented "deep America"—a weighty embodiment of the social and literary tradition on which she too felt she had a claim. In her memoirs, she writes that Wilson came from "the same stock" as her grandfather: "Anglo-Saxon, Presbyterian. His father, like Grandpa, had been a distinguished lawyer. . . . There was a certain feeling of coming home, to my people"; coming home as well to an Arcadia of classical literature ("[W]e were going to read Juvenal together") and Romantic Nature ("We were going to ride horses along the trails above the river; we were going to fish for trout. We would look for wild flowers in the woods"). "It was an idyll he was offering me, and not wholly false." And so she surrendered. The hardest part was breaking the news to Rahv, which she put off doing as long as possible.

McCarthy and Wilson were married on February 10, 1938, a scant four months after they met, in a drab little ceremony at the city hall in Red Bank, New Jersey, where Wilson had grown up and where his old deaf mother still lived. They lunched with Mrs. Wilson ("a stumpy downright old lady with an ear trumpet . . . [who] looked like a warthog," according to McCarthy), after which Wilson repaired, as was his custom, to his old bedroom to read or nap, leaving his young bride to attempt to converse with her new mother-in-law. Then they took the train into New York, where they were to spend their wedding night at the New Weston Hotel. McCarthy gives a harrowing account of the evening in her *Intellectual Memoirs*—the drinks at the hotel bar with her two younger brothers; the staggering retreat to their hotel room, where Wilson proceeded to rant that her brothers were covert agents of the GPU (the Soviet secret police); a volley of grunted threats followed by collapse into stupefied sleep.

> I lay awake, silently weeping. The marriage was over, I had to assume.
>
> In a sense that was true. It was the end of my high hopes for a "classical" life. No more idyll. . . .
>
> During that bad night I assessed my situation. I was alone, with no one to turn to. Philip and my job were gone. Grandpa was dead; my only friends were people like Eunice Clark who were not real friends. . . . My marriage was a mistake. I clearly saw that I never should have married this peculiar man, yet I did not have the courage to take my suitcase and go off somewhere by myself.

The "badly injured marriage lasted seven more years," McCarthy concludes in retrospective amazement, "though it is true that it never recovered."

It was a damaged, and damaging, marriage, but also a fascinating one, especially to McCarthy. For the rest of her life she never got over it or ceased writing about it in both fiction and nonfiction. Elizabeth Hardwick, who usually took her side, at least publicly, recently rebuked her for this unseemly recycling of old marital woes: "Consider the oddity of the amount of repetitive energy put into denunciation of the past by one so pleasantly situated in life, so rich in experience, friendships, new loves, handsome surroundings." The oddity is compounded by Wilson's almost absolute silence: it is McCarthy's version and hers alone that has come down to us. Wilson pretty much kept his mouth shut, while she gave guided tours. And of course the Wilson she put on display is a thoroughly despicable specimen—"a monster," as she brands him in her memoirs, "the minotaur in his maze."

How bad was he really?

Wilson is indeed an easy target, even without the vicious McCarthy texts: the bellowing voice, pitched to his mother's ear trumpet; the heavy hand with which he doled out his "advice"; the empty gin bottles; the heaving bed; the meticulous—and lengthy—ledger of his sexual activity; the fat body; the joyless eyes set in a jowly face (his second wife called him "a cold fishy leprous person"); domestic tyrant; literary autocrat; patriarch; bully. In America's literary pantheon Wilson belongs with Poe, Melville, Mencken, and his ancestor Cotton Mather in the chapel of impossible genius. He is the dead white male par excellence, provoking all the more vexation because he hasn't been dead very long.

Yet to dismember and dismiss Wilson on the grounds of political incorrectness is to miss the deep, strange, stubborn, complex originality of the man. He seduced and controlled and dominated women, but he was also fascinated by the women he slept with and married—by their minds as much as their bodies. "All my life I've been attracted to women of talent," he once mused. McCarthy stood in a long line of talented women that included Edna St. Vincent Millay, Louise Bogan, Anaïs Nin, the poet Léonie Adams. Wilson may have expected women to wait on him and defer to him, fix his meals, and run his homes—he was "old-fashioned," as they used to say, meaning unconsciously, instinctively sexist. But that didn't blind him to the talents and abilities of women. He did not look down on women as inferior beings: in the realm of the intellect, all were equals. Outside bed, a woman's writing was what mattered to him most, and he judged a woman's writing according to the same severe standards he applied to male writers—and to himself, for that matter. He could be generous, sometimes to a fault, with the women whose work he admired, and he went out of his way to encourage young women writers. Diana Trilling fondly recalled the kindness he showed her when she started to write, though she confessed she found him a horror as a man. "He gave candor, and expected it," wrote Edith Oliver, another of the young women writers he was kind to. "One could say anything to him about his own work. . . . He felt that anything in print—and, for all I know, out of it—was discussible. Any piece of writing, whatever its provenance or circumstances, could be dealt with truthfully, even bluntly."

Wilson's priestly dedication to the written word was both a strength and a weakness. As he aged, he used writing more and more as a shield and a refuge from "real life"—a private, impenetrable realm where he alone felt true to himself because he had total control, unbroken solitude, and complete freedom. As the narrator of Wilson's scandalous (literally—it was banned as obscene) novel *Memoirs of Hecate County* says with a sigh of relief as he returns home at the book's end, "I could rejoin my old solitary self, the self for which I really lived and which kept up its austere virtue, the self which had survived through these trashy years." It's a kind of Yeatsian stance, the solitary intellect taking proud possession of its tower; a stance well suited to the composition of scores of books, but not to the daily demands of marriage, especially marriage to a young, ambitious, and demanding wife such as McCarthy.

Whether out of intended kindness or out of a sense of husbandly obligation, Wilson took McCarthy's literary career in hand as soon as they were married. "He was always teaching people," recalls a friend, "not in a patronizing way. He was educating himself by educating others." Mary was to be another one of his tutees, one of the young women who flourished beside his fount of wisdom. That was a mistake. Unlike Diana Trilling and Edith Oliver, McCarthy was anything but grateful for the unsolicited guidance her husband thrust on her. In *Intellectual Memoirs* she describes acidly how Wilson literally "pushed" her into creativity in the first months of their marriage: "shepherd[ing]" her into a small spare bedroom of their house, all but commanding her to write, and then shutting the door firmly behind him. To the stunned new wife, all this was terribly reminiscent of her traumatic orphan years in Minneapolis with the gross, bossy Uncle Myers who imprisoned her in a shabby upstairs bedroom, taped her mouth shut at night to discourage mouth breathing, and beat her with a hairbrush or razor strop "all the time," as she wrote in *Memories of a Catholic Girlhood,* "as a matter of course . . . gratuitously, often, as preventive medicine." The domineering Wilson had made up his mind that McCarthy's true gift was for "imaginative writing"—in his opinion she was wasting her time with the lively theater reviews for *PR*—and so she dutifully set about composing the heavily autobiographical stories that would later be welded into *The Company She Keeps.* In a sense he launched her career, yet she hated him for it—or so she insisted nearly five decades later, when she sat down to write the final volume of her memoirs. Wilson, she recalled, "promise[d] that marrying him would 'do something' for me, that is, for my literary gift. 'Rahv doesn't do anything for you,' he argued, meaning that Rahv was slothfully content to have me do those theater columns, which, according to Wilson, were not up to my real measure. . . . Looking back, I can see that he was right where Philip was concerned. If it had been left to Rahv, I never would have written a single 'creative' word. And I do not hold it against him; on the contrary. His love, unlike Wilson's, was from the heart. He cared for what I was, not for what I might evolve into." Jason Epstein believes the real problem was that Wilson held her, as he held everyone, to too high a standard: "He was very dominating. As a teacher, he never gave you more than a C+. That's what made the marriage so unpleasant."

"Teacher" makes Wilson sound rather academic and dispassionate, perched high above the commercial fray, but in fact he was offering McCarthy a kind of literary partnership—which for her meant a big boost up: "He saw what he perceived as my self-interest, to be furthered by my marriage to him," is how she put it. And indeed, despite the bitter tone of her recollections, she did benefit professionally from the marriage. From Wilson she learned disciplined work habits that stood her in good stead for the rest of her life. "The writing must come first," Wilson's code of conduct, became McCarthy's code too. Wilson never made a lot of money from writing, but he earned enough to support himself and his various families, and McCarthy learned this from him too. In her next marriage, she prided herself on being the main breadwinner, and it pleased her no end when her writing began to outearn Wilson's. But that was years later. During the time they were married, they were less competitors than respectful professionals in the same field. Far more than Tate and Gordon or Lowell and Stafford or Lowell and Hardwick, Wilson and McCarthy were colleagues, laboring productively side by side and often in similar veins: heavily satirical fiction; cultural studies "worked up" from rich historic texts, biographical anecdotes, insights, and observations (Wilson's *Patriotic Gore,* McCarthy's *The Stones of Florence*); reviews of books and plays; political and social reportage.

They were also very much on the same wavelength politically—in accord not only in *what* they believed but in the spirit and attitude of their beliefs. Both considered themselves Marxists during much of the 1930s, but in both cases it was more a flirtation than a committed relationship. Political involvement, or at least political discourse, was all but unavoidable at the time of their marriage: it was how thinking people sorted themselves, what they talked about, how they saw and judged the world. As critic Kenneth Burke remarked, the 1930s was an era when "personal ambitions, sexual anxieties, and metaphysical yearnings were often objectified in political forms." Though Wilson and McCarthy both got swept up in the current, neither was fundamentally a political person—certainly not in the way Philip Rahv and even Robert Lowell were. Arthur Schlesinger Jr., the most politically prominent member of the circle, who knew McCarthy well and admired her very much, believed that politics was more a game than a calling for her: "As a child of the 1920s, she could never really take politics very seriously. Remember her wonderful piece 'My Confession' and you will see what I mean. Though she had sharp political opinions, and was a reliable liberal Democrat most of the time, she really wasn't all that interested in politics per se. She was more interested in the play of personalities on the political stage, in the drama of politics, politics as a theater of irony, hypocrisy, and betrayal. It was the 1920s sensibility, modified a bit by the so-called crisis of capitalism." In many ways this fits Wilson even better than McCarthy—certainly the part about the sensibility of the 1920s, which was of course the decade when Wilson came of age (F. Scott Fitzgerald was a college classmate and lifelong friend) and the era he always looked back on nostalgically.

Wilson, possessed of what one critic calls an "intransigent individualism," was not a joiner, and though he was attracted to the Communist Party in the early 1930s he never signed on. As he wrote Allen Tate on May 28, 1930, "Politically I am going further and further to the left all the time and have moments of trying to become converted to American communism in the same way that Eliot makes an effort to become converted to Anglo-Catholicism. It is not that communism in itself isn't all right, but that all that sort of thing in America seems even more unrelated to real life than Catholicism does in England." And again to Tate on March 22, 1932, commenting on the political and intellectual atmosphere of New York in the early days of the Depression: "Life and people here seem to me to have gotten much more interesting since the Depression. They grow more amiable and have more ideas in proportion as they have less money or less hopes of making it in large quantities. Compared to what it was, the intellectual world is seething. For myself, I am composing a play and in my spare time working quietly at the revolution, of which I will doubtless be one of the first victims."

Wilson never lost his wary detachment—the journalist's practiced eye for the strident, the false, and the absurd. The diction of American Communists and fellow travelers grated on him—their use of sickening euphemisms such as "liquidate" for kill and their mechanical regurgitations of the Party line sent out from abroad. He sneered at the abject sincerity of true believers, a pack of squabbling martinets leading warped little lives in shabby apartments and forever accusing one another of bourgeois backsliding. Visiting Party headquarters in New York, Wilson couldn't help noticing the physical deformities of the staff—a hunchback ran the elevator, a dwarf woman with glasses manned the front desk, and so on. (McCarthy, in a similar vein, records in her memoirs the lament of male Stalinists at the time that the Trotskyites had "a monopoly of 'all the beautiful girls' "—among whom she numbers Diana Trilling, who vehemently denied being a Trotskyite, and Eleanor Clark, who was contributing regularly to *PR* in the late 1930s.) Wilson maintained "complex and ambivalent attitudes toward the left in general," according to Harvard professor Daniel Aaron, who knew him well. He was the "detached witness of the 1930s whose sympathy with the lower orders was maintained from a considerable social distance. . . . [A]lternately angry, curious, bemused" by the events of the day, he retained "his manner of the well-born, well-bred democrat looking downward, whether he was interviewing labor organizers or the hirelings of industry." Looking back from the decade's end on the rigidly partisan literary politics of the 1930s, novelist James T. Farrell praised Wilson for being "one of the exceptions to what happened to many in this decade. . . . In the early thirties, he joined in the spiritual and intellectual migration of writers to the left. However, he retained his judgment, perception, and independence. When new questions were posed, he investigated them in all seriousness. He did not accept ready-made slogans merely because a radical brand was put on them. The result can be seen in his work. Whatever one thinks of various of his conclusions, Wilson's literary criticism has been the finest written in the last decade." He saw "coldly," as Alfred Kazin puts it, "without for a moment allowing [him]self to become cold to America."

The essence of Wilson's politics was not so much Marxist as anticapitalist or precapitalist. The revolutionary tradition he most admired, and with which he felt most at home, was that of the American Revolution—a revolution led by upper-middle-class rationalists like himself. Aaron cites Wilson's proud personal declaration in *The American Jitters* (1932) that his family had "never departed very far from the old American life of the countryside and the provincial cities" and had "never really broken in to the life of machinery and enormous profits." It is this vein of patrician restraint and social obligation that led Wilson to glorify Lenin in *To the Finland Station* for his simplicity, his asceticism, and his dignified virility: "He is the most male of all these reformers because he never weeps: his attitude begins with impatience." Wilson in a sense embraces the Communist dictator as one of his own, an honorary member of the proud old Wilson clan.

To the Finland Station, perhaps Wilson's most unified and narratively compelling book, reflects the excited conviction held by many American intellectuals in the early 1930s that the old rotten capitalist system was self-destructing and a new Marxist/socialist order was about to take its place. As Wilson himself wrote gleefully in his 1932 essay "The Literary Consequences of the Crash": "To the writers and artists of my generation who had grown up in the Big Business era and had always resented its barbarism, its crowding-out of everything they cared about, these years [the onset of the Great Depression] were not depressing but stimulating. One couldn't help being exhilarated at the sudden unexpected collapse of that stupid gigantic fraud. It gave us a new sense of freedom." This sense of freedom and exhilaration fairly effervesces in the pages of *To the Finland Station.* Subtitled "A Study in the Writing and Acting of History," the book reads less like a "study" than like a Victorian novel, with larger-than-life characters, astonishing plot twists, and breathless climaxes. It's a great, sweeping, pageantlike, multigenerational saga in which intellectual titans such as Giambattista Vico, Jules Michelet, Pierre Proudhon, Charles Fourier, Karl Marx, and Friedrich Engels hand down the sacred idea that "the human spirit will be able to master its animal nature through reason," the idea that Lenin finally succeeds in bringing to realization in 1917, when "for the first time in the human exploit the key of a philosophy of history was to fit an historical lock."

For a while, Wilson hoped that the American Left would be able to domesticate and repackage Marxism for local consumption—to "take Communism away from the Communists," as he put it—but his revolutionary idealism drained away in the course of the decade. "Wilson was just a decent liberal," insists Epstein (the same thing Schlesinger says of McCarthy). "He had no interest in abstract ideas after he got over Marx and Freud." By the time he finished and published *To the Finland Station* in 1940, he was thoroughly disillusioned with "the movement": "The whole left literary movement got to be a pain in the neck," he wrote Tate in the spring of 1937, "and now it has been completely demoralized . . . by the Stalin-Trotsky controversy." This controversy, which came to a head during the campaign of mass terror in which Stalin destroyed

political rivals and opponents and mopped up much of the first generation of Bolshevik leaders, traumatized American's left-leaning intellectuals. The news that reached America at the time was sketchy, but we now
know that Stalin exterminated untold thousands of political enemies by
firing squad and in Soviet concentration camps; intellectuals, former
Party officials, and military leaders confessed their "crimes against the
state" in show trials and disappeared into the maw of the "Great Terror."
As a result of Stalinist terror, the American Left splintered into Soviet
apologists, who argued that the "liquidations" and the Moscow trials
were necessary and justified, and the anti-Stalinists, such as Rahv,
Dupee, McCarthy, Wilson, and the Trillings, who were shocked and outraged by Stalin's ruthless consolidation of power. Incredible as it seems
in our current tepid political climate, by the late 1930s, hard-line Stalinism was the ascendant dogma in New York literary circles: it was, as Mc-
Carthy writes in her *Intellectual Memoirs,* "what smart, successful people
in that New York world were." Stalinists such as Malcolm Cowley, Lillian
Hellman, and Granville Hicks held the power to make or break writers,
and they wielded this power along strictly ideological lines. While Stalin
waged war on his perceived enemies inside the Soviet Union, his American supporters were conducting their own metaphorical purges by running down, blackballing, and vilifying Trotskyites and all others deemed
insufficiently hard-line. "Under cover of this Popular Front movement
[the pro-Stalinist bandwagon of the late 1930s] was conducted one of the
most pernicious literary witch hunts in American literary history," wrote
James T. Farrell in 1939. "Practically all American writers of liberal or radical persuasion who opposed the line (the Stalin murders and so on)
were bitterly attacked, often slandered." As critic Christopher Lasch
pointed out in a recent essay, it required "not only courage but an enormous expenditure of intellectual energy" to break with Stalinism at a
time when the Party line not only claimed to be "the last hope of check-
ing fascism" but had managed to associate itself with the "recovery of
America's cultural heritage."

Yet despite the "pernicious witch hunt," the American Stalinist attackers notably failed to silence their targets. The anti-Stalinist Left may have
been a beleaguered minority in New York during the 1930s, but it was a
vocal, literate, and distinguished minority. "In no other Western country
did the anti-Stalinist left play so prominent, if brief, a role as in America,"
writes Irving Howe in his essay "The Thirties in Retrospect," "steadily
breaking away the most distinguished of the writers who had come

within the cultural orbit of the Communist party. . . . At any given moment during the thirties the majority of left-wing intellectuals were likely to be sympathetic to Stalinism, yet the more independent minds among them were constantly drifting into heresy."

For Mary McCarthy it wasn't a matter of drifting since she was heretical by nature. She confessed later that she didn't initially know or care very much about the Moscow trials, but once she found out about the literary witch-hunt that the trials had precipitated in New York, she got her back up. She was scrappy, a born fighter, and she reveled in the intrigue, outrage, and grandstanding of a good political brawl. Later in life she loved to tell and retell the story of how she had stumbled unwittingly into the Trotskyite camp and then refused to budge: at a cocktail party James Farrell asked her whether she believed Trotsky was entitled to a hearing, and when she answered yes "without any clear idea of what he was being charged with," Farrell (or someone) promptly added her name to the letterhead of a pro-Trotsky group. Though peeved that she'd been signed up without her knowledge or consent, she was even more peeved when her Stalinist acquaintances began calling her up and pressuring her to resign. "This only hardened my resolve, as anybody who knew me could have guessed," she wrote in *Intellectual Memoirs*. The decision to let her name stay on the letterhead proved to be epochal: it was, McCarthy wrote, "a pivotal decision, perhaps *the* pivotal decision of my life . . . [though] I was unconscious of having come to a turning point, the great divide, politically, of our time." For McCarthy, the first consequence of crossing "the great divide" was a gratifying upswing in her social life: "I was meeting people—*men,*" as she recollected fondly in her memoirs. The Trotskyites, she discovered, were more fun than the Stalinists: they were more attractive and threw better parties.

Which is not to dismiss McCarthy as a political gadfly. She had strong views about what was going on in the world, and for the rest of her life she would devote considerable energy to expressing and defending these views. But as with Wilson, her politics did not silence her sense of irony—if anything, political engagement fired her satire. The short stories she wrote under Wilson's watchful eye during the late 1930s and early 1940s are not the stern, dogmatic effusions of a committed revolutionary but the sharply pointed digs of the wicked social critic. When politics does enter her work, it is usually a telltale sign of character or character flaw, a trait like taste in clothes or home furnishing or sexual conduct that "places" a person. *Taste*—it was one of the guiding passions of her life, and its realm encompassed everything from cooking to personal hygiene to ethics. As Elizabeth Hardwick wrote in a witty little essay about her, "The reader [of McCarthy's fiction] follows the parade of tastes and preferences with a good deal of honest excitement and suspense, wondering if he can guess the morals of the kind of person who would cover a meat loaf with Campbell's tomato soup." In her fiction and memoirs, politics is like that meat loaf—one more "float" in the taste parade. Thus she dismisses the "Socialist girls" at Vassar as a bunch of badly dressed boors: "their eager fellowship and scrawled placards and heavy personalities bored me—there was something, to my mind, deeply athletic about this socialism. It was a kind of political hockey played by big, gaunt, dyspeptic girls in pants." Meg Sargent, her alter ego in *The Company She Keeps,* is a "violent Trotskyist" not out of carefully reasoned conviction but because she is "temperamentally attracted to unpopular causes: when [she was] young, it had been the South, the Dauphin, Bonnie Prince Charlie; later it was Debs and now Trotsky." McCarthy is even funnier, and meaner, about the left-leaning young men of the thirties in her short story "Portrait of the Intellectual as a Yale Man": "He might even go home with a copy of the *Communist Manifesto* in his pocket—in that period, the little socialist classic enjoyed something of the popularity of the *Reader's Digest. . . .* Marxism was to become for [this] generation what an actress had been for the youths of the Gilded Age." McCarthy may have been more frivolous than some of her leftist comrades, but in retrospect there's something tonic in her ridicule.

It's also refreshing, in an era of deadly self-importance, that she could turn her ridicule on herself. McCarthy placed this brilliant interior monologue in "Ghostly Father, I Confess," the final story in *The Company She Keeps,* in which the unhappy and unhappily married Meg obsessively (and absurdly) analyzes the political implications of her newly acquired tastes:

> There was the class crime, to be sure, yet it was not for having money that she hated herself, but (be honest, she murmured) for having some but not enough. If she could have been very rich. . . . It was the ugly cartoon of middle-class life that she detested, Mr. and Mrs., Jiggs and Maggie, the Norths in the *New Yorker.* And the more stylish you tried to make it, smearing it over with culture and good taste, Swedish modern and Paul Klee, the more repellent it became: the cuspidors and the silk lampshades in the funny papers did not stab the heart half so cru-

elly as her own glass shelves with the white pots of ivy, her Venetian blinds, her open copy of a novel by Kafka, all the objects that were waiting for her at home, each in its own patina of social anxiety. . . .

No, it was not really the humanitarian side of socialism that touched her; though she was moved by human misery when it was brought to her attention, if she went to buy a suit at Bonwit Teller, she was never troubled by irrelevant memories of the slums she had passed through on her way.

Ruthless, almost painfully funny candor was something that McCarthy and Wilson had in common. It was Wilson, after all, who secured a place in the quote books with his quip in the banned *Memoirs of Hecate County* that "Marxism is the opium of the intellectuals." Their minds, though distinctly different in so many ways, ran along parallel political tracks. They even collaborated on a bit of political doggerel entitled "Some Americans Still in Spain to Some Stalinists Still in America," mocking the last gasp of the left-wing intellectuals' doomed campaign against Franco: "You sent us here, and here we rot; / The fight we propped has gone to pot," and so on. Rahv ran it, with only their initials coyly affixed, in *PR*'s Fall 1939 issue.

"For no reason except his intellectual distinction, we endowed [Trotsky] with the humanity which was missing in Stalin and even in Lenin," Diana Trilling wrote in her memoirs, looking back on the calamitous period of the Moscow trials. "It was as if his good prose was the guarantee of a superior morality: he wrote too well to be a tyrant." This is old age shaking its finger at the follies of youth, but even so it gets at the tone and motive of politics in that circle at that time. McCarthy and to a lesser extent Wilson aestheticized politics: style mattered. Political tracts were "texts," as we now say, and their importance lay as much in how they were written and how they related to one another as in how or whether their ideology could be fruitfully put into practice. Wilson explored this concept dramatically and exhaustively in *To the Finland Station*, but even before he finished the book he was sick of the whole business. Though not ordinarily a writer who agonized over his words, Wilson found *To the Finland Station* hell to write (McCarthy nastily attributed his difficulty to the fact that he "didn't have much capacity for theoretical reasoning"). By the time the book came out, its cultural moment had passed—world war had eclipsed socialist revolution—and Wilson's decade-long fascination with Marxism was played out. His next major work, *The Wound and the Bow*, published in 1941, was a collection of literary essays, and during the early 1940s he devoted himself exclusively to literary labors: editing F. Scott Fitzgerald's posthumous volumes *The Last Tycoon* (1941) and *The Crack-Up* (1945) and writing book reviews and fiction. Politics, as a subject for sustained prose pieces, was over.

In the late 1930s and early 1940s, McCarthy joined Wilson in his flight from the tumult of left-wing politics. While Rahv, down in noisy Manhattan, blasted Stalinists and liberals alike in *PR* and wrung his hands over the dire implications of the Moscow trials ("[I]t is not only the old Bolsheviks who are on trial—we too, all of us, are in the prisoners' dock. These are trials of the mind and of the human spirit"), Wilson and McCarthy stayed out of the fray in woodsy, genteel Connecticut. McCarthy's marriage to Wilson and departure from the city promptly got her dropped from the *PR* masthead. But that was a sacrifice she was willing to make. For the moment, anyway, she had thrown in her lot with Wilson, hoping he would make good on his promise to "do something" for her career. She knew he wanted her to distance herself from "Partisansky Review," as he called it derisively, and strike out in a new direction. She had "done" Rahv and the whole downtown, Marxist, immigrant intellectual circuit. Maybe Wilson and the new people she was meeting through him—John Dos Passos, Fitzgerald (who died in 1940), Louise Bogan, Allen Tate, and Caroline Gordon—would open different channels. In any case, by marrying Wilson she had tacitly agreed to give up her world and enter his. Even McCarthy, for all her scrappy independence, understood that this was how things worked between husbands and wives.

"Mary and my father were two supersurvivors," Rosalind Wilson wrote in her memoirs, "who left emotional destruction in their wake." The emotional destruction commenced almost immediately: managing the perpetually scarce money; how much and how often to entertain; alcohol. The two of them clashed bitterly on all of these. Many other couples have failed to find much common ground and yet have survived or at least coexisted in marriage. But Wilson and McCarthy could give each other no peace. They became expert at enraging each other, each peculiarly constituted to be the other's torturer. As Rosalind put it, "Mary longed for the constant reassurance that everything was perfect, and my

father was the last person to give it to her." Both of them loved a good
fight and pulled no punches—but they never figured out how to fight together. Wilson customarily began the arguments with some intellectual
quibble and climaxed, many ounces of alcohol later, in bellowing. Mc-
Carthy jabbed and needled, slapped and cut, and refused ever to admit
defeat or let her husband have the last word. She did her best to drive
him over the edge, and her best could be formidable. They were two
tyrants under a single roof, always amazed that they had failed to cow or
convince the other. Conrad Aiken thought someone should do a cartoon
of Wilson and McCarthy sitting face to face over the caption "The Shock
of Recognition." What was awful was that the shock got worse the better they knew each other.

After the hasty wedding, the couple settled into Trees, Wilson's rustic
rental in Stamford and the site of the drunken seduction that had precipitated the marriage. Wilson got right down to work, and he instructed his
bride to do the same. Her prompt response was "Cruel and Barbarous
Treatment," the autobiographical story of the dissolution of her prior
marriage, written, as McCarthy later claimed, "straight off, without blot-
ting a line." She also, straight off, literally within weeks of the wedding,
became pregnant, and this provoked its own round of torments and anxieties. Children—or at least *a* child—had definitely been on the agenda
when Wilson and McCarthy were contemplating matrimony, and Wilson's ready compliance on the subject counted heavily in his favor (Rahv
had made it clear that he did not want children). Incongruous as it
sounds, Wilson enjoyed children—once they got old enough to appreci-
ate his magic tricks and go to the movies with him—and of course he
was an experienced father (experience of a somewhat theoretical kind,
since his mother had actually raised Rosalind and Wilson saw her only
on weekends and only when he was in the vicinity). As Rosalind herself
recalled, "My father loved his children and his animals but often forgot
about them for long periods of time; and when he looked around again,
after skipping several chapters, was confused by the scenario. Anyone
closely connected with him was likely to develop a helter-skelter way of
life."

But despite his erratic fondness for children, Wilson instantly ran up a
red flag when McCarthy became pregnant. How would Mary "handle"
the emotional and practical commitment of having a baby? What would
it do to their marriage? How would they afford it? In his opinion, a nice
quiet abortion was the most sensible solution—and they could always

try again later, when things had settled down. But an abortion was not in McCarthy's plans; not that she had an aversion to abortion per se—she once admitted to an interviewer that she had had "quite a lot" of abortions—but not this time.

A crisis was swift in coming. It was strange, yet strangely fitting, that the Tates, with their own frayed literary marriage, should have been present to witness the first tremors. Wilson's relationship with Tate had never quite recovered from the nasty essay on "The Tennessee Agrarians" he had written after visiting Benfolly in 1931, but the two men seemed to enjoy quarreling too much to break off altogether. (Shared antagonism was also the basis of a warm, wildly improbable friendship between Tate and Rahv. As Irving Howe recalled, "among [PR's] 'opponents' only Allen Tate responded satisfactorily, since in his own splendidly mad southern way he was always ready to charge into battle. No wonder Rahv and Tate became good friends: nothing but ideas stood between them."). A deep vein of crotchetiness bound Wilson and Tate together—along with a love of modernist literature and an abiding loathing for fools. Both were also renowned lady-killers, though Tate seemed to find being married an incitement to promiscuity while Wilson tended to pursue most of his love affairs between marriages. They did, however, finally fall out seriously over religion. Wilson, despite or perhaps because of his Puritan ancestry, was dogmatically antireligious and not shy about letting Tate or anyone else know it. "We must simply live without religion," he was fond of saying. When he learned that Tate had followed Gordon's lead and converted to Catholicism, he fired off his contemptuous congratulations: "I hope that becoming a Catholic will give you peace of mind; though swallowing the New Testament as factual and moral truth seems to me an awful price to pay for it. . . . Christianity seems to me the worst imposture of any of the religions I know of. Even aside from the question of faith, the morality of the Gospel seems to me absurd." But that wasn't until 1951. Back in 1938, Wilson and Tate were still prickly friends, "bound by disagreement," in Alfred Kazin's phrase; and since the Tates were in Connecticut for the summer, renting a cottage in West Cornwall, they naturally arranged to spend some time with the Wilsons.

The visit, an overnight stay, took place on June 7, 1938, four months into the Wilson-McCarthy marriage and nearly three months into McCarthy's pregnancy. According to Gordon's biographer Ann Waldron, McCarthy served spaghetti for dinner and the company consumed a quantity of Chianti, enough that Wilson felt he could entertain them with readings from the great Russian poets—in Russian—until three in the morning. "I had enough to drink to be able to enjoy it rather but Allen took it pretty hard," Gordon told Katherine Anne Porter in a gossipy letter. At some point fairly early on, while the wine was still swirling out of the bottles, McCarthy retired to bed. She may have been feeling the fatigue of early pregnancy, or possibly she had lost her taste for alcohol, as many women do while pregnant. Or perhaps her husband's Russian performance bored or annoyed her. Whatever the cause, she took herself off to bed and fell asleep. What happened next we have primarily from McCarthy, in slightly contradictory interviews she gave to two biographers forty-four and fifty years after the event. Wilson's version of the nightmare scene, confined to a few sketchy notes in his journal, was never elaborated or published. McCarthy laid it out this way in her 1982 interview with Carol Gelderman: asleep in their bed, wrapped in the blue sheets she had selected, she was rudely awakened when a very drunk and very angry Wilson slammed into the room and proceeded to strip the bed and dump his pregnant wife to the floor. "McCarthy says it was because the sheets were blue, very unusual in 1938, that he became so angry." Somehow they made it through the rest of the night, whether in the same bed or not and whether with the accursed blue sheets or not is unclear. But early the next morning they were at it again. Gelderman: "In the morning . . . she flew at him with 'How could you?' whereupon he punched her repeatedly in the breasts and slapped her again and again in the face. She started crying hysterically and then vomited, thinking all the while, 'What have I gotten myself into by marrying this madman?'" In her 1988 reconstruction of the event for biographer Carol Brightman, McCarthy adds that she had directed Wilson's maid, Hattie, to put the pale blue sheets on the bed "as a surprise" for her husband and that after tearing them off, Wilson had "bounced" her on the floor. According to Brightman, "McCarthy was never sure exactly when the fighting began. Perhaps she had 'made the mistake of complaining [then], which one shouldn't do when a person is like Edmund, and also very drunk.' Or maybe she had cried, 'How *could* you!' the next morning when he woke up, still drunk. In any event, it was later in the morning, after the Tates had left, she claimed, that Wilson had really hit her hard, striking her breasts and stomach." At this point Hattie stepped in, broke up the brawl, and called a local doctor. (McCarthy's memory may have been faulty as to the departure time of the Tates, for Gordon recalls seeing Mary leave the house in "incredible confusion" that morning and assumed that she was dashing off to visit her psychiatrist—this last detail possibly supplied by Wilson in an attempt to cover up the truth.)

Once the medical profession got involved, the marital dispute quickly mutated into something larger and more grotesque. The various accounts and explanations of how and why things transpired as they did are somewhat muddled, but the course of events is clear: the Stamford doctor recommended that McCarthy go to New York for a "rest," Wilson summoned a taxi (his customary mode of travel) and took her to the city, and the battered McCarthy, believing she was going to be admitted to New York Hospital for medical treatment, ended up in a locked cubicle in a psychiatric ward of the Payne Whitney Clinic. Wilson signed her in—"committed" her, in the harsh parlance of insanity—and then left to check into a Manhattan hotel. Wilson later claimed that his wife had been "confined to the ward for violent cases for a period of time," but, as Brightman points out, the fairly cheerful letters McCarthy wrote Wilson about playing pool and Ping-Pong with other inmates and joining in "community sings" contradict this. Two weeks later she was released into her husband's care—the official diagnosis being "Without psychosis; anxiety reaction." While at Payne Whitney, McCarthy had encountered Dr. Sandor Rado, a well-known, rather eccentric Hungarian-born shrink and the head of the New York Psychiatric Institute, and she began psychoanalysis with him shortly after leaving the clinic. The psychoanalysis would continue throughout her marriage, though she switched psychiatrists several times.

What is one to make of this? Did McCarthy suffer a "nervous breakdown"? A brief psychotic episode? A fit of hysteria induced by the hormonal changes of early pregnancy? Was this a marital spat that got blown out of proportion—an argument that mushroomed due to circumstance, misguided medical intervention, and the theatrical bent of the participants? Or was it a case of spousal abuse—a young wife driven off the edge by her rampaging alcoholic husband? Who is to blame? Wilson the monster, bent on beating his new wife into submission? Or McCarthy the bitch, who unleashed her husband's rage by "flying at him" when he was hung over? Or was Wilson in fact trying to help her, to calm her down, and was McCarthy too hysterical to perceive this? It's telling that they came to blows, if indeed they did come to blows, over a set of light blue sheets—just as six years later the marriage would split up in Wellfleet, Massachusetts, over two overflowing garbage pails. Domestic life was ever a bone of contention between them: Wilson demanded peace, comfort, liquor, and regular meals yet despised McCarthy's bourgeois perfectionism; McCarthy craved praise and recognition for her elegant touches—those blue sheets—knowing full well that Wilson would never oblige her. Ibsen-like, they enacted their furious incompatibility in a prim little stage set of flowered curtains and matching cutlery: "the Spode salad plates, the garden, the candy-striped wallpaper," as McCarthy reels off the tokens of domestic order in "The Weeds," her savage short story of marital misery. Though they basically agreed over arrangements of power in the larger world, at home they warred for dominance. In the heat of battle, each would seize on whatever weapons came to hand: fists, missiles, fire, the iron bars of the insane asylum.

The question remains: Did Wilson really hit her? His daughter Rosalind categorically denies it: "I never saw him hit anyone, including Mary McCarthy. He would occasionally raise his hand in an ineffectual way as if he were going to, and perhaps these ladies were so upset they thought he had. . . . Mary was more than a physical match for my father. . . . [She] was a big girl and strong physically. On occasion, her childhood trauma made her think she was about to be beaten, when she wasn't. She would wake up screaming 'Don't hit me' when my father wasn't in the room. Perhaps her therapy corrected this later." Wilson took the exact same line in his play *The Little Blue Light,* in which the character of Judith is modeled closely on McCarthy. Unfaithful, manipulative, castrating, and shrill, Judith is arguing with her older husband, Frank Brock, a beleaguered, idealistic, slightly pompous, liberal magazine editor still fighting the battles of his generation:

> Judith *(screaming)*: Oh, how can you? . . . How can you, you great
> horrible lout! *(She throws a magazine from the table at him.)* You
> pretentious small-time tyrant!
> Frank *(coming over to her)*: Don't—I'm sorry—
> Judith *(hysterical, grasping his hands, as he tries to put his arms
> around her)*: Don't hit me!
> Frank: I'm not going to hit you.
> Judith: You want to kill me! *(Shrieking.)* Help!

Wilson scholar Lewis Dabney notes that with one possible exception there is no evidence that Wilson ever hit a woman (aside from in sado-masochistic sex with a woman identified in the diary as "K.," who encouraged spankings and beatings with a brush—which "rather shocked" him, as he confessed). Dabney is quite emphatic about this: "I talked to Mary about it extensively before she died, and I was never persuaded that he hit her despite what she said. In my view there is no truth to it at all. That morning after the Tates' visit he was not beating her up but trying to control her, which was no easy task with an hysterical Irish spitfire like Mary. Wilson was only trying to take hold of her and calm her down." The clear conviction of the Wilson camp is that this and other violent episodes McCarthy mentioned during the divorce proceedings were figments of her neurotic imagination or deliberate falsifications of the record. But how to explain the black eye she had when she was admitted to Payne Whitney? McCarthy may well have exaggerated the extent and severity of the domestic violence, both at the divorce trial and later in interviews. But the evidence is highly suggestive that Wilson did in fact beat her up in June 1938 and that the beating was traumatic enough, whether physically or mentally, to bring on a psychological collapse.

Wilson moved decisively to consolidate his advantage after McCarthy's hospitalization. He had wanted the pregnancy terminated all along, and the breakdown gave him a trump card. While McCarthy was still in Payne Whitney, he spelled out his position in an extraordinarily stark and revealing letter to her:

> You oughtn't to be let in for relationships and responsibilities which you're not ready for at the present time, and which might ruin your relationship with me as well as interfere with your psychoanalysis. The psychoanalysis is the main thing, and there's no question that it will go better if you get the pregnancy over. There are also the possible difficulties: with a baby you would be badly tied down and the expenses of baby and psychiatrist, too, would certainly be more than we could afford. I think, too, that you and I will get along better with this question out of the way: you won't find your situation with me closing down over you in so oppressive a way as I'm afraid you have. . . . So get the thing over and then you can come out to Stamford and . . . start a gay summer life between New York and the psychoanalyst, and your loving husband.

Money, power, control, responsibility, children: the classic "issues" that married couples fight over come pouring out in this letter. All that's missing is sex, though maybe that's implied in Wilson's urgency to get "the thing over" so Mary can "start a gay summer life." Wilson believed he had McCarthy beat on each issue. Her "breakdown" secured his position. Since Mary was too unstable to make rational decisions, he needed to take over and make decisions for her. He got control of the dividends from the grain elevator stock she had inherited ($1,300 in 1938); he forbade her to drive a car; he tried to eliminate her friends from their social life. It was as if the breakdown demoted her to a lower order of being—the psychological invalid who from now on would require special treatment. Malice may have been part of it, but self-interest was really his primary motive: he could *seem* to be caring for his poor, delicate wife while actually doing everything he had wanted to do all along. In his mind it was the perfect excuse.

It's hard to resist reading this episode as a feminist parable, a cautionary tale of the horrors of marriage in a patriarchal culture: here is the pregnant young wife bullied, possibly beaten, deprived of her status, and literally locked up by her older, shrewder, stronger, brutally oppressive husband. The trouble is that McCarthy would have been the first to ridicule this interpretation of her life. She steadfastly refused to think of herself as a victim: whenever anyone, from her hated Uncle Myers down to Wilson, tried to victimize her, she defiantly fought back. Just as she had triumphed over orphanhood by taking her beatings without a whimper or a flicker of self-pity, so she would get the best of Wilson without whining about women's rights. She proved, to her own satisfaction anyway, that feminism didn't apply to her at all. "Feminism is ridiculous," she told an interviewer. "Feminists are silly idealists who want to be on top. There is no real equality in sexual relationships—someone always wins." Margo Viscusi, one of her literary executors, recalls that she always looked at feminism and feminists with disdain: "Her attitude was—what is this nonsense? A third are lesbians anyway." Or, as she remarked to a reporter from *Vogue* in 1963, a woman "can't possibly have all the prerogatives of being a woman and the privileges of being a man at the same time. . . . I much prefer being a woman, probably for very bad reasons like liking clothes and so on."

With Wilson, McCarthy would win in a womanly way: by being, or at least appearing to be, a good wife. She disguised, as a good wife would, the fact that her husband abused and "committed" her ("Of course I wouldn't tell. . . . You don't. You cover up") and thus canceled out the humiliation. She went dutifully to her psychiatrist, as Wilson had advised her to do. She prepared his meals ("with perfection and trauma," as Rosalind recalls) and kept his houses. And she successfully, stubbornly outmaneuvered him on the "issues": she went ahead and had the baby; she acquired a car (a Chevy she won in a raffle); she kept in touch with her old friends on *PR;* and of course she wrote—the sweetest revenge of all. The fact that she turned out a series of stinging portraits of their marriage—including, in *The Group,* a vivid description of a violent husband who pummels his wife and then commits her to a mental hospital exactly like Payne Whitney—was no more than poetic justice. She was being the good wife *and* the successful author: "In sexual relationships someone always wins."

The marriage, which was "badly injured" the night it began and further mutilated by the events of June 1938, somehow limped along for another six years. After the breakdown, the Wilsons moved out of the large, gloomy Trees and into a more cheerful house on Shippan Point (a spit of land on Long Island Sound south of Stamford). In a kind of geographical Freudian slip, Rado, McCarthy's shrink, was their neighbor for the summer, and he became an awkward friend of the family (Rosalind remembers his compulsive girl chasing). Reuel Kimball Wilson, McCarthy's only child and Wilson's only son, was born on Christmas Day 1938. Despite his resistance to the pregnancy, Wilson prevailed in the naming, Reuel and Kimball both being family names on his side. McCarthy made a devoted if somewhat exacting mother: by all accounts, she had little interest in children until they were old enough to converse and keep themselves clean, but she was determined to master motherhood just as she had mastered cooking, interior design, and gardening, and the baby lacked for nothing. "She had this perfectionism in everything relating to the household, and it extended to Reuel," comments a friend. "She was not motherly, not cuddly, but she did all the right things—the right schools, the right clothing. Reuel was not neglected. She did everything in an exemplary fashion."

As Wilson had anticipated, having a child strained the family's already precarious finances—neither of them held a regular job or a steady reviewing or editing post at this point, and living off book advances and freelance articles was a struggle. Wilson began casting around for an academic position, and he managed to land something at the University of Chicago for the summer of 1939: teaching two five-week courses for a grand total of twelve hundred dollars. In June, father, mother, and baby settled into an apartment in Chicago's Hyde Park neighborhood and proceeded to brawl their way through the steamy summer months (neighbors called the police in twice when their arguments got out of control). Toward summer's end, McCarthy went out by train to visit her grandmother in Seattle, taking Reuel and leaving Wilson in Chicago. The letters she and Wilson exchanged were tart but opaque: a gift of a fur coat from McCarthy's wealthy grandmother provoked another round of fighting over money, Wilson pleading poverty and McCarthy insisting that the fur is actually a savings since her grandmother paid ("You have very strange ideas of economy," he snapped back. "I am down to my last dollar"); Mary proudly recounts Reuel's new skills and accomplishments; Edmund complains that "celibacy is beginning to tell on me" and declares ardently that he "didn't know how much you meant in my life till you left."

For McCarthy and Wilson, this was about as good as it got.

Back in New York, Rahv was entering his "major phase." The gathering political storm of the late 1930s—the show trials in Moscow, Hitler's ruthless consolidation of power in Germany, the nonaggression pact that Hitler and Stalin signed in August 1939, Germany's invasion of Poland at the start of September 1939, and the immediate declaration of war by Britain and France—inspired some of his best work. In 1939 alone, he published such seminal essays as "Proletarian Literature: A Political Autopsy," in which he slammed the rigidly programmatic fiction American writers had been churning out under the direction of the Communist Party ("It is clear that proletarian literature is the literature of a party disguised as the literature of a class"); "Paleface and Redskin," his acute analysis of the two opposing currents in American literature—the highbrow, patrician palefaces such as Henry James and Nathaniel Hawthorne, who are at home only in the "thin, solemn, semiclerical culture of Boston and Concord," and the rough, plebeian, uncultured redskins such as Mark Twain and Walt Whitman, who dwell in the open air and incline to a "gross, riotous naturalism" in their writing; and a brilliant editorial in *PR* in which he considers the possibility of a "new tendency in literature" arising out of the "crisis of our time" ("The revolution may have sunk out of sight and the intelligentsia may be sticking close to its paymaster-mentors, but the impulse to represent experience truthfully persists. . . . [A]ll we have left to go on now is individual integrity—the probing conscience, the will to repulse and to assail the forces released by a disintegrated society").

As an editor, Rahv was filling the pages of *PR* with magnificent writing: poems and stories by Elizabeth Bishop, essays by Lionel Trilling, new work by Wallace Stevens, William Carlos Williams, Randall Jarrell, John Dos Passos, Allen Tate, and Saul Bellow. "Rahv was a brilliant editor in those days," Irving Howe wrote decades later in a short memoir, "partly because he brought to the job not only energy and intelligence but a semiconspiratorial outlook. . . . Rahv wanted his magazine to constitute a public act. . . . Rahv saw cultural life as if it were enacted in a political arena. The imagery of politics was congenital with him, an imagery of definition, conflict, alliance, exclusion. He ran the magazine as if he were heading a movement." In the years to come, Rahv and his coeditor, William Phillips, would clash violently over both style and substance, dividing the *PR* crowd into two wary factions, but in the late 1930s they were still on decent terms and their differences in temperament helped balance and focus the magazine. Phillips was puckish where Rahv was ursine, subtle and mischievous where Rahv was blustering yet paradoxically cautious. Both were convinced of the centrality of the magazine (Phillips once told Diana Trilling that the definition of an intellectual was anyone who wrote for *Partisan Review*). It was an odd but formidable partnership. The magazine they coedited was not always consistent; it lacked the urbane wit (and handsome fees) of *The New Yorker* and the long-established traditions of *The New Republic* and *The Nation*. But for the era immediately before, during, and after World War II, *PR* had authority. What it said mattered to the people who mattered, at least in intellectual circles. *PR* "stood for something," in Howe's words, and that was what its writers and readers valued most about it.

Rahv was not long nursing his wounds over McCarthy's defection to Wilson. Soon afterward, he started seeing her Vassar classmate Nathalie Swan (an architect from a wealthy, prominent New York family—her mother had cofounded the Junior League), and in 1940 they were married. The gossip around *PR* was that Rahv married Swan "on the rebound" from McCarthy, and McCarthy herself claimed that she had expected such a union. The other gossip concerned Rahv's radically improved financial situation: Swan commanded a substantial trust fund, and Rahv could now avail himself of a "perpetual Guggenheim," as *PR* editor William Barrett put it. Rahv and McCarthy remained on good terms, despite the social awkwardness between them, and McCarthy continued to publish regularly in *PR,* including "The Man in the Brooks Brothers Shirt."

Late in the summer of 1939, around the time McCarthy and her infant son rejoined Wilson after her visit to Seattle, Elizabeth Hardwick left her parents' home in Lexington, Kentucky, and arrived in New York City. Thin, smart, and beautiful, Hardwick would follow pretty much the same path Mary McCarthy had taken a few years before: writing precociously assured reviews (as well as less assured fiction), falling in love with Rahv and carrying on an affair with him (among many others), publishing in *PR* and being admitted to the magazine's "inner circle," marrying a famous writer from an old Yankee family. Hardwick and McCarthy themselves were soon to cross paths and embark on a close friendship that lasted until McCarthy's death.

What McCarthy and Hardwick made of their lives over the next three decades—separately, as writers, professional women, wives, and mothers; and together as friends, comrades, and occasionally angry rivals, but always as colleagues intensely aware of each other—speaks volumes about the role and the consciousness of women intellectuals in this era—an era the two of them did a great deal to define.

Country Wives

MCCARTHY CLAIMED she was "dragooned" into the marriage with Wilson, but dragooning was tame compared to the violent, even vaguely sinister force that drove Jean Stafford to agree to marry Robert Lowell. Stafford insisted that she wanted to get away from Lowell. She hid from him and told friends that he was mad and murderous. She bore lifelong facial scars because of a car accident he caused, perhaps deliberately. Stafford knew what she was getting into: she was no wide-eyed innocent, awed by an exalted Boston name, but rather a strong-willed, tough-minded, independent young woman who had every reason to believe she was on the verge of brilliant success. And yet she sat back and let the marriage happen as if it were her fate. Funny and savvy and canny as she was about the world, Stafford had a kind of genius for coming out the loser in her relations with men—especially her relationship with Lowell.

After their brief encounter at the writers' conference in Boulder, Stafford and Lowell went their separate ways—Lowell to Kenyon College in Gambier, Ohio, and Stafford to a one-year appointment teaching composition at Stephens College in Missouri. But before they parted, Lowell had gotten Stafford to agree to correspond with him. Lowell was very much in his element at Kenyon: mentored by John Crowe Ransom, befriended by Peter Taylor and Randall Jarrell, both of whom remained lifelong friends—but he didn't forget about Stafford, nor, apparently, did he pursue other women. Lowell seems to have been a slow starter sexually; though he became breathtakingly promiscuous in middle age, he was rather modest and chaste as a young man—shy, perhaps; and single-minded in his devotions.

The job at Stephens College was a last-minute stopgap for Stafford, better than nothing but definitely not what she'd been hoping for. It was a two-year women's college where the daughters of well-off cotton growers, ranchers, and oil folks from the surrounding states went to acquire some polish before marrying, and Stafford took an instant dislike to the place, ridiculing it as a "charm school" and a "training school for concubines." She spent a lot of time during her cold, miserable semesters there toiling away on her fiction and writing long letters to her friend and admirer James Robert Hightower, who was doing graduate work in Chinese at Harvard and nursing along his passion for her. Lowell seems to have hung fire during the Stephens College period.

At the end of the academic year, Stafford learned that Stephens was not going to renew her appointment, and once again she found herself scrambling. With no offers in sight, she arranged in June 1938 to travel out West with Hightower. They spent a few days together in Colorado and then she went on to Oregon, where her family was now living. Something clearly happened between Stafford and Hightower in Colorado, because the customary comradely sarcasm of their letters suddenly veered sharply to romantic agony. Hers were "*well-written* passionate letters," Hightower says now with a smile. His passion, it seems, was more sincere. Passion aside, it was a bum summer for Stafford—"the worst summer of my life" she later recalled. The novel she had been laboring on was rejected; she failed to get the fellowship from Houghton Mifflin she'd been hoping for; another publisher politely informed her that they could not, after all, publish the interesting journal of her year in Germany; and she didn't have "even a *smell* of a job," as she wrote Hightower. When the University of Iowa offered her a graduate fellowship at summer's end, she took it, even though she knew it was a false step.

She lasted a couple of months in Iowa, and then fled. Hightower describes this juncture in their lives: "Jean was in Iowa, very unhappy, writing me these passionate letters in Cambridge. In one of her letters she announced she was coming to Cambridge. I had some reservations about it, but she needed help and she was in debt and she wanted to turn to me. So she came. It turns out that while she was in Iowa she had been corresponding with Lowell. On her way from Iowa to Cambridge, she and Lowell met in Cleveland and she went to bed with him in a hotel." That's Hightower's version; nobody else mentions going to bed. Stafford's version, recorded in a letter to a friend, is that she and Lowell did indeed meet in Cleveland and drank "a good deal" of beer together and "he said he was in love with me and wd. I marry him and to avoid argument I said sure, honey, drink your beer and get me another one." *To avoid argument:* a fateful phrase. For all her tough-gal bravado, Stafford reveals a soft spot. Attempting to avoid argument was to be one of the hopeless labors in her marriage.

Stafford seems to have been inspirited by the flurry of intrigue that surrounded her flight from Iowa City: the clandestine rendezvous with Lowell, the tense ménage with Hightower in Cambridge, the presence of an ardent lover in the wings were a lot more interesting than "piddling," as she put it, in graduate school. Perched in Hightower's apartment, she made plans to write like mad, pull whatever strings came to hand, and get published promptly. Meanwhile, Hightower became aware that the woman he loved and hoped to marry was being "stalked," and he assumed the role of protector of the beloved, in which Stafford seems to have egged him on. "She told me she wanted to avoid Lowell and get rid of him," he recalls, "that she never wanted to see him again." But this was Lowell's home turf and he easily tracked her down and cornered her. Home from Kenyon for Thanksgiving, Lowell phoned her at Hightower's apartment and insisted on seeing her. Together they went for a harrowing drive out to Bedford, with Lowell, terribly nearsighted and a terrible driver, at the wheel. As Stafford recounts the outing in a letter: "[H]e kept saying if I didn't marry him he wd. just run the car off the road, etc. so I said he cd. go to hell and don't bother me any more and he got savage and I got scared, so I said well I will see you once more but only in the company of other people." In the same letter she brands Lowell "an uncouth, neurotic, psychopathic murderer-poet"—an uncanny mixture of invective and prescience. That's what she put on paper, and maybe even what she was telling herself. But there was that weak spot. She couldn't or wouldn't shake him.

To get her out of Lowell's clutches, Hightower helped find her a room a few miles away in Concord. But Lowell was hot on her trail. "He is laboring under the delusion that I am leading him a Romantic Chase," Stafford wrote a friend, "and that in the end he will carry me home as his bride." The whole business struck her as a bad joke, a *literary* joke, as if her life were a penny dreadful that kept her glued to the page despite herself. Lowell was back in Boston that December for Christmas vacation, and it was then that the relationship changed utterly, drastically, from Romantic Chase to brutal realism. Lowell took her out driving again (Stafford had forgotten or surrendered her demand to see him "only in the company of other people") and he again violently pressed his suit. He'd been drinking and odds are Stafford had too. Stafford once more rejected the marriage proposal, whereupon Lowell crashed the car into a wall that sealed off a dead-end street. Lowell's version, as reported to his friend Frank Parker: "I was driving and then I looked up and saw a dead-end wall." Parker chuckles ruefully today over the part about "then I looked up": where *had* he been looking before? "He wasn't much of a driver anyway," says Parker, "and both were probably drunk." Stafford later told a friend the crash was not an accident but a deliberate attempt by Lowell at murder and suicide—a failed attempt. Lowell survived with no injuries. But the once-beautiful Stafford, though alive, was permanently disfigured. The crash had fractured her skull and jaw and ruined her nose. Stafford spent weeks in a Boston hospital and endured two excruciating operations in which her nose was reconstructed and bits of shattered bone were picked out from near her brain, but her face never looked the same. "Before the accident she had been quite a beautiful woman with a classic profile," recalls her good friend Cecile Starr. "But the accident broke her face. Afterwards she looked crooked and distorted." "Patched together" is how another contemporary put it. She also suffered chronic back pain and breathing difficulties after the accident. And she refused to learn how to drive, probably out of fear of cars.

But far worse and far stranger was the emotional fallout. Stafford in a sense was reborn after the accident. Like the character Pansy Vanneman in her electrifying story "The Interior Castle," Stafford became an ironic spectator of her own ruined life. In the story, as surgery looms, Pansy lies alone in her hospital bed gazing with numb icy clarity at the pink jewel of her own brain: "the physical organ itself which she envisaged, romantically, now as a jewel, now as a flower, now as a light in a glass, now as an envelope of rosy vellum containing other envelopes." It is this treasure that has been defaced, carelessly scratched, and finally stolen from her by the operations. The character Pansy is radically isolated and detached to the point of madness—a girl spellbound by her own pain and indifferent to everything else in her life. Stafford, because of the accident, knew this kind of desperation. But by the perverse alchemy of attraction, she felt bound desperately to the man who had come close to destroying her.

Cecile Starr: "Jean did say that Cal was trouble. She knew this. But something in us all craves what is most destructive to us. Jean married Cal because he had been responsible for breaking her face." Hightower: " 'I can handle it myself,' she said to me about Lowell. She handled it, all right—she handled it by being driven into a dead-end and getting her face smashed up. Yes, he had pursued her, but she hadn't fled seriously."

"[H]e does what I have always needed to have done to me and that is that he dominates me," Stafford wrote to Hightower months later, explaining why she was marrying Lowell. "I was incapable of performing that," Hightower confesses frankly today. "Lowell was the epitome of the dominating male. Early on she claimed to be afraid of him, but she couldn't, or didn't want to, resist him." Lowell's friend Blair Clark scoffs at this business about being dominated and questions Stafford's motive in making such a confession to Hightower. "I never heard her say anything like that," he insists. "That's just Jean accommodating to the cultural clichés of the moment. She didn't mean it—it was just something she tossed off." Maybe. It does sound a little too studied, too much like something one of her characters would say as she got cornered into a doomed marriage. Yet the fact remains that Stafford drew closer to Lowell after the accident even though she believed, or said she believed, that he was trying to kill her. The crash was violent, physical proof of how much power Lowell had over her. It was not the last act of violence in their relationship.

Stafford as victim, Lowell as monster. That's how it looks from the outside, but it was never that simple. Lowell may have been "the epitome of the dominating male," but he was not unfeeling. Guilt and grief tormented him after the accident, and he tried to make amends by behaving more reasonably around Stafford. And he remained loyal to her. He never tried to back out on a damaged, scarred woman, as some men would have done. (Lowell's Boston relatives, who never liked Stafford, believed that "Bobby" had only done "the gentlemanly thing" by marrying her, though they felt "that girl" wasn't worth the sacrifice.) The two of them agreed that she would sue him for her medical expenses, and while the suit was pending her lawyer advised her not to be seen with Lowell. This only seems to have added the thrill of the forbidden to their clandestine meetings. Over Easter vacation, when Lowell was home from college, they secretly became engaged.

In the absence of letters or eavesdropping witnesses, it's hard to know what was going through their minds. Theirs was evidently not a simple love match, but neither was it grounded entirely in masochism, power, guilt, and self-deception. Stafford unquestionably was drawn to what Lowell had and what he represented: a distinguished name, connection to American literary history, Boston breeding, money (though Blair Clark points out with a chummy sneer that "Cal came from a minor branch of the Lowell family with no great intellect or money"). Lowell was Stafford's best shot at crashing the civilization of Boston, something that was very important to her at the time. "She was drawn to Boston but she had serious reservations about it," says Hightower. "She despised it and wanted to be a part of it—to really be able to despise it." Like Mary Mc-Carthy, Stafford was a girl from the western hinterlands, "a flat-heeled country girl" as Clark puts it, spellbound by East Coast prestige. Mar-riage—McCarthy's to Edmund Wilson, Stafford's to Robert Traill Spence Lowell IV—gave both women a box seat in the premier theater. Yet nei-ther match can be chalked up to simple literary social climbing. It was not merely a pact with the devil for either Stafford or McCarthy: the two of them honestly thought they could live with the men who so avidly de-sired their consent. It would be a partnership with advantages—not *for* advantages. The preeminent advantage being brilliance. "There were very few matches for people like Cal and Jean," says Eileen Simpson. "For Jean it had to be someone like John [Berryman, to whom Simpson herself was married at the time] or Randall [Jarrell], someone she could really *be* with intellectually. And Cal had to marry an intellectual, some-one who could follow what he was thinking." Cecile Starr says anachro-nistically that Stafford saw Lowell as the "Mr. Kennedy of the literary world, this forbidden, enigmatic, fearsome guy. He had this wonderful background and wonderful friends such as Peter Taylor, Allen Tate, Ran-dall Jarrell—all people with whom Jean felt comfortable. And there was money or the possibility of money."

Blair Clark puts it best: "There was no aspect of young love in this marriage. It was an arrangement of protoliterary Titans. Cal was always going to marry a literary person—it was the only thing that interested him. It was a strange, strange marriage."

Just as Lowell's Boston pedigree attracted Stafford, so her *lack* of pedigree attracted him. Lowell well knew that his parents were writhing at his choice of this appalling girl from Colorado. In the eyes of the formidably awful Charlotte Lowell, Miss Stafford was a scheming nobody from nowhere—a "common" older woman, the daughter of some unspeakable mother who ran a boardinghouse, a self-styled but still unpublished writer who had managed to get her hooks into "Bobby" by entangling him in a preposterous car crash. Rumors floated back to Lowell at Kenyon that his mother was scheming to torpedo the match. He was furious—and triumphant. Marrying Stafford was a hard slap in the faces Lowell most wanted to slap. It was perfect. He would burn his bridges to home (except, of course, for the modest but useful trust fund) and together he and Jean would find new and better parents, *literary* parents. Home, from now on, would be art.

The wedding infected both of them with an unusually acute case of jitters. For some reason they chose to get married in New York, and there was evidently a frightful scene in the hotel two nights before the ceremony. They had spent the day apart and Lowell was furious that Stafford had stayed out later than he. They had a terrific row when she returned. Stafford, alone in her room with a bottle of rum, recorded events as they unfolded in a rambling letter to Hightower: "He should not have left me tonight and yet at this moment we are so irritated we hate each other." It was a night of ugly revelations. She admitted to Lowell that she had learned little German while in Heidelberg, and "he was absolutely stopped in his tracks and revolted. What wd. he do if he knew me?" The final humiliation comes in the postscript: "He just came in and said you've got to stop drinking and I mean even 1 drink and I was panic-stricken for fear he wd take my rum away. . . . It was very definitely very true and yet I shall perhaps not marry & and if I do not I shall be invisible for the rest of my natural days. Jean." She and Lowell spent the next seven years playing out variations on this humiliating scene.

Lowell's edict on sobriety did no good. The next night both of them got drunk and, as Blair Clark recalls, they had "terrific hangovers" the morning of the wedding. Clark, the best man, came to collect Lowell and found him nursing his head in the bathtub half an hour before the ceremony. Despite her terror and panic, Stafford went through with it. The marriage took place on April 2, 1940, at the charming, poetically resonant old church of St. Mark's in the Bowery. In lieu of family, Lowell's surrogate parents, Allen Tate and Caroline Gordon, attended as witnesses along with Clark. "*Terrified*. Happy," Stafford scrawled to Hightower on the back of a postcard of Radio City Music Hall.

No sooner were they married than they separated—Stafford to visit friends and family in Colorado, Lowell back to Kenyon to complete his studies. "I am very very lonely," Stafford wrote Hightower during a Chicago layover two days after the wedding. "How typical that I should have had a honeymoon on a train and in Cleveland. And while I may lay it all to external circumstance in my soul I know it is only my peculiar genius for the uncomfortable. Poor Cal! What a life he will have with me." All that spring she was intensely, hysterically preoccupied with Hightower's decision to marry her former roommate, an attractive but in Stafford's opinion "cotton-headed" girl named Bunny Cole. From Colorado she poured forth letters of sabotage and slander. Lowell, when she mentions him at all, is a remote apparitional figure—the "absent husband." Though she told Hightower to forget all the "garbage" she wrote from New York about their premarital fights, she remained grim about her married prospects. "I being married, can tell you what marriage is," wrote the blushing bride of eighteen days. "Even with respect, with awe of a superior mind and a shining talent—there is claustrophobia. We are too old, you and I, to expect convenience to endure or comfort to be forever a positive virtue." And later: "I married Cal to save us from ruin" (by "us" she means herself and Hightower). Clearly leery of the future, she was clinging desperately to their past intimacy and her former power over him. Meanwhile, Lowell graduated from Kenyon College with a slew of honors: "summa cum laude, phi beta kappa, highest honors in classics, first man in my class, and valedictorian," as he boasted in a letter to his mother.

The summer, as usual, raised the practical question of what to do next about work and money. Stafford promptly discovered that she had very different job prospects as "Mrs. Lowell" than she had had as Miss Stafford: her immediate options now were either secretary or faculty wife. For a while it looked like they would stay on at Kenyon, Lowell teaching Latin and English while Stafford typed for the *Kenyon Review*. When this fell through, Ransom helped fix them up with a similar arrangement at Louisiana State University at Baton Rouge: Lowell would be a junior fellow studying with Robert Penn Warren and Cleanth Brooks, and Stafford would work as secretary of the literary journal they edited, the prestigious *Southern Review*. Her writing would presumably happen in her "spare" time. It didn't occur to anyone, including Stafford, that as an experienced composition teacher she should have more status than Lowell at LSU. Stafford was always too proud and independent to concern herself with women's rights (a friend from this time of her life writes that the phrase "women's issues" "would have been almost incomprehensible to Stafford et al."). Yes, she was horrified at the idea of being Mrs. Lowell at English Department teas—but mostly because of the prissy absurdity of it. "I will become 'Mrs. Lowell' or 'Mr. Lowell's wife' and it will mean that my fighting will go on the rest of my life," she wrote Hightower as Baton Rouge loomed. It isn't clear what kind of fighting she had in mind here—fighting over her status? for time to write? for recognition or to make a name for herself? In any case, despite serious misgivings, Stafford seems to have resigned herself to typing for the men—and fighting—as necessary evils.

And so their married life commenced in the height of summer in the depths of the Deep South. Lowell was in his element. Warren and Brooks belonged to the tribe of Southern literary gentlemen that Lowell had joined when he apprenticed himself to Tate: in moving from Ransom's Kenyon down to LSU, he was trading one Agrarian outpost for another. Actually, by 1940 agrarianism had pretty much run its course, at least as far as its social and economic platform went. It was clear on the eve of World War II that the South was not going to beat back the devils of industrialization and urbanization and resurrect the bucolic unities of the Old Order. But the Agrarians had allied themselves with certain purely literary ideals—reverence for the modernism of T. S. Eliot and the rhetorical tensions of the English metaphysical poets; close reading of the text as self-contained object rather than as symptom or illustration of historical or social conditions; emphasis on craft over passion—and these furnished some of the essential principles of what came to be known as the New Criticism. When Lowell and Stafford arrived at LSU, Warren and Brooks were engaged in refining the New Critical program and promoting it to their students. Lowell was both intrigued and amused at the intellectual battle cries resounding through the dense Louisiana air. "Here reign the critical approach," he wrote a Kenyon classmate, " 'the aesthetic approach,' 'metaphysical poetry,' 'drama in the lyric' etc. . . . Brooks and Warren/Brooksandwarren are excellent."

(Stafford wrote sardonically that the whole thing boiled down to "the necessity of subordinating historical scholarship to cricicism [*sic*] or vice versa.") Though Lowell imbibed much of the New Critical doctrine, he never became a convert. In fact, his contact with "Brooksandwarren" sent him off in a rather different direction: a brisk immersion in English theology. But Warren became a lifelong friend, and Lowell always looked back fondly on the lunch hours they spent reading Dante together.

Stafford was less enthralled with the LSU atmosphere, intellectual and otherwise. Summer in Baton Rouge was her idea of climatic hell and she complained that the relentless heat and humidity oozed a "mysterious fungoid slime" over all exposed surfaces, fostered "small treacherous insects that house in the skin and hatch," and bred up a race of cockroaches "the size of hummingbirds" (Lowell later wrote of "rats as long as my forearm"). She wrote to Hightower that Louisiana was "lethal, teeming with serpents, disease, spiders, tainted meat." The weather and the vermin spoiled a lot of her pleasure in homemaking, which was complicated enough anyway after the arrival of "23 chairs and 22 imitation Navajo carpets" sent down from Boston by Lowell's grandmother. Homemaking was to assume increasing importance for Stafford as the marriage went on, and this humid three-room Baton Rouge apartment was a distinctly discouraging start. Figuring out her role in the world of "Brooksandwarren" was also problematic. Stafford was not exactly a faculty wife, but she was a *wife* nonetheless with all that implies. Even though she came to admire the Southern circle and embrace some of their literary views, she was never really one of the boys as Mary McCarthy was with the *PR* crowd. And of course she was *typing*, not *writing*, for the *Southern Review* (which was then publishing some of the first and best stories of Stafford's contemporary—and later good friend—Eudora Welty). The journal office was a mess ("hogsty" was Stafford's word for it), the workday long and boring, the pay meager—but at least it was income. Lowell was bringing in little aside from his trust fund dividends and gifts from wealthy relatives. So Stafford was breadwinner *and* wife.

A year before he died, Lowell wrote to "Dearest Jean" reminiscing about that year in Baton Rouge with "Red" Warren, his volatile Italian wife, Cinina, and their bothersome cat. Among the "hundred things" that came back to him from 1940 was an image of himself and Peter Taylor (who had come to live with them) "waiting still in pajamas outrageously for you to return from the office to get our lunch." Lowell's memory was uncannily accurate, for Stafford describes the same situation in a 1941 letter to Hightower: "It has been a dreadful arrangement here and I have not been good about it. It enraged me during the winter to come home at noon and find both him and Peter Taylor still in their pajamas, having spent the morning reading or writing while I had been cutting stencil and wrestling with 'Accounts Receivable.'" This is the quintessential scene from the first year of the marriage. The boys behaving as they did in college (actually Lowell never shook his habit of lounging on a "work bed" and writing in pajamas), only now with a wife to look after them. A wife who is wildly determined not to replicate the penny-pinching tyrannies of her own mother, but who can't let herself chuck bourgeois respectability either. The housework was "an insoluble problem, the first year," Stafford confided several years later to Peter Taylor's new wife, the poet Eleanor Ross. Even though she had help from a series of cleaning women, Stafford was overwhelmed. "Outrageous," Lowell's word nearly forty years later, is exact. The worst part was that she wasn't getting any writing down either. "I'm so up to my ears with working in the Review office, with housekeeping, the heat, etc. that I can't find the time to type up and revise my manuscript," she wrote to Edward Davison, her Boulder professor. ". . . I feel frustrated and angry that the years are going so quickly and I'm still totally unpublished." And to Hightower, now married to the dread Bunny and on his way to study in China, she poured out her heart in a letter written at the end of June 1940, a week before her twenty-fifth birthday: "[O]n that terrible day . . . I will be learning shorthand from 6:30 to 9:30 downtown in an upstairs room, a painful sedative and not a cure for mortality. My life seems annually more fogged and my retrogression is steady—now I'm a secretary. And will the next be a telephone operator or will I be the receptionist in a city laundry? This is not gloom, merely curiosity."

By November, she was hitting bottom. Again, she unburdened herself to Hightower:

I am half dead and the present time and Baton Rouge are like a discomfort of the absence I cannot imagine. There is no day without anger and no night with any articulate hope for the next day. I am resentful and despairing; discouragement is quotidian. I have not had, since I have been here, one experience of joy or one hour of solitude; my life has become subordinate to all other lives to which I am related and has become a monotonous pattern of struggle against rules and frustration so that my desire for anarchy [?] has never been so passionate and the possibility of it has never been so remote.

Even taking into account her penchant for hyperbole and self-dramatization, this is pretty deep misery. In fact, it reads like a formula for clinical depression—depression precipitated by five months of alienation, exhaustion, boredom, and most of all the demands of new marriage. Yet the notion of "women's issues" remained "incomprehensible" to her.

In one way, Stafford had gotten what she thought she wanted. She needed to be married; she was eager to take charge of the domestic front. The housework and entertaining she complains of so often in these first months were in some deep sense a source of satisfaction—and power. Home and the marriage it sheltered were the essential props of her "womanliness," a quality she insists repeatedly is more dear to her than her work, as in this furious letter she wrote to Lowell when the marriage was breaking up: "I know this, Cal, and the knowledge eats me like an inward animal: there is no thing worse for a woman than to be deprived of her womanliness. For me, there is nothing worse than the knowledge that my life holds nothing for me but being a writer." Yet *not* being a writer—being deprived of her writing by the obligations of womanliness—was an equal torment. She had struggled hopelessly with this issue during the long, tortured courtship with Hightower. "[T]hinking of myself as your wife, my daydreams have been those of a woman who had sloughed off all but the essence of womanliness," she wrote him in one of their impassioned periods. "I have wanted domesticity. I have wanted to be your wife and not much more. I have wanted to bear a child for you." Later, in the Boston hospital during her recovery from the car accident: "I want children, I want a house. I want to be a faithful woman. I want those things more than I want my present life of a writer, but I shall have none because my fear will make me unfaithful and desire cannot now be hoped for, it is too late and I have been too much revolted." With Hightower, these womanly desires receded whenever her work caught fire: it was really a rhetorical womanliness. The situation was more complicated with Lowell, partly because he too was a writer ("a superior mind and a shining talent," as she told Hightower) and partly because he was at once so domineering and so totally indifferent to domesticity. In the realm of literature, he was a peer, a fellow artist, an inspiring intellectual companion; but in the living room and bedroom he was a slob and a bully who did exactly as he pleased. He didn't *see* the problem—*her* problem, the galling, solitary problem of the married woman artist—because he didn't have to and she couldn't make him. Her failure to make him see, her failure in both realms—art *and* life— was at the heart of the depression that seized her in Baton Rouge.

"The same old horse and cow debate," she called it in an unpublished novel, "which was better, a creative woman or a homebody." The debate had only gotten fiercer now that she was married. In the years of the marriage to Lowell, she would be both the creative woman and the homebody, and at times succeed at both, but she would never be both together. And she would never really be happy at either. The more she succeeded at one, the more she wanted the other. The old horse and cow debate was at the heart of a lot of what was wrong with the marriage. Other couples of their generation, especially other literary couples, got riled up over this conflict. But Stafford and Lowell never really got beyond it.

Womanliness, that female essence Stafford clung to so fearfully, also meant sex, and that wasn't going terribly well either.

Stafford's biographers believe she was sexually unresponsive with Hightower—"frigid" is the hideous word—and possibly with Lowell as well. "No aphrodisiac has yet been devised to make me desire, to make me submit, yes, but not to revel in it," she wrote Hightower at one of the many critical junctures of their relationship. With Lowell she refrained from explicit revelations, but covert anxieties surface in her fiction. Sonia Marburg, the heroine of her first novel, *Boston Adventure,* desires only men who are deformed or crippled in some way. Molly Fawcett in *The Mountain Lion* hates everything corporeal and stages elaborate rituals to avoid seeing her own naked flesh. May, in "A Country Love Story," creates an imaginary lover to rescue her from the bleak silences of her marriage and then feels bereft when her fantasy fails her. Sexual deprivation ticks like a time bomb in Stafford's works of the 1940s. Rumors and stray remarks in letters suggest that the tension and frustration over sex came right out of the marriage.

The context, and perhaps the cause, of their sexual constraint was Lowell's conversion to Catholicism, which coincided with the beginning of married life. After the divorce, Stafford let drop the remark that Lowell swore off sex with her once he converted to Catholicism. This is hard to credit but also hard to dismiss. Lowell was twenty-four years old when he was "received" into the Church in the spring of 1941, about a year after the marriage. Twenty-four is not a likely age for a vow of sexual abstinence, especially for a man as sexually active and promiscuous as Lowell would become. The marriage lasted for six years after the conversion: six years without sex and without love affairs for two people in their twenties doesn't seem possible. On the other hand, one must reckon with the terrific driving force of Lowell's will—and his mania.

Was Lowell's conversion a symptom of impending mental illness? Possibly. But Catholicism did have a strong intellectual appeal to the young Lowell. With Tate and Ransom, and now with Brooks and Warren, Lowell had apprenticed himself to a literary school in which tradition and the integrity of the text, the word, were paramount. As Hulbert writes acutely, "Implicit in the formalist literary mission, as Eliot's own conversion had already suggested and Tate's would later, was a religious conception of the word as the way to truth." For the New Critics, the text itself was a sacred relic. Lowell initially approached the Church as a literary construct, a constellation of texts with an authority and rigor that superseded that of poetry: here was a complete code of life and belief that had inspired centuries of dense, impassioned commentary and that also required total daily adherence. He read insatiably in the works of Catholic philosophers, apologists, and poets: Etienne Gilson (whose *The Spirit of Medieval Philosophy* and *The Mystical Theology of Saint Bernard* affected Lowell deeply), Thomas Aquinas, John Henry Newman, Jacques Maritain, Gerard Manley Hopkins. Then, at some point, he made the leap from reading to believing—the leap of faith. "I kept swallowing more and more for a number of years" is how he put it years later. Rebellion against his parents may have also played a role in his choice of religion, as it did in his choice of wife. As his cousin Sarah Payne Stuart writes, "When Bobby dramatically changed religion, he picked the religion his family despised, the Roman Catholicism of their Irish maids."

In any case, Lowell had excellent company, for the Church attracted some of his most gifted friends and acquaintances in these years: Caroline Gordon converted; Katherine Anne Porter was an erratic adherent; Flannery O'Connor was born a Catholic and remained devout if ironic; Tate eventually converted under Gordon's influence. Even Jean Stafford, surprisingly, had a Catholic episode during her college years when she studied with a priest named Father Agatho and tentatively entered the Church. "I see why they [the Tates and the Lowells] became Catholics,"

Philip Rahv snorted once. "They're looking for new metaphors." It was a maliciously clever remark, but only partly true. Gordon and Lowell were the real thing (Lowell's friend playwright William Alfred, a Catholic himself, insisted that Lowell remained a Catholic in spirit, if not in practice, "until the day he died"). Tate was pious when it suited him ("he lapsed if it was the slightest bit inconvenient," says Elizabeth Hardwick with a laugh). Stafford tried hard to be pious, but her heart wasn't in it. She wanted to believe, and she went through the motions, but it didn't take. As she wrote Hightower in 1938 of an abortive visit to church: "All that happened was that my knees got sore. I was just dead. . . . I looked at the vigil lights and I listened to the murmuring in the confessional and I tried to tell myself that it was all mysterious and beautiful, but it didn't work. . . . I think that's the last time I will ever go. It's foolish. I expect so damned much and get so damned little." Hightower's comment: "Catholicism might have been more important to her than she admitted, but not so important that she couldn't make fun of it. There was no religious feeling in either of us."

With Lowell, Catholicism "took" with a vengeance. Characteristically, he went to extremes and made himself the best Catholic in creation. His self-imposed Catholic regimen was grueling: two rosaries per day, daily mass, grace at table, prayers before bed, a ban on unclean habits such as smoking and drinking. Patrick Quinn, a Catholic friend in Baton Rouge, recalls the zeal with which Lowell participated in his rebaptism into the Church, at which Quinn served as sponsor: "As I discovered, the initiate has an option: to go or not go to confession. The theory of the baptism is that in the case of an adult, all stain of sin is removed. No need for the sacrament of penance, therefore. It's an option. . . . I think maybe one or two of the other students who were. . . . 'received into the church' that night availed themselves of that option. But Cal, whose turn came last, apparently went all-out. Confession routinely takes a few minutes. Cal was closeted for about thirty minutes. While we all of course waited." "It was all most embarrassing," Quinn told Lowell's biographer Ian Hamilton. This was typical. Tales of Lowell's fanaticism are legion: his banning of newspapers from the household as insufficiently serious; "choice of movies according to the Censor," as Stafford wrote, "choice of books in the same way, and talk of *nothing* but the existence of God"; his insistence on remarrying "in the church" immediately after the conversion; the strict adherence to dogma and rules, particularly rules requiring abstinence from food and pleasure; the religious retreats; the scrupulous observance of saints' days; the endless treks to distant churches by public transportation. Lowell's friends made fun of him behind his back, yet they also respected—and feared—his earnest piety. As Peter Taylor said ruefully to Frank Parker, "One has to laugh, but it is deadly serious." Most deadly for Stafford. "I fell in love with Caligula and am living with Calvin," she told Eileen Simpson. "He's become a fanatic. During Lent he starved himself. If he could get his hands on one, he'd be wearing a hair shirt." She wrote even more damningly to Hightower: "It sickens me down to my soul to hear him talking piously and to see in him none of the common Christian virtues [such] as piety and kindness but only the fire-breathing righteousness that belongs, not to an unbaptized lay brother, but to a priest."

It wasn't enough for Lowell to save his own soul: he required his wife to save hers beside him. Stafford, despite her Catholic sympathies, quailed before his consuming piety. "I thought at first it would satisfy him if I made the gesture—" she wrote Hightower, "he couldn't ask for faith, certainly. But the gestures, if they are all performed, take up your waking hours." Eileen Simpson, herself a practicing Catholic, was one of the people to whom Stafford unburdened herself. "Privately she told me that Cal was a puritan at heart," Simpson writes in her memoir *Poets in Their Youth*. "He had become increasingly and rigidly devout, focusing on the things in the Church she found least attractive: spiritual exercises, retreats, good works. And what was 'maddening and enervating' was that he insisted she follow him in them." It was like his browbeating of Blair Clark and Frank Parker back in prep school, only now he had a higher authority to egg him on. As he wrote with ironclad self-righteousness to Peter Taylor: "[O]ne might almost say common sense is impossible without faith in Christ. . . . [I]t is not foolish to advize [sic] the people we love (O and the people we should love) to plunge into Christianity." And when these loved people failed to take the plunge with him, Lowell blasted them with "wrath and disdain," in Stafford's words. Even priests were alarmed at the depths of this peculiar young man's fanaticism.

Yes, there is the strong intellectual rationale for Lowell's conversion. And it fits emotionally with his desire for righteousness and his fascination with absolute authority (as a child he had been obsessed with Napoléon; later, when he had manic attacks, he raved about the genius of Hitler). Yet Lowell's Catholic zeal, hitting just when it did, must also have been a reaction to the marriage. As he remarked rather cryptically

to an interviewer three decades later, "It came from despair and the ex-
uberance of learning a religion, the despair at my circumstances, a character problem—I was just married and I couldn't get a job. I was too
tense to converse, a creature of spiritual perversity. Christianity was a
welcome." It was, together with the marriage, his first fully independent
act as a adult: he had overthrown or bypassed his mentors; he had flown
in the face of everything his parents held sacred or normal; he had
placed himself beyond the reach of friends, colleagues, and of course
wife. Who could argue with sacred truth? or deny the radiant glory of purity? How strange, and yet how characteristic, that being married should
inflame Lowell with a passion for chastity. In his imagination, the home,
the quotidian, the ordinary were unclean—the wife most of all since she
smoke and drank and cussed and told tall tales and wavered in her faith.
Later in life, whenever he was on the verge of a descent into mania,
Lowell would renounce and denounce Hardwick, swear off sex with her,
and launch himself into a love affair with a beautiful younger woman
whom he publicly beatified as his salvation. Now, in this first marriage,
the Church was the beautiful younger woman. Stafford had a claim on
her husband only to the extent that she joined him as a spiritual partner—a Catholic wife. Quinn recalls being a queasy witness to a scene
between the couple in Baton Rouge when Lowell was trying to get
Stafford to stop smoking (for health as well as religious reasons): "[Jean
was] pleading for a cigarette and Cal [was] doing all he could to persuade
her not to. And doing so with urgency, with patience and 'fellow-feel-
ing.' For he was an addict, too. I was the middle man. Could not but re-
spond to her pleading. And gave her one from my pack. I don't feel
complacent, didn't feel so then, about my gesture. What I'm recalling
now is Cal's efforts to be the protective, 'caring' husband. Not an act. He
was trying to help. I was quite moved, tho, as I confess, I supplied the
wanted article."

What Quinn perceived as marital tenderness and "protectiveness" often felt more like a crusade to Stafford. "I couldn't begin to tell you, con-
vincingly, the extent to which [Cal] will go for a conviction," she wrote
Hightower. "I have been *absolutely* without choice and I have white-
washed the thing to you because I must take all possible precautions
against cracking up completely, which I have done several times anyway
with nearly disastrous results." And later in the same long letter: "I no
better than the thousands of other liberals like me, can speak of Christ as
'Our Lord.' " Yet as always with Stafford, nothing is simple or straightfor-

ward. On other occasions, she confesses to Hightower her yearning to join her husband in belief and absolution: "Cal's Catholicism has been the best thing that has happened. . . . I am apprised of sin and no longer believe my history of it is too old for reparation." (Lowell, in his last book of verse, wrote fondly in a poem addressed to Stafford, "your confessions had such a vocabulary / you were congratulated by the priests.") In another letter she says that the "embarrassing" Catholic rituals of prayer and grace and mass are "only the frame of Cal's day which is, if anything, more intellectual than formerly. My fears were mostly groundless. His poetry is better, his wit has not suffered, he has become more generous and gentle." And then she contemplates the state of her own soul: "I think I can still scoff at aspects of the Church, but I have come to believe in the Passion. . . . I am formless. What else *but* orthodoxy? My life terrifies me. I am saturated with meaningless experience. I hope to have faith eventually." "Eventually"—the qualification of the born skeptic, the outsider, the onlooker. She tells Hightower in yet another letter, "I think I will always be in alien corn" in matters of faith, but then confesses a few paragraphs later that she is haunted by "the possibility of a heavenly book of rewards where my misdemeanours [*sic*] will be added up, in the end, to my ruin and damnation." Even when repeating the words of the Act of Contrition, "I have offended Thee, my God," Stafford still does not believe—but, as she puts it, "I see and am appalled at the *possibility.*"

Piety was not part of her temperament. She knew she harbored some stubborn core of resistance that would always keep her from going all the way: "[I]t is the perverseness of my nature to fight against any therapy advocated for me without my first having discovered it. I may come around in time. Certainly I see no other institution as rewarding." Torn and exhausted, Stafford took refuge in passivity, inertia, and indecision: neither devout nor faithless, she allowed Lowell to lead and herself to follow.

It was a tense situation, and there were battles, especially when Stafford was drinking. One night, on a visit to New Orleans with Blair Clark and Frank Parker, the couple got into a terrible row. Lowell took a swing at his wife—and/or tried to strangle her—and succeeded in breaking her nose again. Frank Parker gave me this account: They were all in New Orleans together and they had run into Harry Brown, "a young poet of great promise," of whom Lowell was rather jealous, for Lowell had not been published yet. Lowell and Stafford went up to their room and had words about Brown. Stafford came back down and "told us how uncivil Cal was. Then Cal came down and ordered Jean upstairs. Later she came down again and her face was bleeding. What provoked it was that Cal didn't want to see her fraternizing with the enemy." Parker laid out the gory details of the aftermath for Ian Hamilton: "She had to start all over again repairing the nose, after the awful time she'd had getting it repaired in the first place. I really don't understand how Cal could have done that. . . . He said he hadn't meant to. But he tried to strangle her. Jean was never afraid of him. I don't know why, because he was one of those people who didn't know his own strength." Blair Clark confirmed "the famous incident" to me, though he was a bit sketchy on the details: "The literature says I took Jean to the hospital, but I'm not sure if Cal came to the hospital or not. It was so traumatic. What did I think about it? I put it down to regrettable drunken behavior. Cal was deeply ashamed. If Jean had said, 'Get me out of this,' we would have done something. But she didn't. I thought the whole Baton Rouge set-up was depressing." The "literature" and surviving correspondence make no mention of any other assault aside from this, but there were ugly rumors of routine abuse. Robert Berueffy, who had known Stafford in high school and college, says that stories of the Lowells' domestic violence spread all the way back to Boulder: "I remember my mother saying to me, 'I hear Jean Stafford is married to that poet Lowell. I hear he beats her up for breakfast every morning.' " Berueffy's own opinion today: "I can believe it. I certainly never wanted to cross him. Lowell was a pacifist except when it came to beating his wife and father." The part about Lowell beating up Stafford for breakfast every morning is vicious gossip; but the pattern of violence is undeniable. Lowell was not a chronic "wife beater," but at least on one occasion he hit his wife hard enough to break her nose; and of course there was the irreparable damage she suffered in the car wreck, which may or may not have been deliberate. Certainly there is a stronger case against Lowell for spousal abuse than against Edmund Wilson. Wilson always denied Mary McCarthy's allegations of beatings, and in fact claimed *she* hit *him;* in the absence of witnesses, it was her word against his. Neither Lowell nor Stafford denied the New Orleans violence; but they seem to have agreed to bury it.

Stafford's characteristic reaction to the emotional turmoil in Louisiana was to take sick: fever that lingered on for weeks in the spring of 1941, and a bout of pneumonia that one doctor misdiagnosed as tuberculosis.

"Oh, Christ, Christ, what an *awful* year," she wailed from her sickbed to Taylor. And to Hightower: "It has been too much to have Baton Rouge, the Catholic church and tuberculosis piled on me all at once."

In the light of everything that was going on in that awful first year of marriage, Stafford's claim that sex ceased once Lowell converted does not look so entirely implausible. She may well have been indulging what Hamilton calls her tendency "to inflate or wittily distort the facts," but if she was, she had good reason, especially once the marriage ended. She was getting revenge for all the Catholic tyranny she had had to endure. She had planted a bomb sure to explode in Lowell's face as he went off with new women. And maybe, looking back, that was how the marriage had felt to her. If Lowell's mania was the Church, Stafford's mania was the marriage. The marriage and the Church were rivals, and it was clear to Stafford which had triumphed in her husband's heart. It was a terrible blow to her pride. To her womanliness. As she wrote Hightower, the grind of Catholic piety made her feel "boxed up and . . . hopeless." Even to attempt rebellion or escape was a sin. "Cal is more Catholic than the church," she later complained to Peter Taylor. "[O]ur conversations and his letters could be written into a case history of religious mania." She meant it literally: Lowell was suffering from a kind of mental illness. She alone recognized it years before it became clinical. It was the unassailable foe.

So she drank and smoked too much and wrote long agonized letters to Hightower. She told long funny, damning stories to anyone who would listen. She got sick. And, once the secretarial job was out of the way, she wrote.

The writing gathered momentum as the end of their time in Baton Rouge approached.

"When I am alone I am very well-off," Stafford wrote Hightower as she was packing up the Baton Rouge apartment ("this death-trap") in the summer of 1941. "The struggle is to be alone. I have a good hour each day when I am in the office in the morning before any of the editors arrive. Then I write—I write at no other time. But this will be changed in New York since Cal will be working, not I." By "working" she means earning money: Lowell had landed a job with the left-wing Catholic publishing company Sheed and Ward, and they were moving to New York in the late summer. Stafford was practically shivering in anticipation of her freedom from clerical drudgery: instead of one "good hour each day," she'd have all day, every day, to write. This was all the more welcome because her writing was going rather well just then. During her convalescence in the spring she had embarked on a major new project, a novel written in the first person and "in *conscious* imitation of Proust," whose works she was devouring along with those of Henry James. It had been ages since Stafford said anything hopeful about her work. Now, as the packing cartons and coat hangers mount up around her, she is almost glowing. "Cal will be working, not I"—she savors the very sound and emphasis of it. Cal will be working, and she will be writing the book that will appear, three years and many drafts later, as *Boston Adventure.*

Coincidentally, or maybe not, Lowell was writing no poetry. There is no natural law that dictates that only one partner in a relationship can be "hot" at a time—but it often works out that way. Wilson floundered around in the toils of dialectical materialism while McCarthy sprinted ahead with the early stories of *The Company She Keeps.* Caroline Gordon's pages mounted daily while Allen Tate suffered from protracted writer's block. Lowell's second wife, Elizabeth Hardwick, published little during her husband's glory days in the late 1950s and 1960s. Even in a marriage of well-matched literary luminaries, one career usually takes precedence over the other. Rivalry poisons the atmosphere or smothers one or another's flame. Financial or domestic burdens fall heavier on one set of shoulders, crushing creative work. Or success itself generates the excuses one needs to shun the empty page: too much mail, too many phone calls, too many friends and parties. So the husband potters in the garden while the wife wrestles with her masterpiece. Or the wife arranges trays of canapés while the husband courts the muse and cracks up. Lowell's "excuse" at the time was Catholicism: "It is not important to me to be a writer," he told Stafford around the time of his conversion. "If I cannot write devotional poetry, then I will not write poetry." It's hard to know whether this self-imposed edict had anything to do with Stafford or with the state of her work. Lowell was, by all accounts, an extremely competitive person, especially in his twenties and thirties. And from prep school on, being a writer had been the most important thing in his life—and always would be. So the Church may have been a cover for deeper anxieties about creation, potency, dominance, fame. He was too pious at the time to admit it, but he can't have been comfortable with Stafford's sudden creative burst.

Meanwhile, they both welcomed the change of scene. Even with the heat and dirt of late summer, New York looked like paradise after Baton Rouge, and by mid-September they were settled in a not-too-shabby apartment on West Eleventh Street in Greenwich Village. Perhaps "perched" would be more accurate than "settled," for the city gave them little peace. Despite Lowell's determination to be "surrounded by Catholics," the couple instantly got swept into the fast, loud current of atheist-Jewish-Marxist-hard-drinking-fast-talking literary New York. Philip Rahv and Nathalie Swan took a shine to Lowell and Stafford, and soon they were getting invited to the Rahvs' combative, whiskey-soaked parties. The jump from the Agrarian New Critics of LSU to the immigrant intellectuals of the *Partisan Review* was not really as implausible as it appeared. The bridge was Allen Tate. Tate and Rahv, behind their fierce public antagonism, liked and respected each other and enjoyed each other's foibles. Both had a gift for spotting new literary talent and an interest in promoting their discoveries—and sleeping with the discoveries when they were attractive females (sometimes the same females: Elizabeth Hardwick was supposedly a partner of both men). Tate and Rahv knew everyone and gossiped like mad about everyone they knew. Gossip about the Lowells must have heralded their arrival in New York, though of course once they got there Cal and Jean more than held their own.

It was a particularly fruitful season for gossip, for the Tates were living just a couple of hours from the city in Princeton, New Jersey, where Allen was winding up a three-year teaching contract. The Princeton position—starting and directing a creative writing program—had more or less fallen into Tate's lap in the spring of 1939, just a few months after he and Gordon had stayed with McCarthy and Wilson on the night of her breakdown. At the time the offer came, Gordon and Tate both held teaching jobs of equal rank at the Woman's College of the University of North Carolina in Greensboro: Tate, when he made up his mind to go to Princeton, resigned these jobs for both of them. "I always left things like that to him," Gordon wrote long afterward. "It was years before it occurred to me that Allen had resigned my full professorship—always a hard thing for a woman to come by—without consulting me!" Though she liked Princeton and lived there off and on for many years, Gordon was not happy at being relegated to the status of faculty wife, and she felt bitter at seeing Tate's reputation soar during the 1940s while her own career foundered. In retrospect, Gordon would look at these three years in Princeton as a time when much of what had been good in her marriage went sour.

Between the Rahvs and their circle in Greenwich Village and the Tates down in Princeton, Stafford and Lowell never lacked for company during their months in New York. Stafford enjoyed the *PR* crowd more now than she would later, but she found the pace of city life hard to maintain. "The main thing about N.Y. is why does *anyone* live here, and how on earth can you ever be human here?" she wrote Hightower. Every poet and critic they'd ever known either lived in the city or came for a visit. They had Randall Jarrell on their hands for a short, exhausting stay. The Rahvs threw a party for Robert Penn Warren, and the Tates summoned them to Princeton to meet British critic R. P. Blackmur. There was much talk of Delmore Schwartz, a *PR* luminary who was up in Cambridge teaching at Harvard, and of Edmund Wilson and Mary McCarthy, now in the third year of their stormy marriage (Stafford thought Wilson was "hot," but she deplored McCarthy's "The Man in the Brooks Brothers Shirt," which she had read in manuscript at the *Southern Review,* as "the dirtiest story I've ever read—of all repulsive things, a Pullman car seduction"). Lowell whacked away at Sheed and Ward manuscripts, wrote jacket copy ("[H]e's hard put to be at once honest and flattering," Stafford remarked), and decorated the apartment with crucifixes. Stafford also took a part-time job at Sheed and Ward to earn some money and, at Lowell's behest, did "Catholic work" at a seedy left-wing Catholic newspaper. Amid the myriad distractions, she pushed ahead with the novel.

By the spring of 1942 she had written enough to submit the manuscript, now called *The Outskirts,* to Harcourt, Brace. Robert Giroux, a young Harcourt editor whom Stafford and Lowell had met soon after moving to the city, took the pages home with him on the train one weekend and became so absorbed that he missed his stop. Giroux persuaded his colleagues to offer Stafford a small advance—$250 on signing, and another $250 on delivery. It was not a lot of money, but for Stafford it finally broke the spell of vague promises, empty praise, and prizes almost won that she had labored under for years. The signing of the contract took place in April at the Tates' house in Princeton: Gordon turned the occasion into a sort of mystic literary rite, placing candles on the desk and summoning her guests to stand by as witnesses. It was fitting that Gordon and Tate, who had witnessed Stafford and Lowell's wedding two years earlier, should now preside over this initiation into the company of professional authorship. It put a seal on the occasion—and marked a deepening of the relations between the two couples.

"Thank God we are both writers and have as a model the superb marriage of the Tates," Stafford wrote to Hightower right after she married Lowell. The superbness of the Tates' marriage was questionable, but they did indeed serve as the younger couple's most intimate model, especially in the coming year when the four of them holed up together in a cottage at Monteagle in the Tennessee mountains. The Monteagle interlude seems to have arisen casually, through an easy confluence of friendship, circumstance, literary alliance, and personal need. By the summer of 1942, Lowell and Stafford had had their fill of New York, and Lowell's job at Sheed and Ward had dried up due to wartime cutbacks. The Tates meanwhile were cast adrift after Princeton failed to renew Allen's contract. Monteagle, a rustic, wooded, mossy genteel Victorian cottage colony near Sewanee, had served as the Tates' retreat before when they were low on funds and desperate to write without distractions, and now was one of those times. "We always start working like hell as soon as we get here," Gordon remarked, anticipating their return. It seemed only natural to ask the younger couple to join them, as they had done before with Hart Crane, Katherine Anne Porter, Ford Madox Ford, and a series of lonely lesser poets and graduate students. The Tates' communal arrangements almost always ended badly, but they—actually it was usually Gordon's idea—persisted in making them. In any case, cottage-sharing in Monteagle now looked like the ideal solution to everyone's most pressing practical and literary problems. Stafford could revise the novel she had just sold to Harcourt; Gordon could plunge into her new novel, *The Women on the Porch;* Tate would embark on the sequel he had envisioned to his recently published novel *The Fathers;* Lowell intended to write a biography of Jonathan Edwards (a distant ancestor). It was an extraordinary, explosive concentration of brainpower, ambition, temper, and personality.

The Tates took first possession of New Wormwood, as they dubbed the cottage, and Gordon sent a couple of nervous, dickering dispatches up to New York. The Lowells' rent was $30, not $25 as originally thought; the decor was alarmingly, appallingly Victorian—"even the fly swatter is embroidered." It turned out that the two separate apartments were not quite separate, and the Lowells' half did not have a working kitchen—"so suppose we eat together," Gordon tosses out. She proposed a room swap whereby Allen would get the storeroom on the Lowells' side of the house as a study "in exchange for the use of our kitchen, dining room, living room and porch." "I know this sounds awfully complicated," she added, but "we need not get in each others' way." And to compensate, there was a pool nearby, farm vegetables trucked down from the mountains, and mushrooms "just popping up everywhere." (Mushroom hunting was a passion of Gordon's, as were gardening, cooking, and painting.) "I think we will all have room enough to work," Gordon wrote after the Lowells had accepted her terms, "and room enough, too, to spread out after we have finished our work."

Reading between the lines, it's clear that New Wormwood was pretty close quarters for any two couples (plus the Tates' teenage daughter, Nancy) to share for a protracted period. Factor in Gordon's domestic tyrannizing, Stafford's fierce, fussy household pride, Lowell's religious fervor, Tate's mood swings, and the penchant all four shared for liquor and gossip, and the whole thing looks like a setup for civil war. Miraculously, it worked for the better part of a year. And *they* worked. It was the "winter of four books" as Lowell put it. Each day, after Cal and Jean attended mass, the four would take possession of their typewriters and pens and have at it. Stafford made steady, crucial progress in revising *Boston Adventure;* Gordon forged ahead with her customary efficiency on her novel; Lowell, soon shelving the Edwards biography, collaborated with Tate on an anthology of English Renaissance and metaphysical verse— and then, at some point in the winter, he began working furiously at his own verse, composing most of the poems that would later be published in his first collection, *Land of Unlikeness.* Tate abandoned the intended sequel to his novel for the sonnets that make up his 1944 volume *The Winter Sea.* "The surges of creative energy . . . shake the house," Gordon reported to Katherine Anne Porter.

In the evening hours, there were surges of a different sort. The women agreed to alternate cooking dinner, leaving the men free to talk poetry (and read aloud from the works of Renaissance and Metaphysical masters) in the living room. Lowell was on the wagon, but the others drank freely—and in Stafford's case sometimes embarrassingly, which prompted Lowell to issue yet another set of temperance decrees. After dinner (Tate washed dishes; Lowell, famous for his ineptitude, probably did not or should not have tried to) they played charades, three-handed bridge, and a parlor game of their own invention—a kind of doubles verbal Ping-Pong character assassination. A name of a common friend or acquaintance would be proposed—"Let's do Rahv" or "What about Berryman?"—and then these four grand gossip masters would go to work on their victim with "amiable venom." Inevitably, as the mountaintop months wore on, they began to flash the knives at each other. The Tates floated vicious little rumors about the Lowells' monastic sex life (was it they who revealed—or imagined—that Cal made Jean sleep under the bed?); the Lowells returned the favor by making Allen's notorious philandering into a running joke. All this was to breed much trouble between them in the coming years.

More important, more enduring, were the literary cross-currents. Lowell had made Tate his "master" ever since he had crashed at Benfolly in the summer of 1937, but the Monteagle year marked the culmination and fulfillment of the apprenticeship. As Steven Gould Axelrod notes in his illuminating study *Robert Lowell: Life and Art:* "Tate gave Lowell a style, a theme, and something greater than either of these—a vision of a life totally committed to art, and an assurance that he too could achieve such a life. . . . Tate taught Lowell what it means to be a poet. It means . . . to put the whole self, the whole of one's imagination and skill and energy, into the act of artistic creation." At Monteagle, Lowell literally lived and breathed Tate: the two men shared a study, collaborated, exchanged works in progress on a daily, hourly basis. Lowell wrote later of watching Tate grit through "the tortured joy of composition to strike the impossible bull's-eye"—and this became his own lifelong model of how to work. Not bardic rapture but vision tempered by infinite agonizing revision: "no one has so given us the impression that poetry must be burly, must be courteous, must be tinkered with and recast until one's eyes pop out of one's head," as Lowell states the exacting credo he learned from Tate in his essay "Visiting the Tates." Up to now, there had always been an element of youthful folly in Lowell's poetic "crushes"—the way he hurled himself at the feet of any great poet within range and patterned his style and manner after his latest hero. But at Monteagle he finally buckled down and took the lesson of his master to heart. The result was stunning.

Much has been made of the "formal" qualities Lowell learned from Tate: his use of archaic forms and meters borrowed from Michael Drayton and Andrew Marvell in poems such as "Satan's Confession" and "The Drunken Fisherman"; the lofty, impersonal expression of lived, intimate experience; the choice of sinewy Anglo-Saxon verbs (strap, bawl, hang, shriek); the dazzling Technicolor symbols that all but blind the reader with multiple meanings. Even deeper, I think, was Tate's influence on his disciple's outlook and temper. Tate was a curmudgeon, a conservative in flight from and in conflict with the modern world. Like Yeats he detested the soulless, mechanized, capitalist state for swallowing up the "ingenious lovely" things of the past. The past was where Tate felt most alive: it was his repository of vanished beauty, his refuge, his source of vital knowledge and inspiration—a tragic source since it was impossible to return to it or to fathom its depths. Lowell was only too eager to join Tate in his plunges into lost time and his rage at the inanities and immoralities of the present. Following Tate's sage advice, Lowell embraced his ambiguous Puritan heritage and embedded it deep into the new poems he was writing. "He seems to be condemned both to read history and repeat it," Randall Jarrell wrote in a seminal early essay on his friend's verse. "His present contains the past—especially Rome, the late Middle Ages, and a couple of centuries of New England—as an operative skeleton just under the skin." Catholicism was Lowell's own personal twist on the usable past, and it had the advantage of putting him on even higher and more hallowed ground (Jarrell: "Such a Catholicism is thoroughly suited to literature, since it is essentially literary, anthropomorphic, emotional").

When the Monteagle poems were finished, polished (with considerable assistance from Tate), and ready for publication as *Land of Unlikeness,* Tate supplied the introduction—a short, strange little document that mixes bile and laurel in equal proportions. In the current state of affairs, with war consuming half the world, "material progress may mask social and spiritual decay," writes Tate. ". . . But the spiritual decay is not universal, and in a young man like Lowell, whether we like his Catholicism or not, there is at least a memory of the spiritual dignity of man, now sacrificed to mere secularization and a craving for mechanical order." Surely the substance of this introduction issued from the endless bull session at Monteagle. Tate might as well have been writing about himself: his benediction here verges on self-congratulation.

Of course it was not all kindly paternal advice and mutual backslapping between them. Tate was notorious for the bluntness and severity of his poetic "advice." "If Jesus Christ should come upon earth and present me with a poem I sincerely thought inferior, I would tell him *just that* to his teeth," Tate once boasted to a friend. He had evidently committed

Lowell's verse to memory during the Monteagle period, all the better to tear it to shreds word by word. Lowell, however, could take it—he later became famous for his porousness, his willingness, indeed eagerness, to absorb multiple streams of advice and promptly recast lines on a friend's suggestion—and he could also dish it out. In his introductory note to his translation of "The Vigil of Venus," Tate credits Lowell for his "constant criticism," and Lowell undoubtedly took potshots at his mentor's original verse as well. But the younger poet delivered his most pointed criticism a few years later when he rejected Tate's style and idiom for the looser, freer, more immediate mode of so-called confessional verse. Traces of Tate would always remain—the historical rootedness, the mournful alienation from the present, the craning after spiritual redemption—but by the late 1950s the ever-restless, protean Lowell had reinvented himself and moved on. The master was not pleased. But this is getting ahead of the story.

Lowell flourished under the intense public scrutiny and friendly fire of Monteagle. Stafford did not. She was ill off and on throughout their stay (as was Gordon). She fell out with Gordon over household matters (not for the last time). She overindulged her preferred vices of smoking and drinking. The close quarters, the domestic rivalries, the abrasive personalities grated on Stafford. But the real problem was that she hated having her work criticized "to her teeth" by the blunt Tates. After the couples had separated, Gordon wrote Stafford to apologize for the way "we were all taking whacks at your novel there on the mountain." And in another letter, Gordon, who was rarely repentant about such matters, blamed herself for precipitating Stafford's recurring illnesses: "I have decided that your mysterious fever came not from sinus or anything else but from having your novel torn to pieces by fiends in the guise of friends." Stafford was too private, too sensitive, too independent a worker to thrive in the glass bowl of Monteagle. She was also too proud and possessive of her own work. Later on, when *Boston Adventure* was published to mostly positive reviews and brisk sales, she wrote Peter Taylor how furious she was at Lowell for claiming that the novel "would have been *much* poorer than it was if it hadn't been for the Tates." It wasn't that she couldn't take criticism: she simply did not want to share any of her glory with "fiends in the guise of friends" or with her ambitious husband either.

The house-sharing, work-swapping arrangement at Monteagle threatened Stafford. The whole thing felt too claustrophobically familial: the

Tates were the exacting yet weirdly bohemian parents, she and Lowell were the children—chaste brother and sister, not husband and wife. Later, after the marriage had ended and Stafford was deep in psychotherapy after a serious breakdown, she analyzed the pathology of their relationship with the Tates in a letter to Lowell. The trigger for this outpouring was an unexpected, and devastating, encounter with Gordon at a party at Cecile Starr's apartment. "It was more than just seeing Caroline," she writes, "it was realizing how you and I together, unable to grapple with the enormous complexity of our problems, took refuge from them in other people—and often it did not matter who the people were. We could not be blamed for that; the Tates, when we first knew them, were delightful company, they were wise critics, they were helpful, they seemed really fond of us. . . . I remembered the anguish of the year in Tennessee and I was struck in a heap to think of how Caroline had always said she thought of us as her children, because we *were* children, we have been everyone's children." Too pat, perhaps; too steeped in officially sanctioned therapeutic insights—and yet there is a nugget of emotional truth here. Stafford didn't *want* another set of parents: the original pair was quite bad enough. Unlike Lowell, she had no use for a mentor to revere and rebel against. Literary family was ultimately just as destructive to her as the ordinary kind. What she *did* want was more of a marriage, more of a solid bourgeois home life. And this Lowell steadfastly refused to give her or let her have. No wonder she was so angry at her husband for crediting the Tates with improving *Boston Adventure*. It was the only thing she had to show for herself—snatched away, as always, by "family."

Strangely, Stafford makes no mention of Lowell's influence on her novel—yet surely this was considerable. During the Monteagle year and beyond it, the two of them wrote side by side about much the same thing: the spiritual and social burdens of Boston, and the plight of the Catholic outsider in a snobbish, hypocritical, Yankee Protestant world. Boston of course was Lowell's turf by right of inheritance. But it came to Stafford as a wedding present and she was determined to open it and use it. Sonie Marburg, her novel's narrator and central figure, is a heavily charcoaled caricature of her creator: her parents are brawling, desperate, impoverished, impossible immigrants from eastern Europe; Sonie herself is a kind of artist who creates no art, a wide-eyed, yearning, but illusionless onlooker, painfully sensitive to the shabbiness of her life in the dull seaside town of Chichester, always gazing across the water to the world of wealth, privilege, and intelligence she imagines Boston to be. Sonie's big break comes when the rich, tight, elderly Miss Pride unofficially adopts her and installs her in her Beacon Hill town house as companion/secretary. Sonie has dreamed of just this escape for years ("I could only imagine myself dazzling Miss Pride with my culture; I had no desire to overthrow her, only to make her welcome me"); yet when the move comes, it instantly proves to be just another prison, even more deadening than her life at home.

What's astonishing about Stafford's heroine is her inertia: the more trapped and hopeless she feels, the less she does about it. Sonie is young, beautiful, intelligent, alive; yet rather than free herself from Miss Pride's "flat, omniscient" eyes, she surrenders to them, withholding just enough of her will and spirit to describe the terms of her surrender with merciless precision. This is pure Stafford: unable or unwilling to escape, Sonie embraces her doom and lets the emptiness and stupidity of her situation consume her.

Stafford identifies with and pities Sonie and wants us to think she is superior to everyone else in the novel, but she still can't resist punishing the girl at every turn. It's typical that Sonie's first visit to Boston culminates not at the statehouse, whose golden dome has been her symbol of salvation for years, but at a cemetery, the Granary Burying Ground, which Miss Pride considers the sole "jewel" of the city. In her Dantesque description of the place, Stafford milks the morbid Boston icons for everything they're worth:

> We entered its iron-bound precincts and advanced down the central path between the splitting gravestones that tilted backwards toward the austere obelisk of Franklin and the eroded sarcophagi. The several trees of the yard, black-trunked, thickly burled, and leafless now, and the naive death's-heads, sprouting angels' wings on the decaying wafers of rock, were dextrous accidents, for they, and the wind we heard when the noise of traffic was briefly suspended contrived to give the place an air so formidable and esoteric that I felt death, at his most facetious unsightliness, walking beside me. I understood why she had said this was the heart of the city. Walled on one side by the Athenaeum through whose black windows a solitary old Bostonian, withered and hewn, was gravely regarding us, the sparse and lowly graves of the harsh garden testified to the city's conviction of its rightness and its adamant resistance to change.

Lowell was also putting Boston cemeteries into the poems he was writing during the time Stafford reworked *Boston Adventure,* and since she usually typed up his verse, it's quite possible that she borrowed something of his mood and manner. There is certainly more Lowell in her Granary Burying Ground passage than in anything else in the novel: the violence of the imagery, the dense plummeting adjectives (iron-bound, splitting, eroded, decaying, dextrous, withered, sparse, harsh), the exaggerated symbolism, the bitter relish of the putrid and diseased, the pleasure in self-mortification. Yet how different are the aims and motives of Lowell's verse. Stafford ends her cemetery passage in ironic stasis: "the harsh garden testified to the city's conviction of its rightness and its adamant resistance to change." She knows the "city's conviction" is false, its "resistance to change" a symptom of paralysis, but she has no alternative vision to suggest. There is no rebellion in Stafford, only weary disillusionment and passive disdain. Lowell's Boston graveyards, by contrast, launch him into a wild apocalyptic orbit. In "The Park Street Cemetery" (later revised and expanded into "At the Indian Killer's Grave") the Puritan dead lie senseless and blind beneath the "Easter crowds / On Boston Common" while the Irish Catholic immigrants flex their new political muscle in the statehouse's golden dome: the rising generation is selling out the true religion for power just as the founders betrayed the "city on the hill" in their day. In the expanded version published in *Lord Weary's Castle,* the "great garden" of the burial ground, "rotten to its root," has become a repository for the violent, misguided sins of the past.

The dead Bostonians who lie in the "harsh garden" of Stafford's cemetery are horrible ghouls who reach out to strangle the spirit of a yearning young woman; but Lowell's dead are the howling damned, burning in a hell of their own creation—a landscape of "green perfection" that they despoiled, spread with carrion and Indian corpses, and finally left to us as a blackened, rotting "great garden" of death. We who inherit are no less culpable than our sinning ancestors: on Judgment Day, we don't have a prayer either. With our world war, our capitalist greed, our overstuffed folly, our pursuit of the godless pleasures of our sham democracy, we have killed Christ "[d]ead as the gods and oaths of yesterday." The only hope Lowell proffers, and it's a remote one for most of us, is the Church. "Us still our Savior's mangled mouth may kiss," he opens the final redemptive stanza of the gruesome "Christ for Sale," "Although beauticians plaster us with mud." Redemption through the Church is, of course, the requisite posture of the Catholic poet, yet it is a *"willed"* redemption, as Tate noted in his introduction, grafted roughly on at the end. Damnation, not salvation, inspired the best lines in Lowell's first book of poems.

Boston Adventure and *Land of Unlikeness,* brilliant as they are in many ways, are both fatally young books—crackling with the strangeness of the original creation yet so tense and intense that they're hard to read. There's something strained and claustrophobic and terribly miserable about them. Later, after the marriage ended and they grew up some, Stafford and Lowell each found a calm, ironic voice for the bewilderments of sorrow, but in these first books they both wrote with a kind of blind fury—the fury of young, self-conscious, unhappy people; unhappily married people. The marriage was neither a cause nor a subject of Lowell's poems or Stafford's novel, but it was the atmosphere in which they were written. Airless, joyless, cut off from the "world." A cramped, unventilated space where the couple labored sullenly side by side. It's not a place one wants to be in very long.

Readers and critics of 1944 did not seem uneasy about *Boston Adventure,* for the book was an immediate and considerable success upon publication in September. Sales approached 400,000 copies after seven months, bringing Stafford $21,000; reviews were for the most part favorable (even before the first notices appeared, Rahv wrote Stafford that the book "struck me as the best first novel by an American writer that I have read in quite a few years"); Harcourt, Brace cranked up the marketing machine to keep the cash register ringing ("I believe they are spending enough money on it to make it sell," sniffed Caroline Gordon in an envious letter). Stafford was "launched." By contrast, Lowell's debut in a pricey, classy, limited edition published privately by Cummington Press barely raised a ripple (at least commercially). The two books appeared within days of each other, and Stafford was acutely aware of how perilous it was to upstage her husband. "I cannot tell you how relieved I was to have him beat me into print" by three days, she wrote a friend in Boulder. "His is a 'fine' edition, very beautiful and so expensive that he's sure no one will ever buy it." The defensive, apologetic tone here is telling. Cal's book, doomed to financial failure, was therefore more genuine, his success more solid. Certainly more Catholic. Beyond this is the implicit assumption that Cal, as the man of the family, "should" have the success that matters. Much as she resented typing her husband's poems, and resented even more being *expected* to type them, much as she insisted that she didn't know or care much about poetry or even *like* it particularly, Stafford wanted to see him succeed as a poet. "Jean was self-centered, but she took pleasure in Cal's success," recalls her friend Cecile Starr. "But Cal felt no gratification because of her success. He was incapable of it. He did not know other people existed." She mustn't "beat" him into print. She mustn't "beat" him in anything.

But she did. In 1944 Cal's success was still nonexistent and, to most of their friends, unimaginable. "After *Boston Adventure* Jean was a best-selling author," says Robert Giroux. "Her success preceded his. Back then no one suspected that Lowell was heading for the success he later attained." "I never heard Cal say anything about Jean's work," says Blair Clark, "but I guess he would have been envious of her. He was in danger of being eclipsed by this girl. She was the coming thing. No one had much interest in Cal's contorted verse." According to Cecile Starr, "Nobody suspected Cal would become bigger than any of them put together. It was Stafford who brought Lowell's work to Giroux; she helped him. But no one had any idea he would be a celebrity. He was the incompetent one around practical affairs. We all thought that publishers and interviewers and people who made celebrities would never see anything in him. He seemed too preoccupied to stand in the limelight. We thought he seemed destined never to be noticed." Lowell's lagging behind in fame and success was a problem for both of them—a marital problem. And together they worked hard to fix it in the coming years.

While the Lowells toiled away on their first books under the watchful eyes of the Tates in Monteagle, the Wilsons pursued country pleasures of their own out in Wellfleet on the eastern forearm of Cape Cod. Borrowing part of the down payment from his mother, Wilson purchased an 1820s white clapboard farmhouse on Money Hill in 1941, and this remained his and McCarthy's primary home for the duration of the marriage—in fact, Wilson lived here at least part of the year for the rest of his life. For Wilson, it was a return to familiar haunts, for he had known and loved the Cape ever since he first trekked out to Truro in 1920 to be with Edna St. Vincent Millay and mingle with the bohemians at Provincetown. Over the years he had spent many summers on the Outer Cape and sometimes stayed on into the colder months. Now that he had a permanent residence in Wellfleet, he slipped easily into an established circle of friends—John and Katy Dos Passos, translator and Yale teacher Charley Walker and his wife Adelaide, the writer Mary Heaton Vorse, and a handful of other writers and artists. They formed a real "community," Wilson mused in his journal, "more closely bound up together than we had realized or perhaps wanted to be." Certainly more than McCarthy wanted to be. Though she reveled in gardening and swimming, she found the Wellfleet social scene oppressively stodgy and faintly ridiculous. Most of Wilson's artsy cronies struck her as "terrible hacks" and "rusting freelancers," and she had a terrific time making mock of them in her Cape Cod novel *A Charmed Life*.

Aside from the satirical character sketches, a bit of local color, and one shocking sexual encounter planted in *A Charmed Life,* the Cape Cod chapter of the Wilsons' marriage remains largely a closed book. McCarthy had little to say about it to biographers or interviewers. And Wilson devoted but a few hasty entries to his young wife in the voluminous diary he kept nearly his entire adult life. Mary looks "pretty and white," Wilson recorded on May 21, 1942, after a picnic on Gull Pond near their Wellfleet house. "But she was ripened by the summer sun where her face and neck and arms had been exposed while working on her garden, and the tan of her forearms and the reddening tints brought out in her rather pale skin were in harmony with her blue suit of overalls." A haze of eros suffuses the scene, the longest entry about McCarthy published in the journals—even the baby pine cones "seemed almost embarrassingly soft, almost like a woman's nipples." On other occasions, Wilson wrote even more explicitly erotic entries about his wife, including a glowing account of sex in a New York hotel, but when the diaries were being readied for publication after his death, McCarthy insisted on suppressing this passage, along with references to her "hysteria," "collapses," "fits," and delusions. All that remains of her in the published diaries of the 1940s are fond fleeting glimpses: strolling their son up and down the sandy hills around Wellfleet, having a drink with him every evening at five, reading magazines at night and ordering from catalogs. This is as close as they got to the "idyll" she had been anticipating when she agreed to marry him four years earlier ("We were going to read Juvenal together. . . . We would look for wild flowers in the woods"). Yet it came too late to make much of a difference. McCarthy by this point was already declaring her independence—from Wilson, from Wellfleet, from the marriage.

In 1942, after a scant year on the Cape, McCarthy rented a Manhattan apartment on Stuyvesant Square so she could keep daily appointments with her impressive new psychiatrist, Dr. Abraham Kardiner (who had been analyzed by Freud himself). She returned home to her husband and child only for weekends, rather like an old-fashioned businessman who parks the wife and kids in a country house for the summer while he swelters it out in the city during the workweek. Wilson had insisted on hiring a nanny so that McCarthy could get her work done and proceed with her analysis, and Reuel was presumably in the nanny's charge while his mother was in town. Years later, McCarthy contemplated the evolution of her uses of New York in a witty letter to Robert Lowell and Elizabeth Hardwick: "I would long ago come to New York to see a lover, then to see a psychoanalyst, then an editor or publisher, then a lawyer, and finally the dentist. I can't quite make this work out to the Seven Ages of Man." (Lowell was so enchanted with this passage that he "versed" it, nearly verbatim, into one of his sonnets.) During this Wellfleet period she straddled the First and Second Ages: she was seeing an analyst *and* a lover—or rather, apparently, several lovers—most notably *PR* art critic Clement Greenberg, with whom she conducted a lengthy and not very enjoyable love affair. As she later told an interviewer, "You know when you have an affair with some man you don't like, somehow they're the hardest to break with." In sleeping with Greenberg, an early and highly influential champion of Abstract Expressionism, McCarthy was betraying not only Wilson but also Rahv, for Greenberg and Rahv were bitter enemies, forever scheming each other's downfall (Greenberg was a key player in an abortive putsch against Rahv that William Phillips orchestrated in 1948). But perhaps that was part of Greenberg's attraction: McCarthy used him to goad a man she cared about but could no longer have.

The affair with Greenberg, however unpleasant, was one sign of McCarthy's growing distance from Wilson; the publication of her first book, *The Company She Keeps,* in 1942 was another. Though Wilson had encouraged her to write the stories that make up this loose-jointed novel and helped her place them in magazines, McCarthy never felt she owed him anything for her success—in fact, just the opposite: she was delighted to be making a name for herself, and a scandalous name at that. With its sexual frankness and breezy irreverence about two of the period's most sacred cows—politics and psychoanalysis—the book made readers, especially male readers, uneasy. Delmore Schwartz went around calling McCarthy's writing "Tidings from the Whore," and William Carlos

Williams, asked by her publisher to supply a blurb, could only splutter that "Mary McCarthy, as Mary McCarthy, is something to be sur-mounted—and a man had better be feeling fit when he takes her on." Clifton Fadiman dismissed the book in *The New Yorker* as "high-grade back-fence gossip." The reviewer for *Time* magazine took McCarthy to task for putting "real people" in her fiction (this was to become a familiar line) and insisted that the novel had stirred up "furious debate among the author's friends and victims." Robert Penn Warren reviewed *The Com-pany* for *PR*—an interesting choice since Warren, though he later threw in his lot with northern liberals, was then an "enemy" Agrarian (and be-sides, he had already seen some of the material in manuscript: as editor of the *Southern Review,* he had published the volume's opening chapter, "Cruel and Barbarous Treatment," as well as "The Genial Host," but he had passed on "The Man in the Brooks Brothers Suit," explaining to Mc-Carthy "with some humiliation" that "the sex episode probably makes it unusable for us." In *PR* Warren tried hard to like the book—he praised it as "shrewd, witty, malicious, original and often brilliantly written"—but clearly he did not. He found the tone "dry, analytical, satirical" and the hybrid structure forced.

There were, however, some appreciative male readers, including Wil-son himself, who seems genuinely to have admired the novel. Obviously, Wilson could not review his own wife's work, but he did his best to drum up enthusiasm among literary friends. Both Vladimir Nabokov and Ran-dall Jarrell praised *The Company* in letters to Wilson, and he gratefully passed their remarks on to McCarthy. "Mary was cheered by what . . . you said," he wrote Nabokov thanking him for his praise, "as she has been getting pretty dreadful reviews. Almost nobody has said that the book was well-written. I don't think people notice the difference nowadays." Wilson also defended the book in a cranky letter to Tate when the *Kenyon Review,* then under the editorship of Tate's Fugitive "brother" John Crowe Ransom, published a "stupid and impudent review appar-ently composed by the office boy" and added insult to injury by rejecting some of her (and his) "best things." In any case, despite the "pretty dread-ful" reviews, *The Company She Keeps* sold 10,000 copies in 1942—a far cry from Stafford's best-selling success two years later with *Boston Ad-venture* but certainly a good showing for a first novel in wartime.

Years later, *PR* editor William Barrett wrote of *The Company She Keeps* in his memoirs, "We did not know it then, but she was in fact fir-ing the first salvo in the feminist war that now rages within our society, though I doubt the movement has since produced any weapon of equal class and caliber. It was also something of a shocking book, or seemed so at the time." Shocking yes; feminist no. McCarthy's protagonist Meg Sargent is neither a victim of patriarchal oppression nor a sexual revolutionary blazing her way to liberation and self-fulfillment. If Meg is humiliated by her encounters with men, she is also, often at the same time, captivated: she doesn't want to overthrow "the system," she just wants to be noticed, rewarded, and crowned with an array of unusual experiences. Especially sexual experiences. What's original in the novel's perspective is not its feminism but its femaleness—its fresh new unblinking honesty about what a woman thinks about and feels in her most intimate moments. As Elizabeth Hardwick wrote with her customary shrewdness, "[T]he 'shocking' frankness of the sexual scenes is very different from the hot prose of male writers. These love scenes are profoundly feminine, even though other women writers do not seem to want to take advantage of this same possibility. . . . [I]t is part of Mary McCarthy's originality to have written, from the woman's point of view, the comedy of Sex. The coarse actions are described with an elaborate *verismo* of detail." The true heroine of these stories is not the character Meg Sargent but the showy originality of McCarthy's performance—this "look at me" quality that drove her to "spill" so many dirty little secrets. Who but McCarthy would follow a heavy-breathing seduction scene with the line "You need a bath"? To quote Hardwick once more: "We might naturally wonder from what blending of bravura and commonsense this tart effervescence has come."

Wherever it came from, tart effervescence was McCarthy's special note. It comes through loud and clear in this first book—in some ways never as loud or clear again. Though the reviews were disappointing, McCarthy would not have been dismayed by the notoriety of being a "shocking" writer. She, like her fictional stand-in, was hungry for recognition, and in *The Company She Keeps* she got it by fashioning an instantly recognizable persona—a kind of trademark that made her a kind of celebrity. Maybe William Carlos Williams had it right after all when he stuttered in his puff that "Mary McCarthy, as Mary McCarthy, is something to be surmounted." Mary McCarthy *as* Mary McCarthy was born with *The Company She Keeps,* and this was indeed "something" to be reckoned with—though never surmounted—for years to come.

• • •

Though he occasionally published in Partisan Review, Wilson never really liked the magazine very much or the "boys" who put it out—in part because his wife was so fond of them. "Potash and Perlmutter" were his snide pet names for Rahv and Phillips, a reference to a pair of squabbling Jewish business partners in a Broadway comedy of yesteryear. This was Wilsonian humor, but he did seriously resent the power and influence they wielded, especially when they wielded it to his or McCarthy's disadvantage. After the magazine declined to publish McCarthy's short story "The Genial Host," Wilson laced into PR editor Fred Dupee: "I've thought there was something wrong in your shop ever since you passed up that short story of Mary's, which seemed to me the best thing she has written. You people owed her a chance to develop, since she was one of your original group."

As if this disloyalty weren't bad enough, Wilson had to endure an invasion of PR writers, editors, wives, ex-wives, and fellow travelers into his beloved Cape Cod haunts. Rahv and Nathalie Swan appeared in Provincetown one summer, and Wilson found himself in the highly unpleasant position of playing host to his wife's ex-lover (he pronounced Rahv's visit in very poor taste; Rahv returned the compliment by calling Wilson a "schmuck" behind his back). Fred Dupee also turned up at some point, for Wilson's daughter Rosalind remembers "some jolly evenings at home with Fred Dupee, Philip Rahv, etc. with everyone screaming about Trotskyism, Stalinism." Though she confesses that she didn't learn very much because she was "always out getting the ice." Alfred Kazin, Arthur Schlesinger Jr., Dwight Macdonald, and Daniel Aaron also began frequenting the Outer Cape in the 1940s, and eventually literary folk, academics, and psychiatrists were so thick on the local beach that one of the more pompous denizens took to calling it "la plage des intellectuels." Rosalind complained that the once wild and lonely Cape was filling up with the "remainders of the Partisan Review crowd, among others, with their new wives, while ex-wives had cottages nearby," which sounds like the kind of thing her father would say. Wilson himself griped that come summer the place turned into "the fucking Riviera."

A "ferocious workaholic . . . buried in a labyrinth at Money Hill" is how Wilson struck Dwight Macdonald's son Michael, who often came to the house to play with Reuel. As he aged, Wilson cut an increasingly eccentric and rotund figure—garbed at home in a ratty bathrobe but buttoned up in tie and jacket when he sallied forth on his rickety bicycle. Kazin remarked, with respect, "a certain seediness" in Wilson's appearance during the early Wellfleet years, "the great bald dome, the lack of small talk, the grumpy concentration on every topic he came to." There's a wonderful photo taken in 1942 of Wilson and McCarthy sitting side by side on the porch of the Money Hill house and smiling rather sweetly and foolishly at each other. McCarthy, with her dark hair long and loose, wearing the open-top shoes that Wilson, a bit of a foot fetishist, loved so much, fairly blooms out of her flimsy short-sleeved dress. Wilson, portly and owlish in tie, jacket, *and* hat, has a newspaper in his lap and his right thumb and forefinger pinched together under his nose. "The pictures of me are downright disgusting and have given me quite a turn," he wrote after he'd seen them. "I seem to be taking snuff in one of them." Whatever he was doing with his fingers, he looks relaxed, happy with his wife, pleased with himself. They *did* have some good times together on the Cape, as even McCarthy admitted. In the absence of letters, diary entries, or revelations from indiscreet confidantes, this photo is about as intimate a glimpse of them as we're likely to get.

It's odd that Wilson and McCarthy's good times in Wellfleet should have coincided with America's entry into World War II. Or maybe not so odd. For as far as they and most of their intellectual friends were concerned, the war barely existed, at least in its early years.

5

The War

■ "WE MISSED the declaration of war, / we were on our honeymoon train west" Lowell wrote in a poem called "Since 1939" published in his final volume. It's a fitting image for the whole crowd. They all missed the declaration for one reason or another—missed it and in most cases opposed it. They didn't, at least at first, consider it *their* war at all, but rather a hopeless conflict between two systems they despised: capitalism and fascism. Of course, they conceded that fascism was worse than capitalism, but they believed that if America joined the war against fascism, it was doomed to become fascist itself. As a number of prominent *PR* writers declared in an open letter published in the magazine: "Our entry into the war, under the slogan of 'Stop Hitler!' would actually result in the immediate introduction of totalitarianism over here." It was not a choice between evils because in their minds the two evils were ultimately the same. In the *PR* circle, Dwight Macdonald was the most outspoken proponent of this antiwar line. Collaborating with Clement Greenberg, Macdonald argued in the July–August 1941 issue of the magazine that the correct response to the world crisis was "not war but revolution": a revolution of oppressed soldiers on both sides against their imperialist war-lord masters. Wilson, who had fought in the First World War and regret-ted it forever after, took a similar stance, insisting that this new war was essentially a continuation of the old war. McCarthy and most of their friends agreed.

Theirs was a classic Marxist position applied to what looked like a classic Marxist situation—McCarthy described it as "the psychology of the 1930s spill[ing] over into the 1940s"—but it threw the *PR* intellectuals in with some strange political bedfellows, including isolationists such as Charles and Anne Morrow Lindbergh. As Diana Trilling wrote later, *PR* "was a Marxist journal and culturally anything but isolationist, yet in its opposition to America's involvement in the war it joined a strange cho-rus." Isolationism of whatever stripe or motive became increasingly un-tenable after the Germans invaded the Soviet Union in June 1941 and the Japanese bombed Pearl Harbor that December. Indeed, before the year ended, Rahv dramatically broke ranks with his fellow Marxists, declaring in an oft-quoted *PR* editorial "And yet in a certain sense this is *our* war" and dismissing Macdonald's antiwar stance as "revolutionary defeatism." "The rest of us were deeply shocked" by Rahv's about-face, Mary Mc-Carthy confessed, "because we regarded it as a useless imperialist war." The reversal blew a hole in *PR:* Dwight Macdonald ultimately quit the magazine because of its position on the war and started his own influ-ential magazine called *politics;* others took it as a sign that Rahv had been "suckered" by the capitalists and looked back on his endorsement of the war effort as the magazine's first step down the road to conser-vatism.

The verdict of history is clear. Macdonald and his fellow left-wing anti-war activists were naive, even delusional, in their dream of an interna-tional workers' and soldiers' revolution. Rahv proved to be prophetic when he wrote that the war "will either be won by the combined might of the Anglo-American imperialism and Stalin's Red Army, or else it won't be won at all; and the military defeat of Germany remains the in-dispensable precondition of any progressive action in the future." But this was by no means so obvious in 1941. Nor was it altogether clear that what the Nazis were doing in Europe was without precedent in modern history. Few Americans at the time understood that Hitler was engaging not only in a war of imperialist-nationalist expansion but in the system-atic extermination of entire populations. As *PR* contributor Lionel Abel wrote in his memoirs, "The facts of the Holocaust were not generally known in the United States during the war. . . . I had no real revelation of what had occurred until sometime in 1946, more than a year after the German surrender, when I took my mother to a motion picture and we saw in a newsreel some details of the entrance of the American army into the concentration camp at Buchenwald." Many others recorded similar stunned revelations.

The American left-wing intellectuals who opposed the war were not, for the most part, callous, cynical, or cowardly, but simply ignorant: a combination of Marxist ideology and understandable incredulity kept them in the dark until the tragedy had ended. But the fact that they were ignorant, whether willfully or not, was to fester and breed terrible dissension and pain in the years following the war. As Alfred Kazin wrote in bitter retrospect of his anguish at idling in New York in 1944, "[T]he world was burning with war, and I was out of it, consumed with guilt. Everything was falling apart. I had a sudden horror of myself. . . . I was as bad as any Nazi. The Jews burned every day in Europe were being consumed in a fire that I had helped to light." The *PR* circle never recovered from the darkness of the war years—a darkness that was especially deep for them because so many were Jewish and so few fought.

Robert Lowell also vociferously opposed the war, but for somewhat different reasons and in a decidedly different fashion from others in the *PR* crowd. In a sense, Lowell's position was the exact opposite of Rahv's: Lowell began by supporting the United States' involvement and then, as the war intensified, radically changed his mind. Many of Lowell's close friends, including Peter Taylor, Randall Jarrell, Blair Clark, and Frank Parker, joined the armed forces, and in the year after the United States entered the war both Lowell and Stafford assumed that it was only a matter of time before he too served in some capacity, preferably as an officer. In fact, Lowell tried repeatedly to volunteer for both the navy and the army in 1942 but was turned down because his eyesight was too poor. Then in August 1943, not long after he and Stafford had decamped from the Tates' cottage at Monteagle, Lowell was notified that he would be inducted into the armed forces the following month. His response to this summons was, he wrote later, "the most decisive thing I ever did." On the day before he was to report for service, Lowell mailed a letter to President Roosevelt that opens with the electrifying salutation: "Dear Mr. President: I very much regret that I must refuse the opportunity you offer me in your communication of August 6, for service in the Armed Forces." Lowell refers the president to the attached "Declaration of Personal Responsibility" and concludes, man to man, patrician to patrician, that "You will understand how painful such a decision is for an American whose family traditions, like your own, have always found their fulfillment in maintaining, through responsible participation in both the civil and the military services, our country's freedom and honor."

In his long, agitated, highly wrought declaration, Lowell argues that America's role in the war has shifted from a justified defensive posture to an aggressive "Machiavellian" endeavor to effect "the permanent destruction of Germany and Japan." As a Christian, he cites his anguish over the "staggering civilian casualties" that resulted from the Allied bombing of German cities. As a supporter of our democratic form of government, he warns that America's collaboration with the Soviet Union—"the most unscrupulous and powerful of totalitarian" regimes—will end in the destruction of "law, freedom, democracy, and above all, our continued national soveriegnty" [sic] as well as leaving China and Europe "to the mercy of the USSR." And as a Lowell, he asserts in closing that "after long deliberation on my responsibilities to myself, my country, and my ancestors who played responsible parts in its making, I have come to the conclusion that I cannot honorably participate in a war whose prosecution, as far as I can judge, constitutes a betrayal of my country."

It's hard to know exactly when or why he changed his mind, although Catholic piety was certainly part of his decision. The Church furnished Lowell with official sanction for two not entirely complementary aspects of his position: humanitarian outrage over German civilian casualties and anti-Communist outrage over the alliance with the Soviet Union. Yet by the terms of the protest, Lowell had also aligned himself with political positions that had nothing to do with Catholicism, including *PR*'s brand of anti-Stalinist Marxism, Edmund Wilson's upper-crust anticapitalist liberalism, and the nostalgic Agrarianism of Tate and Ransom (condemning the United States' insistence on the unconditional surrender of Germany and Japan, Lowell holds up the Civil War as a dire lesson in the long-term consequences of such a policy: "[o]ur Southern States three quarters of a century after their terrible battering down and occupation, are still far from having recovered even their material prosperity"). The same fervent mixing of political agendas finds expression in the war poems of *Land of Unlikeness*—perhaps most vividly in "Christmas Eve in the Time of War" in which Lowell rails against the "good-humored plutocrat" who keeps "the puppets dancing for the state" and rakes in profits while "Blue lines of boys and girls" march to their deaths. Capitalism and militarism in Lowell's vision are the two barrels of the gun that murders Christ in a war-torn world.

Lowell's politics were a "mingled yarn" and always would be. In the 1950s he launched a hysterical campaign against Communists at the Yaddo artists' colony—although the impetus for this may well have been his impending psychotic breakdown. In the early 1960s he was active in the CIA-funded Congress for Cultural Freedom, but by the late 1960s he was a highly visible anti–Vietnam War activist and an influential member of Senator Eugene McCarthy's campaign team. Yet even during his anti–Vietnam War phase, there was something fundamentally conservative, almost Burkean, in his political stance: He believed in the greatness of the democratic tradition and took seriously his individual responsibility for protecting that tradition.

Despite his political eccentricity and seeming contradictions, Lowell never let himself get relegated to a lunatic fringe. He assumed all along that a certain authority belonged to him by right of birth—the "family traditions" he invoked in his letter to Roosevelt—and he saw to it that people in power recognized his authority. The name alone made him a lightning rod: leaders of any faction were always delighted to have a Lowell on their platform. Indeed, Lowell swiftly became a leader of whatever cause he embraced. Considering how inept he was at managing his own practical affairs, he was surprisingly good at political maneuvering. "Cal the public figure—he knew what he was doing," says Blair Clark, who wielded considerable political influence himself as Eugene McCarthy's campaign manager. "I'm sure there were people who were terribly envious of his ability to manipulate himself as a public figure."

The letter to Roosevelt and the "Declaration of Personal Responsibility" marked Lowell's debut as a public figure—a carefully staged, highly effective debut. "He was grandstanding," remarks Clark derisively today. "Well, maybe that's too harsh, but Cal definitely had a temptation to glorify himself which I didn't like. Those organ tones of the Lowell family and military tradition. It's pompous. At the time, though, I assumed Cal had genuine feelings. I thought he was mostly wrong, but I did not feel indignant." Behind the ethical posturing of Lowell's declaration, the basic message is simply this: "I matter." And he was right. The government and the press received the message loud and clear and reacted predictably: newspapers ran splashy stories with headlines such as "Lowell Scion Refuses to Fight"; the government took Lowell into custody and, on October 13, sentenced him to a year and a day at the Federal Correctional Center at Danbury, Connecticut.

Prison, in an odd way, suited Lowell. His fellow inmates at Danbury were mostly "sentenced for a cause," he wrote later, and "all liked nothing better than talking the world to rights." They were conscientious objectors ("idealist felons," he called them), bootleggers, black-market profiteers. The "gang" to which Lowell was assigned worked on building a barn. "The work was mild: the workers were slow and absentminded," he wrote. "There were long pauses." He told an interviewer decades later, "I was thankful to find jail gentler than boarding school or college—an adult fraternity. . . . I found life lulling." Stafford, who took the train up from New York on Saturdays for hour-long visits, became alarmed at the way prison aggravated Lowell's Catholic extremism. "Prison has been dreadful for him: he has become so fanatical," she wrote Peter Taylor in February 1944. "I am frightened, feel that it will be three years before Cal has recovered from the pleasurable monasticism of penitentiary. . . . Last week, sick with loneliness (I see almost no one these days) and with worry, I re-read all of Cal's letters from Kenyon to try to find in them the seeds of this protesting idealism and the letters made me sicker because Cal is nothing like the person he was then when he wrote them."

Stafford was having a rough time of it alone in New York. There wasn't much money coming in, she felt cut off from former friends, and her husband's "protesting idealism" had left her vulnerable to attack or unwanted sympathy from all who disagreed with him. Tate wrote her in the fall to offer money, but he couldn't resist sniping at Cal, who, in his opinion, was trying to effect a "complete escape from his obligations" and "social responsibilities" and was getting away with it scot free. Even though he was in prison, "Cal will never really suffer—" Tate insisted, "unless, of course, he gets into his mother's clutches again." This was irritating; but far worse was the battering she got from the *PR* crowd. In another letter, to Peter and Eleanor Taylor, Stafford recounts the "revolting experience" of attending a cocktail party at the Rahvs' apartment right after returning to the city from a prison visit. Before she arrived, Rahv had gossiped to everyone about Lowell's situation, and as soon as she walked in people started hounding her with nosy questions. Sidney

Hook, a Marxist scholar who would eventually become a staunch anti-Communist, insisted that Lowell was a heretic for "going against the dictates of the Pope" in his antiwar stance, and Hook's wife, "a thoroughly savage and unpleasant woman," began to bait Stafford on the subject of the Spanish Civil War. When Stafford, cornered, remarked that "I am very sure that there is something to be said for Franco," Mrs. Hook erupted in screams—at which point Stafford began to cry uncontrollably. In narrating the events of this horrible evening, Stafford characteristically made no attempt to sort out the political views of her antagonists: what had wounded her was not their ideology so much as their human cruelty. But she did get off a broadside against Jews: "the greatest snobs in the world are bright New York literary Jews," she told the Taylors, "and the name Lowell works like love-philtre."

This is less anti-Semitism, I think, than a sign of how desperately alienated Stafford was feeling. She had her back to the wall defending a political stance that was not her own and that she didn't endorse. Her mother-in-law in Boston was lecturing her about how she must not spend all the money from "Bobby's" trust fund but must use his prison term as "an opportunity for courage, self development, and integrity of purpose." And her husband was telling her that after prison he planned on joining the Catholic Evidence Guilds so he could preach to faithless hecklers in city parks. It's understandable that Stafford should find New York's literary scene hard to take just then.

The heavy drinking of the Rahv crowd was another problem. Stafford could not resist the temptation to get drunk with them, especially since Lowell wasn't there to stop her, but she hated herself for giving in. "The *PR* crowd was too depressing, too drunken, too disastrous for Jean," Cecile Starr remarks. "They were argumentative and philosophical and ran in a pack—but Jean was more of an artist than a thinker. She needed to steer clear of them."

Stafford sensed, correctly, that the *PR* crowd, in fact literary New York in general, would destroy her unless she got away. As Lowell's prison term came to an end, she became obsessed with having a place to escape to—not a room but a *house* of her own. Once *Boston Adventure* started selling, she finally had the means to make this dream a reality.

A catastrophe in Europe, World War II was in many ways a social and economic boon to the United States, especially for women. The war fi-

• • •

nally ended the Great Depression, and the combination of stepped-up production and a manpower shortage created a huge demand for female workers. In the course of World War II, more than 6 million American women entered the workforce, many of them taking over jobs left vacant by men who were fighting overseas. Though there was initial resistance to the idea of a female workforce and skepticism about whether women *could* do men's work, eventually women proved that such concerns were groundless. Production soared at plants employing a high percentage of women, and management was soon clamoring for more female workers.

Employers were not the only ones pleased with the results: women themselves came to value the independence and status of employment out of the home, and many were reluctant to resume their "normal" lives once the war ended. "Work had proved liberating," as social historian William Chafe wrote, "and once a new consciousness had been formed, there was no going back." The social revolution attributed to the women's liberation movement of the late 1960s and 1970s really began with the mass entry of women into the workforce during World War II. Few women or men realized it at the time, but this was the opening of the great divide.

Curiously, women writers and intellectuals were barely touched by the tremors of wartime social change. Rosie the Riveter did not beckon to the likes of Mary McCarthy, Caroline Gordon, Jean Stafford, or Elizabeth Hardwick. They had been working all along anyway, and the war made no difference in their opportunities or conditions. Editorial control of the major literary journals did not shift as a result of the war, nor did the war create a shortage of male literary talent. If anything, the war gave male writers a dramatic new subject that was not available to women. Norman Mailer, James Jones, and later Joseph Heller launched their literary careers by writing about the war, and even Randall Jarrell, though he saw no action, made memorable use of his stateside experience in the army air corps: "In bombers named for girls, we burned / The cities we had learned about in school," he wrote in "Losses," one of his many lyrics about bombing missions. With the exception of a few female war correspondents (Martha Gellhorn, then married to Ernest Hemingway, was the most famous), American women writers remained remote from the action. Caroline Gordon lived in Washington, D.C., for two years during the war (1943 to 1944) while Allen Tate served as poetry consultant at the Library of Congress, but even in the nation's capital she seems largely to have ignored the war. Mary McCarthy, shuttling between her husband in Wellfleet and her psychiatrist and lovers in Manhattan, wrote that "For most of us, the war has been a rather ghastly kind of entertainment," and she pretty much left it at that. Jean Stafford was more deeply affected by the war, for her only brother died in combat and her husband left her poor and lonely during his prison term; but she never felt moved to take a strong position in print or join in any organized protest. Once Lowell was released, she too put the war out of her mind. Elizabeth Hardwick, having left the graduate program at Columbia, was working on a novel, living in a seedy Times Square hotel apartment with a gay male roommate, and spending her evenings at Fifty-second Street jazz clubs. For Hardwick the war years were the era of Billie Holiday, whom she met through her roommate. ("[N]ever was any woman less a wife or mother," Hardwick wrote of the singer in a reminiscence. "Here was a woman who had never been a Christian.")

Not all working women became feminists as a result of their wartime employment, but their lives were changed in a way that made them understand what feminists were talking about. Mary McCarthy, Elizabeth Hardwick, and Caroline Gordon, who went about their lives as usual during the war, never saw the need for or, with the halting exception of Hardwick, the point of feminism. In a way the period of World War II was when the sympathies and alliances of these women hardened into prejudices. After the war, the group as a whole, both men and women, became more politically conservative; but for the women, social conservatism—at least in matters of gender—was already firmly in place.

Things were altogether different for Hannah Arendt. For her, the war was everything: the pivotal event of her intellectual and emotional life; the disaster that stripped her of home, language, political identity; the tragic *fact* that she would try to understand and explain all her life. In the postwar years, after the publication of her masterpiece *The Origins of Totalitarianism,* Arendt became one of the leading lights of the New York intellectuals, an influential political thinker and a highly respected writer. She was an "electrifying presence," as one of the crowd put it, who inspired others as much by her work as by her example: her energy, dedication, intellectual passion. Arendt's close friendship with Mary McCarthy sustained and invigorated both women and became a kind of axis of love and intellectual power that other members of the group recognized and respected (it is one of the only relationships that surviving members of the circle speak of with anything approaching reverence). McCarthy was Arendt's best friend in America, but Lowell, Hardwick, Randall Jarrell, Dwight Macdonald, and Alfred Kazin all knew her well, admired her and her work. Arendt wrote for *PR* and later for *The New York Review of Books;* she and her brilliantly argumentative husband, Heinrich Blücher, became fixtures on the Upper West Side social and intellectual scene. She engaged eagerly in debate and stirred up enormous controversy. In short, she lived the life of the quintessential New York intellectual—but always with the critical, immutable difference that she was a refugee, a German Jew who had been lucky to escape Europe with her life. It was something she never forgot, and she never let the others forget it either. In a sense, Arendt made the war exist for all of them. She made the others *see* the war—its dictators of unprecedented power, its bureaucrat mass murderers, its countless victims—with a political and moral complexity that none of them had dreamed of before. And for this she paid a terrible price.

Arendt was born in Hannover in 1906 to a well-to-do and assimilated Jewish family from east Prussia. Her early childhood was shadowed by the death of her father: he had contracted syphilis and died in its final stages—a death of excruciating pain and mounting dementia—when his only child was seven years old. Martha Arendt raised her daughter with sorrowing devotion, worrying over her emotional withdrawal in the years after her father's death and encouraging her passion for learning. From her mother, she absorbed a tacit understanding of the strange, precarious place of Jews in German society. "The word 'Jew' was never mentioned at home," Arendt later recalled. "My mother was not very theoretical . . . the 'Jewish Question' had no relevance for her." Yet this same mother who avoided any discussion of Jewish identity also taught her daughter how to act when a teacher made an anti-Semitic remark: Hannah was to stand up and silently leave the classroom. The essential contradiction of this attitude toward Judaism—cautious avoidance and fierce pride—stayed with Arendt all her life. "Hannah's family was not religious," a friend remarks. "It was anti-Semitism in Germany that made her aware of her Jewish identity." Yet her identity was always as much German as Jewish, if not more so—German not so much in nationality as in language, literature, philosophy. Throughout her life, long after emigrating to the United States and becoming a U.S. citizen, Arendt considered the German language her true homeland; for her, one of the most painful aspects of exile was being forced to transform herself from a German writer into an American writing in English.

Despite mounting prejudice against Jews in Germany, Arendt received a superb education in classical literature, German literature and philosophy, world history, and politics. "Arendt's education was of an order of magnitude unknown in the United States," says her biographer Elisabeth Young-Bruehl. As a young woman she studied philosophy with Martin Heidegger at Marburg and with Karl Jaspers at Heidelberg, and both men remained crucial intellectual and emotional influences throughout her life—especially Heidegger, with whom she had a brief love affair at Marburg, breaking with him only when she left Germany in 1933, the same year Heidegger publicly embraced National Socialism. Many believe that Heidegger was the great love of Arendt's life— she was eighteen during the time of their sexual relationship—and she has come under vicious attack in recent years for failing to denounce him or cease to love him when he allied himself with the Nazis. Indeed there is speculation that they resumed their love affair after the war. But Arendt was always adamant in her refusal to let politics determine how she loved. The critic Derwent May believes Arendt was referring to her feelings for Heidegger when she wrote, in *The Human Condition,* "Love, by its very nature, is unworldly, and it is for this reason that it is not only apolitical but anti-political, perhaps the most powerful of all anti-political human forces." The thinker and the woman coexisted easily and happily in her: those who knew her best always spoke of her arresting combination of warm, lively, even flirtatious femininity and rigorous intellectual ardor. "What she has canonized all her life—philosophy as a daily activity," writes Alfred Kazin in *A Lifetime Burning in Every Moment.* "Her astonishing expressiveness as an expounder, authority, teacher in her new country is inseparable from her charm as a woman."

Arendt fled to France in 1933 as Hitler let loose the first waves of terror against German Jews, artists, and intellectuals. She had been married as a student to a German Jewish writer named Günther Stern, but the marriage had pretty much broken up before she left Germany. In Paris, Arendt and Stern lived together as friends and comrades with the understanding that both would be free to pursue their own lives. So Arendt was largely on her own, a twenty-seven-year-old political refugee, strikingly beautiful to judge by photos of the period, independent-minded, brilliant, and determined to make some kind of mark on the world. The traumatic, turbulent years in France, which Arendt always spoke of as the most difficult of her life, proved to be critical to her development. The most immediate trauma was the loss of Germany—the country, the language she loved, the culture she had been steeped in, the political state she had belonged to, however precariously. "The loss of a polity itself . . . expels a man from humanity," she later wrote. For Arendt, there was no greater tragedy than such an expulsion. Finding herself stateless was a shock that she never recovered from. Yet characteristically, she reacted not with lethargy or depression, but with a burst of activity. Activity was always her solace: she was by all accounts a person of tremendous energy and vitality, nervous, hard-driving, and intense. She worked "on a high cylinder," as one American friend puts it, "and she had real trouble containing that energy."

In Paris, Arendt completed her extraordinary biography of Rahel Varnhagen, a late-eighteenth-century Jewish woman who had held a fashionable salon in Berlin and struggled to transcend the "the misery and misfortune" of "having been born a Jewess." She was also involved with the growing German refugee community, and she threw herself into "active" social work with the Youth Aliyah organization, assisting young European Jews to emigrate to Palestine (she made a single memorable trip to Palestine on behalf of Youth Aliyah in 1935). The social work for Youth Aliyah, though it was rooted in her beliefs about Zionism and the future of European Jewry, was really a reaction *against* intellectual positions, and especially against the endless empty theorizing and posturing about the "Jewish question" that went on in the refugee community.

Though we think of Hannah Arendt as the epitome of the intellectual, in fact she harbored a deep distrust and dislike of intellectual society as a result of her overexposure to intellectuals during the Paris years. "The life of the mind was not so wonderful for Hannah," remarks her friend Jerome Kohn. "She thought intellectuals tended to be pretentious and terribly ignorant about what was going on and often incapable of thinking and judging. The social work she did in Paris, the work of relocating young people to Palestine, grew in part out of her disgust with intellectuals. In France she came to feel that she never wanted to see another intellectual as long as she lived."

Heinrich Blücher, the German gentile refugee with whom she fell in love in Paris in the spring of 1936, was emphatically *not* a jabbering, paralyzed intellectual—though he was certainly loud and fiercely engaged with ideas. Thirty-seven when they met at a public lecture (she was twenty-nine), the son of a laundress, a former Communist, twice married (in fact, still secretly married to his second wife), explosive in argument, self-taught, a compact but commanding physical presence, Blücher had come of age in the chaos of the German defeat in World War I and the upheavals of the Weimar Republic. Blücher lived life to the full in the heady bohemia of postwar Berlin. He participated in Communist demonstrations and street fighting in 1918 and 1919; he joined a Zionist youth organization, even though he was Protestant by birth; he befriended Expressionist artists, filmmakers, and circus entertainers and mingled freely with them in cafés and clubs; he carried on numerous love affairs; and, whenever he had the money and time, he bought and devoured books. Blücher was every inch the self-made man, the man of the people, the outsider who thumbed his nose at received opinions as he beat a path to a higher, sturdier, strikingly original truth of his own manufacture. Alfred Kazin writes revealingly in his diary of his first impression of Blücher in New York:

> [A]lways wound up, a bit rough in manner but intellectually "pure," a prodigious autodidact and walking philosopher, always trying to make up for his lack of university degree. . . . Bluecher [*sic*] is an unstoppable *mental* creature, orates without stopping in his living room on any "great thinker" who has aroused his attention—from Heraclitus to Joachim of Floris . . . shouting philosophy at you in the sweetest kind of way. . . . Heinrich is given to fantasy and exaggeration, noble lies about his military knowledge. I am told that German Communists thought of Heinrich as their military "expert." But he is the kind of obsessively reflective, altogether human German I no longer expected to meet. My God, the Berlin he encountered in 1919 after the army! In the midst of revolution and counterrevolution, angry mobs all over the place, you could hear Wagner or Bach just by inserting a coin in a box standing on a street corner.

Kazin added more recently: "Blücher was a fantastic talker with a hypnotic style, although you were not always sure what he said." The German novelist Hermann Broch also remarked on Blücher's unstoppable flow of oratory brilliance. "After Hannah had gone to bed Heinrich gave me a lecture until three in the morning," Broch wrote his wife during a visit to Arendt and Blücher. "I did not interrupt his lecture at all. He doesn't let himself be interrupted. It was probably the most enjoyable evening that I have had for months. The thinking of this man is of an uncorruptible clarity such as one finds only in geniuses. He really is a genius in this uncorruptibility."

Arendt fell into intense, consuming conversation with Blücher in the cafes and cramped apartments of refugee Paris and then fell in love with him. "[F]or both of them intellectual argument was part and parcel of passion," writes Young-Bruehl. In a sense their relationship was a never-ending conversation—an intellectual duet that sustained the two of them in a state of perpetual excitement and discovery. "They had a self-absorbed relationship," recalls Kazin. "They were always talking, talking, talking." Theirs was a heated, impassioned conversation, but also "a passion," as Arendt's friend Anne Weil put it. "It was a great love affair," says Jerome Kohn—and evidently an intensely erotic love affair when it began, even though Arendt was not an especially physical person. A year after they met, Arendt wrote Blücher that because of him, "I . . . finally know what happiness is. . . . It still seems to me unbelievable, that I could achieve both—a great love, and a sense of identity with my own person. And yet I achieved the one only since I have the other."

Part of Blücher's appeal for Arendt was that he was *not* a conventional intellectual: the roughness, the bluster, the vehement rawness of his arguments aroused her in every sense. The fact that Blücher had some experience in the world, that he had tested and honed his political beliefs in the trenches of World War I and the streets of Berlin, gave him a charismatic authority that no one else in her circle possessed. Arendt, who had studied with Heidegger and Jaspers, who had secured a doctorate from the university at Heidelberg for her dissertation on the concept of love in Saint Augustine, absorbed everything she could from this self-taught dynamo, whom she began calling "Monsieur." He was, as a friend put it, not only her husband and friend but "the last of her teachers." They became intellectual partners—not equals, for Blücher lacked her discipline, refinement, and rigorous classical training, and though he spoke brilliantly he could not write. Yet in their own unevenly matched way they were collaborators. Arendt once wrote that "in marriage, it is not always easy to tell the partners' thoughts apart," and that's how it was with her and Blücher. When she published her first major book, *The Origins of Totalitarianism,* in 1951, she dedicated it to Blücher and warmly acknowledged the critical role he had played in her writing.

Their friend Kurt Blumenfeld notes that the book reflects "the unwritten political philosophy of the person to whom it is dedicated," a view Arendt totally endorsed.

In this regard, their marriage stands in marked contrast to the other literary marriages under consideration here, perhaps to any with the possible exception of George Eliot and George Henry Lewes. It didn't seem to matter to Arendt that her husband failed to match her success and prominence: she remained staunchly loyal to him and deferred to his judgments on politics and philosophy. "For [Hannah], Heinrich was like a pair of corrective lenses," wrote McCarthy in a memorial piece; "she did not wholly trust her vision until it had been confirmed by his." Arendt's success was not an "issue" for Blücher either. He was not only tolerant of the recognition she received from the world, "but really proud of her," in the words of their friend and fellow German refugee Lotte Kohler, "which was not easily achieved by men of his generation." Not a perfect union by any means, but an enduring and refreshingly healthy one. As the Israeli writer Amos Elon puts it, they had "a love and a marriage that were the 'safe haven' for two hunted fugitives in Dark Times."

Arendt, fondly mythologizing the beginning of their relationship, claimed that their courtship lasted but a single night. In fact, they were rather cautious at first and for several months kept their ardor secret even from good friends. History closely shadowed whatever happiness they enjoyed together. In November 1938, the last hope for Germany's Jews expired when Hitler issued the decree for the coordinated mass violence that became known as Kristallnacht, the Night of Broken Glass. As Arendt later wrote, up until that moment German Jews had been living in "a fool's paradise.... It took the organized pogroms of November, 1938 . . . when seventy-five hundred Jewish shop windows were broken, all synagogues went up in flames, and twenty thousand Jewish men were taken off to concentration camps, to expel them from it." After Kristallnacht, Arendt's mother, Martha Beerwald (she had remarried), was extremely fortunate to be able to arrange an escape from Germany, and in April 1939 she joined her daughter and Blücher in the Paris apartment they shared. Blücher and Martha Beerwald took an immediate dislike to each other: the mother thought this argumentative gentile was crude and lazy; the former street fighter found Frau Beerwald oppressively bourgeois, petty-minded, and sentimental. Arendt was caught in the middle and remained in the middle until her mother's death a decade later.

When war was declared in Europe in September 1939, the French government moved quickly to intern German nationals. Blücher spent almost two months in a labor camp at Villemalard, near Orléans. When he was released, he and Arendt decided to marry. Both had already filed for divorce from their former spouses. The wedding took place on January 16, 1940; a scant four months later, the French government issued another set of internment orders, and Arendt and Blücher ended up in separate camps. Both managed to get out of the internment camps fairly quickly during the chaos that followed the fall of France to the German Army; but in the tumult of events they lost contact with each other. By miraculous good luck they met up by chance in the town of Montauban in the south of France. As Germans began rounding up Jews in occupied France and the weak Vichy government ordered Jews to register with the police as a first step toward deportation, Blücher and Arendt realized that their only hope was to escape. Again luck was on their side (along with helpful connections in America, including Arendt's former husband, Günther Stern). After nerve-racking months of intrigue, hiding from police, frantically negotiating and conniving for the necessary papers, they finally set sail from Lisbon in the spring of 1941 on a ship bound for New York.

Among the few belongings Arendt took with her to New York was a manuscript that the critic and essayist Walter Benjamin had entrusted to her care several months earlier in Marseilles. In many ways, Benjamin's life had run along a track parallel to hers: both were brilliant German Jews who took refuge in Paris when the Nazis seized power; both were steeped in Germany's literary and philosophical tradition; both wrote highly original, influential essays that synthesized a range of disciplines, although Benjamin's work veered more toward literary criticism (Kafka and Baudelaire were his heroes) while Arendt focused on the crosscurrents of history, philosophy and politics. They had known each other slightly in Germany but their friendship deepened during the years of exile in France. Like Arendt and Blücher, Benjamin tried desperately to emigrate to America after the Germans overran France, and he did manage to slip across the border into Spain. But at the last minute, Benjamin got caught in the web of state bureaucracy. The Spanish police informed Benjamin and the friends he was traveling with that their transit visas were void and therefore they had to return to France. Rather than face certain internment in France followed by deportation to a German concentration camp, Benjamin killed himself. He was forty-eight years old.

Benjamin's death haunted Arendt and Blücher as they made their way to freedom and safety in the United States. A single slipup, a missed connection, a twist of the bureaucratic noose, and they would have suffered the same fate. They never forgot how lucky they were. Arendt devoted much of her career in America to fathoming the monstrous convergence of history and ideology that took Benjamin's life, along with so many millions of others in the dark years that followed.

Arendt and Blücher arrived in New York in May 1941 with little money, few contacts, and scant knowledge of English. As in Paris, Arendt rose energetically to the task of mastering and surviving in an alien culture. She immersed herself in English; she made contact with intellectuals and writers in the Jewish refugee community; and within months she landed a job writing a column for the German-language newspaper *Aufbau,* which she used as a platform to argue for the formation of a Jewish army to combat Hitler. A Jewish army in Europe and a Jewish state in Palestine were the two issues that consumed her during the first bleak years in New York: it was as if she had assigned herself the task of rallying fellow Jews to rise to their own defense at the precise moment when history had rendered them most tragically defenseless. Arendt, never a party-line Zionist, frequently and bitterly criticized the Jewish leaders of Palestine and later Israel; and her views about the Jews' role in what became known as the Holocaust would engender terrific public controversy and terrible private suffering for her. But it was clear from her first days in New York that she, who had never heard the word "Jew" spoken in her German-speaking childhood home, had dedicated her intellect to analyzing and explaining the plight and the future of her people. As Kazin writes in *New York Jew,* "[T]his specialist in St. Augustine . . . had turned her life into a voracious political inquiry. How did *it* happen? How had it all happened? How had this modern age happened? . . . Nothing could deflect her very long from her inflexible concentration on the subject. Her uprooting and her need to understand from the modern age the origins of totalitarianism had become the same experience. She lived her thought, and thought dominated her life."

Arendt and Blücher were poor during the 1940s, and their living situation was grim. Eventually they took two rooms in a rooming house on West Ninety-fifth Street on the Upper West Side—one for Arendt's mother, one for the two of them. They cooked their meals in a communal kitchen. Arendt, who was working all the time, didn't seem to care very much about their domestic conditions, but Blücher foundered in the New World. Unlike his wife, he was slow and reluctant to learn English. His first job in America was shoveling chemicals in a factory in New Jersey, labor that left him so exhausted each night he could barely eat, let alone read. He did in time find more agreeable work—researching Nazi atrocities, teaching German history to German POWs, broadcasting in German for NBC Radio—but these were all temporary, stopgap jobs, not avenues to an American career. Blücher, who had led such a vibrant, dangerous, *active* life in Berlin in the 1920s, found himself marginalized in New York in the 1940s. For years he subsisted on scant, ill-paid work, no political connections, and the daily domestic reproach of his mother-in-law. Martha Arendt had never like Blücher; in New York she came to despise him as a loud-mouthed lout who sat around reading, talking, arguing while she and her daughter worked for a living. As Lotte Kohler, Arendt's literary executor and a good friend of both Arendt and Blücher, remarks, "Martha Arendt expected Heinrich to find work, any work, but this was not for him. During those early years in New York all he did was read and read and read." Young-Bruehl writes that once Blücher lost Germany, he lost his direction, his purpose, and his standing in the world: "After he left Berlin, his 'total' inability to write and the frustration of his talents as a public speaker with no party or public forum made him a revolutionary *manqué*. His failure as a political figure was a product more of circumstances than lack of stature: he was a man of action who had no field for action. He may not have thought of himself as a 'dead man on furlough,' but he certainly was, in Paris and during his early years in New York, a man on an unwanted leave of absence." It was extraordinary that Arendt rarely blamed him, turned on him, or felt burdened by his despair. Quite the contrary. Arendt always insisted that she benefited enormously from her husband's period of withdrawal and endless reading—for it was during these years that the two of them talked out the ideas that became her masterpiece *The Origins of Totalitarianism*.

In his memoir *The Truants, Partisan Review* editor William Barrett wrote of his mystification over how Philip Rahv "found" Hannah Arendt "among the crowd of refugees then in New York." But in fact Arendt's meeting with Rahv and her entry into New York intellectual circles was not so much the chance discovery of a hidden talent as the coming together of potentates from curious, mutually suspicious neighboring tribes. Initially, Rahv, Phillips, and Schwartz did not know how to "place" this Prussian female prodigy. She was a "redoubtable woman" in Barrett's phrase—somewhat gruff in manner, combative, a touch arrogant, deeply and widely read, marvelously educated—yet also very much a woman. Expecting some sort of brainy Jewish Valkyrie, the *PR* crowd was surprised to find that she was strongly sexual. Tender, feminine, sexy, romantic, flirtatious, womanly, seductive, vain are the words that come up again and again in gossip and memoirs. Arendt, though not as brash as Mary McCarthy or as yielding as Elizabeth Hardwick, was very much a sexual being. She was "much more womanly . . . and attractive than I had expected," wrote Barrett of his first impression; "she came at things with energy and eagerness. . . . Behind the facade of the stern and intellectual woman there lurked the ghost of a beautiful young girl who had done all the *risqué* things of the 1920s—dared to smoke cigarettes in public, have affairs, charm and tantalize men—and managed to be a very brilliant student at the university. In a way, perhaps, some of that adventurous vitality never left her. . . . I couldn't help thinking throughout that she was a very handsome woman indeed." When Barrett reported this assessment to his colleagues on the magazine, William Phillips thought it over for a while and added a qualification: "I think of Hannah rather as a very handsome man." Phillips was more flattering when he wrote of Arendt in his own memoirs: "I . . . remember being impressed by the unusual combination of gentleness and force which, perhaps, was her most distinguishing trait to the end of her life. It was a very strange and seductive combination: firmness of tone and strength of conviction with a soft, almost caressing manner." Phillips was equally impressed by how formidable Arendt could be on the intellectual battlefield: "[T]here was never any doubt where she stood; and anyone who took her on in debate knew he had taken on a heavyweight and usually found out that he was overmatched. She would begin in a low-keyed, pedagogic tone, and in a gravelly voice, 'Now listen here,' and then go on to demolish her opponent in a mesmerizing combination of persuasion, wit, intellectual authority, and a logic that I can characterize only as a kind of insistent rhetoric. Hannah Arendt had the quality one thinks of as originality, the ability, that is, to put ideas in a fresh form."

Kazin, perhaps her greatest male partisan in the early days, fairly panted into his diary when he first got to know her: "What luck. Hannah Arendt placed next to me at the dinner for Rabbi Leo Baeck, and I have sought her out several times since. Darkly handsome, bountifully interested in everything, this forty-year-old German refugee with a strong accent and such intelligence—thinking positively cascades out of her in waves—but I was enthralled, by no means unerotically. . . . I love this woman intensely—she is such a surprise, such a gift." In *New York Jew,* published shortly after Arendt's death, Kazin fleshed out the portrait with a few more glowing details: "[Hannah] was as arch, witty, womanly as she was acute and powerfully cultivated. When stirred by a new friend, her angular Jewish features and amazingly gruff voice melted into wistful lovingness. . . . The strong, sometimes too commanding mind went with a fiercely imploring heart."

Not everyone was as charmed. "All this mental idealism, fervent with the need to teach and teach, the constant injunction 'to think what we are doing,' produced in Americans either adulators or the bitterest enemies," Kazin wrote. "Saul Bellow found it outrageous to be lectured on Faulkner—*another* novelist!—by someone from *Konigsberg.*" Delmore Schwartz ridiculed her as "that Weimar Republic flapper," and others on *PR* started calling her Hannah Arrogance. Rahv, for once, was at a loss about what line to take. According to Barrett, Rahv was "thrown off stride by encountering an aggressively intellectual woman who talked back to him." Though he published some of her first work written in English in *PR,* starting in 1944 with a piece on Kafka, he remained wary of Arendt's relentless high-mindedness. Some believed that Rahv, always skilled in covert plots and competitive infighting, was biding his time for an opportunity to turn on her. Others said that he feared her because she knew more than he did—that lustrous German education of hers intimidated the autodidact in him. Rahv enjoyed the company of beautiful, smart women and was not shy about pursuing them sexually, but Arendt seems to have left him cold. She was certainly never admitted into the inner circle in the way that Mary McCarthy and later Elizabeth Hardwick were.

Despite Rahv's reservations, Arendt quickly established herself as a force to be contended with in New York: an intellectual emissary from the Old World, a bearer of the torch of the great tradition of classical literature and Romantic philosophy, a well-stocked mind of unusual strength and penetration. According to William Barrett, she had the aura of "speaking for something older and deeper that she understood as European culture." She possessed a command of allusion and a clarity of insight that many literary people, especially poets, found irresistible. Randall Jarrell became her first and closest American poet friend. They met in 1946, when Arendt was working as an editor at Schocken Books and Jarrell was filling in as the book editor of *The Nation*. On the face of it, the eccentric, dapper, tennis-playing, racing-car-obsessed Southern poet and critic had little in common with the German philosopher émigré— but, as they soon discovered, they were very much on the same wavelength. Both of them lived for ideas, for knowledge, for language—and neither had much patience for distracting small talk, a trait they shared with Robert Lowell and Edmund Wilson. Jarrell introduced her to his personal pantheon of English and American poets—Auden, Dickinson, Yeats, and of course his own verse—and made her acquainted, at least by name, with poet friends such as Lowell and Elizabeth Bishop. Arendt got him reading Goethe, Heine, Hölderlin, and Rilke and helped him refine his translations of German poetry. When she wrote reviews for *The Nation,* Jarrell "Englished" them. (Arendt had "Englishing" assistance from several other writers and editors during the forties. Though she mastered the language with extraordinary swiftness, she had trouble with idioms and sentence structure. Her writing style in English was dense, plain, and authoritative, but never elegant.)

Jarrell had a kind of worldly, brainy innocence that appealed to Arendt: it was a quality that she identified as uniquely American and that she came to prize in all her American friends. "Innocence in combination with wide experience," Arendt's biographer Young-Bruehl describes this trait; "innocence preserved." Jarrell's boisterous, contentious enthusiasm for poetry—"the shouting intensity of a football fan" in Kazin's words— was something new and altogether delightful to Arendt. In Europe she had seen such vehemence put to the service of politics—but never in the golden realm of poetry. In a memorial piece, Arendt recalled how Jarrell loved to engage Blücher "in some long, fierce debate about the merits and the rank of writers and poets," their voices ringing "lustily as they tried to outdo and especially outshout each other. . . . As Randall wrote after one such shouting match 'it's always awing (for an enthusiast) to see someone more enthusiastic than yourself—like the second fattest man in the world meeting the fattest.' " "Whatever I know of English poetry," Arendt remarked more seriously, "and perhaps of the genius of the language, I owe to him."

After a few years of lunches in New York and occasional loud weekends together, Jarrell felt close enough, and comfortable enough, with

Arendt and Blücher to use them as models for the characters Irene and Gottfried Rosenbaum in his satiric novel *Pictures from an Institution*. He even admitted as much in a letter to Arendt: "Although the Rosenbaums aren't too like you and Heinrich as individuals, I hardly could, hardly would, have made them up without knowing you. . . . [T]he Rosenbaums' relation to this country is very much understood in terms of you and your husband—and the sentence about Gottfried and Irene 'quarreling' fiercely about Goethe and Hölderlin, etc., applies even better to you two than to the Rosenbaums." (The character Gertrude in the same novel—an icy-cold, neurotic novelist who feeds shamelessly on her friends for material—bears a striking resemblance to Mary McCarthy, though some insist she was actually supposed to be Jean Stafford.) Jarrell's Rosenbaums embody the essence of European strangeness: their home decor, the cookies and coffee they serve, their conversations, their marriage are all intensely, ravishingly exotic. Perhaps the marriage most of all, which Jarrell nailed (through his fictional narrator) in this memorable passage: "When I first knew them I noticed that he did little things to placate or mollify her, or to keep her from being troubled or aroused, and I decided she was the dominant member of their household, but after a while I noticed that she behaved in exactly the same way about him: they were a Dual Monarchy."

Kazin elaborates on this same marvelous marital sharing of power in *New York Jew*:

> They were vehemently involved in working out a common philosophy; any conversation with the two of them could suddenly turn into German and open connubial excitement in some philosophic discovery unsuspected until that moment. Between clenched lips holding a pipe, Heinrich growled his thought out as if he were still on the battlefield—against wrong-headed philosophers. Hannah, despite her genteel training, also talked philosophy as if she were standing up alone in a foreign land and in a foreign tongue against powerful forces of error. She confronted you with the truth; she confronted you with her friendship; she confronted Heinrich even when she joined him in the most passionate seminar I would ever witness between a man and a woman living together.

Kazin spoke more bluntly about the marriage in a recent conversation: "Of course Heinrich was not her intellectual equal—she was a bit of a

snob and there were not many she considered her equal. But Heinrich
was her partner. There was no tension between them over their intellectual standing or accomplishments. They did not compete with each
other. It was not like a typical American marriage." Which may explain
why the Blüchers' marriage endured while the marriages of their American literary friends did not. (It's worth noting that other members of the
circle did not share Kazin's warm feelings for Blücher or his admiration
for the role he played in the marriage. William Phillips compared
Blücher to the neglected wives of the *PR* editors: he was "the husband"
and not much else. Diana Trilling said Arendt kept Blücher "chained to
her bedpost" so he would always be there when she needed him. "Hannah pretended Blücher was her intellectual equal, but he wasn't," insisted Lionel Abel. "He was a nobody.")

Jarrell's friendship with Arendt ended prematurely on account of some
tension in his own marriage. His second wife, Mary von Schrader, resented the way Arendt monopolized her husband when they were together socially. She was not the only wife to feel this way: evidently
Arendt assumed that she, as the ranking intellectual, had a right to the attentions of all prominent husbands she came in contact with. Diana
Trilling also complained bitterly of the "purposeful rudeness" Arendt directed at her while playing up to her husband: "Year after year Hannah
made believe that I did not exist even when we were a few feet apart,
staring into each other's faces—but Hannah was attracted to Lionel . . .
and was therefore . . . resentful of me." Mary Jarrell informed her husband that she had had enough of Arendt's possessiveness, and Randall
instantly terminated the friendship. Arendt was hurt but not offended.
She always spoke of him fondly as one of her dearest men friends and
wrote of him after his death, "Randall Jarrell would have been a poet if
he had never written a single poem."

Mary McCarthy and Hannah Arendt met in 1944 in a hotel bar, of all
places. Clement Greenberg, McCarthy's partner in a glum adulterous affair, introduced them. A year passed before they saw each other again—
at one of Rahv's cocktail parties—and this time they quarreled. It was the
spring of 1945, the Allies were advancing rapidly on the collapsing Nazi
Germany, and McCarthy, recently liberated from Wilson, had the nerve
to wisecrack that she felt sorry for Hitler for craving the love of the van-
quished Parisians. The outraged Arendt left the party at once, muttering

The young Mary McCarthy. "Mary's smile is very famous," remarked her good friend Dwight Macdonald. "When most pretty girls smile at you, you feel terrific. When Mary smiles at you, you look to see if your fly is open."

"My dear, I've got the most Levantine lover!" Mary McCarthy wrote a Vassar friend when she and Philip Rahv began their affair in 1937. Though the affair ended when she left Rahv to marry Edmund Wilson, McCarthy insisted that she never ceased to love Rahv—and that she always preferred him to Wilson.

Mary McCarthy and Edmund Wilson in Wellfleet on Cape Cod, their home from 1941 until the end of their marriage. McCarthy was spending much of her time in New York during these years, seeing her psychiatrist and carrying on a halfhearted affair with *PR* art critic Clement Greenberg.

Caroline Gordon and Allen Tate. Four years older than her husband, Gordon was as vehement in her faithfulness as Tate was in his philandering. They divorced in January 1946, only to remarry three months later.

"A rabid Southerner of the old school," as one friend described him, Allen Tate became more irascible, waspish, and rabidly reactionary as he aged.

The young Jean Stafford before the terrible car accident that left her face scarred for life. "She was always trouble. Wherever she was, things happened," remarked James Robert Hightower, who loved her and hoped to marry her before she met Lowell.

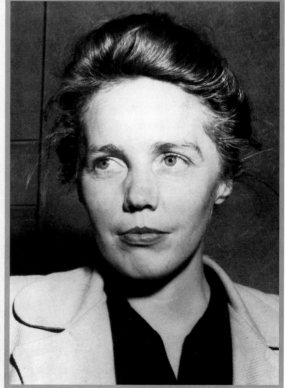

Robert Lowell around the time his marriage to Stafford broke up. Stafford once described Lowell as "an uncouth, neurotic, psychopathic murderer-poet," but she was shattered when he left her.

Lowell, Stafford, and their editor and friend Robert Giroux in front of the house in Damariscotta Mills, Maine, that Stafford loved so dearly. This photo was taken early in the summer of 1946—the summer of the "influx of poets." By autumn, the marriage was over and Stafford was in a mental hospital.

Diana Trilling in 1950. Though she published in the same journals as Mary McCarthy, Elizabeth Hardwick, and Hannah Arendt, and went to the same parties, Trilling was never accepted by them as an equal—and she knew it. McCarthy, who tangled with her several times in print, praised her beauty in her posthumous *Intellectual Memoirs*.

The young Hannah Arendt. A formidable intellect, Arendt was also beautiful, flirtatious, and intensely feminine.

Hannah Arendt and her husband Heinrich Blücher in New York. They met as refugees in Paris in 1936 and emigrated together to America in 1941, just escaping the Nazis. Alfred Kazin, who knew them well, described their relationship as "the most passionate seminar I would ever witness between a man and a woman."

Mary McCarthy in maturity. "I've always liked being a woman," McCarthy once told an interviewer, explaining why she opposed "women's lib." "I like the domestic arts, cooking and gardening. I like clothes very, very much."

Lowell and Hardwick at Harvard graduation during the 1960s.

McCarthy and some of her best friends in the 1960s. Back row left to right: Heinrich Blücher, Hannah Arendt, Dwight and Gloria Macdonald. Seated left to right: Nicola Chiaromonte, McCarthy, Robert Lowell.

Courtesy Harry Ransom Humanities Research Center, the University of Texas at Austin; print by Pratt's Photo Service

Lowell at his desk in Castine, Maine, during the summer of 1967. Lowell, stabilized on lithium, was entering the highly productive period of his "fourteen-liners." This was also the summer when Mary McCarthy and her fourth husband, James West, bought a house in Castine. The pace and grandeur of summer entertainments escalated whenever McCarthy was in residence.

McCarthy and Hardwick in 1984 at the McDowell Colony in Peterborough, New Hampshire, where Hardwick presented McCarthy with an award for literary achievement. After McCarthy's death, Hardwick commented, "I was always being called upon to introduce her. At her funeral I was tempted to say, 'This is my last introduction of Mary McCarthy.' "

Courtesy Special Collections, Vassar College Libraries

about how appalling it was for this woman to make such a remark "in front of me—a victim of Hitler, a person who has been in a concentration camp!" They kept up their private cold war for three years until Arendt finally made a peace offering: having just attended an editorial meeting of Dwight Macdonald's magazine *politics,* the two women were standing in silence on a cold subway platform. Arendt approached McCarthy and said abruptly, "Let's end this nonsense. We think so much alike." "From this richly productive lie," writes the critic Claudia Roth Pierpont, "grew one of the literary world's most loyal friendships, lasting until Arendt's death, a quarter of a century later."

Dear friends, intellectual allies, political comrades, confidantes, devoted correspondents (their two and a half decades of letters fill a volume), occasional houseguests, commentators on each other's work, Arendt and McCarthy were true "literary family," to borrow Elizabeth Hardwick's phrase. Perhaps "family" carries the wrong connotations, for even though they became intimate and affectionate with each other, there was always an element of the foreign, the unfamiliar in their attraction. Each represented for the other the finest flowering of an alien culture: for McCarthy, Arendt was Europe, with everything that implied in 1948 of tragedy, antiquity, complexity, wealth, and waste; in Arendt's eyes, McCarthy epitomized the bright, brash, clean-slate goodness of the New World. As Elizabeth Hardwick writes in her foreword to McCarthy's *Intellectual Memoirs,* Hannah "saw Mary as a golden American friend, perhaps the best the country could produce, with a bit of our western states in her, a bit of the Roman Catholic, a Latin student, and a sort of New World, blue-stocking salonniere like Rahel Varnhagen." To Arendt, McCarthy possessed the same qualities she so admired in America's Founding Fathers: high seriousness and honesty combined with a revolutionary conviction that the ideal was within our grasp.

Arendt, in turn, became McCarthy's "intellectual conscience," according to her son, Reuel, and an inspiration to pursue serious projects on European history, politics, and art (*The Stones of Florence* and *Venice Observed,* McCarthy's two finest sustained nonfiction works aside from her memoirs, were written during the first flush of her friendship with Arendt). They came to know and understand each other well as writers, as women, as fellow wives—but fantasy figured almost as large as knowledge in their extraordinary friendship. Each "stood for" something the other very much admired and desired to be near. Jerome Kohn, Arendt's last research assistant and a close friend, feels that "an essential element in their mutual attraction" was McCarthy's deep recognition of Arendt's sense of herself as a "stranger . . . literally as a visitor from somewhere far away." In Kohn's view, this self-perception is a crucial aspect of Arendt's character, and McCarthy's understanding of it "accounts to a considerable extent for the intensity of their friendship." Of course it wasn't all empathy and admiration between them. Lotte Kohler notes that Arendt was rather appalled at McCarthy's attitudes toward love and sex: "There were no limits to what Mary would think, speak, or do sexually and Hannah was very conservative in social matters. She could not understand how it was possible for Mary to be so promiscuous." But for the most part, their deep differences made their mutual approval all the more gratifying.

Arendt and McCarthy basked in each other's light. And their friendship was to become an important source of illumination, amusement, and consolation to both of them in the years to come. Fascinating in its own right, their friendship also opens a fascinating perspective on the inner lives of intellectual women of their generation.

Divorces

MARY McCARTHY'S friendship with Hannah Arendt was a sign of the marvelous sense of freedom she felt after breaking with Wilson. It was pure chance that the end of the marriage coincided with the end of the war, but in McCarthy's mind the events were linked: she was free and the world was a different place, with new people, new ideas, new connections to be made. The war and the long prelude to war had flooded America, and especially New York, with European refugees, among them some of the most brilliant minds of the twentieth century: Albert Einstein, Arnold Schoenberg, Bertolt Brecht, Thomas Mann, Walter Gropius, Simone Weil, Paul Tillich, and of course Arendt. "The whole character of New York was changed by the appearance of these refugees," McCarthy wrote. Certainly the refugees changed the character of her own life. Even before she befriended Arendt, McCarthy had become enthralled by the conversation and writing of Italian journalist and anarchist Nicola Chiaromonte, a refugee whom she met in 1944 and grew close to on Cape Cod during the summer of 1945. The deepening of her friendship with Chiaromonte that summer—a love affair of the mind, never consummated physically—laid down what she called the "dividing line" between her old life and her new. As she wrote Chiaromonte years later, "Nicola, I've long wanted to tell you . . . that seeing you on the Cape in the summer of '45 was a crossroads in my life. In fact, *the* crossroads. I became a different person." "I mean inner change of course," she went on to say—but outer change, particularly the break with Wilson, was just as important in this reinvention of herself.

It's somehow fitting that the breakup of this impossible marriage should have been precipitated by garbage—literally: two overflowing garbage cans that had to be carried out of the kitchen after a party. Here is McCarthy's version of the July 1944 evening, written in a deposition filed during their divorce proceedings:

> Everybody had gone home and I was washing dishes. I asked [Edmund] if he would empty the garbage. He said, "Empty it yourself." I started carrying out two large cans of garbage. As I went through the screen door, he made an ironical bow, repeating, "Empty it yourself." I slapped him—not terribly hard—went out and emptied the cans, then went upstairs. He called me and I came down. He got up from the sofa and took a terrible swing and hit me in the face and all over. He said: "You think you're unhappy with me. Well, I'll give you something to be unhappy about." I ran out of the house and jumped into my car.

Garbage, the reeking detritus of the domestic scene, reduced the two of them to slapping, screaming children—drunk children, which made it all that much worse. Wilson evidently chased McCarthy (who had apparently taken Rosalind with her) to Gull Pond, the locale of picnics in rosier days, where the car may or may not have run out of gas; at some point the women seem to have gone for a swim, and at some other point Wilson punched out one of the car's windows, possibly by accident, possibly in a drunken rage. Whatever really happened that night, this was *the fight* and it was followed by the inevitable aftermath: McCarthy's flight to New York, where Wilson pursued and recaptured her (an episode eerily foretold in McCarthy's short story "The Weeds"); faltering attempts at reconciliation ("I have really loved you more than any other woman," Wilson wrote her on July 13, "and have felt closer to you than to any other human being"); the unhappy family's unhappy move that autumn to an apartment on the Upper East Side; the "final" farewell note that McCarthy wrote in January 1945, when she snatched up Reuel and ran for her life ("Dear Edmund, This is the note in the pincushion. I'm afraid I don't see what else there is to do. . . . I'm sorry. This could probably all be managed with less éclat, but the only way I can ever break off anything is to run away. . . . Perhaps the fighting is mostly my fault, but that's not a reason for our staying together").

Wilson, desperate to get her back despite everything, replied that she had nothing to gain from divorce "except the satisfaction of feeling that you have somehow scored off me," but McCarthy went ahead and filed suit in New York for "extreme cruelty" in February 1945. Divorce was actually rather tame compared to what she had been fantasizing. "How many women had poisoned their husbands," ponders the nameless heroine of her short story "The Weeds," "not for gain or for another man, but out of sheer inability to leave them. The extreme solution is always the simplest. The weed-killer is in the soup; the man is in his coffin. One regrets, but now it is too late; the matter is out of one's hands. Murder is more civilized than divorce; the Victorians, as usual, were wiser." Twenty-two months would elapse before the divorce finally came through in December 1946.

The Wilsons made the most of their large stage and ample time to mount a really bang-up divorce, surely one of the ugliest in modern letters. Domestic violence, insanity, alcohol abuse, mental cruelty, and infidelity were the charges they hurled at each other. Wilson accused McCarthy of being a "psychiatric case," with a "progressively aggravated condition of hysteria, which resulted in violent outbursts toward me. . . . Plaintiff is the victim of hysterical delusions and has seemed for years to have a persecution complex as far as I am concerned." McCarthy countered by accusing Wilson of inflicting "physical and mental humiliation" which included not only beating her but charging her with infidelity in front of Reuel. (Significantly, she does not deny that she was unfaithful; her affair with Clement Greenberg was more or less an open secret in New York, and there were rumors of an affair with Wilson's old friend John Dos Passos, among other men.) Wilson turned the tables, insisting that his wife was in fact the physical aggressor: "At no time did I ever attack her. I have found it necessary to protect myself against violent assault by her in the course of which she would kick me, bite me, scratch me and maul me in any way she could." McCarthy was indeed taller and certainly a good deal fitter (and younger) than Wilson—so it's not implausible that she did knock him around some; in her sworn deposition she did, after all, admit slapping him.

Wilson kept harping on his wife's "insanity" because he knew it was the best way to get sole custody of Reuel—the ultimate revenge. Things got so brutal between them that, as Dwight Macdonald put it, Wilson's "insistence that she was insane was one of his pleasanter accusations." Unfortunately for Wilson, McCarthy's psychiatrists all denied the insanity charge and nobody came forward to corroborate his claim that she hit him. McCarthy had better success than Wilson in getting friends to testify on her behalf. Nathalie Rahv, Philip Rahv's wife, wrote in her deposition that Wilson "appeared to take delight in scolding and upbraiding his wife for petty matters. He humiliated her in my presence and in the presence of other friends by attempting to belittle her efforts at running the household and performing her wifely duties." It's hard to imagine a judge being terribly impressed by this, but an accusation of domestic incompetence and failure at "wifely duties" must have cut McCarthy to the quick. Adelaide Walker, the wife of a good friend of Wilson's, also publicly took McCarthy's side, a betrayal that Wilson was slow to forgive.

And so their legal battle of attrition dragged on. During the two years it took to effect the divorce, McCarthy and Wilson were really engaged in a solemn creative endeavor: turning their failed marriage into a work of fiction, or rather two works of fiction, his and hers. The depositions they composed and solicited from friends sound uncannily like their novels and short stories—stark, caustic, satirical, barbed with malice, painfully self-conscious. And competitive. Each was hell-bent on winning by writing better than the other. The relationship that had begun with words—"I only wanted to talk to him"—ended with words, ferocious competing narratives intended to cancel each other out. Each wanted to have the final say while discrediting the other. But of course the very existence of two versions has the effect of undermining both. Ultimately we believe neither. It's like the polemical, propagandistic fiction of the Marxist 1930s: we get the message, but we have no faith in the characters. In the end, neither scored a complete victory. McCarthy was awarded custody of Reuel, but Wilson got the boy during the summers and parts of his school vacations. Wilson also won the privilege of deciding which schools Reuel would attend. It was not exactly "joint custody," but neither was it a clean break for either side. The financial settlement was burdensome but not ruinous: $85 a week that Wilson had to pay for "maintenance."

What they really succeeded in proving in their protracted war of words is that they never should have married in the first place, which ought to have been obvious to both of them all along. In their next marriages, which followed hard on the heels of the divorce, both found partners who, as Reuel Wilson puts it, "were living for them to a large extent"—partners whose primary "job" was to attend to the details of daily life so the writing could progress smoothly. Wilson's daughter, Rosalind, recalls hearing her father say "somewhat wistfully and enviously" of McCarthy in later years, "I think she's got her life arranged so she can work"—an odd remark because McCarthy had done quite a lot of good work during their marriage. Maybe what Wilson meant was work in peace and security and without worrying about *his* work. "He casts a long shadow," says McCarthy's alter ego in the novel *A Charmed Life* of her Wilson-like husband, "I don't want to live in it. I feel depreciated by him, like a worm, like a white grub in the ground." McCarthy learned and gained a lot from Wilson, but she was afraid of him and she hated him for making her afraid and hated herself for being vulnerable to this fear. She hated how he split her into the wife and the writer, always rasping away at the wife for failing to "perform her wifely duties" and critiquing the writer as if she were some minor prose stylist he was working up for a review. A performer, an assumer and inventor of roles, McCarthy wanted to be *believed,* and she hated Wilson because he never really fell for the act. The hatred lasted her entire life. "She continued to dwell on the pain years later," says Margo Viscusi, who was McCarthy's secretary during the late 1960s. "It was not something she forgot. She could never go deep enough to explain what it was about the marriage that left such a scar."

As for Wilson, who was at once simpler and deeper emotionally than his wife, he hated being hated. If Mary had only piped down and stopped throwing fits, he could have lived with her forever. But piping down was not her style. As she reveals in a memorable passage of her brilliant *Memories of a Catholic Girlhood,* her favorite role from high school dramatics was Cataline, the vilified Roman revolutionary, "the damned soul, proud and unassimilable" who vowed to "extinguish the flames of my own ruin in the conflagration of all Rome." Better to torch and run than endure being married to a man who had the power to make her afraid.

Thus the marriage burned to a cinder and blew away.

Inevitably, a few traces remained. The former couple were still connected by their son and linked, perhaps even more intimately, through their literary circles. Though they rarely encountered each other face to face, even during the awkward period when McCarthy and her third husband, Bowden Broadwater, lived in Wellfleet, they heard about each other all the time. It infuriated Wilson that so many of McCarthy's *PR* cronies had gotten summer places on the Cape, and he made a point of glowering at them whenever he ran into them on the beach. Later on, Robert Lowell and Elizabeth Hardwick, who were friends with both Wilson and McCarthy, passed gossip back and forth. Jean Stafford also entered both of their spheres. And of course they couldn't help seeing, and couldn't resist reading each other's work, much of which appeared in *The New Yorker* during the 1950s and 1960s. There is nothing quite as queasy-making as reading a story or memoir by a former spouse. What intimate little secret would she next reveal? Would he parade her through one of his anatomically exact sex scenes? The ghost of the marriage lived on for years on the printed page and in the living rooms and kitchens of their crowd.

McCarthy made a big deal later in life about how loathsome Wilson was, but in her writing and interviews she really treated him no worse than many another and better than some. In her fiction he's a bastard with little pig eyes, but he's a smart, tough, *commanding* bastard. As the writer Mike Macdonald, Dwight's son, puts it, "Despite her reputation for literary malice, Mary's portraits of friends and foes are usually accurate." As for Wilson, even the deleted entries from the diaries are tepid compared to what Lowell wrote—and published—about Hardwick at the time of their divorce. Wilson and McCarthy did a lot of snarling, but they refrained from biting. This may have been out of fear or respect, or maybe they'd gotten the worst rancor out of their systems during the hideous divorce proceedings. In the end, this spectacularly ill-suited couple may have had more in common than either of them ever cared or dared to admit.

The Wilsons' divorce naturally became one of those irresistible gossip topics at *PR* cocktail parties and farther-flung literary gatherings—and even in the news media once it got to court. Certainly Jean Stafford was acutely conscious of the Wilson case as her own marriage to Robert Lowell fell apart around the same time. "I am thinking of the horrifying account of the Wilsons' divorce," she wrote Lowell, referring to a smirking squib in one of the newsweeklies, "but I am certain now that half of that was because of their awful books." Stafford dreaded being subjected to similar treatment if she and Lowell filed for divorce in New York. But as things turned out, bad press and nasty gossip hardly made a difference to Stafford, since the divorce itself so devastated her. If McCarthy's split with Wilson was a liberation, Stafford's separation from Lowell was a meltdown—an excruciating ordeal that very nearly destroyed her emotionally, mentally, and professionally. She lost nearly everything she had in the divorce and never fully recovered any of it. Like McCarthy, she would brood about the marriage and its demise for the rest of her life. Unlike McCarthy, she avoided publishing her broodings. It wasn't until the end of her life that she could bring herself to write about how the marriage came apart—just once, but unforgettably. Stafford's brilliant, savagely funny short story "An Influx of Poets," published discreetly soon after Lowell's death, was just about the only consolation she got out of the whole mess. She waited thirty years to collect it.

Lowell and Stafford remained together for two and a half years after Lowell was paroled from prison in March 1944, but it was pretty much a long slide downhill. Never very strong or healthy to begin with, the marriage unraveled as the two of them outgrew the compulsions and illusions that had made the relationship possible. Perhaps "outgrew" is the wrong word, for neither of them matured emotionally or attained a fuller sense of self in the breakup. But each changed, partly in response to the other, and in changing they put the marriage behind them. Lowell came into his own as a poet and began to crave contact with and recognition from a larger literary world. He also emerged from his monk's cell and resumed an active sex life—active, that is, outside the marriage. Stafford threw herself into creating her dream house, her frenzy for domestic perfection mounting as Lowell pulled away from her. And she drank— covertly, guiltily, defiantly, punishing herself with alcohol and demanding punishment from her husband. Increasingly, they cast each other as the enemy—the ancient familial enemy dragged out of childhood: the controlling, castrating mother; the improvident, heedless father. It was as if they set out together to re-create their worst family memories in their relationship with each other.

And yet, in the bizarre economy of the self, both of them did some of their finest work in the months immediately preceding the split: the words poured out in brilliant streams as the great iceberg of the marriage fissured and sank.

Lowell, on his release from prison, moved into a dingy room in Bridgeport and took up the final labor of his sentence: cleaning the nurses' quarters at Bridgeport's St. Vincent's Hospital. Stafford cleaned and closed up her apartment in New York and came to Connecticut to begin house hunting in earnest. Though she was actively fantasizing about acquiring an atmospheric old house "with its original floors and many fireplaces" set on lawns sloping down to Long Island Sound, she had to content herself for the moment with a series of provisional rental flats and cottages: a one-bedroom apartment near the water (and the dump) at Black Rock, Connecticut (whence the titles of two superb poems by Lowell, "Colloquy in Black Rock" and "Christmas in Black Rock"); a spacious barn converted to a house in Westport, Connecticut, where they lived from October 1944 to the summer of 1945; and then, in July 1945, a furnished cottage in the midcoast Maine tourist and boating town of Boothbay Harbor.

Stafford, now flush with funds for the first time in her life, thanks to *Boston Adventure,* was determined to do better. And she promptly did. She struck gold in Damariscotta Mills, a fine old town perched on the edge of a long, chilly lake near a stretch of tidal coves and deeply indented peninsulas on the Maine coast. The house she lit on was a rambling white clapboard green-shuttered Greek Revival affair—"large and grandly Hellenic," as she wrote a friend, and "too wonderful to be believed in." Built in 1820, it came with a barn (which she planned to convert into "two vast studios"), four fireplaces, "wonderful oaks and elms and blue spruce," and, as she bragged, was "within a stone's throw [of] the oldest R.C. church north of southern Maryland."

They took possession in early September, more or less camping out in a couple of rooms they were able to clear out and make habitable. After a month Lowell wrote to Peter Taylor, "Not even you could imagine the state of sustained extasy [*sic*] Jean is in. Every day I say: 'let's make a list of things that don't absolutely *have* to be done.' " But Jean was for doing everything. Her idea was to get the place fixed up to her liking over the winter, move in for real the following spring, and settle down to protracted tandem literary labors in that converted barn, with a few considerate friends coming up to visit at well-spaced intervals. But of course nothing worked out this way at all.

Since the house was not winterized, Stafford and Lowell planned on traveling down to Tennessee for another house-sharing stint with the Tates, this time in Sewanee. But this arrangement collapsed in October, when Tate and Gordon each posted letters with the startling news that they were getting divorced. "It all came up quite suddenly," Gordon explained in a curt letter to Stafford. "It is his idea, not mine. And I do not think he understands himself, or is frank with himself. At any rate he feels that we can no longer live together. I do not bolster his ego in little ways, he says—I have too high an opinion of him, an opinion he cannot live up to." Tate was even more tight-lipped about it: "Caroline has left me—permanently," his letter to Cal and Jean begins, and that's all he says about it. What neither of them wrote the Lowells, or needed to write, was that there had been trouble between them for years. Tate's infidelities and the long slack periods when he couldn't write; Gordon's resentment at being overshadowed, her involvement with her exhausting, eccentric Southern relatives, her exalted opinion of her husband's genius, her inability to write when Tate was playing the violin—which he did for interminable stretches when he couldn't work: all this had been dragging down the marriage for a long time. During that summer when the war ended, the strains became intolerable. Tate, as usual, was involved with other women, including the young Elizabeth Hardwick, who was just coming into her own as a writer. Gordon, as usual, knew or pretended to know nothing about it, though everyone else did. There were fights and violent scenes, and then one day Tate suddenly decided he had had enough and ordered Gordon to leave at once—literally, to clear out of the house and take the next train out of town. Gordon fled to New York with $500 in her pocket and no place to go. Characteristically, she blamed herself—her work, her self-involvement, her failure to anticipate her husband's needs—for what had happened. As she wrote to Malcolm Cowley, "One usually looks for the other woman. In this case I think there are two: Allen's mother and my muse. I'd have done better if I hadn't been so absorbed by my own work and so drained by it. Allen's mother looms larger in the picture. She so tortured him when he was a child that he is literally afraid to commit himself to any woman. I might have done something about that years ago if I had been wiser, but it is too late now."

Miserable and broke in New York, Gordon soon moved down to Princeton, where she found a room in the house of a widowed college professor and tried to write. She barraged friends, including Lowell and Stafford, with letters about her dire situation. Until that summer she'd had a husband, a house in Sewanee, a daughter, and a baby grandson she'd been helping to raise; and now, all at once, she had nothing but the prospect of a December divorce. The Lowells took pity on her. They had an empty house on their hands up in Maine. It seemed only charitable to invite Gordon to live in the place for as long as she could stand the cold and rather primitive conditions. "I have always wanted to live by the sea," she wrote them, accepting swiftly and gratefully. "I am delighted with the prospect of a winter up there." Her delight, as it turned out, was premature.

Gordon duly installed herself in Damariscotta Mills (which, she discovered, was not "by the sea"), and late in November, Stafford—who'd been in New York shopping, drinking, welcoming friends back from service overseas, and nursing Lowell through an appendectomy—joined her. Disaster swiftly ensued. "After three days of intensity, there was a final spectacular explosion," Stafford summed up the scene in a letter to her friends the Thompsons in Boulder. "Everything crashed in a most terrifying event," she wrote another friend. From the various oral and written accounts, one can splice together a rough picture of what happened: It was cold and bleak, and the two women consumed a quantity of alcohol. Gordon was naturally preoccupied with the dissolution of her marriage. By the third night she was prodding Stafford to tell her what she knew about her former husband's prodigious philandering, whereupon Stafford named names, and there were lots of them. Gordon became enraged by what she was hearing, threw a glass of water into Stafford's face and then threw the glass at her head. "It crashed on the wall above my head," Stafford wrote Tate later, "and she then got up and said, 'I'm going to break every goddamned thing in your goddamned house.' She did not say 'in *the* house.' She said, 'in *your* house.' " Gordon proceeded to let fly with a barrage of crockery—glasses, pitchers, peanut butter jars, whatever came to hand; after she broke a window, Stafford took fright, bolted to the house next door, and summoned the police. Gordon, once she disentangled herself from the law, fled south to attempt a reconciliation with her husband. This failed and on January 8, 1946, the divorce was finalized (although they remarried three months later).

"Everybody feels wretched," Tate wrote Stafford mournfully from Sewanee once the dust had settled somewhat. "We shall never know the whole truth . . . I simply don't think you should have called the police, regardless of the consequences. I have never thought for a moment that anything you said or did actually caused any of our troubles; you simply made deep trouble deeper." Lowell was just as stunned and hangdog as

Tate. "As you probably know Caroline's visit here was a disaster," he wrote Peter Taylor from Maine after Gordon had left. "I don't want to go into details, but I am sure there is nothing more we can do for the Tates. The whole business is very sad and grim." Gordon, for her part, kept holding out for a genuine apology. "I do not think that either of you . . . realize, or will admit, the enormity of Jean's offense," she wrote stiffly to Lowell. "What she did puts her beyond a pale within which we all move and have our being. Only a genuine act of contrition could bring her inside the pale again."

Yet despite Gordon's profound sense of injury, the one who ended up suffering most was Stafford. No doubt she had goaded and provoked Gordon. And calling the police *was* extreme. But she had panicked when faced with someone who was enraged. The house was important to Stafford; it was payback for the poverty and barrenness and "all the humiliation, the half-hunger," of her childhood, as she wrote in a letter; a reward for a decade of literary labor; an outward sign of what she wanted her life—and her marriage—to be. "You do not know and you never did know why that house is of such importance to me," she told Lowell later. "I worked my whole life toward its acquisition and toward all it should have brought." "I never owned anything so beautiful," she wrote a friend after she had lost it, "nothing was ever so completely *mine* as that house and those trees and those marvelous scenes from all the windows." Having Gordon there, destroying the beautiful, sacred place from within, was a terrible violation, made more terrifying by the specter of divorce. The end of the Tates' marriage, and the end of the friendship between the two couples, kicked a critical support out from under the Lowells. "Thank God we are both writers and have as a model the superb marriage of the Tates"—Stafford's good-luck charm as her marriage began, now a cruel piece of mockery.

Something snapped inside her that night as the crockery broke on her kitchen floor. The blowup left her shaken, vulnerable, scared to death of going mad—and drinking more than ever. It was a sad, grim prelude to the breakup of her own marriage.

Somehow, amid the turmoil and dislocations of home renovation and domestic battles, work got done—excellent work for both of them. Lowell had spent much of the time since his release from prison revising *Land of Unlikeness* and writing new poems. By October 1945, right before Stafford's blowup with Gordon, he had a new book in hand that he titled *Lord Weary's Castle*. Though still Catholic, still difficult, overloaded, and intense, still high-pitched and highly wrought, the new verse had shed the hysterical preaching of the earlier volume. In the finest poems—"The Quaker Graveyard in Nantucket," "Colloquy at Black Rock," "Christmas Eve Under Hooker's Statue," "Mary Winslow," "After the Surprising Conversions"—he masterfully welded together his deep reading in American literature, his religious passion, and his family connection with New England history to arrive at something new and totally assured. Randall Jarrell, with his uncanny sixth sense for poetry's inner workings, declared that the new poems convey "the contrary, persisting, and singular thinginess of every being in the world. . . . The things in Mr. Lowell's poems have, necessarily, been wrenched into formal shape, organized under terrific pressure, but they keep to an extraordinary degree their stubborn, unmoved toughness, their senseless originality and contingency."

The eyes that stare out at us from these poems bear an altogether different expression from those in *Land of Unlikeness*—sadder, wiser, less challenging, at once more puzzled and more acute. Lowell's true and abiding gaze. There is suffering, as well as learning, behind these lines, a sense of urgent apprehension and a burning need to give words to the workings of the mind. Lowell had found his voice, as well as the forms and postures he would carry through his career. The naked recounting of personal moments—as in "Rebellion"; the portraits and memorials of family members and meditations addressed to dear friends ("To Peter Taylor on the Feast of the Epiphany"); the loose translations and "imitations" of European and classical poets (Rilke, Propertius, Rimbaud); the sweeping gestures and global thoughts inspired by current events: Here were the germs and sketches and outlines for the next three decades of his work. It was an extraordinary achievement—and an astonishing advance.

All that was missing—conspicuously—was marriage, which would become a preoccupying subject in Lowell's later volumes. Though *Lord Weary's Castle* is dedicated "To Jean," not a trace or a shadow of her shows up in the verse. Lowell at this point in his life wrote best by writing outside his marriage. Home life was perhaps too raw and hot and worrisome to be wrestled into poetry. Or perhaps he needed to absent himself from the marriage, to divorce himself psychologically, in order to create. Lowell was growing and moving fast in these years; and every

change took him farther away from his wife. In his own mind, he had
nothing to gain from looking back.

Stafford was acutely aware of how hard and how successfully her husband was working after prison; "his intensity and industry make me feel
completely worthless," she confessed to Eleanor Taylor, while she told
Peter Taylor she was feeling "sick of the way I write." But in the summer
of 1945, just as Lowell was beginning to wind down, Stafford caught fire.
She had lit upon a new subject, the story of a girl's painful, abortive coming of age, and over the next nine months she brought the novel to swift,
sure completion. *The Mountain Lion,* her masterpiece, is also her most
intimately revealing fiction—not strictly autobiographical, despite some
obvious correspondences with her own life, but extremely close to the
bone. She pours into her young heroine, Molly Fawcett, all her own
thwarted brilliance, painful self-consciousness, loneliness, loathing, and
self-loathing. Molly is indeed a hateful creature—ugly (which Stafford
never was), spiteful, neurotic, peevish, easily wounded, viciously vindictive, emotionally stunted, impossibly snobbish—yet what's extraordinary
about Stafford's presentation is that we neither hate nor pity her. Rather,
we come to understand her from within and long to protect her and save
her from herself.

As she grows up (the book covers roughly the period between ages
eight and fourteen), Molly systematically burns every bridge behind her.
Her life is split between two irreconcilable camps: the fussy, precious, in-
door, feminine world of her mother's house in Covina, California (where
Stafford had lived as a girl), and the rough, gruff, masculine, outdoor
world of the Colorado ranch ruled by Molly's grandfather and, after his
death, by his son Claude. Molly and Ralph, the older brother she adores
and identifies with, despise the niceties of Covina, and long to escape to
the Colorado ranch—but when they get their wish one summer, Molly
finds that she doesn't really fit in there either. As she sadly discovers, the
only thing her two worlds have in common is that both are emotionally
repressive, especially for girls, and this discovery proves catastrophic for
her. Summer after summer, Molly watches Ralph grow up and drift away
from her into the silent, stoic, masculine realm of long rides into the
mountains and hunting expeditions with Uncle Claude. Molly had always assumed that she and Ralph would marry; on the day she finally re-
alizes that this won't happen, she sneaks into a garden shed and pours
acid on her hand—to punish Ralph, to draw attention to her plight, to
demand some sort of emotional recognition from her family. And of

course it backfires. Ralph is disgusted by his sister's folly. And with the onset of puberty he turns on her and effectively kills their relationship, the only real affection Molly had ever known. Molly devotes the remainder of her short life to ingenious, embarrassing expressions of her grief and rage, taunting Ralph publicly and mortifying her own hated body in private.

The Mountain Lion is a kind of portrait of the artist as a doomed girl. Molly writes poetry and stories, reads fine "literature," and brags insufferably about her taste and erudition. But there is no hope or future for her. Even had she not been killed—she dies in a tragic, heavily symbolic accident when Ralph and Claude fire on the mountain lion they have been stalking for years without realizing that the girl is hiding nearby— she is not a likely candidate for success or fulfillment. You get the feeling that she's heading for insanity, or a miserable dead-end job somewhere, or, at the very best, a life of hell as the wife of some impossible genius. But Molly is not allowed to live. The Kenyon men finish her off—inadvertently with a bullet, but she would have suffered a slow death anyway, for in their world there was no place for an imaginative girl. It may be pushing it a bit to suggest that the family name Kenyon popped into Stafford's mind because of the college attended by the male writers she was closest to: Lowell, Peter Taylor, Randall Jarrell, men who admired her but who instinctively shut her out of their tight chummy camaraderie. But even without the Kenyon association, there's no question that *The Mountain Lion* is a powerful cautionary tale about the perils of being brilliant and different and emotionally extravagant and female.

That Stafford wrote it so quickly is a sign of how close to the surface these unconscious issues had risen. Like *Lord Weary's Castle,* the novel contains no overt references to the marriage. But it does afford a harrowing glimpse of the emotional bind Stafford had gotten herself into— had, in fact, been in all her life. Rage that can only turn inward. Talent that rouses scorn and laughter and incomprehension in those close to her. Love that opens wounds. Idiotic vengeful pride that keeps wounds open forever. It's a kind of case history of female vulnerability, though Stafford deliberately undermined any impulse to read a social agenda into the book by making it so oddly buoyant, so lacking in bitterness or blame. Still, it's there if you want to see it: the repression and sacrifice of a fierce rebellious female sensibility practically leaps off the page. Had Stafford not ridiculed "women's lib" in the 1960s and '70s, the novel might have found a place on feminist reading lists instead of assuming the shabby-genteel status of a neglected classic. It's hard to think of another American novel that strikes a similar note—unless perhaps *Huckleberry Finn*. Huck and Molly are distant cousins: smart, funny, damaged, outcast, misunderstood, forever gazing with wide, level eyes at the strange goings-on of the adults around them. But of course Huck in the end regains his freedom by "light[ing] out for the territory," while Molly dies.

How typical it is of Stafford that she should pull off this stunning accomplishment while she herself was on the brink of collapse.

The winter and spring during which Stafford finished *The Mountain Lion* were rough times for her, and the summer ahead would be rougher. The November debacle with Gordon ushered in a series of mishaps and domestic calamities: frigid temperatures and burst pipes in Maine; a hectic, drunken midwinter stretch as housemates of Delmore Schwartz in Cambridge; fraught dinners with the Lowell family in Boston ("I am more thoroughly, more icily, more deeply disliked than ever, on account of [*Boston Adventure*]," Stafford wrote her friend Cecile Starr); long smoky evenings of exalted musings on fame and low-down literary gossip ("we talked away our friends," as Lowell put it in a poem); Delmore's mounting hostility and rumor-mongering aimed at poisoning the Lowells' marriage. Stafford, sleeping badly and drinking too much, slid into depression. "I really need my house to keep me from stultifying gloom," she wrote a friend in March.

But the rapture of possession was brief. Stafford moved up to the Damariscotta Mills house in April 1946 and completed *The Mountain Lion* soon after settling in. As she recalled years later in a fond author's note written for a reissue of the novel, "The last sentence of *The Mountain Lion* was written on a misty April day in 1946 in Damariscotta Mills, Maine, while a local carpenter was screwing handles on the drawers of a desk he had made for me." Whatever satisfaction she may have felt at the simultaneous attainment of house and book perished in the civil war that broke out as soon as Lowell arrived. "When he came back and found the house fresh with all this wallpaper and its new paint, he exploded and said that it was cheap," she wrote Peter Taylor, "that it was immoral, and that I had done the whole thing out of a sadistic desire to stifle him." Lowell was not a man you could stifle with paint and wallpaper. According to Stafford's biographer Ann Hulbert, he lashed out violently just after his return to Maine, possibly striking Stafford or threatening to kill her or strangle her in bed. No one was present aside from the two of them, and neither left any record of the "incident," as Stafford later referred to it darkly, aside from ugly scenes of marital violence buried in their work (Stafford's "A Country Love Story" and Lowell's long poem *The Mills of the Kavanaughs*). Lowell's biographer Paul Mariani places "the incident" in December and attributes it to sexual tension and jealousy. Stafford had been dreaming of a "former lover," writes Mariani, citing an interview with Lowell's friend Frank Parker, and "Cal had awakened her to make love and, still half asleep, she'd repeated her lover's name. In a perfect frenzy, Cal tried to strangle her." That's more or less what happens in *The Mills of the Kavanaughs:* "Who, who, who?" the enraged husband Harry Kavanaugh demands when his wife, Anne, stirs in sleep murmuring of a boy whose unshaven chin has "gored me black and blue"; Anne, musing on the incident decades later, recalls how her husband "shook the bed" and raved about shaking her "dead / As earth" and how she jumped up and threatened to shout "from the housetops" that Harry had sought to kill her "for dreaming."

Stafford's rendition of the "incident" in "A Country Love Story" is more muffled and oblique: there is no climactic physical outburst but rather a rigid regime of suspicion, silence, disdain, and withdrawal that tortures the wife, May, worse than any beating. Stafford does a superb job of conjuring up the frigid loneliness of a country winter and the madness that insidiously seduces the young wife as her husband alternately ignores her and barrages her with barbed accusations: "Will you tell me why it is you must badger me? Is it a compulsion? Can't you control it? Are you going mad?" Stafford's character May, who ends up feeling "[c]onfounded utterly, like an orphan in solitary confinement," bears a striking resemblance to Mary McCarthy's nameless heroine in "The Weeds": both are wives who watch in helpless, fascinated rage as their husbands take control of their lives and with seeming kindness drive them to the brink of insanity.

Whatever actually happened between Lowell and Stafford and whenever it happened, the "incident" left their marriage shattered beyond repair. There had been violence between them before and bitter arguments, but this was worse than anything they had been through and both of them knew it.

There was to be no relief. They were still seething when Lowell's par-

ents showed up for a visit—the first in a long, unbroken, clamorous parade of guests. Cal and Jean had acquired a good many literary friends in
the five years of their marriage, and just about all of them piled up to
Maine that summer on protracted and sometimes unannounced visits.
The Taylors, Robert Giroux, Eileen Simpson and John Berryman, James
Robert Hightower and his wife, the Clarks, the Parkers, Philip Rahv and
Nathalie Swan, and Delmore Schwartz were among their more prominent houseguests. Stopping at Lord Weary's Castle, as the house became
known, was a vacation highlight for a generation of poets, critics, and
editors. "The idea was to get away from the distractions of New York and
have people come up to visit in pairs," says Cecile Starr, "but everything
went wrong. Cal did not want to be so far from New York, and he felt
stuck with Jean. She was drinking too much. People came in overwhelming, unmanageable bunches. Cal was not interested in the pine
chest and brass lamp on which Jean lavished so much care. And they
were surrounded by Maine neighbors who weren't compatible but who
made lots of invitations and requirements; Cal left all of this to her. They
were in a little village where social amenities were expected. Everything
went wrong." Stafford confessed to Starr as the summer was nearing its
end that there had been "such a stream of visitors ever since Memorial
Day that I was half out of my mind and so was Cal. . . . No work done at
all since April. . . . I thought I was at the end of everything in my life."

"That awful summer," as Stafford called it, has become something of a
literary legend, rather like the Tates' house party at Benfolly in the summer of 1937, with variant versions appearing in the memoirs, reminiscences, fiction and fabrication of those involved. Fittingly, Stafford's own
account, the short story "An Influx of Poets," is the most highly colored
and certainly the best written. Published in *The New Yorker* in November
1978, a little more than a year after Lowell's death, the story created
something of a sensation for its thinly veiled and scathingly intimate portraits of the marriage, of the young Lowell and his young poet friends,
and of the adulterous love affair that brought the marriage down. In fact,
"An Influx of Poets" is a curious, insidious mixture of truth and invention, a kind of black comedy in which a good deal of the humor derives
from the distortions and departures and exaggerations. Stafford's alter
ego, the narrator Cora Savage, appears shorn of her art: she is "just" a
wife; the Lowell character, Theron Maybank, is an impossible Boston
prig, deeply, dully conventional and hideously snobbish under his Romantic poetic facade. "My nesting and my neatening were compulsions

in me that Theron looked on as plebeian, anti-intellectual, lace-curtain Irish," declares Cora, skewering both herself and her husband. "I did not know how to defend myself against his barbs, the cruellest of which was that I could not sin with style. . . . God almighty! Never was a man so set on knocking the stuffing out of his bride!" Cora's character is her voice—the rasping, scathing, smoky voice of late middle age looking back in amused disgust on the follies of youth. Theron, on the other hand, is not so much a character as an exquisitely fashioned act of revenge—a punching bag wearing Lowell's clothes.

Stafford put into the story a lot of what really happened in the course of her marriage: their meeting at a writers' conference; the initial residence in fetid Baton Rouge followed by frequent moves ("[we] changed the scene of our travail each year from the beginning"); Lowell's onerous Catholic piety and her own sheepish faithlessness ("I was God-forsaken"); the purchase of the lovely old house in Maine ("I was thirty now, and I had achieved at last what I had striven for from the beginning: a house and a lawn and trees"); the painstaking remodeling and decorating of this "temple" of the marriage. But what rings most true in the story is the *feeling*, or at least Stafford's feeling as she suffered the bardic invasion of her precious home and the dissolution of her marriage. "All day I'd cook and wash the dishes and chop the ice and weed the garden and type my husband's poems and quarrel with him," her narrator recalls in retrospective fatigue. When she's not slaving to keep the poets fed, Cora is forced to listen to them recite their works in progress—"I admit they were brilliant poets, if you happen to be interested in that sort of thing"—while her thoughts stray into "fields far distant from those bounded by the barbed-wire fences (some of them electric) of my marriage."

The voltage in those electric fences rises dangerously when Theron falls in love with a pretty, petite, kittenish Jewish critic named Minnie Rosoff, an episode lifted pretty much intact from Lowell's affair with Gertrude Buckman. Cora sees where things are headed between Theron and Minnie—she'd have to be blind not to—and part of her rejoices. She's been casting around for a pretext to leave her marriage, and this budding affair looks like her ticket to freedom. While drinking herself into a stupor one night, the forsaken wife fantasizes about the "sinful" lovers and schemes to turn their crime of passion to her own advantage: "Dishonored, I would ascend refreshed, putting aside the ruin of this marriage shattered so ignominiously by *the other woman,* by that most unseemly of disgraces, above all by something *not my fault,* giving me the uncontested right to hate him." The psychology here is twisted but revealing: Stafford's stand-in believes that she cannot leave the marriage until she has been issued some absolute, unassailable justification—until she has been victimized and humiliated so painfully and undeservedly that at last she is free to act. But the denouement is even more revealing, for when her fantasy comes true, it destroys her. Far from triumphing over the squirming adulterous pair, Cora is plunged into the "vilest degradation, the bitterest jealousy, the most scalding and vindictive rancor"—as was Stafford herself.

What Stafford leaves out of the story is that she and Buckman had been close friends during the time Lowell was in jail—so it was a double betrayal. "I helped in every way to make the match," Stafford's fictional self confesses in stunned self-discovery, "which was already a fait accompli and which, when I discovered that it was, was to hurtle me off the brink on which I had hovered for so long into a chasm." This is "Cora" speaking, of course, but the mask is quite transparent here. For Stafford was indeed an accomplice in her unraveling that summer, and the disclosure of the affair did indeed hurtle her off the brink. Perversely, she craved punishment, and cruelly, she got it.

Stafford was a victim, both of her own psychology and Lowell's. But she didn't suffer in silence. Evidently, she gave back as good as she got. "I had the tongue of an adder and my heart was black with rage and hate," states Cora, almost proudly. Houseguests confirm how true this was to Stafford's own mood and behavior. Eileen Simpson recalls Stafford's "black tongue" that summer—the cutting remarks tossed at Lowell and the long, mocking anecdotes about his domestic crimes and follies. And everyone noticed the drinking and the sleepless nights. Stafford drank in company, she drank in private, she had bottles stashed all over the house: she was giving every sign of drinking herself to death or insanity. Cora in the story speaks of her "secret boozehead side," but Stafford's boozing was no secret. The alcohol, as much as the affair with Buckman, hurled her off the brink.

The plunge came toward the end of August. "I don't care for confessions, but I suppose I must tell you that everything is chaos with us," Lowell wrote to Peter Taylor on August 19. "Jean is driving like a cyclone, and we both have had about all we can stand and more. . . . We have got to *leave each other alone.*" Stafford, writing to the Taylors on the twenty-eighth, confirmed that chaos had descended and blamed herself for the catastrophe: "I love Cal too much now to allow him any longer to be subjected to what seems to amount almost to insanity. . . . I am almost altogether to blame for my life being the ruin that it is." Later she wrote that it was her "too great necessity" that drove Cal away. In haste and misery they left the Maine house on September 20 and took the train down to New York. Their parting, after a single night together in the city, must have been excruciating. Stafford later wrote the Taylors that they stayed up all that night while Lowell told her repeatedly that she was "possessive like his mother" and that "he did not love me and believed that he never had." The next day, she said, he "drove me out." Shades of the first Tate divorce. The relationship dragged on for months through a couple of abortive attempts at reconciliation, a "cooling-off period" brokered by Peter Taylor, and a series of fraught, and, on Stafford's side, voluminous negotiations; but the marriage was over.

Lowell's side of the story is curiously blank. The distaste for "confession" that he mentioned to Peter Taylor (an odd remark coming from a practicing Catholic and later the most celebrated of the confessional poets) kept him from saying much about the breakup in his letters. And his verse is also mostly silent. References to the final stretch of the marriage surfaced only years later in his poem "The Old Flame," in which he recalls Jean's summoning the Damariscotta sheriff to drive her to the State Liquor Store in nearby Bath; the "imaginary lover" whom she alone saw (Stafford made this apparition the central motif of "A Country Love Story"); their sleepless nights in "one bed and apart," "simmering like wasps"—but by then time had mellowed his voice and rosied his vision. "Everything's changed for the best—" he sighs with the wise irony of middle age.

Back in the autumn of 1946, when the wounds were fresh, Lowell was not ironic at all but grim, stony, and determined to put as much distance as he could between himself and Stafford. His life was opening out in every direction; he was back in New York, albeit it in a seedy, bug-infested apartment on Third Avenue; *Lord Weary's Castle* was about to be published; Buckman adored and admired him. Under the circumstances, an estranged, hysterical, alcoholic wife was a serious encumbrance. And so, he shuffled her off as efficiently as possible. "Jean has suffered a lot in her lifetime from the feeling she is unwanted," Peter Taylor wrote Lowell in a vain attempt to spark some sympathy. "The effect of divorce might be disastrous." But Lowell remained unmoved: he had made up his mind and that was it. The marriage was over. All of this makes Lowell sound heartless, calculating, and single-mindedly ambitious, which was not entirely the case. Stafford was, plainly, impossible: "driving like a cyclone." Lowell's remoteness was in part simple self-protection. Had he not gotten away and stayed away, Jean's cyclone would have demolished him as well. But perhaps he carried his severity further than he needed to. In her letters to Peter and Eleanor Taylor, Stafford accuses Lowell of a "calm, Olympian brutality." While she is "perfectly wild with despair," he "has remained so immovable, so utterly, so absolutely utterly unaware of what I might be suffering. . . . It is Cal's doing, all of it, in his serene greatness. He will be unsmirched. He will always be a Lowell. . . . [H]e has never shown me anything in any of his letters but cold, self-justified hatred." This is bitterly partisan, but it does have the ring of emotional truth (unfortunately Stafford destroyed most of Lowell's letters to her). The marriage was over and Lowell had nothing to gain from mourning its demise, nothing to gain from writing about Stafford or even speaking to her. He now wanted the cleanest, fastest break he could get. No poetry; no nostalgic anguish; minimal contact: just his freedom. It's worth remarking that he took precisely the opposite tack twenty-five years later, when he left his second wife, yet tried so desperately to keep the relationship alive—and recounted the endeavor so nakedly, so obsessively in his verse.

The final chapter of the marriage—the dismantling of it—belongs to Stafford. Whatever Lowell was feeling he kept to himself. But Stafford let fly with a string of electrifying letters, both to Lowell and to the Taylors, in which she criticized husband, self, and marriage. It's a magnificent, excruciating literary performance—by turns a laying bare of the soul in torment, a frantic plea for help or at least pity, a bid for revenge, a shrewd psychological analysis of what went wrong, a justification of her rage and despair. Page after page of rapid-fire, flawless, merciless prose, the letters could almost be the script for a one-woman play—a play about the shipwreck of a woman, writer, and wife in a man's world. Despite the epistolary format, one senses that Stafford really wrote for herself: to play back the marriage in her own mind and to fill the terrible void its dissolution left in her life. The void was more than loneliness, for during the time she composed the letters, Stafford was a kind of nonperson—

an inmate at a mental institution. She had signed herself in to Payne Whitney (the hospital to which Edmund Wilson had committed Mary McCarthy and where Lowell would soon be a patient as well) at the end of November, having suffered what used to be called a nervous break-down compounded by uncontrollable drinking. She was under the sur-veillance of a nursing staff and in the care of psychiatrists. And she was in hiding. During her first few weeks at the hospital, no one, aside from Cecile Starr and the Taylors, knew where she was, and no one but Starr came to visit; certainly not her estranged husband. The disgrace, in her own mind, was total.

In this situation and this frame of mind, Stafford sat and typed bril-liantly. "Wife," "woman," "love," "marriage" are the words that rise to the surface over and over in the letters to Lowell. "What do I care if Randall likes my book?" she demanded, responding to a letter in which Lowell evidently tried to soothe her with secondhand praise. "Or anyone? Why should it console me to be praised as a good writer? These stripped bones are not enough to feed a starving woman." I've already quoted the final sentences of this searing paragraph: "I know this, Cal, and the knowledge eats me like an inward animal: there is no thing worse for a woman than to be deprived of her womanliness. For me, there is noth-ing worse than the knowledge that my life holds nothing for me but be-ing a writer. But being a writer and being a robbed woman whose robber will doubly rejoice in her stolen goods." And later: "In your letter you say that you hope I will be recognized as the best novelist of my generation. I want you to know now and know completely that that would mean to me absolutely *nothing*. . . . I shall be grateful for what-ever praise I get, but I shall never be so confused as to think that this is life or that, if one looks closely, it bears any resemblance to life"—a tragic statement coming from a woman who had just published her mas-terpiece. Underneath the bombast and bile she blamed herself. "It only adds to my torment," she writes the Taylors, "to know that if I had been smart in the way Mackie [Randall Jarrell's first wife] is smart I could have made it work." She was convinced that if only she had been more of a "woman" and less of a writer she might have held on to her husband. But here she misunderstood her husband. Lowell *wanted* and *needed* to be married to a writer. His next two wives were also writers. He just didn't want to be married to Stafford anymore.

With the help of the Payne Whitney psychiatric staff, Stafford was try-ing to figure out why her marriage failed. The fundamental problem, she explained to the Taylors, was that Cal had married his mother and she had married her father. And when "these people really emerge[d] in us," the marriage dissolved. "And I suppose they emerged because we dug them out, we probably wanted it to be like this." Though it sounds like "psychiatric cant," as she put it, there is a core of truth here. Lowell had been treating his wife with the same cold, petulant, adolescent arrogance he had used to keep his mother at bay. And he was sick of it. He didn't want to be the priggish domestic tyrant anymore, meting out the drinks, hauling Jean off to mass, raging against the lace and muslin in which she tried to swaddle him. The marriage in a sense had been an act of youthful rebellion that ended up replicating and enshrining the worst of his youth. Lowell wanted to grow up and Stafford wouldn't let him. Her failure to fight back, to stand up to him as an equal, to be as strong as he was, forced him into the role of surly, sneering bully. And the more he bullied, the more she shrank from confrontation. Stafford mused in her journal over this tight knot in their relationship: "Sometime, he said, I would lose my temper and stop letting people knock me about. 'As you have always done?' I asked and he replied, 'Yes, it's all that could be done with someone like you.' But I did not know how to refuse to accept the mistreatment. If I fought back with anger, it only made things worse; yet my submissiveness maddened him. I apologized for everything; I had no center and therefore I had no self and therefore I did not lead a real life. His vanity and passionate self-devotion fascinated me evilly."

Lowell would always be a difficult husband, but he was never again as sour, glum, and vain as he had been with Stafford. None of his other brides got the stuffing knocked out of them so badly. But of course Stafford was a full and willing partner.

"Being a writer and being married to a writer is a back breaking job and my back is now broken," Stafford wrote one of her sisters during "that awful summer." First her back was broken, then her heart, then her mind. Stafford never fully recovered from her marriage to Lowell, either emotionally or professionally. She continued to write, creating some wonderful stories, and another novel and later turning to journalism, but most of her best work was behind her. She married twice more, but neither marriage brought her much lasting satisfaction. Losing Lowell, she lost a good deal of her standing in the literary world—lost or deliberately renounced or perhaps surrendered it. In the painful, shaky months after emerging from Payne Whitney, she steadfastly refused invitations to the

Rahvs' cocktail parties: "I know that I had already been to that party up-
ward of a hundred times," she wrote Lowell after meeting Rahv on the
street. "How long ago it all seems, and how very, very unimportant." She
hid from the Tates and crumpled when she unexpectedly encountered
Gordon at a party. She realized, after running into Delmore Schwartz in
the city, what a stranger she had always been in literary New York. Being "without money and without friends . . . is harder for a woman than
for a man," she wrote Lowell as she contemplated the misery of her existence in Manhattan. "A man who is called a scoundrel remains, to most
people, attractive, but a woman who is called a bitch is shunned." While
she watched Lowell embark on his "very fabulous life" of praise, honors,
prizes, and growing fame—*Lord Weary's Castle* won the Pulitzer Prize in
the spring of 1947, and Lowell's handsome face was all over the newspapers and magazines—Stafford moved out to the margins where she
felt safer and less exposed. Though she repeatedly declared herself well
rid of Lowell, she remained "evilly" fascinated by him—as he was,
though perhaps without the evil, by her.

The divorce was slow in coming, and there were many months of
wrangling over property, alimony, and the disposition of the beloved
house in Maine. Stafford was determined to have a more dignified and
above all quieter legal severance than the publicized debacle that Mc-
Carthy and Wilson staged in 1945. A New York divorce looked too risky,
so Stafford reluctantly agreed to remove herself to St. Thomas in the Virgin Islands at the end of April 1948 and stay there for the requisite six
weeks. According to the terms they finally settled on, Lowell paid Stafford
a lump sum of $6,500. And that was it; On June 14, they were free.

Lowell, as it turned out, did not marry Gertrude Buckman, as Stafford
expected. In the summer of 1947, while Stafford was winding up her
treatment at Payne Whitney, he went up to the Yaddo writers' colony,
and from there he moved down to Washington, D.C., to take up the
post of poetry consultant to the Library of Congress. Separated from
Buckman, Lowell started an affair with an older woman named Carley
Dawson, a divorcée with a son, but he didn't marry her either, though
he talked about it for a while. He also talked and fantasized about marrying Elizabeth Bishop, Mary McCarthy's Vassar classmate, whom he
met and fell in love with around this time, though he never quite got
around to proposing.

Lowell was still in Washington when the divorce came through. Stafford, winding up her stay in the Virgin Islands, boasted of her tan and insisted, with hollow-sounding levity, how strong and fit she felt. "I want us both to marry again, don't you?" she wrote Lowell. "We'll be so much wiser and so much calmer." Her wish for remarriage came true promptly for both of them; but wisdom and calm were not to be their fate.

The Tranquilized Fifties:
Insanity and Liberalism

JEAN STAFFORD wrote to her friends Dorothy and Paul Thompson on November 10, 1949, "Cal, who, as you may know, was dreadfully sick last spring, got out of his sanitarium after being there less than three months (although he was so sick that he had electric shock) and within a week married a literary baggage called Elizabeth Hardwick. After a ten-day honeymoon, he fetched up in the hospital again where he has been ever since." This was the juiciest bit of gossip making the rounds of literary New York that fall. Not malicious "creative" gossip for once, for the truth was every bit as appalling as Stafford's rather arch (and only slightly exaggerated) account. With the fearful symmetry of a work of art, Lowell's first psychotic breakdown—the first of many—coincided with his marriage to Hardwick, just as his feverish Catholic conversion coincided with his marriage to Stafford. Madness was to be the dark star of the second marriage just as religious fanaticism had ruled the first. It's a wonder and a tribute to Hardwick—her sanity, toughness, and determination to hold on to Lowell—that the second marriage endured more than twenty years: twenty years with a volatile, tortured, incurable madman at the center of a high-voltage, high-profile literary scene.

Hardwick met her husband pretty much as Lowell described it in the memorable lines of his poem "Man and Wife": there was a party at the Rahvs' apartment "in the heat / of Greenwich Village"; he was drinking a lot and wobbly with repressed desire: "fainting at your feet— / too boiled and shy / and poker-faced to make a pass." Boiled and shy and poker-faced are *exactly* how one imagines Lowell during the tense Stafford years; the pass, however, was out of the question, since Stafford was also present, no doubt drinking hard herself. It would be the Rahvs who brought them together, for Lowell, Stafford, and Hardwick were closely connected to Rahv and *Partisan Review* at this time. None better connected than Hardwick, who had quickly been ushered into the *PR* "inner circle" and more or less remained there until she jumped ship in the 1960s to found *The New York Review of Books*. A native of Lexington, Kentucky, and a graduate of the University of Kentucky, Hardwick had come to New York in 1939 at the age of twenty-three to do graduate work at Columbia. She'd also been accepted at LSU in Baton Rouge— Lowell and Stafford's old haunt, then a powerhouse of English literature with Robert Penn Warren and Cleanth Brooks on the faculty and a more obvious choice for a Southern woman—but Hardwick wanted New York. Hardwick, who had briefly been a member of the Communist Party, later joked that she had come to New York because she wanted to be a Jewish intellectual. In fact, she was an auburn-haired Presbyterian girl from a large family (eleven children in all, of which she was the eighth). But the qualities she admired in Jewish intellectuals—"a certain deracination," as she told an interviewer, "an angular vision, a love of learning," intellectual independence, skepticism about received values and opinions, a sense of irony, an affinity for the important cities—were hers as well. Hardwick also had a taste for the quick, barbed exchange, a gift for devastating gossip, a commitment to serious political discourse, and a beguiling gracious modesty that concealed a restless, often brilliantly original mind. She could be quite nasty when she wanted to be, cutting others down to size with a smile, never a snarl. As *PR* editor William Phillips wrote in his memoirs, "A marvelous talker, she has usually managed—like the English—to be charming even when most devastating or malicious." "She'll spit in your eye as quick as look at you," a friend remarked. Sylvia Plath wrote in her journal in the late 1950s that Hardwick struck her as "charming and high-strung," although she overheard one of Hardwick's women friends telling her, "Next to me I hear you're the biggest bitch in Cambridge."

Though Hardwick dropped out of the Columbia Ph.D. program after a couple of years, she stayed on in New York to try to live by her wits. She hoped to make her way as a fiction writer, and she duly produced a novel, *The Ghostly Lover,* an eerie, rather labored bildungsroman about a Kentucky girl who breaks away from her unpleasant family (a pair of wan, drifting, absentee parents; a handsome, self-absorbed, apparently homosexual brother; a vain, foolish grandmother) and comes to New York for graduate school and then for life. After the book appeared to mixed reviews in 1945 (Lowell's future flame Gertrude Buckman deemed Hardwick "a new writer of great talent and promise"), Rahv took notice of her and asked her to write reviews for *PR.* "I weighed about ten pounds then, skinny, smoking, and he was quite surprised that I had read everything," Hardwick reminisces today. Rahv, whom she remembers as "curious, sly, and prying," asked her in the course of that first interview what she thought of Diana Trilling's reviews in *The Nation.* "Not much" was Hardwick's response, which was evidently what Rahv wanted to hear, for her first reviewing assignment came shortly afterward. As usual, it was a smart move on Rahv's part, for the critical essay turned out to be Hardwick's true métier—certainly more so than fiction.

Hardwick quickly developed a reputation for critical ferocity: Katherine Anne Porter called her a hatchet man ("Hatchet woman sounds too gentle for her") and Peter Taylor quailed under a stinging review of his first short-story collection. "Articulate, witty, very clever, freewheeling, she became a master of the slashing critical style of the politicized literary intellectuals," wrote Phillips. "She was one of our more cutting minds, and she made us aware of our faults as well as our virtues." Like Mary McCarthy before her, she developed a reputation for getting around sexually and for her (relatively) uncomplicated enjoyment of her love affairs. Jason Epstein says Hardwick was "the prettiest and sexiest and the easiest to have a love affair with" of all the women in that crowd. "She was a cute little kid. Very feminine. There was a Betty Boop quality to her—in those days women could still be feminine in that way." Other men recall being stunned by how beautiful she was—graceful, slender, animated, fair, wide-eyed, pleasurable to watch and to be with. There was an affair with Rahv and a liaison with Allen Tate around the time of his first divorce from Gordon.

"Sure, Lizzie slept with Rahv," Epstein remarked. "Everybody slept

with everybody in those days. She went more for the fun of it. Mary Mc-
Carthy, on the other hand, would have made a project out of her sex
life." The comparison with Mary McCarthy was obvious: both were
young, smart, promiscuous, ambitious literary women who instinctively
knew their way around town. Both had broken the gender barrier at *PR*
and made the male editors not only publish them but respect and listen
to them. Both were intimate with Rahv—indeed, both were in love with
him at different times, Hardwick so much that she asked Nathalie to
"give him up" so she could have him, much to McCarthy's amusement. It
was inevitable that McCarthy and Hardwick would become either friends
or enemies. Somewhat warily, they settled on the former, friends as well
as rivals. Hardwick still laughs when she recalls McCarthy's leaning over
to Rahv when he introduced the women to each other and whispering
loudly, "I don't see what's so good about *her!*" Hardwick and McCarthy
never considered each other "so good"—they were too familiar, too critical for that—but there was affection between them and almost always
respect.

By the time Hardwick met Lowell and Stafford at the Rahvs' heated
party, she was a force to be contended with in the literary world—not famous or successful in a worldly way (this never really happened to her),
but known, admired, sometimes feared by those who mattered. She was
promising, pretty, eager to be with the best people, and not afraid to
make her opinions known to them. "[T]he shrill verve / of your invective
scorched the traditional South," Lowell writes of her in "Man and Wife":
clearly she could more than hold her own with the vociferous *PR* crowd.
The "traditional South" was a sore subject for Hardwick then, for she had
been criticized by Tate, among others, for not being "southern enough"
in her writing. But she didn't care. "I never considered myself a southern
writer," she said blithely. "Being a southern writer is a choice, not a fate."

In New York in the early 1940s, with Rahv, McCarthy, Dwight Macdonald, Clement Greenberg, and Delmore Schwartz—and now, briefly,
with Robert Lowell and Jean Stafford—Hardwick was in her element. Far
more in her element than Stafford was. Stafford and Hardwick and Mc-
Carthy bumped up against each other in the 1940s, and the impressions
they made are revealing. Women from the provinces—Boulder, Lexington, Seattle—they were all determined not to be dazzled by the women
they met in the city, including each other. They certainly had no sense of
sisterly comradeship; and yet they were keenly aware of what and how
other women writers were doing and where they stood. Hardwick re-

members going out to dinner alone in New York with Stafford before she separated from Lowell, possibly during the time when Lowell was in prison. She thought much of Stafford's work was brilliant (with the exception of *Boston Adventure,* which she attacked in *PR* for its use of a "poor little rich girl" stereotype in the character Hopestill Mather. But in her opinion Stafford was not an intellectual: "She had the fictional talent, but she had none for intellectual life. Never." Stafford, as we've seen, dismissed Hardwick as "literary baggage," though this is probably sour grapes. McCarthy came in for much rougher handling. McCarthy struck Stafford as "ignited ice" when she turned up with her new husband Bowden Broadwater at a talk Stafford was delivering at Bard College—the pair of them sitting in the front row "grinning like cats." "Your speech had a great deal of charm," McCarthy told her afterward, sending chills up her spine. "I wanted almost to reply that I was glad," Stafford wrote Lowell about it, "that to be a charming woman was my principal ambition. . . . There is something so dead and dreary about all one hears of all the Rahv set—thank God, I've encountered none of them except Mary McCarthy."

The Rahv set: how deeply they all cared about their standing in that circle. Especially the women, who were allowed in only by special dispensation. In a sense the Rahv set *had* no women—only wives and writers, and if a writer happened to be female, she became one of the boys. Being a wife in that crowd was a fate worse than death. "They were treated badly," Hardwick admits. "No one paid attention to the wives at the parties; they just sat there while everyone was drinking cheap whisky and battling over politics." That was Diana Trilling's problem: she started off as a wife and then tried to gain recognition as a writer, thus irritating both sexes, especially the women. As she writes in her memoirs, attempting to explain the ridicule and scorn she inspired when she started to publish, "People will celebrate one member of a household but not two. To celebrate two members of a single household doubles the strain on generosity." In the *PR* set, Stafford, McCarthy, and Hardwick were definitely *not* wives (it's telling that they all published under their maiden names, while Diana Trilling used her married name). They got in because of their talent and they didn't give a hoot about how other women were treated. "Of course I didn't think of advancing womanhood," remarks Hardwick. Their work was getting published—why worry about womanhood? Style was what mattered, not gender. It didn't occur to them to protest the fact that the editors were all men, that the meaty pieces and editorials were written almost exclusively by men, that men had the power to promote or kill them professionally. The main thing for the women in this crowd was that they weren't wives—except at home. Neither McCarthy nor Hardwick felt or admitted to any sense of conflict over this literary-domestic split. If anything, they were proud of managing both so well. Only Stafford had a terrible time separating the two sides of her life so radically, which may explain why she found the Rahv set "dead and dreary."

Or maybe it was just the booze. Hardwick and McCarthy belted back the cheap whiskey with the best of them, but hard social drinking was never really a problem for them as it was increasingly for Stafford. Once the marriage to Lowell ended, Stafford avoided *PR* and moved on to a more comfortable and more lucrative arrangement with *The New Yorker*. Rahv, Jarrell, Berryman, Delmore Schwartz, and other old cronies accused her of selling out, for in the eyes of the *PR* crowd *The New Yorker* was irredeemably unserious and fatally haute bourgeois—at heart a humor magazine catering to Park Avenue matrons and trust-fund dilettantes. "Deliberately . . . its editors confine their attention to trivia," sneered Dwight Macdonald in his critique of the magazine published in the first issue of the reborn *PR*. "Its readers are expected to buy Paris gowns, airplanes, vintage wines, movie cameras, Tiffany jewelry, air conditioning, round-the-world trips, et cetera. Interlarded with the advertisements are various 'departments,' devoted to practical advice on the great problem of upper-class life: how to get through the day without dying of boredom."

Macdonald wrote this in 1937. A decade later, *The New Yorker* had changed considerably. The tone sobered up during the war as editor Harold Ross, somewhat reluctantly, began to run in-depth, fact-filled reports by the likes of A. J. Liebling, E. J. Kahn, Jr., Rebecca West, Janet Flanner, and John Hersey. And William Shawn, who took over the editor's post from Ross in 1952, went much further in this direction, to the point where long, heavily documented, topical articles overwhelmed the ephemeral "departments." Nonetheless, the *PR* faithful still regarded *The New Yorker* as basically the humor magazine of "our ruling class" (Macdonald's phrase). This is all the more curious considering how many of these faithful "crossed over" and wrote for *The New Yorker* at one time or another (and happily accepted their relatively princely fees). Macdonald himself was a longtime staff member (Diana Trilling claimed that *The New Yorker*'s editors hired him on the strength of his attack in *PR*); Edmund Wilson signed on as book reviewer in 1944 and remained with the magazine for years; and eventually Mary McCarthy, Hannah Arendt, Elizabeth Bishop, Diana Trilling, and Elizabeth Hardwick would all publish in *The New Yorker* as well. Only Lowell steadfastly held out, refusing to see his verse sandwiched in among the Tiffany jewelry and Paris gown ads.

Yet even after Shawn made *The New Yorker* a widely respected, if somewhat eccentric, "intellectual" and "literary" presence (two house pejoratives during the Ross years), the magazine remained a world apart, socially, stylistically, in outlook and in attitude—urbane where *PR* was urban, casual where *PR* was committed, remote where *PR* was in the trenches, protective of its writers and their quirks where *PR* was brutal and embattled. Stafford, in the care of motherly fiction editor Katharine White, was happy to take refuge there—and glad for the company of Wilson, along with Peter Taylor and Eudora Welty, who also became regular contributors around the same time.

Hardwick was altogether better suited than Stafford to the world Lowell wanted to be in. She was happy to live in New York. She straddled the Tate and the Rahv factions, as did Lowell. She liked and understood poetry much better than Stafford ever did and felt easier with the people who wrote it. She was only too glad to share what Stafford contemptuously called Cal's "very fabulous life"—the growing fame that followed the Pulitzer Prize, the contacts with august figures such as Eliot, Pound, Frost, George Santayana, the high-profile political involvement, the sense of momentousness and authority that flowed from the name Lowell. The fact that madness was part of the bargain did not at first trouble her, for how could she know that this demon would be with her for the next twenty years? She wanted Lowell and everything he accomplished and stood for and had access to. She loved him and she loved his mind, his sane mind anyway. Though she was thirty-two when they crossed paths again at Yaddo in the fall of 1948, Hardwick was still young enough to be swept off her feet by the attentions of Robert Lowell. And in the early stages of love, Lowell could be very attentive indeed.

Lowell was up at Yaddo to complete his long, tortured narrative poem *The Mills of the Kavanaughs*—my "immense Maine-Catholic-dramatic narrative" he called it—and Hardwick was one of the few writers in residence who amused him. He was especially delighted to discover in her a fount of gossip about Tate's hyperactive love life: as he wrote Elizabeth Bishop, Hardwick's tales summoned up "those days—when it was glorious and horrible to be alive—of the Tate divorce." (The "days of the Tate divorce" were brief: the couple remarried after only three months and stayed married for thirteen more years, then they divorced again and for good.) Lowell told Peter Taylor that "Miss Hardwick" struck him as "slip-shod, good humored, malicious (harmless), and humorous—full of high-spirits rattling a lot of sense and sheer stuff—very good company." Before Hardwick left, Lowell got her to agree to return to Yaddo after Christmas. But, as it turned out, they had another brief encounter before the holidays. Early in November, a crowd of high-powered poets de-scended on Bard College for a weekend marathon of readings and talks. Lowell and Elizabeth Bishop, in the first flush of their almost romance, attended, as did Richard Wilbur, Louise Bogan, William Carlos Williams, Jean Garrigue, Richard Eberhart, James Merrill, and Kenneth Rexroth. Mary McCarthy was also on the scene, and so was Hardwick for some reason.

The event generated a famous, though possibly apocryphal, story of the Lowell-Hardwick courtship: on Saturday night, Lowell drank so much of the lethally spiked punch that he needed an escort back to his room, and Hardwick and Bishop shouldered the burden together. When they got him into bed, Hardwick loosened his tie and opened his shirt, then stood marveling at the recumbent figure. "Why, he's an Adonis," she supposedly murmured. Bishop told James Merrill that she realized at that moment that Elizabeth Hardwick was going to be "the next Mrs. Lowell." "This is the outcome of Cal's helplessness," Bishop remarked with some astringency. "Someone will move in and take him over."

Helplessness—a myopic incapacity for anything practical, domestic, or nonliterary—was one facet of Lowell's character. Another facet, one that opened out alarmingly when he was in the throes of mania, was an overwrought, domineering fanaticism. Soon after Hardwick rejoined Lowell at Yaddo in January 1949, this fanatical side took over and fixated on Yaddo's director, Elizabeth Ames. Lowell concluded on the basis of paltry but not implausible evidence that Mrs. Ames was a Communist sympathizer who had been harboring Communists at Yaddo, including Agnes Smedley (accused by U.S. Army higher-ups of being a Soviet spy but ultimately cleared of this charge). With Hardwick's loyal support, Lowell launched a vigorous anti-Ames campaign, demanding her resig-nation and threatening to involve his powerful New York allies (Rahv and the *PR* crowd) if the Yaddo board failed to take swift action. FBI agents appeared at Yaddo to investigate, though Hardwick insists that

Lowell had nothing to do with them: "It's untrue that Cal called the FBI. I spoke to the agent but Cal did not. He is wrongly blamed." The uproar that ensued polarized the literary community. Eleanor Clark, John Cheever, Alfred Kazin, and Katherine Anne Porter, among others, rose to Ames's defense. Angry petitions circulated. Ames retreated to a nursing home. Yaddo, in the words of Malcolm Cowley, "was left like a stricken battlefield."

Lowell and Hardwick promptly decamped for New York, but Lowell kept blazing away in the city—"shooting sparks in every direction," as a friend put it. He went to mass for the first time in months. He plagued his friends with phone calls and telegrams about the burning need to fight the twin evils of communism and the Devil. He was "wound up," sleeping little, talking too much and too loudly, in love but also obsessed with sexual purity—all clear warning signs of a descent into mania, though no one knew it at the time. Lowell suffered a serious blow toward the end of March when he lost the Ames campaign: the Yaddo board found the director innocent of wrongdoing. Lowell, stunned, became more overwrought. On March 26, he and Hardwick made another foray into anti-Communist politics at the Cultural and Scientific Conference for World Peace at the Waldorf-Astoria Hotel. The conference was essentially a rally sponsored by the Soviet government to demonstrate the vitality of the arts under a Communist regime. A. A. Fedayev, secretary of the Union of Soviet Writers, was in charge of the Soviet delegation, and, as Hardwick recalls, "they hauled out poor old Dimitri Shostakovich and propped him up on the stage." Lillian Hellman, Dashiell Hammett, W. E. B. Du Bois, Leonard Bernstein, Frank Lloyd Wright, Aaron Copland, Marlon Brando, and Howard Fast, among others, turned out to represent America's pro-Soviet arts community. Lowell and Hardwick infiltrated the panel on writing and publishing along with Mary McCarthy and Dwight Macdonald to present the "other side": they planned to disrupt the proceedings by demanding to know what Stalin had done to Boris Pasternak, Isaac Babel, and other dissident Russian writers. It was serious business, but carried out, says Hardwick, in the spirit of fun. According to the various histories and biographies, Sidney Hook, wise in the ways of political machinations, instructed them to bring along umbrellas to pound on the floor to attract attention and to bind themselves to their chairs in order to make it hard for the Stalinist goons to eject them. In the event, each was granted access to the microphone for two minutes. Lowell (who was not manic that evening, according to Hardwick) apparently used his time to identify himself as a poet, a Roman Catholic, and an anti-Communist. McCarthy engaged Harvard American literature scholar F. O. Matthiessen in a debate about Emerson and Lenin. Hardwick recollects that the Communists countered accusations of Soviet repression with their standard line about the persecution of blacks in the South. In short, it was the party line all around. The only deviation from the script came when the young Norman Mailer got up to attack both sides: "I don't believe in peace conferences," he declared. "They don't do any good. So long as there is capitalism, there is going to be war. Until you have a decent, equitable socialism, you can't have peace." The response to this, predictably, was loud booing.

The attempt by Hardwick, McCarthy, Lowell, and Macdonald to undermine the proceedings of the Waldorf conference was a sign of the times, an expression of the fervor with which the New York intellectuals would attack communism in the postwar era. The *PR* crowd, of course, had spoken out vociferously against Stalinism since the late 1930s. But this protest was different because the political climate had altered so radically in the intervening years. Back in the 1930s, Rahv and company had been left-wing rebels, attacking Soviet repression from a Marxist perspective and within a Marxist context. But by 1949, with a hysterical Red scare paranoia sweeping the nation, the distinction between the ideology of Karl Marx and Soviet-style totalitarian communism was forgotten: anything stained with red was poison. In a political arena dominated by Joseph McCarthy and the House Un-American Activities Committee, liberal intellectuals who spoke out against the Soviet Union found themselves in uneasy alignment with the knee-jerk better-dead-than-Red fanaticism of Middle America. Or in some cases not so uneasy. As Rahv wrote presciently in 1952 at the height of the anti-Communist witch-hunts, the "ex-radicals and ex-Marxists, who have gone so far in smoothly readapting themselves, in unlearning the old and learning the new lessons" are now "scarcely distinguishable from the common run of philistines. . . . The old anti-Stalinism of the independent Left . . . has lost its bearings, continuing to denounce the evils of communism with deadly sameness and in apparent obliviousness of the fact that in the past few years anti-Stalinism has virtually become the official creed of our entire society."

What Rahv was describing was the emergence of "liberal anticommunism" as the dominant postwar political creed of the New York intellec-

tuals. It was, as Rahv suggests, liberalism hiding behind conservative protective coloring, and in many cases it ended up becoming indistinguish-
able from conservatism—and eventually, as many liberal anti-Communists
set themselves up as neoconservative pundits, even more conservative
than conservatism. Liberal anticommunism was a kind of mass amnesia,
a tacit agreement among a generation of intellectuals to shed their recent,
embarrassing, and unprofitable political past and join the mainstream. As
Alan M. Wald writes in *The New York Intellectuals: The Rise and Decline
of the Anti-Stalinist Left from the 1930s to the 1980s,* "[T]he postwar envi-
ronment—filled with disappointments and fear as well as opportunities
for new careers in publishing and academe—precipitated the final stage
in their collective change of political allegiance. . . . In the Cold War atmosphere the careful distinctions that the New York intellectuals had
once made between criticizing Communism from the left and criticizing
Communism from the right tended in some cases to dissolve into epithets
that equated the Soviet Union with Nazi Germany." It was the era when
being "soft on communism" was the ultimate political sin. Diana Trilling,
one of the leading lights of liberal anticommunism, caused a sensation by
standing up at a party to declare, "There's not a man in this room who's
hard enough for me!" "I had to flee the room before I burst out laughing,"
recalls Jason Epstein, "but the funny part was that no one else was even
smiling. It passed them right by." Ambition and greed played a part in this
turn rightward, for the U.S. government generously (though often
covertly) rewarded anti-Communist intellectuals, especially former Marxists, with grants, appointments, travel stipends. Both sides profited: the
government got excellent press in the most prestigious journals from a
formerly dissident faction, and the cooperating intellectuals found themselves with more money and stimulating professional opportunities than
they had dreamed of back in the grubby 1930s. Of course there were embarrassment and finger-pointing when some of these subsidies and funding arrangements came to light in the 1960s. But by then it was too late:
the New York intellectuals had been pushed to the margins of the culture,
and liberalism had withered away to something flabby, formless, and uni-
versally reviled.

Elizabeth Hardwick, in an essay about sociologist David Riesman,
breathlessly evokes the euphoria her generation felt in espousing its new
all-American political credo and enjoying the country's newly minted
riches just after the war:

Our prosperous, unique, odd society was wild, we felt, but splendid, too, like a run-away horse. Right after the war, the therapy for all our moral discomforts was a daily recital of the sins of Communism and the Soviet Union and the subsequent healthy enjoyment of our own virtues, or at least of our absent sins. Nothing much was asked of us beyond that, no other sacrifice beyond reminding ourselves how good we were as a people and a system and that we did not need to suffer the infection of despairing self-criticism. These easy days did not last long. . . . Sometimes one has the feeling of an almost supernatural character to the shifts and changes in our national mood. They appear beyond the prose of cause and effect; to live through them is to know the ineffable pain and fascination of tragedy. It was such a short, short time.

For Hardwick, there was an urgent, intimate subtext to these "almost supernatural" political shifts and changes. For this "short, short time" of blissful, self-righteous anticommunism coincided with the extraordinary drama of her "engagement" and marriage. She had never been involved in anything quite like it—though "involved" does not cover the depth of her entanglement in the surreal pageant of Lowell's mania. Lowell may have been rational and composed the night of the Waldorf conference, but within weeks he had become violently delusional. Leaving Hardwick behind in New York, he embarked on a kind of crusade to chastise and stir up old friends in the heartland. First he descended on the (remarried) Tates in Chicago and immediately opened old wounds by reeling off the lengthy list of Allen's lovers. In a fit of insane inspiration, Lowell suspended Tate outside a second-story window while reciting Tate's most celebrated poem, "Ode to the Confederate Dead." Tate, once he'd gotten Lowell off his hands, wrote furiously to Hardwick that Cal was suffering from "a purification mania, which frequently takes homicidal forms."

Next stop was Bloomington, Indiana, for a visit with Peter and Eleanor Taylor. By now Lowell was totally out of control. Eluding Peter Taylor, he embarked on a rampage that ended when he assaulted a police officer at a movie theater, whereupon he was beaten by another policeman, straitjacketed, and locked up in the Bloomington jail. Lowell's mother, accompanied by faithful Boston psychiatrist and poet Merrill Moore, flew out from Boston and took him back to Baldpate, a small private mental hospital north of Boston. He remained there through early July, three months in all. On July 28, a little more than two weeks out of the hospital, Lowell married Hardwick in a small (non-Catholic) ceremony held at his parents' home outside of Boston. The Tates were absent this time; instead Lowell had Frank Parker as his best man. Mary McCarthy stood up in a chic black dress as Hardwick's maid of honor.

Marriage did not bring tranquillity. Lowell remained depressed and shaky, and by September he had to be hospitalized again, this time in New York's Payne Whitney, the mental hospital where Stafford had spent so many agonizing months when their marriage broke up. "[M]ornings, the unbearable; afternoons, the numb," he wrote Hardwick of his days in the ward. It was nearly Christmas before he was discharged.

Neither of them had any idea how familiar this pattern would become: the "gruesome, vulgar, blasting surge of 'enthusiasm,' " as Lowell later described his manic phase, "[when] one becomes a kind of man-aping balloon in a parade—then you subside and eat bitter coffee-grounds of dullness, guilt, etc." Despite therapy, medication, electric shock, and a succession of psychiatric treatments, the "attacks" came nearly every year, usually at the onset of winter, and progressed along the same worn tracks. Almost invariably, Lowell latched onto a woman during the "surge of 'enthusiasm.' " He would proclaim his love publicly and passionately. Hardwick, the wife, represented everything he loathed and needed to escape. His new love would make it all better. They would marry and start a new life together. But first he must phone everyone he knew in the middle of the night, roam the streets, start fights, shout from windows. At some point, Hardwick usually had to call the police. There was the ritual of the straitjacket. The exaggerated charade of humoring "Mr. Lowell" to come along quietly. Then the hospital, the Thorazine, the "bitter coffee-grounds of dullness, guilt," the weeks or months of shame and inertia and forgetfulness. And finally the slow painful climb back to sanity. It began in 1949 and it lasted for the rest of his life.

How, one wonders, did Hardwick stand it? "I didn't know what I was getting into," she said later, "but even if I had, I still would have married him. He was not crazy all the time—most of the time he was wonderful. The breakdowns were not the whole story. I feel lucky to have had the time—everything I know I learned from him." And two decades after Lowell's death, she remarked, "Of course I suffered a good deal in the alliance, but I very much feel it was the best thing that ever happened to me." A telling passage. She really did admire him, even after the first lovely illusions burned away. But she also knew how to manage him, at least when he was sane. It wasn't a matter of cringing wifely docility; Hardwick was never the type to fade gracefully into the background. She loves to talk and argue and gossip and laugh hard at a good joke. With Lowell, she could and did hold her own, emotionally and intellectually. She didn't submit to him, she didn't spare him, but she did defer to him, perhaps most of all in her own mind. It may have been part of her heritage from the "traditional South" to think of herself as being in a "woman's place" and to make a virtue of it—feminine wiles, in the mean old sexist phrase. From somewhere she found the strength and the wit to keep the marriage going. "Her head was screwed on perfectly tight," remarks Frank Parker. "She didn't want to give up Lowell."

She was *so tough,* everyone says in amazement as they look back over the decades of insanity and infidelity: tough and tough-minded. She had no illusions about herself. She controlled her ambitions or kept them under wraps. It's commonly said that she married Lowell for the prestige, for the boost to her own status, but in fact she swiftly realized how little she stood to gain professionally from a prominent literary marriage. She might move in a wider circle, command greater "clout"—but the trade-off was that a lot of people took her less seriously. Being "Cal's wife" was a notch down from being Elizabeth Hardwick; no one thought to rechristen him "Lizzie's husband." "I had started writing before I was married to Lowell, but I was not interested in having a reputation of my own," she insists now. "I had more reputation once he left me. I worked harder. Only inferior people are always thinking of their role and whether they're getting enough attention. I find that degrading." She told an interviewer in 1979 that she "never felt competitive" with Lowell, always assuming his was the greater intellect: "[I]t was a privilege to be overshadowed. I felt intense dedication to him, to his life, to his brilliance." "You can't be competitive with someone so gifted and special and dedicated as he was as a writer," she explained patiently to another interviewer. "It just didn't occur to anyone, especially to me as a wife, to be competitive with someone like that." And in response to yet another interviewer who asked if she felt "overpowered by Lowell's work": "Well, I should hope so. . . . Because I had actually such great regard and admiration for it . . . [and for] the quality of his mind, which was certainly the most exciting and the most extraordinary and deepest of . . . anyone I've ever been close to."

In this regard she was very different from Jean Stafford, who for all her conflicts over writing and "womanliness," cared deeply about her reputation, competed with Lowell, and resented the way he put his work before hers—and resented typing his work for him (something Hardwick scoffs at, pointing out that poetry doesn't require much typing anyway— though of course what Stafford really resented was not its volume but the expectation that she would take care of it). Frank Parker believes that Lowell rated Stafford's writing higher than Hardwick's and respected her more as an artist—but he came to despise Jean as a woman, and he did everything he could to control and reform her. With Hardwick he was only too willing to surrender control into her capable hands. "If you wanted it, you were in complete charge of everything with Cal," she says, laughing. "The money—everything." Marriage to someone as sane and competent and tough as Hardwick allowed Lowell to grow up at last. He relaxed and expanded under her caustic admiration. The fastidious Catholicism gave way to a disheveled urbanity and wicked, grinning charm. The mellowing of Lowell was not all Hardwick's doing, but she was definitely a major influence. She made him a brilliant wife, with enough brains to understand him and not take him too seriously. But brilliant as she was, during the two decades of their marriage, she was first and foremost a wife. Unlike Stafford, unlike McCarthy, unlike Caroline Gordon, certainly unlike Hannah Arendt, Hardwick maintained a front of modesty and offhandedness about her professional self. She preferred to toil out of sight, without obvious effort or large claims.

Yet this woman who found it "degrading" to think about her "role" as a literary wife chose so often as her subject the tortured literary woman—Sylvia Plath, Jane Carlyle, Dorothy Wordsworth, Zelda Fitzgerald, Charlotte Brontë—and the "text of the family" as the focus of her analysis. Not her own family—Hardwick was much too private and guarded to employ the confessional mode. (As she told her friend Darryl Pinckney when he interviewed her for *Paris Review* in 1985, "In general, I'd rather talk about other people. Gossip, or, as we gossips like to say, character analysis.") But in her most searching, lucid essays she wove in strands of her intimate knowledge of the lives of writers' wives, "gifted, energetic" women who devote themselves to "collaborating in the very private way of love or the highest kind of friendship" and who end up, always, perplexingly, shortchanged. Her essays form a covert autobiography tucked away in her confident, frankly personal, but unconfiding prose.

The marriage was inspiring and puzzling for Lowell as well. Inspiring artistically. Starting in the mid-1950s, his verse became increasingly absorbed in the relationship with Hardwick and in his various incarnations as husband, father, son, and finally ex-husband and new husband to another woman. Between *Lord Weary's Castle* (1946) and *Life Studies* (1964), the common deities of daily life—wife, child, parent, and above all the self in torment—took the place of Jesus and Mary. As Elizabeth Bishop wrote, Lowell's verse made "family, paternity, marriage, painfully acute and real."

This strange marriage, though it began most inauspiciously under the dark star of madness, turned out to be astonishingly enduring and, in its own way, successful. It certainly proved to be a boon to the creative life of both husband and wife.

"I leave the hospital on Wednesday forever," Lowell wrote Peter Taylor optimistically from Payne Whitney on December 29, 1949. He had secured a teaching job at the University of Iowa, and both he and Hardwick were looking forward to leaving New York—"anxious to get out of the dump we're in and into a new one," as Hardwick put it in a postscript to the letter to Taylor. Iowa, the first in a series of teaching appointments for Lowell, was a mixed bag for both of them. Iowa City itself struck Lowell as a "bare stretching gray place" and Hardwick as "flat and ugly," but Lowell rather warmed to teaching. He enjoyed the human contact and the captive audience of a classroom, and his students, for the most part, were enthralled. "Week after week we came away staggered under a bombardment of ideas, ideas, ideas," recalled the poet W. D. Snodgrass, an Iowa student on whom Lowell made a deep impression (and vice versa). Others noted Lowell's eerie and endearing tendency to treat all poets, living and dead, as colleagues—as if he had just been chatting with Browning or supplying Wordsworth with a verb moments before class. "Teaching is rather awful—boning up on what you can't use, then faking," he wrote Peter Taylor with false modesty. "My greatest success has been reading Burns aloud with a Scotch accent." Lowell kept at it for the next twenty-five years, guiding and grading and cajoling the poetic generation that came of age in the 1950s and 1960s: Adrienne Rich, Anne Sexton, Sylvia Plath, Richard Tillinghast, Frank Bidart, Helen Chasin, and Jean Valentine, among many others.

While Lowell "boned up," taught, and wrote, Hardwick immersed herself in a lurid local murder trial. As Lowell described it to Taylor, "Last November a girl was strangled, or maybe not. And now the trial—gruesome, blurred, silly, pitiful—sororities, fraternities, 'pinned,' 'chained,' 'they seemed happy' psychologists, Irish policemen—money, justice, and no good answer. Elizabeth goes eight hours a day as an accredited reporter for the New York Post, and has talked a book." She did, eventually, get a book out of it—*The Simple Truth,* her second novel, a fictional reconstruction of the murder and trial and its impact on two Iowa City residents who become fascinated by it, which was published in 1955. It took her three years of intermittent labor to finish (Hardwick was forever complaining of how slowly she wrote and how susceptible she was to interruption). Lowell seems to have regarded her efforts with a mix of bewilderment and condescension. As Hardwick prepared to give a public reading from the book in Iowa City late in 1953, Lowell wrote to Tate that the project was "rather tiklish [*sic*]" since "the victims are really the Iowa City mind." And he worried that the audience would "feel that both Elizabeth and her subject are mere prose," a feeling he more or less shared. "Mere prose" pretty much sums up Lowell's attitude toward his wife's work. Only poetry, in his view, counted.

For Hardwick, the lesson of *The Simple Truth,* if there was one, was that fiction was not her calling after all; she turned out a few more short stories during the 1950s and then pretty much abandoned fiction until the late 1970s. Perhaps the most interesting thing about this now-forgotten novel is that it presaged Hardwick's abiding fascination with gruesome, highly publicized murder trials: decades later she wrote memorably in *The New York Review of Books* about the Menendez murders (two wealthy young brothers from Los Angeles accused of brutally killing their parents) and less memorably about the O. J. Simpson trial. Thanks to cable television, she was spared the chore of sitting eight hours a day in courtrooms and instead, along with millions of her compatriots, absorbed the legal dramas comfortably, via live television coverage.

The single semester at Iowa was enough, at the moment, for both of them. Rather than settle into the responsible academic grind, Lowell and Hardwick decided to pull together what they had saved from Lowell's Iowa salary and the balance of a Guggenheim fellowship he had been awarded in 1947 and take off for a "frugal year abroad." Neither had ever been to Europe, and they were dying to feast on the old cultures, especially Italian. But the planned late-August departure was delayed by the death of Lowell's father: Commander Lowell died suddenly in the Beverly, Massachusetts, hospital on the day they were scheduled to sail. "Father's death was abrupt and unprotesting," Lowell wrote later in the poem "Terminal Days at Beverly Farms." And in an unpublished memoir he marveled over the swift, unheralded departure, "Not a twist or a grimace recalled those unprecedented last words to Mother as he died, 'I feel awful.' " Lowell and Hardwick spent about a month in Beverly Farms with the widowed Charlotte. Lowell remained calm and rather stoic about the loss: his vague, smiling, weak-willed father had always been a difficult man to get close to. The biggest shock was that the commander had failed to mention his only child in his will. Lowell inherited a small trust fund on his father's death, but that was all—no gold watch, no token of love or family pride. "He was not a suffering or heroic man," Lowell told Elizabeth Bishop grimly, "but rather as someone said 'happy-seeming,' . . . and deep under, half-known to him: apathetic and soured." Hardwick endured the month with her mother-in-law with characteristic grace and resilience. She would always cope better with her difficult in-laws than Stafford had—and the Lowell and Winslow clan liked and admired her. "She wasn't 'common,' " Lowell's cousin Sarah Payne Stuart wrote recently of the family's verdict. "She was opinionated, yet she had manners. And as my mother said, Charlotte knew Elizabeth would take care of Bobby." Hardwick herself recalls her in-laws murmuring appreciatively, "She's a nice little thing." "And I would think, Oh, yes?"

Lowell and Hardwick finally embarked for Italy on September 28, their craft a freighter bound for Genoa. "We lived like students, really hand to mouth," Hardwick remembers, although at thirty-four they were well beyond even graduate student age. They behaved a bit like students too, dutifully toting around dog-eared guidebooks and recording their awe and reverence in journals and letters back home. "It's overwhelmingly astonishing," Lowell gushed in a letter to Jarrell, "—so much that is harmonious, unbelievably wonderful, odd, unforeseen, varied. . . . It's like going to school again—I fill up on everything indiscrimently [sic], and hope it will settle." They spent the first delirious autumn months in Florence, where it rained a lot. Like scores of their compatriots, from Henry James to Allen Tate and Caroline Gordon to Mary McCarthy, the Lowells paid homage to Bernard Berenson at his villa, I Tatti. Hardwick, unimpressed, later wrote in a caustic essay that "you had the belated feeling you were seeing the matinee of a play that had been running for eight decades." There were awkward encounters with the local literati—in Hardwick's words "several sweaty, mute evenings of language difficulty" with the Italian poet Eugenio Montale "and great displays of blundering affection." They had lots of free unstructured time on their hands, and they pondered and toyed much over the questions of where to go next, how to live, whether to join the expatriate colonies permanently. Here is Hardwick again, sounding perhaps more world-weary than she felt, in the essay on Berenson: "The possibility of escape never entirely deserts the greedy dreams of the 'self-employed.' It flares up and dies down, like malaria; it is a disease arrested, not cured, a question without an answer. The thought that one might himself settle far, far away gives a kind of engrossing sub-plot to one's travels." Late in November they traveled to Rome, for Lowell was eager to meet the aging New England philosopher-novelist George Santayana, with whom he had been exchanging letters. The brief visit yielded "no new impressions," Lowell confessed, "except that, in this post-War era, the Roman ruins looked at last contemporary."

The other discovery they made that winter was how difficult it was to be together so much and so unrelievedly, stranded in a foreign land, relying almost entirely on each other for conversation and diversion. The strains surfaced by late winter—bouts of heavy drinking, raw-nerved hangovers, quarrels. In the spring of 1951 they embarked on a long swing through Turkey and Greece and then proceeded on to Venice, Vienna, and Paris. In a letter to Bishop, Lowell made a list of all the cities they'd covered and then confessed that the summer had in fact passed in "a tremendous whirl—like going through college and graduate school in one year on pills that prevent your sleeping at night." Late in the summer, Lowell's mother arrived for a protracted visit. As their second European winter loomed, Lowell announced his intentions: they would settle in a northern clime—preferably Holland—a place with recognizably wintry weather, removed enough from the main tourist avenues so they could write in peace but not so remote that they would "drown in ourselves," as he put it, and, above all, not Catholic. Hardwick, who had been looking forward to another winter in Italy, was appalled. But Lowell was adamant. In a situation straight out of Henry James, Lowell and his mother holed up in the resort town of Pau in the French Pyrenees while Hardwick, miserable, frightened, and alone, trekked north to Amsterdam to seek out suitable winter quarters. Judging from the letters they exchanged, their parting had been bitter, teetering on a breach. Lowell admits that their recent relations have been a "snarl of confusion, squabbles and inertia" but promises this will change. He's dreaming "with anguish . . . of sunlit rooms, busy, perceptive, productive days and calm and joy between us." Three days later, sheepish, tongue-tied, he backs off a little: "It comes over

me that I mustn't give you orders. I have been pressing in that direction almost to the point of madness. . . . Our marriage or you are/is the only opportunity I want." Nonetheless, orders or no, he prevailed. Hardwick
dutifully found the quarters that her husband wanted, and he promptly
left his mother and joined her in Amsterdam.

It proved to be a strange, damp, cocoonlike winter. They spent most
of the time immersed in books; Lowell, on a World War II jag, read
straight through all twenty volumes documenting the Nuremberg trials
and devoured Hannah Arendt's recently published *The Origins of Totalitarianism*. They acquired some Dutch friends. They fell in love with
opera. And, as winter wore on, they quarreled. Lowell confessed ruefully
to Peter Taylor that "During the . . . rain-every-day months we both suffered from the spleen and mastered . . . every wrincle [*sic*] of domestic argument and sabotage." And in a letter to Bishop he quotes Hardwick's
grim pronouncement on the married life: "The only advantage of marriage is that you can be as gross, slovenly, mean and brutally verbose as
you want." Years later, in her autobiographical novel *Sleepless Nights,*
Hardwick looked back in wonderment at this gloomy, intense season of
their lives: "From Holland I wrote many complaining letters. . . . How
cold the house is. How we fight after too much gin, etc., etc. Complaining letters—and this one of the happiest periods of my life. . . . At night,
feeling uprooted because so much was familiar, we would tell each other
the story of our lives. The downy, musty embrace of the bed set us
afloat, not as travelers, but as ones somehow borne backward to the
bricks and stuffs of youth."

It was a relief, especially to Hardwick, when the seven-month Amsterdam adventure ended. Spring took them down to Paris for an international writers' conference on totalitarianism and twentieth-century art,
with many American friends in attendance, including Allen Tate and
Katherine Anne Porter. Despite their pleasure in spinning around Paris
with Tate, neither Lowell nor Hardwick could resist taking potshots at
him. Lowell observed wryly that his former mentor had recently jumped
on the Catholic bandwagon, though the conversion, far from reforming
Tate, had only "freed [him] from all his inhibitions." "Tate's Catholicism
was a joke," Hardwick insists. (Gordon, however, who had converted in
1947, would always be in deadly earnest about Catholicism—as fanatical
in her way as Lowell had been.)

Summer set them wandering again, this time to the German-speaking
countries—a boat trip down the Rhine followed by a three-week stint in

operatic Vienna. By early July they were in Salzburg, where Lowell was to teach for six weeks at the Salzburg Seminar in American Civilization. It was here that trouble caught up with them. All the warning signs of an incipient psychotic episode surfaced: Lowell was "speeding up" again, racing from classes to musical performances to interviews to boozy celebrations, and he was madly in love with another woman, a young Italian music student named Giovanna Madonia. The breakdown was, by Lowell's standards, mild and brief. After only a few weeks in a mental hospital, Lowell was well enough to travel, and the couple sailed home to America soon after, arriving in New York on January 19—the beginning of the Eisenhower era. Their immediate plans were to return to Iowa City for two more semesters and then look around for something more permanent.

Hardwick had congratulated herself on steering Lowell so smoothly through the Salzburg episode, but it turned out her relief was premature. Lowell returned to Italy alone in February 1954, when his mother died suddenly of a stroke in Rapallo, and in the excitement and sad confusion of arranging to take her body back home, he began to unravel again. In Milan, he looked up Giovanna Madonia, and his feelings for her came back in a blasting surge. By March, back in the States, he was writing Taylor that he and Hardwick were separating—Hardwick was going to New York, he was to teach in Cincinnati. "There are no 'sides.' There's no great story to tell; we just exhausted each other. I more than Elizabeth, but we both did." But in fact there *was* a story. Madonia, Lowell now told anyone who would listen, was the great love of his life; for nearly two years he had been "waiting half-dead" to be reunited with her. Hardwick was all wrong for him, had been all along. Madonia would come from Italy, dispose of the husband she had acquired in the meantime, and marry Lowell. But before this could happen, Lowell slid off the rails into mania—speaking compulsively about Hitler, turning on friends and colleagues and setting them against each other, frequenting strip joints, blazing away at all hours with no sleep or food. This time the breakdown was protracted and serious. Hardwick came out from New York and had him committed to a Cincinnati mental hospital. He was subjected to the agony of electric shock treatment, but to little effect. In June he was worse and had to be moved to a locked ward at Payne Whitney. The initial diagnosis was acute schizophrenia. Later the doctors changed their minds and rediagnosed him as manic depressive, although as Hardwick, a veteran of his breakdowns, notes, "[H]e was never as clinically depressed as he was clinically manic." The discharge from Payne Whitney did not come until September, nearly half a year after he had been committed.

In the spring of 1961, having lived through more than a decade of her husband's mental illness, Hardwick wrote Mary McCarthy a long, extraordinarily revealing letter about "this business of Cal's" and her role in it. Lowell was in the throes of yet another manic attack with all the woefully familiar elements—the nonstop monologues, the uncontrollable energy, the love interest, the shattering anticipation of the new life. Hardwick had been through it all before, several times. Only now, in a sudden burst of illumination, she believed she had discovered "the key," the psychological explanation for Lowell's marital and sexual behavior during madness. And in her excitement, she poured it out for McCarthy.

Lowell's pattern, she explained excitedly, was to leave home and loudly proclaim his love for another "girl," making it look as though he was in the throes of a passionate love affair, whereas actually he was not having sex at all—neither with the "girl" nor with Hardwick. "These attacks are not explosions of uncontrollable sexuality," she insists, "but explosions of uncontrollable desire to repress sexuality." It's not that Lowell is impotent, but that in some way she doesn't quite understand the mania makes him fear sex and "wonder about himself." Boasting about his new "false" love affair becomes a way of hiding the truth from himself and from the world: that he is terribly afraid of women. Hardwick now sees that this pattern of abstaining from sex went all the way back to the the start of their relationship at Yaddo. With Stafford it was somewhat different, she continues, for "when the repressive urge, the fear, came on him, he had The Church and could practice continence. . . . [H]e didn't need to go mad."

It's a sign of how desperate Hardwick was that she wrote this letter at all, and to McCarthy, of all people, who was then on the eve of her fourth marriage. Hardwick knew perfectly well how frank McCarthy could be in person and how indiscreet in print, a quality novelist Thomas Mallon called her "radical candor." Hardwick must have understood the risk she ran of Mary's pouncing on this "material" and thrusting it into her next novel or short story. Secrets and lies, sexual betrayal and masquerade, the Catholic Church lurking in the background—it was right up her alley. But Hardwick felt she *had* to expose herself as the only way to clear her name of Lowell's manic slanders and rehabilitate herself from the "most awful sense of sexual humiliation" that he had inflicted. Perhaps she chose McCarthy as her confessor because of their own overlapping sexual histories—partners they had shared or passed on to each other "as if there weren't enough desirable men to go around," as Carol Brightman puts it, "or enough women of their caliber to save them the awkwardness of sharing lovers." Hardwick wanted McCarthy, of all people, to know the truth, or at least her side of it. Though in fact it was not the truth. Hardwick was lying or deceiving herself about the manic affairs: Lowell *did* consummate at least some of them, and some of the women have spoken of him as a sensitive and passionate lover. Hardwick, clearly, did not want to face this—or couldn't. She needed McCarthy to understand that she was not the castrating "mother" who withheld sex and drove her frustrated husband into the willing arms of younger women. Rather, she was the baffled victim, the wronged wife who was herself deprived of sex whenever Cal's "purification mania" seized him. Jean was comparatively lucky: it had been the Church instead of manic depression in that marriage and Lowell at least had been faithful to her in his fashion. There was no "Mary Magdalene" in the picture yet. That pattern would begin with Hardwick. And it continued for as long as the marriage lasted.

Yet she stood by him. She wrote to a friend during the 1954 breakdown (the Giovanna Madonia one) of the "dread" she felt at having to go through "all these months and months of agony" when Lowell suffered his next relapse. But she never did anything. Part of it was that, despite the "torture," she never ceased to love and admire Lowell and to love being married to him. As she wrote to McCarthy, "the most desolating fact is that Cal and I have, by some strange miracle, a good marriage and great love for each other, except in these manic months and just before they come on." But part of it had to do with her sense of herself as a woman and a wife. For all her liberal-left politics and promiscuous young womanhood in New York, Hardwick harbored an old-fashioned, conservative ideal of duty and decorum. She was the responsible one, loyal, forgiving, willing to put up with and "take" a lot. Being a wife was something she treated seriously. She had a "by now arcane notion of fidelity," writes Hilton Als in *The New Yorker.* "Hardwick had chosen Lowell, and she accepted responsibility for that." Hardwick once told an interviewer that she married "very late, even for a Bohemian . . . I was afraid of getting married, afraid of losing something."

But once she was married, she was even more afraid of what she would lose by ending it. Her female peers in the literary world tended to

marry over and over again or not at all: McCarthy racked up four husbands, Stafford three, Katherine Anne Porter also four; while Eudora
Welty, Flannery O'Connor, and Elizabeth Bishop remained unwed for
various reasons. But Hardwick married once and stuck with her choice
forever. Only Caroline Gordon, among her fellow female bohemians, re-
stricted herself to a single husband—but as an observant Catholic convert, she really had no choice. Religion did not figure in Hardwick's
loyalty to Lowell. As Tate wrote her, marveling at how she had forgiven
yet another marital slap, "You, as a Presbyterian atheist, have evidently
the compassion that we expect only of the Blessed Virgin."

In a curious way, Hardwick turned the emotional predicament of her
marriage into an intellectual position. In essays and book reviews written
during her years with Lowell, she scrutinized the social and economic
underpinnings of the married state, pondering its costs and rewards, uncovering the hidden agendas of wives and husbands, picking apart the
arrangements that couples, particularly smart, well-matched couples, take
for granted. Her most arresting, and disturbing, statements on the subject
come in a 1953 attack on Simone de Beauvoir's *The Second Sex*. Of
course Hardwick would hate the classic feminist tome: Beauvoir's argument that women are not *born* but *made* the way they are by male-dom-
inated social structures threatened the very assumptions and terms by
which Hardwick and her generation lived. "Are women 'the equal' of
men?" Hardwick writes in her review titled "The Subjection of Women."
"This is an embarrassing subject. Women are certainly physically inferior
to men and if this were not the case the whole history of the world would
be different. . . . Any woman who has ever had her wrist twisted by a
man recognizes a fact of nature as humbling as a cyclone to a frail tree
branch. How can *anything* be more important than this?" This all-impor-
tant physical inferiority explains, to her mind, why women's writing is
weaker than men's: deprived of the military campaigns, the "first-hand
knowledge of vice," drinking bouts, dueling matches, firing squads, pub
crawling, and "gross depravity, obscenity, brawls" that great male writers
engage in as a matter of course in their "experience of life," women simply have less to write about. "In the end, it is in the matter of experience
that women's disadvantage is catastrophic"—catastrophic, and yet, as she
insists paradoxically elsewhere, ultimately irrelevant to her own literary
career. Hardwick, like most of the recognized American women writers
of her generation, felt it was necessary to go on record stating that being
a woman was absolutely no impediment to her work or success. "Of all

problems writers have," Hardwick told an interviewer, "being a woman is the least grave." Welty voiced the same view: "All that talk of women's lib doesn't apply *at all* to women writers. We've always been able to do what we've wished." Stafford asserted that she had never "suffered from discrimination by being a woman." And Mary McCarthy laughed the whole subject to scorn: "As for Women's Lib, it bores me"; feminism is "bad for women in its self-pity, shrillness and greed . . . it induces a very bad emotional state." It's a "competitive ideology born of desperation." It was embarrassing even to think about whether women were the "equal" of men. The very question was absurdly irrelevant, these successful, re-spected, widely published women proclaimed—certainly irrelevant to *their* careers. Talent will out no matter what gender. In essence, the an-tifeminism of these exceptional women is an elitist, exclusionary posi-tion, rather like the staunch anti-Communist liberalism that the old Trotskyites and socialists embraced after the war. The "system" was working for *them,* so why knock it?

Hardwick cuts even closer to the bone when she tangles with Beau-voir over sex and marriage. Beauvoir's notion that "if it were not for the tyranny of custom, women's sexual life would be characterized by the same aggressiveness, greed and command as that of the male" is dead wrong in Hardwick's opinion. Men obviously want sex more often than women, and women, just as obviously, pour a tremendous amount of energy into making sure they don't get it. Woman, Hardwick seems to ar-gue in a particularly hot passage, is a "reluctant, passive being" by na-ture, and she "really has to be . . . wooed, raped, bribed, begged, threatened, married, supported," before she'll yield to "man's voracious appetite." "After she has been conquered she has to 'pay' the man to re-strain his appetite, which he is so likely to reveal at cocktail parties, and in his pitifully longing glance at the secretary—she pays with ironed shirts, free meals, the pleasant living room, a son." Isn't this the whole erotic history of the hopelessly unliberated 1950s in a single blistering sentence? A sentence more electrifying still when read in the context of Hardwick's own marriage, in which the husband "cut off all sex" and subjected the wife to the "most awful sense of sexual humiliation" whenever madness seized him.

This passage on sexual commerce, indeed the entire Beauvoir review, is at once savagely honest and supremely disingenuous—or perhaps merely self-deceiving. McCarthy acknowledged that in ridiculing femi-nism she was a "sort of Uncle Tom"—after all, she'd made it in a man's world, she could afford to sneer at these shrill, competitive, self-pitying, badly dressed "women's libbers." And so could Hardwick. They both enjoyed the privileges and exemptions of "the special case." McCarthy, whose own attacks on Beauvoir were more personal and more vicious than Hardwick's, shrewdly pointed out that the great French *écrivaine* had "made it" in the exact same way she herself had—"through her sex by attaching herself to this man [Jean-Paul Sartre]." At least *Mary* had the good grace not to squawk about it. Something about Beauvoir incensed McCarthy—her views, her standing, perhaps most of all her gender. As Carol Brightman notes, McCarthy devoted considerable energy and ink over the years to her campaigns against "female archvillains." Beauvoir was a warm-up for the coming matches against Diana Trilling and Lillian Hellman.

"Elizabeth has just finished a wonderful crucifying polemic on the Second Sexe," Lowell wrote to Peter Taylor from Iowa City on March 25, 1953. "She proves with all the eloquence of Shelley that no woman can ever be as good as a man. It's quite gone to her head she walks around with her nose in the clouds, and I am dirt under her feet. What man could ever have thought up anything so sensible?" Beneath the fond, sweetly patronizing teasing, Lowell is onto something. There was a certain power and superiority to be gained from proving that "no woman can ever be as good as a man"—the secret power of the wife who knew better. Hardwick had nothing to gain from equality, and she knew that too. Two decades later, after the women's movement of the late 1960s precipitated what Hardwick described as a "psychic and social migration, leaving behind an altered landscape," she retracted some of what she had written in her review of *The Second Sex*. "Women proved they could get drunk in the gutter if they want to," she says today, "so I was wrong about that part." But she still maintains that she finds the whole subject mostly irrelevant: "I'm a feminist, of course, but it's not my interest to look at things from the woman's point of view. You write as who you are." Hardwick had been one of the boys since the old *PR* days back in the 1940s, and she never really renounced her membership in the club. She'd always gotten too much out of it.

It's strange that McCarthy should have been so vehement in her antipathy toward feminists, for she, far more than Hardwick, lived the life of a liberated woman. "For my generation she was a kind of icon," remarks

New York Review of Books editor Barbara Epstein. "She was beautiful, she led a glamorous life, she was very talented—and she was a real professional. She got up every morning and wrote, and she seemed totally professional about her work. But she was not a preacher, and she would not describe herself as a feminist or use any kind of label about herself. It would have boxed her in. Anyway, feminism was less an issue for strong women." The novelist Alison Lurie writes of the example McCarthy set for younger women, "Before Mary McCarthy, if an educated girl did not simply abdicate all intellectual ambitions and agree to dwindle into a housewife, there seemed to be only two possible roles she could choose: the Wise Virgin and the Romantic Victim." But McCarthy managed to be "both coolly and professionally intellectual and frankly passionate." McCarthy would probably have taken exception to Lurie's opposition of intellectual ambitions and housewifeliness, for she prided herself on pursuing and succeeding at both. As her old friend Arthur Schlesinger, Jr. puts it in a fond reminiscence, "A truly liberated woman, she rejoiced in her femininity. She loved to cook, she cared about her dress, she had beauty, sex. All these things meant a great deal to her and she saw no reason to apologize for them."

"I've always liked being a woman," McCarthy told an interviewer. "I like the domestic arts, cooking and gardening. I like clothes very, very much. . . . [O]ne of the problems of a lot of feminists is that they don't like being women." The domestic arts and literary arts were not incompatible for McCarthy or other talented women in those days, says Schlesinger: "It was part of the full female existence."

McCarthy also liked being married very, very much—"she'd been married every day of her life," Hardwick says, with fond malice, "she never could spend a night outside." But unlike Hardwick, she didn't let marriage interrupt or sidetrack her career. Even the oppressive Wilson, as we've seen, proved to be more help than hindrance professionally, holding her to disciplined work habits and insisting on hiring a nanny so she could keep writing. Competition with Wilson may have been another goad. McCarthy knew that Wilson was the greater figure when they married—and when they divorced as well—but it galled her. Hardwick's remark that "it was a privilege to be overshadowed" by Lowell because of her "intense dedication to him, to his life, to his brilliance" is inconceivable coming from McCarthy. Indeed, Wilson accused McCarthy of seeking to "destroy" him as a writer, and their Wellfleet friend Katy Dos Passos reported to her novelist husband that McCarthy had "undermined

[Wilson's] work. She kept telling him it was worthless and getting worse." For her next husband McCarthy found someone who felt intense dedication to *her* life and brilliance. Bowden Broadwater, whom she married in December 1946, was Wilson's opposite: younger than McCarthy by seven years, tall, rather slender and boyish-looking, well dressed in crisp Brooks Brothers suits, unfocused professionally, bisexual or perhaps predominantly homosexual (something everyone but his wife seems to have known). After graduating from Harvard in 1941, he'd taken various editorial jobs in New York, including a stint at *PR,* but his true avocation seems to have been literary gossip. "Bowden was not nice," writes Brightman; "he had a fork in his tongue that could gore an ox." "A nasty wit—and a kind of social arbiter" is how *PR* editor William Phillips summed him up.

But that suited McCarthy fine. It was ideal for her after Wilson to have an adoring, waspish husband who was proud and supportive of her work and protective of her time. Broadwater arranged the domestic side of their lives so that her work would always come first. As Lionel Abel recalls, the talk around town was that McCarthy married Broadwater because "she needed a wife. Everybody noticed that her prose became more grammatical after she started living with Bowden." Perhaps more important, Broadwater had complete faith in his wife—her work, her superiority, everything about her. During the Broadwater years, McCarthy was the household's main breadwinner, and being out in the world made her tougher and more hard-boiled about her career—like Wilson. She was not the wife of the genius, "collaborating in the very private way of love," in Hardwick's phrase, but the genius herself. "I'm now convinced that the elementary duty of a writer, after a certain age, is to make money," she wrote Hardwick in October 1953, "enough to insure him against the daily heart-palpitations over the mail, which are *too* ignoble. Anybody who doesn't take this precaution, in my opinion, is not serious; all the good ones did, if they didn't inherit it or cotton on to a steady private patron." McCarthy used the masculine pronoun, but surely she was thinking of herself, hard up and married to a low-achieving, low-earning man, when she wrote this. Hardwick, on the other hand, explained that women of her generation "expected a lot of financial support" in return for the domestic work they did alone: "Women don't expect this anymore." McCarthy, antifeminist though she was, took pleasure in earning money herself. She was equally adept at spending it—on clothes, houses, furniture, food, travel.

McCarthy once praised Hardwick for looking "through the eyes of those wronged or not considered." But this was not her approach, either in work or in life. When she looked at "those wronged" it was never through their eyes, except when she herself was the wronged party. *Memories of a Catholic Girlhood,* considered by many her finest book, is one long hard lucid look at the wrongs done her in childhood after her beloved parents died. She sometimes puts herself in a bad light, and she is frank about her failings—pride, stubbornness, deceit, vanity, selfishness—but the narrative is suffused by a rosy glow of fondness. No one devotes six hundred pages to her first twenty-six years, as McCarthy did in her three volumes of memoirs, unless they find themselves the very best of company. When she scrutinized other women, however, especially the women she put in her fiction, she was merciless: no fondness, no rosiness tempered her zeal as she exposed their failings and vulnerabilities, their embarrassing fantasies and delusions, their self-inflicted wounds and well-deserved punishments. Think of the nameless wife in "The Weeds," the silly, fluttery little painter Dolly Lamb in *A Charmed Life,* all those wretched Vassar women in *The Group.* "Most of her women," writes one critic, "have internalized their inferior status, and are plagued by self-doubt, self-contempt, guilt, dependence, and competition with other women."

Hardwick and McCarthy were close friends, intellectual family, political allies; but there was a fundamental difference in the way they saw themselves as women, writers, and wives. A certain wariness, a shade of constraint existed in their relationship. Hardwick admired McCarthy but she also found her faintly ridiculous and overreaching. McCarthy, for her part, was not fully engaged by Hardwick or her concerns. McCarthy concerned herself with her intellectual heroes, most of whom were men. The great exception was Hannah Arendt.

After a false start following their quarrel at Rahv's party, McCarthy and Arendt decided to "end this nonsense" between them and become friends—shy, rather formal friends at first. It took a while for the relationship to warm into real affection. The first letters they exchanged concerned work—Arendt's note praising McCarthy for *The Oasis,* the savage little utopian satire that almost cost her her friendship with Rahv, and then, two years later, McCarthy's rapturous reaction to *The Origins of Totalitarianism,* which, she told Arendt, she "absorbed, for the past two weeks, in the bathtub, riding in the car, waiting in line in the grocery store." The book struck her as "a truly extraordinary piece of work, an advance in human thought of, at the very least, a decade, and also engrossing and fascinating in the way that a novel is." Nearly half a century later, Arendt's magnum opus remains "truly extraordinary," most of all for its originality. The rise of the totalitarian state—Stalin's Soviet Union, Hitler's Germany—was the crucial political phenomenon for this generation: this was what Rahv, Phillips, Wilson, Lowell, McCarthy, Kazin, Hardwick, Jarrell, all of them had to one degree or another been arguing about, writing about, and worrying about for almost their entire careers. Yet only Arendt dared tackle the subject of totalitarianism head-on and attempt to account for its nature in the twentieth century. As she explained in the preface to the second edition, she composed the book at the "first possible moment to articulate and elaborate the questions with which my generation had been forced to live for the better part of its adult life: *What happened? Why did it happen? How could it have happened?*"

Her approach was marvelous in its idiosyncrasy: she traced Nazi ideology back to the racism embedded in nineteenth-century European imperialism; she analyzed the peculiar place of Jews in European culture as pariahs and parvenus, the social "others" who deliberately blinded themselves to the political implications of their ambiguous role; she used figures such as Benjamin Disraeli and Alfred Dreyfus to make sweeping points about historic movements; she set the Soviet Union and Nazi Germany on a par as twin manifestations of the same "radical evil"—"the unpunishable, unforgivable absolute evil which could no longer be understood and explained by the evil motives of self-interest, greed, covetousness, resentment, thirst for power, and cowardice"; she identified the concentration camp as the crucial "innovation" of the totalitarian state, not just a convenient tool for the perpetration of political terror but the essential, defining institution of totalitarianism; she excluded, seemingly arbitrarily, huge swaths of history, ideology, theory. Marxism and economics are largely absent from the book; Russian history leading up to Stalin's regime gets short shrift. Isaiah Berlin, who once called her the most overrated writer of the twentieth century, claimed that she got every fact about the Soviet Union wrong.

Arendt did not write an evenhanded or nonpartisan book. But she did write an incredibly compelling and groundbreaking one. McCarthy was right to compare it to a novel: the quirky, intuitive structure, the unexpectedness of the movements from part to part, the emotional ferocity, and the austere passion that holds it together make it "feel" like a product of the kindled imagination. Kazin, once again, was acute in his assessment: "[Hannah's] conception of totalitarianism as 'the burden of our time' is powerful, a stupendous literary idea, like the structure of Dante's hell. No one else has recognized the essentially arbitrary, make-believe nature of the reality that Nazism and Communism alike have imposed on their submissive victims, and how much the essence of the matter is 'total domination.' . . . Simply as a vision of the horror visited upon our century, admitting the selective nature of the phenomena that fit into her theory, the last chapters are overwhelming, apocalyptic."

Lowell vividly recalled his first encounter with the book during that isolated, gin-drenched winter he and Hardwick spent in Amsterdam. "I felt landless and lone, and read Hannah as though I were going home," he wrote in a memorial essay after Arendt's death in 1975. "Writing when Stalin was still enthroned and the shade of Hitler still unburied, Hannah believed with somber shrewdness, like Edmund Burke, that totalitarian power totally corrupts."

Literary people have always been more enthralled by the book than philosophers or political scientists. Arendt, whose own political stance has been described as a blend of the revolutionary and the conservative, followed no party line and thus opened herself to attack from both sides. Leftists in particular jumped on her for failing, or refusing, to distinguish between Hitler's Germany and Stalin's Soviet Union. As Alan Wald writes in *The New York Intellectuals,* "Into the charged atmosphere of this historical moment [the early Cold War] came Hannah Arendt's book *The Origins of Totalitarianism* (1951), which among intellectuals in New York may have performed a conservatizing role. . . . The book could be read in such a way as to bolster the anti-communist hysteria of the 1950s, reinforcing the view that the Soviet Union was to be expected to behave as Nazi Germany had in the 1930s." Heightening the tensions of the Cold War was not Arendt's intent; in fact, she and Blücher were appalled by the Communist witch-hunts and repressive atmosphere of the McCarthy era. But the book took on a life of its own, independent of the author's intent or personal views. According to historian Alexander Bloom, *The Origins* became a "key foundation for the emerging liberal anti-communist ideology of the postwar years." Certainly it had a profound and lasting effect on the political thinking of Lowell, Hardwick, Mary McCarthy, and their crowd. The book launched Arendt in a major way. Both intellectually and socially she was now a very formidable figure on the New York scene.

Blücher was only intermittently employed during the years when Arendt was writing *The Origins* (roughly from 1945 to 1949). His primary occupation seems to have been to help his wife with the book: reading during the day at the New York Public Library, talking endlessly with her during the evening, gathering ideas and gossip from their tight circle of émigré friends. For Blücher, contributing to the book was a labor of love, and also a labor of desperation; according to Arendt's biographer, he was suffering from an "almost paralyzing melancholy" during these years, a depression precipitated by the situation in Europe (it "erupted immediately over the gas chambers," Arendt confided to a friend) and deepened by his own sense of aimlessness and disconnection in America. It was no coincidence that Blücher came suddenly to life again after Arendt's mother died in 1948. "While Martha Arendt was alive, Blücher was like a man in mental bondage," wrote Young-Bruehl. "After her death, he felt free; he charged out of the domestic prison." He experienced a tremendous surge of physical and intellectual energy—a "surprise attack of productivity," as he put it—and soon he found an outlet in lecturing at the Eighth Street Club (an informal artists' organization in Greenwich Village), the first step toward his distinguished teaching career in America. Blücher also, around this time, began a love affair with a younger woman—one of many affairs he pursued in the course of the marriage.

"Heinrich liked women, and he was not always faithful," their friend Lotte Kohler says delicately. Arendt knew about her husband's erotic life and kept up a calm, "philosophical" front, but Kohler believes that she was deeply hurt by the betrayals, particularly this one: "In her diaries from this time she jotted down thoughts on faithfulness and musings on the double meanings of the word 'true.' There was pain over the feeling that his thoughts and emotions were going in a different direction. It was particularly hard to be cast out of your own country, feel that you're lost in the world, that your only anchor is your husband, and he is being unfaithful to you. It's a terrible feeling if you're uncertain about your marriage." But according to Kohler, it never occurred to Arendt to divorce Blücher for his adulteries—a practice she found absurdly American. "Can you imagine getting divorced over a love affair?" Arendt demanded of Kohler whenever she heard of another foundering American marriage. To her "Old World" way of thinking, it was better to turn a blind eye than cause a marital rift. Better still was to be open, tolerant, honest. "These fools who think themselves loyal if they give up their active lives and bind themselves into an exclusive One," she declared to Blücher in a letter boasting of their own "unison"; "they then have not only no common life but generally no life at all. If it weren't so risky, one should one day tell the world what a marriage really is." "What a marriage really is," apparently, meant a philandering husband and a silently suffering, tolerant wife. Arendt herself seems to have refrained from love affairs; those who knew her well concur that she was a romantic, emotional woman but not especially passionate in a physical sense.

Blücher and Arendt remained devoted to each other after their own fashion, but from the 1950s on they led increasingly independent lives with long periods of separation while one of them taught or lectured or pursued research away from New York. They were never again to collaborate with the intensity and fervor they had brought to *The Origins of Totalitarianism*.

The publication of *The Origins of Totalitarianism* consolidated Arendt's position in the American intellectual world and brought her many new friends and admirers. Lowell, during his New York decade, spent many hours deep in conversation in the Blüchers' apartment. Hardwick used *The Origins* as the basis for an odious (and rather far-fetched) comparison in her review of *The Second Sex:* "if one is expecting [from Beauvoir's book] something truly splendid and unique like *The Origins of Totalitarianism* by Hannah Arendt, to mention another woman, he will be disappointed." Randall Jarrell told Arendt that he read the book "the day I got it" and assured her that "It's one of the best historical books I've ever read—if it doesn't make you famous, at least *moderately* famous, this is an unjust world." Lowell, McCarthy, Jarrell, Kazin, and Hardwick didn't always get on very well with one another, but after *The Origins of Totalitarianism,* they all became zealous Arendt partisans. She was the intellectual's intellectual, all the more prized for being Jewish and European. As Lowell wrote in a letter to McCarthy, "Hannah is really a Hebrew prophetess, a sort of Prussian Deborah. Still, I guess she's close to being the moral heart of the country."

Of course there were dissenters, among them Diana Trilling, who declared herself revolted by Arendt's "illegitimate pride" and insisted that Arendt harbored a deep strain of Jewish self-hatred, even anti-Semitism. Trilling also claimed that Arendt was "very promiscuous sexually" (though Arendt's friends and biographer deny this), and she was convinced that Arendt wanted to seduce Lionel. "She was incredibly rude to me," Trilling remarked, "far worse than Mary McCarthy was. I couldn't stand her stupidity, arrogance and condescension." Above all, Trilling could not stand the way Arendt naturally assumed male prerogatives. In Trilling's mind, Arendt stood for everything she hated about successful female intellectuals—self-importance, unscrupulous ambition, snobbism, and what she called a "defective sense of reality" in which work came before ordinary daily life. In her memoirs she praises William and Edna Phillips because "One could talk with [them] about an illness, a family crisis, a social dilemma and they knew what one was talking about." Arendt never stooped to such mundane solicitude, certainly not with Trilling.

The *PR* crowd, particularly the women, considered Trilling the epitome of fussy, self-righteous bourgeois bombast. She was always up on her high horse about *something,* especially some slight to her status, morals, or aesthetic judgment. As Kazin wrote in *New York Jew* about his one and only evening at the Trillings' apartment, "Diana had been writing book reviews for *The New Republic* before my accession and, on her most recent appearance in the paper, had without my knowledge been described in the contributors' box as 'the wife of Lionel Trilling.' Despite all my efforts to explain away this stupidity and to make amends, Diana fixed me with an unforgiving stare that was to last forever. She was a dogged woman and looked it, with a passion for polemic against all possible dupes of the Soviet Union that in the McCarthy era and the heyday of the American Committee for Cultural Freedom was to make her the scourge of all mistaken ill-thinking 'anti-anti-Communists.' " In a sense Arendt, McCarthy, Hardwick, and their pals were in the opposite camp from the Trillings inside the tiny, incestuous *PR* fiefdom. Arendt and company felt that Lionel might have been one of *them* if it were not for Diana. Not only did she burden a gifted man with her neuroses and phobias, she had the temerity to demand respect and consideration for her own gifts. The *PR* "girls" really did have it in for her. Diana Trilling was right when she complained in her memoirs that "Women, in particular, were likely to feel that I had enough good fortune in being married to someone as attractive and agreeable and distinguished as Lionel without, in addition, having distinction of my own. It has indeed been my impression that more envy has been directed to me than to any woman writer of our acquaintance, Hannah Arendt, Lillian Hellman, Mary Mc-

Carthy, all of them infinitely more successful than I, and that Lionel was the cause."

Trilling remarked disdainfully that Arendt and McCarthy "deserved each other," but in fact their relationship was so fond and sweet it robs the insult of its venom. Even though Arendt's American circle widened following the publication of her book, Mary McCarthy remained firmly at the center—the acknowledged "best friend," a role that took on new and deeper shades of meaning in the course of the 1950s. A 1954 exchange about "the ritual of doubt" in Western philosophy prompted McCarthy to confess that she felt Arendt peering over her shoulder as she wrote a racy scene in her novel *A Charmed Life:* "I have you horribly on my conscience every time sex appears. You are tugging at my elbow saying 'Stop' during a seduction scene I've just been writing. And your imagined remonstrances have been so effective that I've rewritten it to have it seem from the man's point of view" (this is the famous scene in which the character modeled on Edmund Wilson more or less rapes his former wife). By 1959 the women abandoned Descartes and compositional quandaries to plumb the depths of McCarthy's love life—an unhappy affair with a dishonest English writer, the breakup of her marriage to Broadwater, and the excited but complicated commencement of her relationship with James West, a U.S. foreign service officer in Warsaw (and later Paris) who would become McCarthy's fourth and final husband. In the many lengthy letters they exchanged over these intimate and often painful matters, Arendt is the wise, worried, forgiving, maxim-spouting, sometimes exasperated mother to McCarthy's fluttered, guilt-ridden, blazing, headstrong girl in love. Once McCarthy made up her mind to divorce Broadwater, Arendt found herself in the awkward position of go-between: Broadwater, in New York, cried on her shoulder, while McCarthy, in Europe, raged over his treachery in dragging his heels about the divorce. Arendt played her part with dignity and tact, soothing Broadwater into behaving reasonably, standing loyally by McCarthy without getting swept up in her "anger, disappointment, and incredulity" over Broadwater's stubbornness. It was the loyalty and protectiveness that McCarthy most prized.

The wrenching period of McCarthy's divorce, remarriage, and new life in Paris (in a rather grand apartment on the rue de Rennes) put the women's relationship on a different footing, especially on McCarthy's side. From now on they were confidantes, with all that implies. Theirs was a friendship that, in Carol Brightman's words, "border[ed] on ro-

mance; not sexual romance, but not entirely platonic either." William
Phillips agrees that there was a passionate, almost "love-like" aspect to
their attachment: "There was something girlish in their relationship, the
way girls attach to each other. They had a gushiness with each other." It's
hard to square this image with the graying, somber-eyed, middle-aged
Arendt (she was fifty-four in 1960) and the tough-minded, sharp-
tongued, disarmingly honest McCarthy. Yet Lotte Kohler agrees that
there's something to it: she recalls Arendt rushing about excitedly on the
eve of a visit from McCarthy, all but panting, "Tomorrow Mary is coming—my best friend!" "Gushy" or not, their friendship was indeed unique
in the nasty, seething world of intellectual New York. Arendt and Mc-
Carthy proved to be more considerate and protective, and certainly
kinder, in what they wrote for and about each other, than most husbands
and wives.

Their mutual protectiveness peaked in the early 1960s, during the
crises that followed the almost simultaneous publication of their most
controversial books: McCarthy's *The Group* and Arendt's *Eichmann in
Jerusalem*.

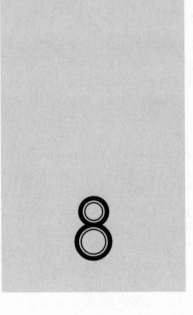

The Early 1960s: Firestorms

■ ELIZABETH HARDWICK once remarked that growing up in Lexington, Kentucky, she felt like "some provincial in Balzac, yearning for Paris." Instead she ended up with the next best thing: New York. Or maybe the best thing. Hardwick arrived in New York as a young woman and has lived in the city on and off for sixty years—a span that has taken her from *Partisan Review* in the war years to the founding of *The New York Review of Books* in the early 1960s and on into the era of Vietnam War protest, black power, and women's liberation. Hardwick experienced these cultural changes from the perspective of the New-Yorker-by-choice. For her, New York was everything, including a welcoming shelter, one that in her opinion was especially accommodating to women. New York is "a very good place for women," she once told an interviewer. "There is more work for you, more pay, and you are more free." With this attitude, Hardwick could only feel a sense of banishment during the years when she and Lowell lived in Boston.

The Boston chapter of the Lowell-Hardwick marriage in the 1950s represented a retreat into respectability, tradition, quiet, and stability.

They had been nomads for the first five years of their marriage, during which time Lowell had suffered four shattering mental breakdowns. The 1954 collapse—the one precipitated by the death of his mother and the affair with Giovanna Madonia—was especially severe, and the recovery painful and slow. When Lowell was finally discharged from Payne Whitney in mid-September, the couple decided that the solution to their practical problems and emotional tensions would be to settle down properly in Boston. Lowell had inherited some money after his mother died—$50,000 in cash and the proceeds from a modest trust fund—and with both parents now gone, Boston, the town he had abandoned in 1937 after socking his father in the face over his engagement to Anne Dick, was finally a *possible* place to live. Indeed, in Lowell's mind, it was a logical, eminently suitable choice. In Boston he had position, standing, *roots*.

Settling there took a while, for during their first Boston year they shuttled awkwardly between an apartment on Commonwealth Avenue and a large suburban house in Duxbury. But eventually they found a single dwelling that answered their needs: a nineteenth-century town house at 239 Marlborough Street in Back Bay, a block from where Lowell had grown up. Lowell wrote proudly to Elizabeth Bishop that the house was "rather Parisian . . . [with] white, neat, dainty Italian fireplaces, a lovely foyer, a sort of stream-lined Victorian." Quite a change from the grubby graduate student apartments and sagging faculty housing he had been camping out in ever since the marriage to Stafford. Lowell and Hardwick felt obliged, or perhaps inspired by ownership, to rise to the level of their new setting: they became, in Lowell's self-mocking words, "very pretentious and sociable, sort of Poobahs." Lowell rejoined the Episcopal Church. Hardwick presided over tasteful literary entertainments. "[W]e are somehow expected to do our part," Hardwick wrote her husband's beloved cousin Harriet Winslow (actually his mother's cousin), "and so we are always giving luncheons and cocktails for the visitors and actually enjoying it all," though she confessed to Tate that she felt "some bewilderment" over the "great splendor" of their lives. Randall Jarrell couldn't resist flicking a little mud at the newly resplendent Brahmin poet and his charming wife. He reported in a letter to Elizabeth Bishop that Hardwick (whom he disapproved of) was "very cordial, poor disingenuous thing, and Cal was joylessly being good, good, the properest Bostonian imaginable." Soon enough the Back Bay splendor would lose some of its shine.

In those years, Boston was fairly teeming with poets—Robert Frost,

Richard Wilbur, W. S. Merwin, Maxine Kumin, Donald Hall, Adrienne Rich, Sylvia Plath, Anne Sexton, and Philip Booth, among many others, were writing, teaching, studying, and publishing poetry in and around town then—and Lowell promptly took his place at the center of the "scene." He began teaching classes at Boston University in the fall of 1955, and poets both native and exotic peopled the Marlborough Street luncheons and cocktail parties. It was a busy, stimulating period, but not a productive one. While new verse was being written and read all around him, Lowell himself was in the midst of a prolonged poetic dry spell, a "slack of eternity" he called it. Since *The Mills of the Kavanaughs,* published in 1951, he had written very little poetry—"five messy poems in five years," as he told an interviewer—and now he was stuck. The old style, the triumphant "trumpet blast" of the *Lord Weary's Castle* poems, suddenly appalled him: "Their style seemed distant, symbol-ridden, and willfully difficult," he wrote later. "I felt my old poems hid what they were really about, and many times offered a stiff, humorless, and even impenetrable surface. . . . [M]y own poems seemed like prehistorical monsters dragged down into the bog and death by their ponderous armor." But he didn't know what or how else to write. So, during the first couple of years in Boston, he tried his hand at translations and prose— "delightful prose reminiscences of his youth," as Hardwick reported nervously to Allen Tate. At first, the autobiographical pieces were meant to be therapeutic, a coming to terms with his heritage and awkward childhood—"a sort of immense bandage of grace and ambergris for my hurt nerves," as Lowell put it—as well as an exercise regime to keep his imagination supple until the poetry flowed again. And then, suddenly, wonderfully, toward the end of the summer of 1957, new poems came pouring out of him. He was composing "furiously," Lowell wrote Bishop from Cousin Harriet's white clapboard house in Castine, Maine, spending "whole blue and golden Maine days in my bedroom with a ghastly utility bedside lamp on, my pajamas oily with sweat, and I have six poems started." "Skunk Hour," "Sailing Home from Rapallo," and "My Last Afternoon with Uncle Devereux Winslow" were among the six—poems in which the "ponderous armor" had been stripped off and the self, the "blear-eyed ego," laid bare. At some point in that season, Lowell fell on the pages of prose autobiography he had written and, as Hardwick recalls with some dismay, began chopping them up into lines—turning them into verse simply by putting them down on the page in a different way. "Cutting it down into small bits, I could work on it much more carefully and make fast transitions," Lowell later told an interviewer. But in turning the personal narratives into verse, he wanted to keep the looseness and freshness of the prose. "I couldn't get my experience into tight metrical forms. . . . I felt that the meter plastered difficulties and mannerisms on what I was trying to say to such an extent that it terribly hampered me."

In the new poems Lowell is quiet, lucid, almost eerily restrained as he monologues about the terrible things he's been through—the death of parents, recurrent insanity, family unhappiness, illness of the spirit beyond hope of cure or recovery. What's startling after the early books is the perfect clarity and accessibility of the voice: we know at a single read exactly what he's talking about. It's only on the second or third time through that we begin to puzzle over the imagery, the detritus of common objects and unnerving juxtapositions: ten dollars and a car key tied to a woman's thigh, garbage cans patrolled by skunks that "will not scare," his mother's corpse "wrapped like *panetone* in Italian tinfoil," a nuptial bed "big as a bathroom," a town house bordered by "a coffin's length of soil," weedy suburban sumac trees "multiplying like cancer" at the edge of his parents' last garden. *Life Studies,* as Lowell called the volume in which he collected these new poems, is a book of quiet desperation, its power arising not so much from confession as suppression. There are no shocking revelations or frantic outbursts here: the intimacy is in how intensely we feel Lowell's mind working, most of all to stay sane. "I myself am hell; / nobody's here, " those unforgettable lines from "Skunk Hour," might stand as epigraph for the entire book. Milton's princely Satan shadows these lines—"Which way I fly is hell; myself am hell"; but there's also an ironic nod to Whitman's "Song of Myself"—"I celebrate myself, and sing myself." (Lowell acknowledged in an essay on "Skunk Hour" that the stanza about watching for "love-cars" came "from an anecdote about Whitman in his old age.") Lowell is not singing but whispering, and celebration is the last thing on his mind. In this stripped-down poetic idiom the reader is not so much audience as eavesdropper; and the poet is not bard but fellow sufferer.

Life Studies, one of the pioneering volumes in what became known as confessional verse, was, in the opinion of Lowell's friend the playwright William Alfred, "as great as Wordsworth's *Lyrical Ballads.* It was as important a milestone." It marked a shift in style and stance as much as in subject. Lowell brought to verse the snapshot immediacy of letters or conversation or case histories. "Why not say what really happened?"

Hardwick supposedly asked her husband when he was groping for a new voice, a new mode of expression in the mid-1950s. Why not? That's a question, really a dictum, at the heart of a literary revolution that is still going on: *say what really happened,* the anthem of confessional verse, is now the fluttering banner under which our legion of late-twentieth-century memoirists and autobiographers march. The artifices of fiction "feel" false to us today. *Our* truth is personal, intimate, singular, and at the same time verifiable, shared, exposed, "out there." Truth is what happened to us that we can make known to others—in a word, confession.

It's hard to know what Hardwick thought of the two searing marriage poems in *Life Studies,* "Man and Wife" and "To Speak of Woe That Is in Marriage," the first addressed to her after a sleepless, tortured night on Marlborough Street—"All night I've held your hand, / as if you had / a fourth time faced the kingdom of the mad— / its hackneyed speech, its homicidal eye"—and the second, whose germ was a translation from Catullus, written in the voice of a frantic wife of a screwball husband, who "might kill his wife, then take the pledge." Not *her* voice, certainly, but a kind of funhouse mirror distortion of their marriage at its worst: "Oh the monotonous meanness of his lust." She must have known the poems intimately in draft, perhaps even memorized them, as William Alfred suggests, since Lowell was in the habit of reading his work repeatedly to anyone within earshot. "He always showed everybody what he was working on, certainly to me," Hardwick recalls. "You got it day after day." Stanley Kunitz, a poet friend and ally, notes that Lowell's "method of composition was uniquely collaborative. He made his friends, willynilly, partners in his act by showering them with early drafts of poems. . . . It did not seem to matter much, for the end-product always presented itself as infallibly, unmistakably Lowellian." So Hardwick was under no illusion about what was coming in *Life Studies.* And she can't have been pleased by the exposure—who would be? Although she defended the book passionately in a letter to Tate, who had thundered that the poems were "definitely *bad*" and too "terribly intimate" to be published, today she admits that it is "not my favorite." Some of the lines now strike her as "a little slack."

Lowell expected, and got, a good deal of consideration from those around him. He was "unaccountable," Hardwick once said, meaning not just unpredictable but not subject to an ordinary reckoning. Certainly, when it came to editorial feedback, he did not square his account with Hardwick for the "day after day" commentary she provided, nor did she especially want him to. Lowell "wasn't that interested in my work," she acknowledges. "He did read my work, of course," she told an interviewer, "and he was very encouraging, and nice about it, and all of that, but it wasn't going over each little part. . . . I didn't find his suggestions so useful; perhaps I should have." His most pointed and repeated suggestion, it seems, was that she was "too snippy" in her judgments, and apparently he asked her to tone down a few of her reviews, especially reviews of friends. William Alfred recalls a memorable pan that Hardwick wrote of a play by Lillian Hellman, who was an old friend of Lowell's: " 'Why did you ever let Lizzie bring out that review?' I asked Cal. And he answered, 'You can't stop her when she has that kind of streak on.' " Loyalty to Mary McCarthy may have had something to do with Hardwick's savaging of Hellman—or perhaps she was merely honoring her own critical standards. Snippy she remained.

In any case, Hardwick was not doing very much writing during the time Lowell was working on *Life Studies,* for in January 1957, at the age of forty, she had given birth to their only child, a daughter they named Harriet. Lowell was delighted to be a father, and by most accounts he was a benevolent if at times rather remote parent, in the classic paternal mode of the 1950s; Hardwick, on the other hand, even with the help of a succession of nurses and nannies, felt overwhelmed by the demands of a new baby. "I am exhausted," she wrote her friend Susan Turner in April. "My life is so taken up with chores I find it hard to know what I'm about." And in September, back in Boston after a summer in Castine, she complained that she was occupied from six in the morning to six at night "just on the baby!" a regimen she found "simply killing." In the throes of baby care, Hardwick may have forgotten her rather lofty views on the suitability of women to domestic duties in her review of *The Second Sex:* "A life of chores is bad luck. . . . In the home at least it would seem 'custom' has not been so much capricious as observant in finding that women are fairly well adapted to this necessary routine. And they must keep at it whether they like it or not." Several years after Harriet's birth, in a brilliant piece about Sylvia Plath, Hardwick was more sympathetic about the consequences of a "life of chores," especially the chores of child rearing. She dismissed as pure fallacy the notion that Plath, or any other woman, experienced a surge of artistic energy after becoming a mother. "The birth of children opens up the energy for taking care of them and for loving them. The common observation that one must be prepared to put off other work for a few years is strongly founded"—her own version of "confession."

Lowell's breakthrough in *Life Studies* ended, predictably, in madness. The mania erupted in early December 1957 with an act of domestic sabotage so perverse as to rank almost as absurdist theater: without telling Hardwick, Lowell telephoned everyone he could think of in Boston and summoned them to a crushing cocktail party at the Marlborough Street house. "Every time the door opened Elizabeth would look down and groan, because Cal had not warned her about anything," W. S. Merwin, who was one of the guests, told poet Peter Davison. She, of course, quickly realized what was really going on, and her ingenious stratagem was to enlist William Alfred to keep pouring stiff drinks so that the guests would not notice how "excited" their host was. And, amazingly, no one did. Edmund Wilson got so soused that he fell and hit his head on the floor. Robert Frost tried unsuccessfully to get Lowell to calm down. Hardwick, who had been drinking as much as everyone else, got into an argument with Merwin over Alger Hiss (a member of the State Department who had been accused by former *Time* editor Whittaker Chambers of participating in a Soviet spy ring), which Lowell did his best to inflame. As Merwin remembered it, Lowell came over while they were standing and talking, and "threw himself down, sort of pushing people out of the way, threw his legs up onto the coffee table, knocking off about twenty drinks, which got a lot of attention, looked up at the two of us, and said, 'Bill [Merwin] thinks Hiss was innocent.' " Hardwick started crying. Arthur Schlesinger Jr., glaring at Merwin, led her away. "That was Cal's doing the most mischievous thing he could think of," says Merwin. The whole "nightmarish cocktail party," as one guest called it, was a brilliantly cruel blow at Hardwick, at the marriage, at the temple of decorum on "hardly passionate Marlborough Street."

The breakdown that followed was one of the more harrowing ones for Hardwick: reluctantly, after a three-day sleepless marathon, she had to summon the police, who were rude and rough with Lowell. There were two episodes in McLean's (the Boston sanitarium for "thoroughbred mental cases" described with merciless realism in the poem "Waking in the Blue"), in the course of which Lowell fell in love with one of his "damned girls," as Hardwick wrote Cousin Harriet. He insisted that he wouldn't submit to treatment until he had been to Reno for a divorce. At one point Hardwick left Boston briefly to take refuge with Blair Clark in New York. Finally, three months later, Lowell returned home, "frizzled, stale and small" to wife and daughter. He documented the whole psychotic episode in *Life Studies,* yet another of the book's breakthroughs.

Hardwick, as noted, was writing little during these years, but she did find the time and energy for one memorable outburst, an essay about the cultural climate of Boston that she published in the winter of 1959. The piece is a glorious act of devastation, a perfect little bomb packed with her own inflamed feelings about this chapter of her life and marriage. Furious, but covert. She laid waste impersonally, satirically, from on high, very much in the spirit of Stafford's *Boston Adventure* (which she now singled out for praise, having derided it earlier in *PR*):

Boston—wrinkled, spindly-legged, depleted of nearly all her spiritual and cutaneous oils, provincial, self-esteeming—has gone on spending and spending her inflated bills of pure reputation, decade after decade. Now, one supposes it is all over at last. The old jokes embarrass, the anecdotes are so many thrice-squeezed lemons, and no new fruit hangs on the boughs. . . . Boston is defective, out-of-date, vain, and lazy.

How dare this shallow backwater style itself a center of culture, creativity, civilized appreciation? Compared to New York, dead and deadening Boston scarcely deserves the name of city: "In Boston there is an utter absence of that wild electric beauty of New York, of the marvellous excited rush of people in taxicabs at twilight, of the great Avenues and Streets, the restaurants, theatres, bars, hotels, delicatessens, shops. In Boston the night comes down with an incredibly heavy, small-town finality." New York is "cocktails, reality, life, taxis, telephones, bad connections" while Boston is "a culture that hasn't been alive for a long time."

What Hardwick leaves unsaid is her personal history in the two cities—for her, New York was youth, freedom, love affairs, *Partisan Review,* jazz clubs, and seedy atmospheric hotels, while Boston was middle age, literary luncheons, family furniture, Harvard professors, motherhood, and marriage to a man entering his second decade of mental illness. A nostalgia for the past suffuses the essay, as well as a sense of restless, bored disgust with the present—an emotional state familiar to many new mothers.

"Robert Lowell has done something very extraordinary," Edmund Wilson wrote after reading *Life Studies;* "he has made poetry out of modern Boston." In the essay she titled "Boston: A Lost Ideal," Hardwick made her own poetry out of modern Boston—a prose poetry of ridicule, rebellion, exposure, and revenge. Proper Bostonians writhed under her lashing, but this time Lowell backed her up, snippiness and all. Indeed, he gave voice to similar sentiments in his celebrated poem "For the Union Dead," which he wrote the following year. The poem records Boston's betrayal of its vaunted past: the monument to Colonel Robert Shaw, who died leading the Union's first black infantry regiment in the Civil War, is stranded in the wasteland of urban renewal ("Puritan-pumpkin colored girders"); World War II, the "last war," goes uncommemorated except for an ad showing a mushroom cloud "boiling / over a Mosler Safe, the 'Rock of Ages' "; the south Boston Aquarium Lowell loved as a boy is boarded up and abandoned. "The Aquarium is gone," Lowell writes dry-eyed in the final stanza. "Everywhere, / giant finned cars nose forward like fish; / a savage servility / slides by on grease." "Savage servility" is the stage that follows hard on the desiccation Hardwick described.

Hardwick insists that it was Lowell's idea to move back to New York in September 1960, but it seems unlikely that she objected.

They tested the waters in Manhattan for a few months that autumn, trading their Boston house for an apartment on Riverside Drive while they figured out whether to relocate permanently. By Christmas they had decided. They had found an ideal place to live—a "baronial" apartment, as Hardwick called it, in a turn-of-the-century artists' studio building on West Sixty-seventh street off Central Park and around the corner from the mammoth construction site of Lincoln Center. Grandly bohemian, the duplex apartment had a spacious two-story-high living room, four bedrooms, and a maid's room at the top where Lowell could work. It just suited them: more elegant than the dark, cavernous West Side apartments most New York intellectuals lived in, but a far cry from the plutocratic splendor of Fifth Avenue. The notion that the Lowells were rolling in money is false, especially by New York standards. With a trust fund and income from teaching and writing, they were well off compared to most writers, but hardly filthy rich.

After half a decade in Boston, New York was "like discovering . . . oxygen in the air," wrote Lowell, "—people to talk to, plays, opera, and something in the air that somehow makes the same people very different here from what they are in Boston." Lowell was moving in many different directions at once. He threw himself into translations of European poetry, and he secured funding from the Ford Foundation to study opera. He was seeing a lot of Stanley Kunitz and his old prep school friend Blair Clark. In January 1961, the Lowells received an invitation to attend John F. Kennedy's inauguration—a event that meant a great deal to Lowell. Lowell felt a strong personal connection to JFK: they were exact contemporaries, both Boston-bred, and had been at Harvard at the same time; they had friends in common, notably Blair Clark and Arthur Schlesinger, Jr., and shared at least some political ideals. "With a lot of reservations, I feel like a patriot for the first time in my life," Lowell wrote Elizabeth Bishop after the inaugural festivities were over.

New York brought the Lowells back into the orbit of Philip Rahv and what was left of the *PR* crowd. Ever the sardonic observer, Rahv couldn't resist spreading a little gossip about the rising star poet. "New York has gone to Cal's head," Rahv wrote Mary McCarthy around the time of the Kennedy inauguration, "—he's being feted everywhere as the big new name in poetry—but I don't believe that New York is good for him. It plainly overexcites him." There were both spite and truth here. By March 1961 Lowell was spinning into madness again. The breakdown followed the now predictable pattern, with one new twist: this time not only did he declare his intention of starting a new life with the young woman he had fallen in love with (a poet named Sandra Hochman), but he had actually found an apartment where he and Hochman could live together. This was the affair that inspired Hardwick to write the long letter to Mary McCarthy (quoted above) about Lowell's sexual behavior during madness. Two weeks after composing this letter, Hardwick announced to Tate that she was divorcing Lowell. And she actually took Harriet and returned to Boston for a while. Whether this was a calculated piece of strategy or an act of desperation, it worked. Lowell promptly broke with Hochman, and Hardwick "took him back" (a phrase she hated). The first six months in New York gave fair warning of what the coming decade would be like for them: fast-paced, lived on a public stage, emotionally turbulent, saturated with gossip, increasingly political, and riddled with mental illness.

The stage expanded notably early in 1963, when Lowell and Hardwick, together with their friends and neighbors Jason and Barbara Epstein, decided to start a new literary magazine called *The New York Review of Books*. As Jason Epstein recalls the moment, "We were sitting over dinner in our apartment. New York was in the midst of a long [newspaper] printers' strike and we were talking about what a relief it was not to have the *Times* anymore, and especially not to have the *Times Book Review,* which was even worse then than it has subsequently become. We all decided, *now is the time to do something.* It was like a Judy Garland movie." The idea was to fill the void left by *The New York Times Book Review* during the 114-day strike, but fill it with something different: not the reviews churned out week after week by "tired hacks, lame professors, breezy illiterates," as Jason Epstein snorted but hard-hitting, opinionated, learned, savvy, and, when necessary, lengthy reviews written in their own individual voices by "real" writers and intellectuals of standing. The Epsteins and the Lowells settled on Robert Silvers, a brilliant and highly regarded veteran of *Paris Review* and *Harper's,* to edit the new magazine along with Barbara Epstein. Jason Epstein assisted with publishing expertise and contacts, but quietly, to avoid conflict with his book-publishing commitments. Hardwick herself, billed on the masthead as "advisory editor," was from the first more staff writer than editor, although she also had a hand in assigning pieces and setting editorial policy. Lowell's major contribution was financial: he guaranteed the initial bank loan of $4,000 against his trust fund and helped line up wealthy investors, including his old friend Blair Clark, who put up $20,000 and kicked in $5,000 more when the magazine refinanced in 1965.

The venture was a terrific boon for Hardwick and an ideal outlet for what Lowell called her "wonderful energies." The energy required to get the thing off the ground was considerable. The *NYR* founders worked like mad to put out the first issue, lining up pieces from an all-star cast that included Mary McCarthy, Philip Rahv, Fred Dupee, Irving Howe, Alfred Kazin, Dwight Macdonald, Norman Mailer, Susan Sontag, Robert Penn Warren, Lionel Abel, John Berryman, and Gore Vidal. The articles, written gratis on extremely tight deadlines, descended on the editors in an avalanche. The first issue was pasted up during a round-the-clock marathon in the Lowells' dining room on West Sixty-seventh Street and hit the newsstands in February. In a brief explanatory note above the masthead, the editors declared that their intent was "to suggest . . . some of the qualities which a responsible literary journal should have" and warned that their writers would pull no punches as they set out "to reduce a temporarily inflated reputation or to call attention to a fraud."

The *NYR* put Hardwick at the center of New York literary life and gave her a reliable forum for her serious work (she published her slighter pieces, including film and theater reviews, in *Vogue* and *Mademoiselle,* presumably for the money). She now had some power and "clout," and with it came an irresistible temptation to make mischief. No sooner was the *NYR* off the ground than Hardwick used her newfound editorial muscle to tweak her old friend Mary McCarthy. The occasion was the publication of McCarthy's novel *The Group,* a titillating examination of the marriages, sex lives, birth-control devices, careers, ambitions, domestic interiors, dreams, and terrors of eight Vassar girls from the class of 1933. McCarthy had been struggling with the book off and on for over a decade, but her efforts paid off handsomely in the end. William Jovanovich went to press in August 1963 with seventy thousand copies, and the book perched on best-seller lists for months, eventually selling more than five million copies in hardcover and paperback. McCarthy was suddenly a "real" celebrity, both rich and famous, and her fellow intellectuals naturally responded by declaring open season on her. Ridicule (along with some rave reviews) came from many quarters; but no publication was more savage than the *NYR.*

In fact, the *NYR* editors saw fit to deal McCarthy a double blow: first, on September 26, 1963, they ran a parody of *The Group* called "The Gang," published under the pseudonym Xavier Prynne but actually composed by Hardwick; then, in the next issue, Norman Mailer's hyperbolic pan appeared as the cover story. Hardwick's piece was a stinging slap that zeroed in on McCarthy's most annoying verbal tics and silliest pretensions: "Maisie had always, rather demurely, thought of the great event as a 'defloration,' from the Late Latin, *defloratio.*" "She put on her Lord and Taylor bias-cut cocktail dress, (all the rage this year, just as Hitler was threatening to reoccupy the Rhineland)."

But Mailer's review was a hatchet job, steaming with rage and venom. "These piss-out characters with their cultivated banalities," he growled after running down the Vassar lineup. The premise of the book struck him as "a flaccid spring-board from which to jump into a major novel of the thirties." Like Hardwick, he took McCarthy to task for her snobby obsession with consumer goods and brand names: "The real interplay of the novel exists between the characters and the objects which surround them, until the faces are swimming in a cold lava of anality, which becomes the truest part of her group, her glop, her impacted mass." But he was far more savage about the author herself than about her work. "Our First Lady of Letters," the piece opens (the *Newsweek* reviewer had rather grudgingly bestowed this epithet), "our saint, our umpire, our lit arbiter, our broadsword." McCarthy's exalted, untouchable reputation was what most incensed Mailer, and he deflated it not with a pinprick but with a bludgeon: "[McCarthy] is simply not a good enough woman to write a major novel; not yet; she has failed, she has failed from the center out, she has failed out of vanity, the accumulated vanity of being overpraised through the years for too little and so being pleased with herself for too little. . . . She has been a very bad girl these years, mean and silly, postured and over-petted, petty in the extreme." It was the pan of pans: vicious, nasty, sexist, lowdown, and also quite funny. " 'Tis strange the mind, that very fiery particle, / Should let itself be snuff'd out by an article," Lord Byron wrote in *Don Juan,* spreading the myth that Keats had been killed by a bad review. Snuff-out by an article was exactly what Mailer had in mind for "Our First Lady of Letters."

McCarthy was, understandably, incensed and baffled by her treatment in the *NYR,* to which she was a contributor, after all. Mailer, she knew, was no friend and could be counted on to be outrageous—but Lizzie? The bitchy little parody was especially strange since Hardwick had written her in August congratulating her on the "tremendous accomplishment" of *The Group:* "I'm so happy to have this wonderful book finished and so happy that you will make money on it as we all 'knew you would!' Your long, brilliant career had to bear money fruit as well as all the real fruit." To make matters worse, McCarthy was convinced that Hardwick was the one who had given the book to Mailer to review. This was probably a misconception, fostered by Hannah Arendt, who had her own reasons for being angry with Hardwick. Robert Silvers recalls that it was actually *Lowell's* idea to pair Mailer with *The Group,* but this is difficult to fathom since Lowell *liked* the book and stood staunchly by McCarthy during the mud-slinging that ensued. Lowell and Hardwick both read the novel in Maine in early August, and four days after Hardwick penned her rather tepid congratulation, Lowell weighed in with a far more heartfelt and high-flying letter of praise: "I think you have done something I've always wanted to do, and never had the knowledge or slant to try—you show these cloistered, pastoral souls breaking on the real rocks of the times. What is troubling, shocking and hard to swallow about your story is realizing that we were so compact and ignorant,—dependable little machines made to mow the lawn, then suddenly turned out to clear the wilderness." Two months later, after the Mailer review appeared, Lowell wrote again to assure McCarthy of his solidarity with her: "Please believe I am your loyal friend and I hope a formidable one."

Hardwick, for her part, blushed furiously at being caught out as the author of "The Gang" but did not really recant. "It was meant as simply a little trick," she wrote McCarthy at the end of November, "nothing more. I did not mean to hurt you and I hope you will forgive it. . . . I don't know how else to express the sense of deprivation I would feel if this could not be put aside." But McCarthy was in no mood to forgive and forget. She wrote to Lowell (not Hardwick) in January 1964 that she was still angry at the *NYR* and still reeling from the barrage of publicity generated by *The Group:* "I can scarcely open a book, newspaper, or magazine without feeling like the president of a personal anti-defamation league." As for the "little trick" Hardwick had played: "Please give Elizabeth my New Year's wishes, good ones, I mean, not bad. That's the best I can manage just now. . . . I think it's easier to forgive your enemies than to forgive your friends, and that is not just a remark. With your enemies you don't feel a sense of betrayal, and what is at the bottom of a sense of betrayal but bewilderment—a loss of your bearings? I would not know how to act with Elizabeth yet; that is, I feel I would start acting falsely."

"What a roar, what a forest fire, of praise and abuse!" Lowell wrote McCarthy in his next letter about the fighting over her best-seller. It was a sign of the times, he felt, when "the entire Partisan Review world seems to be throwing bricks at one another." In a few years, the roar over *The Group* would seem very tame—indeed, *The Group* itself, which shocked Kennedy-era Book-of-the-Month Club types with its flying diaphragms, rough sex, and artistic lesbians, would, by the late 1960s, seem rather dowdy and old-fashioned. A great fissure was about to zigzag through American society, a fault line that buckled the ground beneath McCarthy, Lowell, Hardwick, and their generation. *The Group,* coinciding as it did with the Kennedy assassination, turned out to be one of the last works of the *ancien régime,* devoured with greedy curiosity for a season or two and then crowded out by a strange new creations. The wilderness that Lowell wrote of attacking absurdly with a lawn mower was about to shoot up all around them into rank, impenetrable jungle.

• • •

The "roar" over *The Group* was sweetly civil compared to the inferno of insult, accusation, denunciation, and pure hatred that raged over Hannah Arendt's *Eichmann in Jerusalem,* published that same year. At the height of the furor McCarthy and Arendt saw themselves, with some justification, as paired victims of vicious literary assassins and foul circumstances. "[W]hat surprises and shocks me most of all is the tremendous amount of hatred and hostility lying around and waiting only for a chance to break out," Arendt wrote McCarthy in the autumn of 1963. And McCarthy to Arendt: "If I am upset, I can imagine what you must be. And combining being upset for you and upset for myself has made my head spin. In this revolving door one is caught without an exit, and in this multiple vision—like a Picasso image—there is no cheek left to turn." In their first round of letters on their double ordeal, Arendt and McCarthy singled out Elizabeth Hardwick from among the many who had betrayed and disappointed them both. For it was Hardwick, according to Arendt, who had arranged the very worst reviews of their two books: Mailer's slam of *The Group* in the *New York Review of Books* and Lionel Abel's highly influential attack on *Eichmann in Jerusalem* in *PR.* "I am afraid that Elisabeth [*sic*] had the brilliant idea to ask [Mailer]—just as she had the brilliant idea to ask Abel to do the PR piece," Arendt informed McCarthy in an undated letter from the fall of 1963. "I asked her and she said 'yes'—so no doubt about PR. But she probably would not have done either if there had not been fertile ground for precisely this kind of stab-in-the-back."

This is perplexing, especially the part about Hardwick's supposed admission of guilt, since it squares with no one else's recollection of the events. Robert Silvers, as noted above, remembers that Lowell suggested Mailer as the reviewer of *The Group;* the story of how Abel got to review *Eichmann* is muddy—but nobody aside from Arendt blames Hardwick. William Phillips, admitting that he has no precise recollection of the circumstances, speculates that "Rahv arranged it—he was out to put Hannah down. In any case, Lionel originally said he liked the book and I said he didn't have to write a plug for it." Abel in his memoirs, however, remembers things differently. He notes that before *Eichmann* came out he had already published an extremely negative review of Arendt's *Between the Past and the Future,* and so he concludes that "when the *Partisan Review* editors asked me to review Miss

Arendt's *Eichmann in Jerusalem,* they must have been *expecting* a piece that would be very critical of Arendt." Again, there is no mention of Hardwick.

In wrangles of this sort, truth is ultimately less important than perception: Arendt, whom even friends describe as a bit paranoid at times, believed Hardwick had deliberately betrayed both her and McCarthy, and she tried to persuade McCarthy of this belief. Hardwick's treachery, whether imagined or real, was shocking because she had been an old friend and ally. But whatever Hardwick did and with whatever intention paled beside the attacks launched in the next few months by Arendt's new, numerous and highly organized enemies.

Eichmann in Jerusalem was a departure for Arendt, because it originated as a work of reportage. When she learned that the Israeli government had kidnapped former S.S. officer Adolf Eichmann in May 1960 from the suburb of Buenos Aires where he had taken refuge and transported him to Israel to stand trial, she decided she had to attend the trial. As she wrote at the time, "To attend this trial is somehow, I feel, an obligation I owe my past." She asked *New Yorker* editor William Shawn if she could cover the trial for the magazine, and to her amazement he promptly and generously complied. *The New Yorker* was an odd choice for Arendt, since many intellectuals still dismissed it as essentially lightweight and frivolous (Ved Mehta in a memoir of his involvement with the magazine recalls a dinner in December 1962 during which Robert Silvers, Lowell, and Hardwick "all turned on *The New Yorker* [and] said that the magazine suffered by not publishing hard-hitting articles"). Yet in fact under William Shawn the magazine had begun publishing work of exceptional quality and originality—Rachel Carson's *Silent Spring,* John Hersey's *Hiroshima,* James Baldwin's *The Fire Next Time* all ran originally in *The New Yorker.* And as the 1960s went on, the magazine took an increasingly "hard-hitting" stance against the war in Vietnam. Arendt's series of articles on the Eichmann trial in a sense ushered in *The New Yorker's* decade of fiercest controversy—though no one had any idea just how controversial her "report" would become. The trial dragged on through most of 1961, the death sentence was handed down at the end of that year, and after the appeal failed, Eichmann was hanged in Israel at the end of May 1962. Arendt's articles appeared in five issues of *The New Yorker* in February and March 1963 and reappeared, with some changes, as a book later that year.

Arendt subtitled *Eichmann in Jerusalem* "A Report on the Banality of

Evil" and though she came to rue her use of the phrase "banality of evil" (which was misunderstood and misinterpreted by most critics), she always insisted that the book was nothing more or less than a *report:* a record of the circumstances, evidence, and background of a single trial. Her book was *not* a history of the Holocaust or an analysis of the morality and politics of genocide or a consideration of the reasons why the Germans tried to rid their territory of Jews. In fact, her central question is not *why* but *how:* how Eichmann went from being a bumbling traveling salesman for the Vacuum Oil Company in Austria to the S.S. officer in charge of the deportation of Jews throughout the Reich; how such an ordinary man—not a raving, fanatical monster but an ill-informed, inarticulate, ideologically apathetic, unimaginative bureaucrat—could have brought himself to participate so willingly, so happily in the slaughter of millions; how the Nazi high command carried out an insidiously gradual policy of anti-Semitic persecution, first depriving Jews of their civil rights, then revoking their citizenship, then rounding them up and registering them, then stripping them of their property, then forcing them to emigrate (usually from west to east), then collecting them in concentration camps, and finally killing them either in gas chambers or by gunning them down in masses or by working them to death in factories.

The book also documents how the implementation of the so-called Final Solution differed from country to country—how the Danes and Bulgarians, for example, sabotaged Hitler's orders and managed to save most of their resident Jews while the Romanians exceeded even the Germans in their murderous zeal and greed. Most controversial is Arendt's discussion of how some European Jews inadvertently fostered and indeed cooperated in the destruction of their own people: how Jewish police rounded up fellow Jews and handed them over to the Nazis; how Jewish councils and Jewish leaders prepared lists of resident Jews that the Germans used in emptying the ghettos; how "Jewish commandos" were forced to carry out "the actual work of killing in the extermination centers." It was the Jewish leadership Arendt held most accountable for moral failure, as she wrote in what her critics considered the book's most incendiary passages: "Wherever Jews lived, there were recognized Jewish leaders, and this leadership, almost without exception, cooperated in one way or another, for one reason or another, with the Nazis. The whole truth was that if the Jewish people had really been unorganized and leaderless, there would have been chaos and plenty of misery but the total number of victims would hardly have been between four and a half and six million people. . . . To a Jew this role of the Jewish leaders in the destruction of their own people is undoubtedly the darkest chapter of the whole dark story."

Arendt knew that *Eichmann in Jerusalem* was controversial, but she was totally unprepared for the scale and the ferocity of the campaign to discredit and denounce the book. The Anti-Defamation League of B'nai B'rith, accusing her of writing about "Jewish participation in the Nazi holocaust," tried to "excommunicate" Arendt and directed rabbis throughout America to preach against her during the Jewish high holy days. A cadre of lecturers (some brought in from overseas) toured the country to denounce the book and castigate Arendt as a "self-hating Jew." The more extreme reviews accused her of defending, even praising, Eichmann while she blamed and attacked the Jewish victims. As Norman Podhoretz wrote in *Commentary,* "In the place of the monstrous Nazi, she gives us the 'banal' Nazi; in the place of the Jew as a virtuous martyr, she gives us the Jew as accomplice in evil; and in the place of the confrontation of guilt and innocence, she gives us the 'collaboration' of criminal and victim." According to Lionel Abel, Arendt had made Eichmann "aesthetically palatable, while his victims are aesthetically repulsive." And so on. As the editors of *PR* wrote in a prefatory note to the first salvo they printed on the subject: *Eichmann in Jerusalem* "has provoked as much controversy as any other book we can think of in the last decade." The uproar over the book raged in the intellectual press for the better part of three years, dying down briefly around the time of the Kennedy assassination in November 1963, only to flare up again afterward. "[T]his Eichmann business . . . is assuming the proportions of a pogrom," McCarthy wrote without exaggeration to Arendt in September 1963.

McCarthy rose loyally to her friend's defense, publishing a long, emotional rebuttal to the attacks on the book, especially Abel's, in *PR.* McCarthy asserted, with some justification, that reaction to the book divided along religious lines: Jews by and large hated it while gentiles failed to "understand" what was wrong with it. "It is as if *Eichmann in Jerusalem* had required a special pair of Jewish spectacles to make its 'true purport' visible." And she referred several times to the "hate campaign" being waged against Arendt and the "slanders" circulating in books, articles and gossip "intended to destroy the reputation of a living woman." (In his memoirs, William Phillips wrote that McCarthy's defense of her friend was "brilliant, especially in the writing, and honest in stating her bias, though her division of the protagonists into Jewish and gentile only fueled the polarization.") Lowell also went to bat for Arendt in letters to the editors of *PR* and *The New York Times Book Review*. Lowell wisely skirted the issue of the Jewish Councils and focused instead on Arendt's portrait of Eichmann. The *Times* letter reads in part, "That Eichmann is no monster on a heroic scale, but only a strangely numb and nerve-wrung part of our usual world makes him all the more appalling. Mediocre, banal, unable in the end to speak or even think the truth, he moves through his inferno, now wriggling in his confusion, now flying on his 'gusts of elation.' His life is as close to living in hell as I can imagine, and I am able to see it as such because Miss Arendt has refused to simplify the picture with melodrama or blur it with clichés."

But in a curious way, defenses based on the merits, the accuracy, and the intent of the text were beside the point. Arendt had hit an exceedingly raw nerve in the Jewish community. As Irving Howe wrote in his memoirs, Arendt had tapped into a huge hidden reservoir of guilt among American Jews—"a guilt pervasive, unmanageable, yet seldom (until then) allowed to reach daylight." According to Howe, the "long-suppressed grief evoked by the Holocaust burst out" in the storm of protest over *Eichmann in Jerusalem:* "It was as if her views, which roused many of us to fury, enabled us to finally speak about the unspeakable." This is the crux of it. During the war, many American Jewish intellectuals maintained a remarkable silence and diffidence about what was happening to the Jews in Europe: for years, relatively little of what Hitler was doing was known or understood or believed; left-wing Jews had ideological reasons for opposing yet another capitalist-imperialist war; the atrocities, once they were revealed through newsreels and newspaper reports, were indeed "unspeakable" in every sense of the word. Rather than dwell on the horrors of the past, many Jews chose to look to the state of Israel as their salvation and their guarantee that nothing like this could ever happen again. As Abel wrote in his memoirs, "Certainly, the Holocaust was a *tragedy*. . . . Some good must come of so much evil; and for the Jews, this good was found only in the setting-up of the state of Israel. What came out of the Holocaust was the success of Zionism. And this success was essential to the self-respect of all Jews in all parts of the world." This was the party line in Jewish-American intellectual circles.

Arendt broke with the party and broke the silence—especially on the vexed question of how so many Jews could have been slaughtered so efficiently and seemingly easily, "arriving on time at the transportation points," as she writes in one of the book's more harrowing passages, "walking on their own feet to the places of execution, digging their own graves, undressing and making neat piles of their clothing, and lying down side by side to be shot." At no point does she blame the victims for their deaths; in fact, she follows this passage on the Jews' "submissive meekness" with an even more harrowing description of what happened when the victims dared to resist: how the Nazis slowly tortured 430 Dutch Jews to death in revenge for a single act of defiance in Amsterdam. For Arendt, breaking the silence, reporting on the "banality of evil" that she saw in Eichmann and its tragic consequences for the victims was a kind of cathartic experience. As she wrote McCarthy after reading her defense of *Eichmann* in *PR,* "you were the only reader to understand what otherwise I have never admitted—namely that I wrote this book in a curious state of euphoria. And that ever since I did it, I feel—after twenty years—light-hearted about the whole matter." The euphoria must have come from the act of composition itself—from the release of revealing what she knew—and not from her feelings about the subject at hand. For the emotion that pervades the narrative voice of *Eichmann in Jerusalem* is not joy but sarcastic, bottled-up fury—fury most of all at the Nazi leadership for devising the Final Solution; fury at the German people for allowing themselves to be cowed and blinded into carrying out Hitler's orders; fury at the herdlike passivity that afflicted whole populations who never dared to protest because no one else did (in Denmark, where protest was widespread, starting with the king, even the S.S. officers became "demoralized," inept at the business of death, and ultimately humane); fury at Eichmann for being so stupid, so deluded, so clownishly incapable of grasping the reality of his actions and situation; and fury, finally, at the Jews themselves for their long, tragic history of hope and delusion, for the terrible circumstances that trapped and destroyed so many of them, for the impossible moral choices the Nazis forced them to make. As Lowell wrote of the experience of reading the book, "Hannah's rage against Eichmann's mediocrity was itself enraging."

Eichmann in Jerusalem is indeed harsh, arrogant, and confusingly oblique. Arendt looks down on the proceedings from a very high vantage point, preaching at the prosecution, hissing at the defense, making bold judgments about events she has failed to research completely (most important, the controversial role of the Jewish councils), insisting over and over that she and she alone is telling the "whole truth." It's not hard to see why her critics charged her with failure of sympathy and lack of "soul." As Daniel Bell wrote in a largely sympathetic piece in *PR,* the book has a "cold force" and an "abstract quality" that make it difficult to take: "[H]er response to the unbearable story reduces a tragic drama to a philosophical complexity. . . . The agony of Miss Arendt's book is precisely that she takes her stand so unyieldingly on the side of disinterested justice, and that she judges both Nazi and Jew."

But the vehemence of the attacks on *Eichmann in Jerusalem* ultimately had more to do with the attitudes of readers than with the style or substance of the book. Those who most hated the book simply did not want to hear what she was saying. It was easier to attack Arendt as an anti-Semite, an anti-Zionist, a defender of the Nazis than to confront the shame of being a nonparticipant, an innocent or ignorant bystander, a baffled survivor.

American Jewish intellectuals, especially those in the *PR* group, fought Arendt far more zealously than they had fought Hitler. Whether or not guilt fueled the antipathy toward the book, it's probably fair to conclude that Arendt found few objective readers in the American Jewish community. *Eichmann in Jerusalem* tapped into tensions that a generation of American Jews had been unable to resolve, tensions that were indeed at the heart of their double identity as Americans and Jews.

A sign of the time: In 1959, Allen Ginsberg, rising to fame as a Beat poet, gave a reading at his alma mater, Columbia University, in company with his friends Gregory Corso and Peter Orlovsky. Diana Trilling attended out of curiosity and anticipatory pique and was so moved by the proceedings that she composed an essay about it entitled "The Other Night at Columbia" (published in *Partisan Review*). Trilling was not a wholly objective or disinterested observer, for she had known something of Ginsberg from his undergraduate days when he had studied under her husband and gotten himself suspended for a year for writing "fuck the Jews" in the dust of his dorm room windowsill, among other infractions. Professor Trilling had done what he could for young Ginsberg and succeeded, with the help of the college dean, in keeping him out of jail on a drug-related charge. But there was obviously no great love between them—and very little agreement about the value and uses of literature.

Diana took her seat at the Beat reading expecting the poets to smell bad, and she duly recorded the fact that they didn't. She also wrote that the lot of them struck her as "miserable children trying desperately to manage" and other remarks that many people, not just the Beats but lots of *PR* people and nice literary liberals, found smug, condescending, defensive, narrow-minded, haughty, and unimaginative. More than thirty years later, still brooding in her memoirs about the "considerable hostility" the essay aroused, she singled out Mary McCarthy as the most memorable of her attackers. McCarthy at a party told Trilling that the problem with the essay was that "no one knew from whose point of view" it was written and that she "should have started it by identifying [herself] as the wife of Lionel Trilling." Trilling commented that she found this remark "senseless except as an insult."

Ginsberg's own response to Trilling's piece was less insulting and more interesting. He sent a letter to the editors of *PR* that read *in toto,* "The universe is a new flower." Years later he told an interviewer that what he had meant was that "the world and our understanding of it was changing. . . . Our consciousness was getting beyond fights between Communists and anti-Communists, beyond the radical disillusion of the thirties intellectuals. . . . We were worrying about the more universal police state that comes through technology." While the *PR* crowd was still locked in the old fights and looking at the world through the old grid, Ginsberg and company had stepped around them and moved on to something new—a "consciousness" that did not so much challenge *PR* as dismiss it as irrelevant. It was as if the two "sides" were speaking different languages even as they lived and worked blocks apart in the same city. It wasn't just Diana Trilling. For all their ridicule of Trilling's Columbia essay, McCarthy and Rahv and the others didn't *get* the Beats any better than she did. Nor did any of them really *get* the fractured, loopy, antiserious surrealism of the so-called New York School of Poets—Frank O'Hara, John Ashbery, Kenneth Koch, and James Schuyler—who were coming of age at the same time and in the same city, but in yet another wildly alien cultural patch.

By the late 1950s the likes and dislikes decreed in *PR* were being challenged in many quarters: Ginsberg and O'Hara, different as they were, represented a vital, vibrantly new style of radicalism that thumbed its nose at everything *PR* stood for and assumed. In the coming decade, cultural and political radicals would go well beyond nose-thumbing—and *PR* would crumble before the onslaught.

The year 1963 also brought the publication of Betty Friedan's *The Feminine Mystique,* as controversial, eye-opening, and influential in its way as

• • •

Eichmann in Jerusalem, which appeared the same year—that queer watershed year of the Kennedy assassination, *The Group,* and the founding of *The New York Review of Books.* "As disruptive of cocktail party conversation and women's club discussions as a tear-gas bomb," *Life* magazine reported breathlessly in November as *The Feminine Mystique* climbed best-seller lists (sales would top 3 million by 1966) and made an instant celebrity of Friedan. Some cocktail parties were more disrupted than others. Even if Friedan's book was talked about in the *PR/NYR* circle, the talk was not deemed spirited or important enough to merit any notice in print: no review of the book appeared in either journal, no mention of it in the memoirs of the leading figures. Here was yet another brand of radicalism that the crowd, men and women alike, simply did not get. Though *The Feminine Mystique* is generally credited with sparking the women's movement of the late 1960s, it failed to show up on the radar screens of the New York intellectuals.

The almost simultaneous publication of *The Feminine Mystique* and *The Group* is a fitting coincidence, for the two books bear an eerie kinship. Both were inspired by the experiences in the "real world" of the graduates of the very fine women's colleges their authors attended—in Friedan's case, Smith College. Both books were shocking at the time for their revelations of the fraught inner lives of seemingly privileged, outwardly happy American women, though of course Friedan took a journalistic approach while McCarthy wrote a novel.

Friedan got the idea for *The Feminine Mystique* during a forced hiatus in her career. Having been fired from her job as reporter for a labor newspaper in 1949 when she requested a second maternity leave, Friedan retreated to the life of suburban wife and mother and took to mulling over the lot of women. Starting in the mid-1950s, she began circulating questionnaires among Smith graduates to find out how her peers felt about the issues that were troubling her: career, family, personal fulfillment, the role of intelligent women in society. She discovered that most Smith alumnae who had given up careers to devote themselves to homemaking shared her sense of emptiness, depression, and disappointment. They felt they had been sold a lie—the myth perpetrated by women's magazine editors, schoolteachers, editorial writers, and husbands that women should find contentment and self-realization in the duties of marriage and child rearing. It was this lie that Friedan named "the feminine mystique," and in her book she exposed its devastating effect on the psyches of women from all over the country and in all social classes. Far from reveling in their tidy suburban villas and glossy "labor-saving devices," American housewives, according to Friedan, were leading lives of quiet desperation, debilitating depression, alcoholism, drug addiction, suicide, and rage. But change was in the air. As she insisted, "We can no longer ignore the voice within women that says: 'I want something more than my husband and my children and my home.' " Friedan analyzed why earlier feminist movements had failed to change women's lives, and she encouraged contemporary women to throw off their shackles and live up to their full human potential. "Don't be an appliance, a vegetable or a service station," she exhorted. "How will you get a man? If you find yourself first you won't need any trickery." Millions of women would soon be following her advice, even if they didn't know it came from her, even if they did so not out of ideological conviction but rather from the simple, practical desire to get a decent job for a fair wage. *The Feminine Mystique* is flawed and slick and superficial in many ways, but it fell on fertile ground. It was the right book at the right time, and it had an overwhelming and enduring impact on the American social scene.

But Mary McCarthy, Hannah Arendt, Elizabeth Hardwick, Jean Stafford, Diana Trilling, and most of the women they knew and listened to didn't notice, weren't interested, or actively opposed "women's lib" until it was a fait accompli. In fact, the whole business irritated the hell out of them.

The Late 1960s: Dispersal

HANNAH ARENDT was traveling abroad when the furor over *Eichmann in Jerusalem* broke in 1963, and Lotte Kohler remembers her friend's dismay at returning home to her apartment on Riverside Drive and finding a mountain of mail stacked up on the dining room table. "Hannah asked me to come the next morning and help sort the mail," says Kohler, "and the first task was to separate it into three heaps. The first heap was for the crazies, people who were threatening to kill her and so on, and this heap was sizable—there are a lot of sick people. The biggest heap was for attacks, emotional attacks of the 'How could you?' sort, and attacks over facts—'there were not three thousand killed that day but four thousand.' Then there was a small heap of acknowledgments, people expressing gratitude for what she had written. For Hannah it was the saddest and most serious shock in her life. She suffered about it terribly."

Many intellectual friendships ended on account of *Eichmann in Jerusalem,* and wounds remained raw for years. Arendt never forgave Irving Howe or Lionel Abel, to name only the most prominent, for what they said or wrote about the book, and Jewish leaders never forgave Arendt for publishing it. She had made herself, unwittingly, a pariah within a group she had characterized as pariahs.

But Arendt still had her allies and partisans in literary New York, including the editors of *The New York Review of Books*. The Lowells remained firmly in her camp, and Arendt apparently decided to forget about whatever behind-the-scenes scheming Elizabeth Hardwick might have engaged in over *Eichmann in Jerusalem*. Even so, a chill seems to have lingered between the two women. The few references Arendt made to the Lowells in her letters to McCarthy are veiled and guarded, but she definitely sounds miffed whenever circumstances threw her and Hardwick together. Something about Hardwick's voice and social manner rubbed Arendt the wrong way. Perhaps it was Hardwick's silky venom—the way she smiled and laughed and threw up her hands as she demolished yet another literary reputation. Or it might have been the way she clung to Lowell for "the prestige," as Arendt put it, of being married to a great man. In any case, there was strain but no breach between them, and McCarthy herself in time forgave Hardwick for her betrayal over *The Group*.

About Lowell, Arendt's feelings were deeper and more complicated. She had tremendous admiration for his verse and delight in his brilliant, serious, associative conversation; but she also felt intense discomfort over his mental illness. As a girl, Arendt had witnessed her own father succumb to madness in the final stages of the syphilis that killed him, and perhaps as a result she was always tense and self-protective around anyone suffering serious mental imbalance. Even garden-variety neurosis raised her guard. "She was deeply skeptical toward psychoanalysis and therapy," notes Young-Bruehl. "When everyone in New York was going to an analyst, she always spoke of it as a waste of time. The fashion among New York intellectuals of telling their dreams at cocktail parties was in her view beneath contempt." Arendt admitted in a letter to McCarthy that she was "rather obtuse in all purely psychological matters." She never wanted to look into the dark corners of the psyche—but with Lowell this was unavoidable, and so she made sure to keep some distance between them. They saw each other at dinner parties, especially when mutual friends were visiting from abroad. And Lowell stopped by Arendt's apartment now and then to chat, occasions he remembered fondly in a memorial piece he wrote about her: "Hannah's high apartment house high on the lower Hudson always gave me a feeling of apprehension, the thrill, hesitation, and helplessness of entering a foreign country, a north German harbor, the tenements of Kafka. . . . How unconsciously Hannah held the straying mind. Though a philosopher in every heartbeat of her nervous system, she belonged, like all true thinkers, to culture and literature." Lowell and Arendt were allies in politics and literary politics; Lowell "basked in Arendt's admiration," as Kazin put it, and dedicated several poems to her. But they were never as easy with or close to each other as Arendt and Jarrell had been.

Lowell and Hardwick had come back to New York in 1960, they said, for the scale and the pace and the adrenaline of a big city—"the marvellous excited rush of people in taxicabs at twilight" that Hardwick had written of wistfully in dim, stately Boston. But the marvelous rush brought distress to both of them along with exposure and celebrity. By the time his volume *For the Union Dead* appeared in 1964, Lowell was accustomed to seeing the word "greatest" linked to his name: greatest American poet, greatest poet writing in English, greatest poet of the age, the era, the postwar period. His collection of free translations of poems by Villon, Heine, Baudelaire, Montale, and others—Lowell called the work *Imitations*—gave him a claim to the European tradition as well. (The book was controversial, with some reviewers expressing outrage over the liberties Lowell had taken while others praised the freshness of his approach. Edmund Wilson, who liked Lowell a good deal and spent an occasional evening with him in deep talk and heavy drink, wrote admiringly that *Imitations* was "the only book of its kind in literature . . . really an original sequence by Robert Lowell.") Lowell also staked out a place for himself in the theater during the early 1960s. His three one-act plays, collected under the title *The Old Glory,* were in a sense "imitations" as well, for Lowell had taken short stories by Hawthorne and Melville and "versified" them into dramatic speeches and dialogue. Lowell's first biographer, Ian Hamilton, wrote dismissively of the project, "[I]t is a measure both of his standing as '*the* poet' of the day and also perhaps of the enfeebled state of the American theater in the early 1960s that *The Old Glory* should have been greeted as a major cultural event."

Professionally, Lowell was in his prime—but meanwhile, privately, the breakdowns and wrenching love affairs continued. "I am tired. Everyone's tired of my turmoil," he wrote in the poem "Eye and Tooth" in *For the Union Dead*. But universal fatigue brought no relief, least of all to Hardwick. She was now a hardened veteran of a seemingly end-less war—actually, war would have been straightforward compared to being the wife of Robert Lowell in the 1960s. Jailer, target, nurse, the betrayed and the betrayer, the wounded, the furious, the fury, and al-ways in the end the fount of forgiveness, solace, security, Hardwick was desperate but powerless to make a break. The "line" on her around town was that being married to Robert Lowell—"*the* poet of the day"—was by her own reckoning worth any pain and humiliation. In fact, she was often in agony about whether to leave him, give him "one last try," insist on further treatment, or put up with a cycle that seemed as relentless as the seasons. In the end, the decision to "put up" looks less like hope or resignation and more like bafflement, grit, and stub-bornness. She *could* manage him most of the time. He *was* tender, de-voted, charming, and brilliant when he was sane. She *had* soldiered through fifteen years of this, so why not stick with it? Of course we'll never know the "real" reasons unless Hardwick chooses to reveal them, and so far she hasn't.

In June 1965 Lowell suddenly became a lot more famous outside lit-erary circles when the news media reported his refusal of an invitation President Lyndon B. Johnson had extended to attend a White House Fes-tival of the Arts. In his letter of explanation and apology, Lowell told the president that he had originally accepted the invitation "somewhat rapidly and greedily," but that upon reflection he felt "conscience-bound" to decline because of his "dismay and distrust" over "our present foreign policy"—i.e., the escalation of the war in Vietnam and the bomb-ing of the North that had commenced in February 1965. Edmund Wilson, who had also been invited to the White House festival, refused at once, brusquely and almost rudely, but it was Lowell's presidential rebuff that got the attention. The story appeared on the front page of *The New York Times* (Lowell had helpfully sent a copy of his letter to the paper), and a follow-up article reported that a distinguished group of writers and artists had sent a telegram to Johnson in support of Lowell's action: signers in-cluded Arendt, McCarthy, Lillian Hellman (one of the rare occasions that found Hellman and McCarthy on the same side of an issue), Alfred Kazin, Peter Taylor, Stanley Kunitz, John Berryman, and Robert Penn Warren. All this stood in striking contrast to Lowell's previous rebuff of an American president—his 1943 letter to President Franklin D. Roo-sevelt refusing to serve in the army, which friends and colleagues had either scoffed at or ignored. Lowell was now officially, publicly, an "antiwar activist," a role he played with dignity, circumspection, and increasing skepticism as the 1960s wore on.

The irony of Lowell's taking a stand as a leader of the antiwar movement was not lost on his old friends. "Boy, Cal's politics—they're a study," Blair Clark commented, laughing. From "fire-breathing Catholic C.O." to fervent post–World War II anti-Communist to anti–Vietnam War marcher on the Pentagon (Lowell figures prominently in *Armies of the Night,* Norman Mailer's account of the 1967 Pentagon demonstration). Yet, as Clark noted, Lowell knew what he was doing: he had an "ability to manipulate himself as a public figure. He did it without any pomposity—but he definitely believed that he *was* a public figure." Certainly Lowell was more successful at it than most of the other members of the crowd. Mary McCarthy also got swept up in the antiwar movement, publishing a series of soul-searching, breast-beating essays in *The New York Review of Books* based on her trips to South Vietnam in 1967 and, far more daringly, to North Vietnam in 1968, engaging in a wordy wrangle with Diana Trilling over the consequences of the United States' withdrawal from Vietnam, arguing at cocktail parties, organizing and agonizing behind the scenes. But she never appealed to the young the way Lowell did: in the minds of campus radicals and would-be revolutionaries, she was not a charismatic emissary from the older generation but the author of the supremely uncool novel *The Group,* a smiling, soignée, well-heeled woman-of-the-world who appeared faintly ridiculous as she picked her way across rice paddies and visited bomb sites in war-torn Vietnam. As McCarthy herself admitted to Carol Brightman years later, "My dear, I arrived in Hanoi wearing a Chanel suit, and carrying many suitcases!" The two collections of her essays about the war—*Vietnam* (1967) and *Hanoi* (1968)—raised scarcely a ripple in either the "establishment" or the alternative press. Privately, her peers and old comrades in the anti-Communist Left muttered that she had gone too far: it was embarrassing to read Mary hymning the praises of the elegant, erudite North Vietnamese leadership while she castigated America (and herself) for being too rich, too complacent, too homogenized, too plastic, too numbed by the allures of consumer culture. If the Old Left cringed at McCarthy's radical chic, the New Left sneered at her self-conscious efforts to be more-radical-than-thou. In half a decade, McCarthy had gone from being the "First Lady of American letters," the hot author of a scandalously sexy best-seller, to being an irrelevancy— unheeded, unshocking, and out of touch with the spirit of the day. It was a strange, queasy sensation for "Bloody Mary" of the icy smile and merciless candor to find herself shouldered from center stage into the wings.

Arendt fared slightly better in the shifting winds of 1960s politics, though for reasons she did not entirely approve of. Members of the fledgling New Left latched onto the notion of spontaneously generated local councils and grassroots discussion groups that Arendt had put forth in *On Revolution,* her paean to America's Founding Fathers, and the SDS (Students for a Democratic Society) rechristened the concept "participatory democracy." For a few seasons at Berkeley, *On Revolution* became a required text for participants in the Free Speech movement, the vanguard groundswell of campus protest. In addition, some of the young Jewish radicals within the New Left defied their elders and endorsed Arendt's *Eichmann in Jerusalem:* in the heated rhetoric of the day, the United States was like Germany on the brink of the Nazi takeover and the engineers of the expanding war in Vietnam were banal bureaucrats who, like Eichmann, routinely and efficiently wiped out alien populations without worrying about morality or ideology. Arendt the iconoclast, the glorifier of the young republic, the explicator of totalitarianism, was fashionable, sort of, but only for a fragment of her work. The gruff, opinionated, hyperabstract refugee from the Old World made an exceedingly strange political bedfellow with the rank and file of the SDS, which historian John P. Diggins describes as a mélange of "gifted graduate students and sophomore dropouts, Christian pacifists and militant confrontationists, weekend potheads and midnight mystics." But such was the tenor of the times.

In the 1960s, as always, Arendt went her own way politically for her own reasons. On Vietnam, she was clear-eyed and prescient, writing McCarthy as early as April 1965 that "This is a civil war situation and it is a lie that two nations, South and North Vietnam, are involved. . . . If we only would let well enough alone, we would get there a variety of Socialist to Communist regimes with which we could live very well." And she realized that the critical problem that the United States would eventually face in the region was "how to get out: we cannot simply let all people down and without protection who ever were on our side; they would simply be massacred." All of which came to pass more or less as she imagined it. The following year, in response to a political questionnaire, she expressed her unequivocal opposition to the United States' involvement in the war: "I am against the intervention of the United States in the civil war in Vietnam. . . . The way to resolve an armed conflict is always the same: cease fire—armistice—peace negotiations—and, hopefully, peace treaty." Arendt also endorsed some of the early student sit-ins and takeovers at universities—hardly a popular position among members of her generation. Mark Denneny, a student of hers at the University of Chicago, recalls Arendt flying up a staircase two steps as a time, "as excited as a girl," to address student protesters who were occupying a campus building. And when the far more controversial student uprising broke out at Columbia University in the spring of 1968, Arendt was initially a zealous supporter—"The students are demonstrating and we are all with them," she told a friend breathlessly the day Columbia students took over campus buildings—though she soon felt the protesters had become too violent in their threats and demands.

The Columbia riots gave Arendt, McCarthy, Lowell, and friends another excuse to disparage Diana Trilling, who was wild about the students' desecration of campus property and furious at old *PR* cronies such as Dwight Macdonald and Fred Dupee for coming out in support of the demonstrators and physically joining them. Trilling and Robert Lowell went head-to-head in print over the student sit-ins, with Lowell at one point denouncing Trilling as "a housekeeping goddess of reason," which was patronizing but far kinder than what the others were saying about her privately. Like Macdonald, Arendt was mesmerized by the spectacle of revolutionary theory being put into practice on the Upper West Side; but unlike Macdonald, she did not herself mount the barricades, either literally or figuratively. "I don't think that you should do anything," she wrote McCarthy rather peevishly as demonstrations were heating up across the country. "I don't do anything either, except when I am on campus. I signed one of the many protests and that is that. I don't intend to make a profession of it."

Arendt had less foresight and insight on questions of race. She had broken ranks with liberals in coming out against forced school desegregation in Little Rock, Arkansas, in 1959 (she argued, perplexingly, that "government has no right" to block discrimination in the social realm even though it has a "duty to make sure that these practices are not legally enforced," and further that it was unfair to make black schoolchildren the pawns in a social and political conflict that subjected them to hatred and possibly violence). A decade later she took a strong stand against the violence advocated by leaders of the Black Power movement and against the campaign to introduce "Black Studies" programs and open-admissions policies into America's universities. African literature was, in her view, a "nonexistent subject," and she believed that America's blacks would in time come to see Black Studies as "another trap of the white man to prevent Negroes from acquiring an adequate education." Arendt wrote frankly about her fears of the goals and methods of black activists in a letter to McCarthy: "Negroes demand their own curriculum without the exacting standards of white society and, at the same time, they demand admission in accordance to their percentage in the population at large, regardless of standards. In other words they actually want to take over and adjust standards to their own level. This is a much greater threat to our institutions of higher learning than the student riots." The New Left and "the old liberals" had, she believed, the same "trouble" in grappling with "the Negro question": lack of common sense, dishonesty, "complete unwillingness to face facts, abstract talk, often snobbish and nearly always blind to anybody else's interest." She wrapped up this diatribe by singling out Elizabeth Hardwick's review of a biography of George Wallace for its "monumental" hypocrisy. This letter sounds like another outbreak of the old revulsion against the jabbering of intellectuals that had first seized her in Paris during the 1930s, only now the object of her scorn is not the German refugee community but New York "opinion-makers," and the "enemy" is not fascism but Black Power. McCarthy, in despair, wrote back that "*all* utterances on the subject of student violence, black power, etc. fill me with nausea. The 'moderates' are almost the worst." She added, with characteristic frivolity, that she was "having an odd reaction on a personal scale" to the stomach-turning political situation: "to go and order a lot of dresses made, as though they would be my last. The reverse of a hope chest."

Arendt's disgust with old liberals and New Leftists was widely shared by New York intellectuals in the 1960s. This was, after all, the period when neoconservatism rose from the ashes of the anti-Communist Left, with figures such as Irving Kristol, Norman Podhoretz, Daniel Bell, and Nathan Glazer leading the charge to the right. (Actually, as John P. Diggins recounts in his excellent study *Up from Communism,* the roots of neoconservatism go back to the mid-1950s, when William F. Buckley, Jr. founded the *National Review* and enlisted former radicals such as John Dos Passos and Max Eastman to serve on the editorial board.) The standard line is that the neoconservatives abandoned liberalism in reaction to the excesses of the New Left, although some have argued that it was actually the other way around—that a deep strain of conservatism and elitism had always lurked beneath the surface of postwar liberalism and that the radicals of the New Left were bent on exposing this and replacing it with "people power." No doubt there is some truth on both sides. The crucial point is that liberalism as it had been known and advocated for nearly two decades by the likes of McCarthy, Hardwick, Wilson, Dwight Macdonald, the Trillings, and to some extent Lowell and Arendt, expired in the 1960s. And as it died, it killed off the cultural authority of the group that espoused it.

The revelation in 1967 that the CIA had all along been secretly funding the Congress for Cultural Freedom, an international organization from which Lowell, McCarthy, Dwight Macdonald, William Phillips, and many other intellectuals had received generous travel funds and other benefits for years, was a serious blow. But far more destructive was the increasingly bitter and entrenched divisions in the ranks: the Epsteins and the Podhoretzes, once bosom buddies, fell out over political differences; the *PR* group, what was left of it, was furious at the *New York Review* group for jumping on the radical bandwagon (there was a terrible howl from the old guard when the *NYR* ran a drawing of a Molotov cocktail on the cover of the August 24, 1967, issue with annotations on the ingredients); Tom Wolfe ridiculed the "radical chic" of Norman Mailer, Leonard Bernstein, and their cronies; and the young thumbed their noses at all of them. As William Phillips wrote in his memoirs, "One felt assaulted not only by the contempt for the past on the part of the new radicals, but by the cultural fragmentation that made tradition look like an outdated custom. . . . The blossoming of the new left and the counterculture not only drove the conservatives more to the right, but further splintered the remnants of the left." Rahv, in disgust, distanced himself from both the "swingers" and the "hipster writers" who were mouthing off regularly in *PR* and the *NYR* and from the disorganized, amorphous, overhyped New Left, which he dismissed as "little more than a mood and an oppositional rhetoric" and "an inchoate mass of political groupings ever ready to engage in scenes of melodramatic confrontation, but extremely short on theoretical insight and principle." In 1970 he severed his ties with the magazine he had edited since 1934 and let the "swingers" run amok.

God knows there had never been anything like consensus among the New York intellectuals, on either political or social issues; but there *had* been a shared outlook, a common sense of what and who mattered, an agreement that written discourse, especially their own discourse, was central to the culture as a whole. They had always written primarily for one another, yet they felt with some justification that their words streamed forth from New York to define and illuminate the issues of the day—*their* day. The New York intellectuals were never a monopoly. There were many other voices, competing outlets, and arenas. Even among this crowd, the sense of who belonged, what they stood for, who held power was always shifting. But there *was* power, and now it was largely gone. A new generation had arrived to grapple with the Vietnam War, the defining issue of the day. McCarthy, Lowell, Hardwick, Arendt, and the rest still wrote and published, spoke and argued, met and gossiped, won and awarded prizes. But their cultural moment—a long moment stretching back to the 1930s—was past.

In this charged atmosphere, the demise of the Lowells' marriage was both a symptom and a symbol of what was wrong. By the late 1960s, both Lowell and Hardwick were getting burnt out on politics and New York. Lowell marched on the Pentagon with Dwight Macdonald, Norman Mailer, and thousands of less celebrated protesters in the fall of 1967; and he played a prominent, though perhaps not very effective, role in Eugene McCarthy's brief, thrilling campaign for the Democratic presidential nomination the following year. But as the Vietnam War dragged on and the social programs of the Great Society went up in flames in America's inner cities, a sense of futility set in. America was sick; American politics was sickening; the world seemed to be changing fast, but nothing was getting better. The jittery hope that swirled around the uprisings of 1968 had crashed by 1970. You can hear the mood shift in two letters Hardwick wrote to Mary McCarthy in these years. In the first, from May 3, 1968: "Here, news, events, take up all of one's time. . . . This hateful sense of crisis, or of just something new happening every minute, destroys the mind and the sense of wanting to do anything except wait for the next 'happening.' " Less than two years later, the crisis atmosphere has given way to an ominous dead calm, an eerie, depressing "feeling of emptiness and fear":

> New York is both quiet and very tiring. . . . You feel as if you'd been in a play running for years and then it closed and you went uptown and no one called. That is the feel of the political scene, an utter, odd, shambles, a nothing. . . . There is something wrong with every appearance and setting.

By way of example, she describes the incongruity of a party for a Vietnamese Buddhist poet held at the "town house of some very rich people, all of the guests, rich, famous, listening to this plain young woman." Destructiveness, emptiness and fear: the 1960s were over, and this is what remained.

Lowell's personal experience of the late 1960s was colored by a new treatment for his mental illness: lithium carbonate. Introduced in America in 1967, lithium was touted as a "wonder drug" that kept manic-depressives on an even keel by restoring their salt balance. As Lowell wrote skeptically to Peter Taylor when he started on it, "I even have pills that are supposed to prevent manic attacks, something . . . which supplies some salt lack in some obscure part of the brain and now for the rest of my life, I can drink and be a valetudinarian and pontificate nonsense." Lowell is teasing here, but lithium has indeed had stunning results in stabilizing manic-depressives, and for a while it worked wonders with him. The winter of 1967–1968 passed without a "manic attack," the first sane winter in years, and Lowell and Hardwick were cautiously optimistic. But Mary McCarthy sounds a note of alarm about Lowell's "improved" condition in a letter to Arendt from September 12, 1967:

> [W]hat is disclosed, by keeping him "normal," is how mad he is all the time, even when on his good behavior. . . . He's very tense and, when he's drinking, quite grandiose; he oughtn't to drink and has stopped for the moment, but I don't think he can keep it up. It's as though the drug were depriving him of his annual spree and he compensates for the deprivation rather cunningly by using the license given to drunkards. My opinion is that it would be better to let him be crazy once a year, be locked up, then emerge penitent, etc., than to have him subdued by this drug in a sort of private zoo—his home—with Lizzie as the keeper. But she prefers it that way.

But as it turned out, "that way" was not to last very much longer.

What McCarthy failed to mention, and perhaps didn't know, is that lithium did not subdue the love affairs that invariably attended Lowell's breakdowns. There was a new young woman in Mexico during a trip Lowell took in January 1968 and others at Harvard, where he had been teaching for a semester each year since 1962. Lowell made no secret of these amours: they surfaced quickly and candidly in the verse he was writing at the time—"sex indelible flowers on the air"—along with every-

thing else that was happening to him every day. Lowell's poetry under-
went a sea change around the time he started taking lithium, though it's
unlikely that the drug was the sole cause of the change. Unrhymed sonnets—"fourteen-liners," as he called them—began pouring out of him in
a torrent in 1967, often several sonnets a day composed during the summer in long sessions at his seaside "work barn" in Castine or dashed off
in the gaps between classes, rallies, love affairs, and parties. As he told
an interviewer, "I did nothing but write; I was thinking lines even when
teaching or playing tennis. . . . Ideas sprang from the bushes, my head;
five or six sonnets started or reworked in a day." Lowell deliberately left
the poems rough, slapdash, ragged, studded with non sequiturs and
great swoops of association: the intent was to capture the mind in the act
of thinking, the body in the act of doing. "I want words meat-hooked
from the living steer," he declared pungently in "The Nihilist as Hero."
Not crafted, polished verse—the "well-wrought urn"—but life grappled
into art as it was being lived. In the *Notebook* Lowell mixed the public
and private: intimate sonnets about his marriage, childhood, friendships,
love affairs, daughter alternate with sonnets in which the poet leaps from
his daily life to the events and personages of Western history and culture—Robespierre, Abraham Lincoln, Julius Caesar, Eugene McCarthy,
Mary Stuart, Harpo Marx. Later he winnowed the public from the private
poems, publishing the former as *History* (with many new additions) and
the latter as *For Lizzie and Harriet.*

Just as Lowell made family life an acceptable subject for American poetry in *Life Studies,* so in the various versions of *Notebook* he made marriage an acceptable, indeed obsessional, poetic theme. Loose and
scattershot as they are, the marriage sonnets quiver with the paradoxes
of twenty years of shared life: love and cruelty, exaltation and disgust, fa-
miliarity and strangeness, deceit and remorse, misty fondness and rutted
despair. "Life is too short to silver over this tarnish," he writes in "New
Year's Eve" about an epic quarrel at a party ushering in the new decade
of the 1970s (possibly Arendt and Blücher's annual New Year's Eve
bash). This is the prevailing tone: a weary acknowledgment of age and
pain, and a wistful longing to "silver" over these hurts. Heart's-Ease, dear
heart, prickly hedgehog, heavenly shiner, old campaigner, unsteady
swallow: Hardwick flits through the lines as ancient adversary, beloved
friend, drinking companion, wary partner. Their love, after twenty years
of marriage, has grown "leathery." In the lovely, sorrowing "Obit" that
closes the volume, Lowell faces the end of marriage—and the end of

life—from the other side, and seizes the final moment just as it passes. The poem opens with a declaration: "Our love will not come back on fortune's wheel." And closes with an aching question: "After loving you so much, can I forget/you for eternity, and have no other choice?"

"My plot rolls with the seasons, but one year is confused with another," Lowell wrote of the progression of the sonnets in the "Afterthought" to *Notebook*. "Accident threw up subjects, and the plot swallowed them—famished for human chances." The plot. The inevitable, conventional denouement for the plot Lowell had set in motion was separation, divorce, and new life with another woman. And sure enough, all of these "human chances" came up in turn. In the spring of 1970, Lowell went to England on a visiting professorship at All Souls College, Oxford, and it was during this sojourn that he met and fell in love with the other woman: Lady Caroline Blackwood, a thirty-eight-year-old writer and a member of the Anglo-Irish aristocracy (her father was the fourth marquis of Dufferin and Ava, and her mother was a Guinness, a member of the wealthy stout-brewing family). Beautiful, rich, twice-before married (her first husband was the renowned painter Lucien Freud, her second the musician Israel Citkovitz), the mother of three daughters, careless in her personal habits, deeply dependent on alcohol, talented, troubled, and well connected, Blackwood was decidedly *not* another of Lowell's "girls," much as Hardwick tried to convince herself of this. She inspired him and, for a time, rejuvenated him; he believed, for a time, she would keep him sane. His love for Blackwood consumed him and beguiled him: when his time was up at Oxford, he could not bear to leave. For her he would give up Hardwick and start a new life in England.

"To Cal, it seemed an alliance made in heaven," says Stanley Kunitz. "Caroline had literary power, social power, money power. She was a fit culmination of his romantic history." The writer Jonathan Raban, then living in London, recalls that when he first met Lowell and Blackwood, they were "very happy with each other. They were the two happiest people on the face of the earth, though it didn't last." But Mary McCarthy, who had seen Lowell and Blackwood together in England soon after the liaison began, took a more jaundiced view. In a long, gossipy letter to Arendt, she gaye her version of the Lowell-Hardwick split and the Lowell-Blackwood romance, along with wonderful verbal snapshots of the principal parties and attendant complications. Blackwood is "a beautiful, odd girl, somewhat like a blonde Carmen, somewhat schizoid, history of psychiatric treatment, mysterious, childlike, innocent, candid. . . . [S]he isn't stupid but what you might call self-educated, like so many daughters of the very rich that become Bohemian. A waif." She tosses in the odd detail that *New York Review of Books* editor Robert Silvers had loved Caroline for years and "for years she has refused to marry him." Silvers evidently introduced her to Lowell, and Lowell proceeded to "steal" her away. (According to Blackwood, Lowell harbored a fantasy that Silvers actually arranged the whole thing—that their romance was "fate, organized by Bob.") As for Lowell, McCarthy writes that "he doesn't seem to me to be manic, though naturally somewhat excited." "My doubts aren't so much about Cal's seriousness," she continues, "as about Caroline's ability to bear the weight of his personality, which can be crushing, overbearing, and so on. I wouldn't have the strength to live with him twenty-four hours. But he seems to feel in Caroline or in a life with Caroline some source of potential change, renewal. . . . He seems quite ready to turn his back on everything, all his old myths, including the Maine one. He's renounced, with slight sadness, any thought of returning some day to Castine."

And then Mary moves on to "poor Lizzie": "To me, his finding another wife could be a blessing for Lizzie. For both of them. . . . [S]eeing her as I've done so exhausted, beaten, and unhappy, one couldn't have much hope for a miraculous improvement of the marriage. At least she has the *New York Review*. That interests her (or did) a lot more than coping with Cal, who I think more than anything else has *bored* her the last few years, to the point of excruciation, though he cannot have guessed this. And maybe she not either."

Good old Mary. In fact, this is one of the most sympathetic paragraphs she ever devoted to Hardwick—and one of the more perceptive. Did she suffer from excruciating, though probably unconscious, boredom with Lowell's madness? Yes. Would divorce be a blessing for her? Yes, in a way it did eventually prove to be that. But before the blessing came the curse and humiliation of finding herself the scorned wife, a curse compounded by Lowell's determination to make the whole debacle public in his poetry. McCarthy makes another interesting connection in a letter to Lowell: "The coincidence of Women's Liberation with what [Lizzie's] been through, over Caroline, has played, I'd guess, quite a role." Coming from McCarthy, an avowed antifeminist, this is a very interesting statement, with several shades of meaning. Hardwick, as we've seen, was no feminist either, even less so than McCarthy in the way she lived her life; yet finding herself thrust into the role of the unwanted older wife inevitably raised feminist "issues." Why was a man still viable and desirable at fifty and a woman not? What was the "value" of twenty years of keeping house for a husband who "didn't lift a finger"? Who would end up with the money and the property? How could she face the world alone? What status would she command in the literary world without Lowell, who had always been "the star attraction," as Rahv crassly put it? Where could she summon the power to hurt Lowell as much as he had just hurt her? Power, money, work, prestige, sex, domestic labor, body image, freedom: this is what the "women's libbers" were talking about in 1970. And though Hardwick despised the shrill verve of feminist invective and sneered at the crude poses struck by the young female firebrands, she could hardly deny the fact that a lot of what they were saying suddenly, disconcertingly "fit" the circumstances of her own life.

Her feelings on this score must have been complicated by having witnessed, at close hand, her (and Lowell's) dear friend Adrienne Rich transform herself from long-suffering poet-wife to radical lesbian feminist. Rich first declared her rebellion against the oppressions of 1950s-style wifeliness in her ten-part poem "Snapshots of a Daughter-in-Law"—"that savage, those first attacks," as William Alfred put it—which sent shock waves through placid, sexist literary Boston in the early 1960s. At the end of the decade, Rich left her husband of many years and the father of her three sons, the economist Alfred H. Conrad, who committed suicide in 1970. In the poetry she was writing at this time, Rich spoke out openly, angrily as a woman newly aware of "the tragedy of sex" and the hideous power of men and their machines; and she dared to tell the terrible sad secrets women kept from each other as they "walked the floors of their lives in separate rooms"—women such as herself and Hardwick, who had been wives and mothers side by side in Boston, passed down maternity clothes, "bathed their children in the same basin," as she wrote in "After Twenty Years." In telling the truth at last, she felt herself "flow into history" as a woman "living in the prime of life."

Hardwick wrote to a friend in 1971 that Rich was "more feminist and radical than I am, but something very special and right." Looking back today, Hardwick speaks of her amazement at what Rich went through from the late 1950s to the early 1970s: "She was a wonderful mother and wife, one of the most brilliant and beguiling women I've ever known. I don't know what happened. She got swept too far. She deliberately made herself ugly and wrote these extreme and ridiculous poems." "Adrienne was so alert, so intelligent, so witty," Hardwick told the poet

Peter Davison. "We were great friends, but that all changed later on."

To Hardwick and the literary women of her generation, Rich's "defection" was horrifying—hideous, shameful, but also fascinating, like public nudity or violence in the streets. They could dismiss Betty Friedan and Gloria Steinem as polemicists, but Rich was a *poet*—a woman who loved language and used it with power and precision—and her work was electrifying: *Diving into the Wreck,* the collection of poems she wrote right after the breakup of her marriage and her husband's suicide, won the National Book Award in 1974 (she refused the award for herself but accepted, in a statement cosigned with poetry nominees Audre Lorde and Alice Walker, in the name of all women). Rich crossed a line that Hardwick could hardly bear to contemplate. Rich addressed the dilemma women of Hardwick's generation had been living all along and refusing to think about or acknowledge. But now that Hardwick was no longer a wife, she began to look at things differently. She acknowledged, in a letter to a woman friend, that being on her own—as a single mother, as we now say—had altered her attitude toward her work. She now felt "more as men feel" about writing professionally—that is, for money. "I always knew Mary McCarthy *wanted* to be the money earner—that was a spur, a necessity. I could not do that in relation to a man." But now that she too is "compelled" to write, she worries that it's "too late! Jamesian—'The Beast in the Jungle.'"

Not "too late" at all, as time has proven, for almost three decades later she's still at it. Hardwick, unlike Lowell, would never write openly, recognizably about her marriage and its demise: even her autobiographical novel *Sleepless Nights* circles maddeningly around "the huge fact of Cal," as McCarthy put it in a letter to Hardwick praising the novel. But in the essays she composed around the time of the breakup, she inserted strands of her own feelings, coded passages from her own book of days. As Lowell wrote her in 1971, praising the pieces on Ibsen she was publishing in the *New York Review,* "I think you should be vain of having put so much of yourself into the classic plots; I'm envious." This was an oddly detached statement, given the furious clarity with which Hardwick analyzes the love triangle in *Rosmersholm,* "putting in" not only herself but also Lowell and Blackwood and the whole wretched, wrenching mess of their entangled lives:

There is always something vulgar about a triangle. Even in the most elevated circumstances, the struggle is one of consumption, of "having" or "getting" something that is not, so to speak, on the free market. The victors are degraded by slyness, corruption, and greediness; the loser by weakness and humiliation. Heartlessness, ignobility, and ambition are the essence. It is a struggle for the experienced, not for the very young. Only those who have lived and endured have the understanding of the narrowness of opportunity within one lifetime. This experience provides the energy and the brutal decisiveness necessary to persist.

Hardwick put more of herself and more of Lowell into her essays on Zelda Fitzgerald and Sylvia Plath—different parts, disguised, but still there. In the piece on *Zelda,* a review of Nancy Milford's 1970 biography, Hardwick considers the hidden costs of being the literary wife—the artistic woman loved and valued privately by the artistic husband because she can "keep up" but brusquely elbowed aside in public when she threatens to declare herself his equal or dares to outshine him:

> In the case of artists these intense relations are curiously ambivalent, undefined collaborations—the two share in perceptions, temperament, in the struggle for creation, for the powers descending downward from art, for reputation, achievement, stability, for their own uniqueness—that especially. Still, only one of the twins is real as an artist, as a person with a special claim upon the world, upon the indulgence of society. Many writers seem to long for these trembling, gifted, outstanding hand-maidens, for they are aware that the prosaic, the withdrawn, the demanding, are terrible daily deterrents to art.

Hardwick was not Lowell's "twin" in the way Zelda was Scott Fitzgerald's twin; yet she was indeed one of the "outstanding hand-maidens" and she knew all too well that of the two of them, Lowell was the one who had the "special claim upon the world." A claim he exercised not only through genius but through madness. Here too the Fitzgeralds' marriage is painfully relevant. As Hardwick writes with insight born of twenty years of coping with mental illness: "[S]ick persons create guilt of a mysterious kind, whether by their own wish or merely by the peculiarities of their often luminous fixity. The will to blame, to hold them to account, soon appears futile to those closest. Instead the mad entwine their relations in an unresolved, lingering, chafing connection, where guilt, exasperation and grief for the mysteries of life continue to choke. Perhaps the nearest feeling is the immensely suffering and baffling connection between those living and those slowly dying."

Mental imbalance, feverish marital competition, domestic destruction also figure in Hardwick's extraordinarily perceptive essay about Sylvia Plath. Rather in the manner of Edmund Wilson, she knits together character sketch with a shrewd assessment of how Plath's life and times impinged on her work—but unlike Wilson, Hardwick writes very much from the heart. Plath stalks through the essay as a kind of deranged cousin, a fellow "literary wife" who labored and raged her way through the tranquilized 1950s:

> I myself do not think her work comes out of the cold war, the extermination camps, or the anxious doldrums of the Eisenhower years. If anything, she seems to have jumped ahead of her dates and to have more in common with the years we have just gone through. Her lack of conventional sentiment, her destructive contempt for her family, the failings in her marriage, the drifting, rootless rage, the peculiar homelessness, the fascination with sensation and the drug of death, the determination to try everything, knowing it would not really stop the suffering—no one went as far as she did in this.
>
> There is nothing of the social revolutionary in her, but she is whirling about in the center of an overcharged, splitting air and she especially understands everything destructive and negative.

Again, it is difficult not to see something of Lowell in this frantic household cyclone that destroys everything in its path and makes art of its acts of destruction. Plath, in a sense, straddled both sides of the chasm: bound to home, but rootless and homeless; the mother and the maniac; the wife who went farther than anyone else.

Interestingly, Lowell also wrote about Plath, a brief introduction to her final, posthumous volume *Ariel* (1966)—one of the very few times he and Hardwick crossed paths professionally. Lowell's piece has some delicate touches—"the manner of feeling is controlled hallucination, the autobiography of a fever"; Plath as a student sitting in on his class was "a brilliant tense presence embarrassed by restraint"; she had "an air of maddening docility that hid her unfashionable patience and boldness"—but overall it comes off sounding rather forced and wooden next to Hardwick's inward, intuitive analysis. Lowell's shrewdest insight deals with an issue that was occupying more and more space in his own mind—the overlap between life and art:

> Sylvia Plath's poems are not the celebration of some savage and de-bauched existence, that of the "damned" poet, glad to burn out his body for a few years of continuous intensity. This poetry and life are not a career; they tell that life, even when disciplined, is simply not worth it.

This was a position he contemplated deeply but would never endorse for himself.

Lowell saw Plath, as he saw all women poets, as a woman first and a poet second (he infuriated Elizabeth Bishop by ranking her again and again among the best *women* poets). Lowell does indeed catch the thrashings of Plath against the circumstances of her time and place—marriage, daughterhood, motherhood, the long months of domestic des-olation—but he misses the way she "jumped ahead of her dates," as Hardwick put it. Plath in her final poems invented a voice that still sounds new, new in a way that Lowell's own voice no longer sounds, and Lowell didn't hear it.

"This poetry and life are not a career," Lowell wrote knowingly of Plath; but by 1970 his own poetry and life increasingly *were* a career, the same career. As he lived it, he rolled it out in fourteen-liners. Mary McCarthy described this ravening of life for "material" in a letter she wrote to Hardwick on April 5, 1972: "Cal is not a sacrificing man, least of all, I suppose, where his poetry is concerned, which means more to him than any people. People in fact are sacrificed to *it,* to keep the flame burning. It is a Jamesian subject, I guess—the Moloch-artist." Mc-Carthy is especially exercised on the subject because she has just seen Lowell's new poems, the sonnets that chronicle his split with Hard-wick, his new life with Blackwood, her pregnancy, their marriage, his return to New York for a visit, and so on. Hardwick is more than a "character" in these poems; she is, in a sense, coauthor, for Lowell quotes extensively, and in many cases verbatim, from her letters and phone calls. "It wasn't hard to recognize your voice, certainly," Mc-Carthy informed her rather breezily. But the breeziness would vanish, on all sides, once the poems were published as *The Dolphin* in 1973. Hardwick's voice is the loudest in the book: where Lowell ruminates mournfully on the impossibility of choosing one woman over another and scours his soul for signs of doubt and insincerity, Hardwick howls. Hers is the voice of fury incarnate, slashing, sarcastic, writhing in pain and spewing venom; the voice of the discarded wife. "What a record year, even for us—" she sails into him in "Voices," the first of her letters. "That new creature / when I hear her name, I have to laugh." *"Don't you dare mail us the love your life denies,"* she rages italically in "Exorcism"; *"do you really* know *what you have done?"* And so on.

Strangely, Hardwick had contemplated a similar situation in her essay on Zelda Fitzgerald. Describing how Scott used Zelda's letters and portions of her diary in his novels, Hardwick quotes Zelda's pronouncement that "Mr. Fitzgerald . . . seems to believe plagiarism begins at home." But plagiarism was the least of Lowell's offenses in Hardwick's eyes. He had betrayed a sacred trust; he had violated her privacy and the sanctity of their marriage; he had made her a laughingstock; and, in her view, he had written not only offensive but *bad* poetry. "If Cal was going to break all the rules, I wish the poems were better," Richard Wilbur recalls her telling him. And she wrote to Elizabeth Bishop that the parts of *The Dolphin* that relate to her and Harriet strike her as "inane, empty, unnecessary." How, she wonders, could Cal have worked so hard on the verse and still left in "so many fatuities, indiscretions, bad lines. . . . That breaks my heart, for all of us." "The poems from my letters seem to me quite silly," Hardwick told an interviewer recently, still brooding about Lowell's offense, "and perhaps I should be glad they are not in the mode of fury of some of my communications at the time."

The Dolphin is unquestionably indiscreet, even indecent in parts—but it is not fatuous or inane. In fact, the volume may be the best of Lowell's sonnets, the most alive, supple, accessible, true to life. Truest of all, perhaps, in the way the poems turn inward to scrutinize the acts of creation and narration. Life and art flow into each other, exchange molecules and substance, like air entering the lungs and fortifying the bloodstream with oxygen. "My words are English, but the plot is hexed," Lowell writes in "Exorcism 2"; "one man, two women, the common novel plot." He poses himself variously in *The Dolphin*'s "plot" as a Victorian hero, Hamlet sick with vacillation, the aging bigamist who would be happy only with both women—the old familiar "heart's ease" and the elusive, destructive dolphin. He has come down off the Olympian heights of his early 1960s mode—"Pity the planet," as he intoned in "Near the Ocean"—and cast himself in the "humanly low" station of ordinary actor.

These poems are very fine and at the same time very brutal. As Stanley Kunitz told Lowell after reading the manuscript, "There are details which seem to me monstrously heartless . . . passages I can scarcely bear to read: they are too ugly, for being too cruel, too intimately cruel." There's a greediness in Lowell's eagerness to tell all, make everything public, dress every deed instantly in words. "In a central way, Robert Lowell was not quite civilized," said Frank Bidart, who was in a prime position to know. "He knew that his poems destroyed the decencies, the privacies of family life as these are ordinarily understood. He was haunted by the pain the poems caused." *"Art just isn't worth that much,"* Elizabeth Bishop wrote him in a long, frantic letter urging him not to use Hardwick's "personal, tragic, anguished letters"—but he went ahead and did it anyway. He couldn't help himself: the "material" was too good.

The book caused an uproar when it was published, especially among those who had been close to Lowell. Adrienne Rich was already angry at him for leaving Hardwick and fathering another child ("[h]aving children must be a profound thing if it's anything," she lectured him in a letter when she heard the news of Blackwood's pregnancy, "and right now in history it is a strange thing to do. . . . Men and women are having such a hard time with the intense fragility of their own relationship that adding a complication seems foolhardy"); now she let him have it publicly in a stinging review in the *American Poetry Review*. What, she demanded, could "one say about a poet who, having left his wife and daughter for another marriage, then titles a book with their names, and goes on to appropriate his ex-wife's letters, written under the stress and pain of desertion, into a book of poems nominally addressed to the new wife? . . . I have to say that I think this is bullshit eloquence, a poor excuse for a cruel and shallow book. . . . The inclusion of the letter poems stands as one of the most vindictive and mean-spirited acts in the history of poetry, one for which I can think of no precedent." Another poet accused Lowell of living his life solely "in order to provide material for poems; one sees with horror the cannibal-poet who dines off portions of his own body, and the bodies of his family." Richard Wilbur was repelled; Mary McCarthy sided, cautiously, with Hardwick; Arendt was fed up with his self-indulgence and self-pity. "[H]e talked about Lizzy [*sic*]," Arendt wrote McCarthy from London after an unpleasant evening with Lowell around this time, "that his having deserted her would haunt him until his grave, that he would die soon. . . . And for the first time I did not like him." Hardwick, who was devastated by the hideous publicity attending the book's publication, wrote Bishop of her "dread [of] the future with biographies and *Lizzie,* to say nothing of Cal. . . . Fortunately I'll be dead before most of them come."

The Dolphin, the last of Lowell's sonnet books, marked the end of an era, not only for him and Hardwick, but in a sense for their generation. In its deliberate, desperate assault on decency, *The Dolphin* was extremist art, very much in the spirit of the late 1960s and early 1970s. There was shock value in publishing an ex-wife's letters, in going all the way in pursuit of truth. But beneath this radical, daringly amoral narrative ploy, the book is deeply conventional—"The common novel plot," as Lowell himself acknowledged. Unlike Adrienne Rich, he did not leave a marriage to find a new kind of intimate freedom—rather, he left one marriage to bind himself into another one. And as he left, he threw open all the doors and cupboards and peeled back the drapes and bedspreads. It was a startling, insulting act—and ultimately a futile one. At the heart of *The Dolphin* is the sickness that afflicted all the marriages in this book: the husband's desire to have both handmaiden and partner; the woman's need to be both wife and artist. Blackwood, the shimmering, dangerous dolphin, "all muscle, youth, intention," promises to cure Lowell of the sickness—until they marry and the fever spikes again. "I'm manic, she's panic," Lowell told a friend shakily when the delirious happiness of new love was gone. Lowell and the literary men of his generation were all bigamists of a sort and their marriages broke under the weight of their double desires, for the women they married could never really play both parts and still hold on to their sanity. Either they drank and cracked up, like Jean Stafford; or they divorced and had affairs, like Mary McCarthy; or they toughed it out for as long as they could stand it, only to be chucked in the end, like Hardwick. The Arendt-Blücher marriage endured, perhaps, because the roles were reversed: she was the "star attraction," and he, despite his love affairs, was "the husband" who supplied brilliant conversation and intellectual companionship but never threatened to overshadow his wife. Or maybe it was just that they were Europeans.

Feminism did not solve these marital problems—succeeding generations of wives and husbands are still desperately trying to figure things out; marriages are still blowing apart over these sorts of conflicts—but feminism brought the problems of marriage to the surface. The expectations are different now; more people seem to know what's going on; handmaidens are hard to find these days. The marriages that McCarthy, Lowell, Wilson, Hardwick, Stafford, and most of their writer friends made were prefeminist, really antifeminist; they were the last generation to reach maturity before the social landscape changed thanks to the women's movement. For feminism *was* the only revolution that survived the 1960s and remains a part of our daily life. As Hardwick wrote in a brilliant essay examining America's "domestic manners" after the incendiary 1960s had guttered out into the dazed, bewildering 1970s:

> The inner changes within women can scarcely be exaggerated. . . . The arrival of women's ambition, transforming as it does private life, inner feeling, and public life is not at all simple but instead resembles the subtle shiftings of human thought and life brought about by enormously challenging ideas such as evolution and Freudianism. . . . Husbands cannot take the responsibilities for wives as an immutable duty, ordained by nature. Women's liberation suits society much more than society itself is prepared to admit. The wife economy is as obsolete as the slave economy. . . . The women's movement is above all a critique. And almost nothing, it turns out, will remain outside its relevance. It is the disorienting extension of the intrinsic meaning of women's liberation, much of it unexpected, that sets the movement apart. It is a psychic and social migration, leaving behind an altered landscape.

The culture, as Hardwick perceived with acuity and dismay, had moved on. New voices sounded more compelling. New issues commanded more urgent attention. It wasn't just the "swingers" and the "hipster writers" Rahv was always fuming about. The American literary world had broken up into a mixed, dissonant chorus: James Baldwin and John Updike, Bernard Malamud and Ken Kesey, Thomas Pynchon and Toni Morrison, Jack Kerouac and Adrienne Rich, all of them backed up by rows and rows of newly minted, wildly contentious academic theorists. There was no longer a coherent discourse or a recognized cultural center. The idea of a "best literary magazine in America"—an epithet that belonged to *PR* for decades—was passé. *The New York Review of Books* did not succeed to the throne: it was too high-brow to tune in to 1960s popular culture, too narrow to let in those speaking in different dialects, too provincial to comprehend life and thought outside New York (and London). "Art as a religion—Rilke—seems to be passing," Elizabeth Hardwick wrote in a 1963 essay published in one of the *NYR*'s first issues; "not the work of Rilke, but the style of life, the austere dedication, sustained by the hope that poems and novels would save us. Those holy pages produced in pain . . ." It was Lowell's religion as much as Rilke's, and if it was passing in 1963, by 1970 it was past. There was nothing sacred about literary culture anymore; in fact, there was nothing sacred and there was no literary culture but rather many warring cultures happening simultaneously and often in total ignorance of one another. The times were—briefly—too rebellious to endorse anything smacking of cultural authority and then, from the mid-1970s on, too indifferent.

Those who came of age in the 1960s and early 1970s had no need of the truth that Lowell told in *The Dolphin,* with its sorrowing exposures and agonized self-consciousness. Truth telling would become faster, dirtier, more haphazard, more suspicious than anything Lowell imagined: less formal; less learned; above all, less literary. In the decade between *For the Union Dead* and *The Dolphin,* Lowell and the New York intellectuals moved from the center to the sidelines. There had always been something fundamentally elitist about the *PR/NYR* crowd, despite their left-wing politics; but increasingly they were an elite who impressed and provoked only one another. The sense of excitement and momentousness in who said what and wrote what about whom was over: the latest movie or blockbuster was more of a cultural "event" than the table of contents of *Partisan Review.* In the 1960s, mass culture—movies, television, commercial fiction—took center stage. By the end of the 1960s, Rahv and McCarthy, Hardwick and Lowell, Wilson, Arendt, and Tate were beginning to look like survivors, old warriors whose commands went unheeded, misinterpreted or openly derided by the young. Their "domestic manners"—their drinking and adulteries, their slashing gossip, their publicized couplings and uncouplings, their devout worship at the shrine of the written word, their pugnacious variations on the theme of liberalism—"placed" them like period pieces in a house museum. Authority—diffuse, covert, denied, sometimes unwanted—passed away from them. And no other group has taken their place. They were the last generation for whom, in Alfred Kazin's words, "writing was everything."

As for the generation's women, they had won their first battle without fighting and lost the war without realizing there was one. They managed to get published and to become famous, formidable intellectuals without challenging or offending the males who published them: they succeeded because they were "good" in a way that the men appreciated and respected. But their unintended victory proved to be perishable, personal, bound up as it was with their own gifts, sway, charm, intimate connections, powers of persuasion. They were exceptional in both senses of the word and they knew it and didn't care. They made no common cause with one another as women, at least in what they wrote for publication. To them, gender was not an issue: talent, brains, and beauty were what mattered. Those who did not come by these qualities naturally were not worth considering. Never mind the odds, the "system," the social context; when the great "psychic and social migration" of feminism came, altering the place of women, the relations between the sexes, the meanings of wife and mother, the women of this generation were left stranded. They were an aristocracy of intellect who suddenly found themselves in a hostile new order—not quite a true democracy, but a clamorous, young, fluid republic. They might have been heroes had they known what was coming and fought for it. But instead, to the rising generation, they were the *ancien régime:* they drew the first and fiercest fire because they were so brilliant, so distinguished, so privileged, and so intensely, maddeningly familiar.

Epilogue: Deaths

DEATH, the ultimate loss of authority, claimed most of the crowd rapidly in the course of the 1970s. The women, as they usually do, outlived the men.

Heinrich Blücher was the first to go. He died of a heart attack in New York's Mount Sinai Hospital in the autumn of 1970. Hannah Arendt's friends were surprised that her first desire was to give her Lutheran-born husband a Jewish funeral, with the chanting of the Kaddish, the Jewish prayer for the dead. Instead the funeral was a simple, nonreligious ceremony at New York's Riverside Chapel. Mary McCarthy flew over from Paris to be with her widowed friend and speak at the service. Arendt had had her differences with Blücher over the years, and his adulteries had pained her, but she felt very lost and alone without him. She was free, she wrote sadly to McCarthy, "free like a leaf in the wind," but it was a thin, haunted kind of freedom. After Blücher's death, McCarthy's friendship became more important to her than ever—the women traveled together and corresponded more frequently, and Arendt enlisted Mc-

Carthy's editorial advice more urgently as she embarked on her final work, *The Life of the Mind.*

Edmund Wilson, who had spent the 1950s and 1960s battling with the IRS over his failure to pay income tax for nine years and writing about such diverse topics as the Dead Sea Scrolls, the Iroquois Indians of upstate New York, the great American writers of the Civil War era, and the sins of the Modern Language Association, died in his beloved family home at Talcottville, New York, on June 12, 1972. He was seventy-seven years old. Wilson's last marriage, to the half-Russian, half-German Elena Mumm Thornton was his longest and, by most accounts, his happiest. He had finally found a brilliant, beautiful woman who, unlike Mary McCarthy, knew how to handle him and refrained from competing with him or, usually, crossing him.

McCarthy and Wilson necessarily maintained a certain amount of contact through their son, Reuel, and as the years went by they relaxed a lot of their hostility toward each other. They heard about each other through common friends—the Lowells, Arthur Schlesinger, Jr., Dwight Macdonald—and they crossed paths now and then professionally and socially (McCarthy's fourth husband, Jim West, remembers a brief encounter with a very drunk and tired Wilson in a Paris hotel bar). And of course they read each other's work with interest. But the old wounds did not heal entirely. When Doris Grumbach was preparing her early biography of McCarthy, *The Company She Kept,* for publication, Wilson wrote her publisher, John J. Geoghegan, that "Miss Grumbach ought to be on her guard against Miss McCarthy's constant tendency to distort and exaggerate." That "constant" speaks volumes—a warning only a former husband would have issued.

Wilson rumbled on from beyond the grave, for the diaries he had been keeping all his life began to appear in decade-long installments, starting with *The Twenties,* published in 1975, and ending with *The Sixties* in 1993. Amid the voluminous, hasty sketches of dinners, debates, drunken evenings, love affairs, travels, quarrels, sights seen, and politics endured are snapshots of members of the crowd, whom Wilson identified in the mid-1960s as "a whole sort of *Cultural Establishment*" in New York, with the Lowells and the Epsteins (Jason and Barbara) running "the headquarters of the literary department." Lowell, on the verge of a breakdown, strikes Wilson as "precariously high. It was like hurricane

warnings on the Cape." Jean Stafford is "amusing but . . . becomes fa-
tiguing with her continual complaining ridicule." And so on. "Extraordinary thing to publish actually," Hardwick wrote to McCarthy when
Wilson brought out a section of the diaries in his 1971 volume *Upstate*.
McCarthy herself was largely absent from the published journals—at her
own insistence.

Philip Rahv was only sixty-five when he died in Cambridge, Massachusetts, in December 1973. His last years had not been happy ones. Living
in the Boston area, where he taught at intervals at Brandeis University,
Rahv had had to content himself with long-distance blasts at New York
about the sorry state of literature and politics. Hardwick and McCarthy
rolled their eyes in letters to each other about the shambles of his private
life—his third wife, Theo Stillman, dead in a house fire in 1968; his
fourth marriage, brief and miserable, ended in bitter divorce after eighteen months. But his death was a terrible blow to both of them. Hardwick wrote a long letter about it to McCarthy, blaming the rancor of
Rahv's final divorce for the "suffering and rage of the last year" and for
his descent into the "treacherous habit" of mixing sleeping pills and alcohol: "The horrors of indulgence in full middle-age. No doubt it all
comes from depression and it is awful to be really fouled up in your personal life at that time. To make a mistake [in a late marriage] is to be really, truly miserable." McCarthy, privately, cast a cold eye on these lines.
As she wrote Arendt, she had gotten a very different picture of Rahv on
his final night from her friend Frances FitzGerald. FitzGerald's account,
she said, "leads me to doubt Lizzie's picture of his utter '*isolation,*' heavy
drinking, sleeping drugs, total disintegration. I had suspected her account anyway, so hysterical and insistent—a good deal of projection, I
think, of her own assessment of her position onto him." Hardwick's "position" in 1973 being the desolation that followed the rancorous breakup
of her own marriage—this was the year *The Dolphin* appeared.

There may be some truth to what McCarthy says about Hardwick's
projection. But it's also possible that Mary's rush to discredit Lizzie here
rose from their long rivalry for Rahv's affection and approval. It was important to McCarthy to establish herself as closer to Rahv than anyone
else, especially Hardwick. She was extremely proud that her vivid, intimate memorial piece ran on the front page of *The New York Times Book
Review:* "So he's gone, that dear phenomenon," she opens. "A powerful

intellect, a massive, overpowering personality and yet shy, curious, susceptible, confiding." She had designated herself the official mourner. McCarthy wrote of Rahv again, even more intimately, in her posthumous *Intellectual Memoirs* (1992), in which she reminisces about their love affair and wonders, coyly perhaps, why she ever left him, when she loved him so much, and married Wilson, whom she loathed.

"I must admit that I mind this relentless defoliation (or deforestation) process," Arendt wrote to McCarthy the day that Hardwick telephoned her with the news of Rahv's death. "As though to grow old does not mean, as Goethe said, 'gradual withdrawal from appearance'—which I do not mind—but the gradual (or rather sudden) transformation of a world with familiar faces (no matter, foe or friend) into a kind of desert, populated by strange faces. In other words, it is not me who withdraws but the world that dissolves—an altogether different proposition." The world dissolved appallingly for McCarthy when Arendt died two years later, on December 4, 1975. Like her husband, she had suffered a heart attack, and death came swiftly. She was sixty-nine years old.

In the five years since Blücher's death, Arendt had ridden herself hard, lecturing at conferences and universities in Europe and America, teaching at the New School for Social Research, working on her final opus, *The Life of the Mind*, smoking heavily. Angina first afflicted her, apparently, in the winter of 1971, and she suffered a serious heart attack while lecturing in Scotland in the spring of 1974. She chose never to quit smoking. "Since I am certainly not going to live for my health," she wrote McCarthy, "I'll do what I think is right." Doing *right* meant, above all, thinking and working. The night she died, December 4, 1975, she was entertaining dinner guests at her New York apartment on Riverside Drive. Dinner was over and the friends were conversing over coffee when Arendt began coughing. It was the onset of the heart attack that killed her.

McCarthy came at once from Paris to attend Arendt's funeral. The eulogy she delivered, later published as "Saying Good-by to Hannah" in *The New York Review of Books,* was an odd, charming blend of the intellectual and the emotional, just like their friendship. McCarthy's "placing" of Arendt's work was at once shrewd and reverent:

> The task that had fallen to her, as an exceptionally gifted intellect and
> a representative of the generations she had lived among, was to apply

thought systematically to each and every characteristic experience of her time—*anomie,* terror, advanced warfare, concentration camps, Auschwitz, inflation, revolution, school integration, the Pentagon Papers, space, Watergate, Pope John, violence, civil disobedience—and, having finally achieved this, to direct thought inward, upon itself, and its own characteristic processes. . . . Hannah was always more for the Many than for the One (which may help explain her horrified recognition of totalitarianism as a new phenomenon in the world). She did not want to find a master key or universal solvent, and if she had a religion, it was certainly not monotheistical.

But the personal, emotional aspect of the eulogy, especially McCarthy's evocation of Arendt as "a beautiful woman, alluring, seductive, feminine," was what most struck and surprised mourners in the Riverside Chapel. William Phillips recalls how strange it was to hear Mary praising Hannah's legs at the funeral service (actually it was her "charming ankles, elegant feet," of which she was rather vain). "She liked shoes," McCarthy went on in her tribute to Arendt as "a physical being"; "in all the years I knew her, I think she only once had a corn. Her legs, feet, and ankles expressed quickness, decision." It was a side of Arendt only her dearest friends saw. How like Mary McCarthy to notice and to talk about it on an important public occasion.

After Arendt's death, McCarthy shouldered the considerable task of editing and annotating the work Arendt had been in engaged in when she died, the projected three-volume *The Life of the Mind.* McCarthy set aside the novel she'd been writing (*Cannibals and Missionaries*) and devoted the better part of three years to preparing the first two volumes, *Thinking* and *Willing,* for publication. *Judging,* the conclusion, was never written. The first page of the manuscript was in Arendt's typewriter the day she died. She had gotten as far as the title and the two introductory epigraphs.

Robert Lowell was next. He died of a heart attack in a taxicab in New York City on the evening of September 12, 1977. He had celebrated his sixtieth birthday six months earlier.

The circumstances of Lowell's death are characteristic of the way things had been happening to and around him in his last years. The marriage to Blackwood did not bring Lowell the renewal he had hoped for, or not for long anyway. In a way, Blackwood was too much like him—unstable, slovenly, fragile, egocentric, cut off from ordinary, practical things—to give him the kind of care he had been used to with Hardwick. "They seemed to be two of a kind," recalls Stanley Kunitz. "Spontaneous, feckless, dangerous. When I visited them in England, it seemed like the most reckless and haphazard household." "They existed in a state of destruction," says the writer John Malcolm Brinnin. Their son, Robert Sheridan Lowell, born in the autumn of 1971, added to the turmoil. When Lowell got sick, Blackwood couldn't stand to be around him. "I'm no use to him in these attacks," she told a friend. "They destroy me." There was a good deal of drinking—innocent enough when they kept themselves to white wine, wildly out of control when they moved on to vodka. Lowell could usually hold his liquor, at least when he was sane, but Blackwood became something of a zombie when under the influence. A friend remembers that during the vodka-drinking periods Blackwood would appear thinner each day, her clothes hanging on her body: there was less and less flesh and more and more vodka.

In January 1977 Lowell, back in America to teach a semester at Harvard, suffered congestive heart failure and spent ten days at Massachusetts General Hospital. He recovered but remained shaky. His parents had both died in their early sixties, and Lowell was convinced that the same thing would happen to him. The poems he was writing in these years, collected in his final volume, *Day by Day,* are weary and meditative—poems of "ache and twilight," as critic Helen Vendler put it. In the book, he addresses all three of his wives, dedicates poems to dear old friends, Peter Taylor, John Berryman, and Robert Penn Warren, and records the illness and confusion and heavy drinking that snarled his relationship with Blackwood. The breakup of this marriage was as fraught and vacillating as its inception. For a year or more, Lowell and Blackwood played an agonized tug-of-war with the marriage, parting and reconciling, threatening and forgiving each other, declaring love one moment and dread the next. "They were both in bad shape at the end," says Jonathan Raban, who was with them often in England. "For Cal it was an impossible oscillation, not knowing what he wanted or what to do." There were torturing transatlantic phone calls, suicide attempts, breakdowns, depression, pills, and always an overflow of alcohol. The two of them had become, in Lowell's word, "two eruptions, two earthquakes crashing." Lowell, feeling desperate, turned to Hardwick for support, which she happily gave him. Lowell and Hardwick were together a good deal in New York during the spring of 1977, and they went up to Castine together and remained together there that summer.

Hardwick attempted to unravel the new situation and the "arrangements" in a letter she wrote to Mary McCarthy that June: "There is no great renewed romance, but a kind of friendship, and listening to his grief [over losing Caroline]. . . . It could be said we 'are back together,' but the phrase is not really meaningful—at least in the way it is commonly used." Hardwick felt that Lowell's sufferings over Blackwood, the feeling of being "unwanted," had humanized him: "The passion and the grief he knew from Caroline and from his feeling for her have made him more like the rest of us. We are trying to work out a sort of survival for both of us, and both are sixty. . . . We, together, are having a perfectly nice time, both quite independent and yet I guess dependent." To another friend she wrote, "I don't feel vulnerable, don't feel sent out on approval . . . don't talk or care about contracts and commitments . . . we are just going along, having a very agreeable time . . . day by day it seems real just as it is."

And so things went along for the last months of Lowell's life. A "perfectly nice" summer in New York, in Maine for the hot months, and, briefly, in Moscow to attend an official conference with the wife he had left seven years before. What happened at the very end is somewhat clouded in conflicting versions. This much is known: In September, Lowell went to see Blackwood in Ireland (where she had moved after selling her estate in Kent), and apparently she pleaded with him to stay on with her. Lowell found the visit "sheer torture" and telephoned Hardwick in New York to tell her he was returning to America earlier than he had originally planned. He flew from Dublin to New York on September 12 and took a taxi from the airport to the West Sixty-seventh Street apartment he had shared with Hardwick for nearly a decade. He was dead before the cab arrived. Among the belongings he had with him was a portrait of Blackwood done by her first husband, Lucien Freud, that she had asked him to have appraised in New York. Blackwood apparently believed he would come back to her. Lowell probably didn't know what he was going to do.

A story circulated that all three Lowell wives sat and wept together at the packed funeral mass at the Church of the Advent on lower Beacon Hill in Boston. In fact, Jean Stafford wanted to attend and considered arranging for a car to drive her up from her home in East Hampton. But she was ill, and Robert Giroux, her first editor and Lowell's, persuaded her that she had better not attempt the journey. Black-wood, however, was there, plunged in deep alcoholic grief. The jour-ney from Boston up to the Winslow family graveyard in Dunbarton, New Hampshire, was harrowing, with stops along the way to scare up drinks. But the real nightmare, for Hardwick, descended afterward. As she wrote at her wit's end to McCarthy after the funeral, "Caroline somehow moved in with me for 8 days and nights to prepare the Memorial Service. I don't think any single night I slept more than two hours. Her poor drunken theatricality hour after hour, day after day, night after night was unrelieved torture for me and I am sure for herself much more." It wasn't until Hardwick escaped to a furnished apart-ment she had in Storrs, Connecticut, that her own grief overwhelmed her: "[O]nly then could I burst into sobs and realize that Cal was truly gone forever. It is terrible."

Ailing when Lowell died, as she had been for much of their marriage and many of the years before and after it, Jean Stafford died in New York City in the winter of 1979. She was sixty-four years old. Stafford, after her marriage with Lowell ended, remained close to two of Lowell's best friends, Peter Taylor and Blair Clark, but professionally she threw in her lot with the lighter-toned (and higher-paying) *New Yorker,* which had al-ways been anathema to Lowell. She was friendly during the 1950s and 1960s with Edmund Wilson (who was also associated with *The New Yorker* for many years) and she pops up occasionally in his journals, usu-ally with glass in hand.

It would be an exaggeration to say that Stafford's life after Lowell was a long anticlimax, but she seems never to have matched the creative and emotional intensity she knew with him. Like Lowell, she married twice more—both times literary people. Her second husband, Oliver Jensen, an editor at *Life* and *American Heritage* magazines, at first appealed to her as a welcome relief from the wild-eyed poets and antagonistic essayists she had consorted with in the 1940s. But Jensen was stodgy and Stafford quickly began to scorn his efforts at keeping her healthy, sober, and pro-ductive. "I am all you say, a liar, a breaker of promises, an alcoholic, an incompetent . . . a hypochondriac," she wrote him in 1952, when the mar-riage was breaking up. "Do you imagine that knowing this and knowing it full well—I can also love myself and wish to go on living, making your life an incessant disappointment?" The marriage lasted two years.

In 1959 Stafford married *New Yorker* writer A. J. Liebling, a portly journalist and bon vivant ten years her senior, who was as famous for his ap-
petites as for his prodigious output of prose. *Between Meals,* his
best-known book, recounts a year of adventures in and out of Parisian
restaurants during the 1920s, but he also wrote memorably about box-
ing, the racetrack, politics, war, and the seamy side of life in New York
City. The marriage was, for the most part, a happy one for Stafford, but
her writing all but ceased. It's possible that Liebling's seemingly effortless
flow of prose paralyzed her, as Lowell's creative bursts had years before.
She claimed she didn't want to write for fear of interrupting Liebling's
high-speed production of articles and sketches, but this was probably an
excuse. She was also drinking more and more heavily, and Liebling, who
loved to drink and eat himself, did not try to control her as Lowell had
done so disastrously. Liebling died in New York in December 1963, four
years after they married. He was fifty-nine years old.

After Liebling's death, Stafford moved out to his house in the Springs
in East Hampton and set herself up as something of a curmudgeon—a
crusty, reclusive literary "lady" deliberately out of step with the hideous
barbarisms of the day. She marveled, sarcastically, over Lowell's phe-
nomenal power and glory in the late 1960s. "It is a little hard to keep up
with R.T.S.L., Jr. these days," she wrote Peter Taylor in 1968, when Lowell was campaigning nationally for Eugene McCarthy. "I like the image of
a president-maker lolling about with his loafers off (you can imagine
what condition they're in) and fetching up with that definition of acedia."
The student takeovers at Columbia, where she taught creative writing for
a time, horrified her, and she vowed to go on assigning Henry James,
Kafka, and Chekhov and to make "absolutely no reference to the troubles" no matter what her students said or did in class. Her writing in
these years dwindled down to reviews and the odd journalistic assignment, though her *Collected Stories,* issued in 1969, won the Pulitzer Prize
in 1970.

Stafford and Lowell had a bittersweet, wary rapprochement in these
years. Soon after Liebling's death, Stafford wrote Lowell a lovely, nostalgic letter thanking him for his gifts and flowers and forgiving him for the
ugliness of their past: "My dear, please never castigate yourself for what
you call blindness—how blind we both were, how green we were, how
countless were our individual torments we didn't know the names of."
Yet when Lowell adopted a similar tone in the letter/poem he wrote to
her in *Day by Day,* she got angry. The poem concludes wistfully, almost

like a eulogy: "You have spoken so many words and well, / being a woman and you . . . someone must still hear / whatever I have forgotten / or never heard, being a man." Perhaps what really galled her was a report of the condescending prefatory remarks Lowell made when he read the poem at New York's Ninety-second Street Y at the end of 1976. "Men may be superior to women," Lowell told the audience, "but women always do better in college, I think, and are much more precocious. . . . [Jean] could punctuate, and do all sorts of things. . . . She is one of our best writers, and her talent developed early." Stafford, in the hospital recovering from a stroke, muttered that Lowell was a "son of a bitch" and complained that "my only role was typing for him." She was still fighting the old battles.

Stafford got in the last lick, however. A year after Lowell's death, she published in *The New Yorker* her brilliant, lacerating, wickedly funny story "An Influx of Poets" about the demise of their marriage. It was the only section of a long-stalled novel ever to see the light of day. And it was the last piece published in her lifetime.

Her involvement, one might almost say obsession, with Lowell held her in thrall until the very end. When Stafford died at the Burke Rehabilitation Center in 1979, three books were found at her bedside: two works by Mark Twain and Lowell's *The Mills of the Kavanaughs,* the difficult volume he had written in the aftermath of their marriage. In the margins of the long title poem she had scribbled in her corrections and comments, tallying up how much he owed her and how little he had given. But at one point, overcome by the sheer beauty of the verse, she submitted once more to the old feelings: "How marvelous this is. It's the kind of writing that reminds me why I married him."

Caroline Gordon, Stafford's sometime mentor, friend, and finally nemesis, died two years later in 1981 at the age of eighty-five. The final two decades of Gordon's life had not been happy or especially productive ones. All her adult life, even during the period between their divorce and remarriage, Gordon thought of herself as Allen Tate's wife, and when Tate left her for good in 1959, she was devastated. "The divorce was the tragedy of her life," according to novelist Walker Percy, a devoted friend and protégé. Tate divorced Gordon to marry a much younger blue-blooded Boston poet named Isabella Stewart Gardner—a "bone stupid" woman, in the opinion of Robert Lowell, who was Gordon's junior by twenty years. Gordon was left with the house in Princeton and the Catholic Church, which sustained her as much as anything, even though hers was a tortured, hounding faith, as fanatical in its way as Lowell's had been. Tate's new marriage proved to be short and miserable, and he was divorced and married again, this time to a former nun named Helen Heinz, who bore him three sons, one of whom died tragically in a choking accident. Lowell and Tate were old men and new fathers at around the same time, and Lowell grieved with Tate when his little boy died before his first birthday, leaving a twin brother behind.

Gordon wrote and taught as she had done for years, taking a teaching position at the University of Dallas in 1972. But her earlier modest fame had dimmed and many of her students resented her fierce, opinionated, old-fashioned, intolerant style. Gordon had never been one to pull punches, and she wasn't about to start in her seventies. She and Tate remained in fond, occasional contact, and supposedly Tate proclaimed in the hearing of his third wife that Gordon had always been his *only* wife. Tate died in Nashville in February 1979, angry, bitter at many old friends, and obsessed with money. Gordon, who had moved down to Mexico to be with her daughter, Nancy, suffered a debilitating stroke two years after her husband's death. She died in Mexico on April 11, 1981. Her tombstone bears a fitting—and revealing—quotation from Jacques Maritain: "It is for Adam to interpret the voices which Eve hears."

Eight years later, on October 25, 1989, Mary McCarthy died of lung cancer in New York Hospital. She was seventy-seven years old.

McCarthy remained active right up to the end, writing fiction (*Birds of America, Cannibals and Missionaries*) and in-depth journalistic pieces (on the trial of Captain Ernest Medina for his role in the My Lai massacre and a series about the Watergate fiasco), publishing collections of her essays and stories, forging ahead with her memoirs (in three volumes, totaling more than six hundred pages, she got as far as her marriage to Wilson when she was twenty-six). But, unfortunately, it was her legal battle with Lillian Hellman that dominated much of the last decade of her life. The enmity between Hellman and McCarthy went all the way back to dinner-party disagreements over the Spanish Civil War and to the famous Waldorf conference of 1949 (the one McCarthy had crashed more or less on a lark with Lowell and Hardwick)—and probably farther back than that. Hellman was a Stalinist, McCarthy was an anti-Stalinist; both were powerful women with many influential friends and lovers; both of them wrote, among many other works, memoirs of their political involvements in the 1930s. They had both good reasons and bad reasons for hating each other—jealousy, professional rivalry, political and social antagonism—and no reason at all aside from the pure mean pleasure of vituperation. But their shared contempt, however heartfelt, would no doubt have remained in the realm of cocktail party sniping had McCarthy not opened her mouth to talk-show host Dick Cavett. McCarthy, with some prodding from Cavett, declared in front of the television camera that Hellman was a "dishonest writer" and that "every word she writes is a lie, including 'and' and 'the.' " Two weeks after the show aired in January 1980, Hellman sued for libel, demanding $2.25 million—$1.75 million for "mental pain and anguish" and injuries suffered "in her profession" and $500,000 for punitive damages.

The lawsuit would have ruined McCarthy financially, even if she had won it, for the fees involved in moving a libel suit through the legal system into trial are enormous. Financial ruin, and every other kind of ruin, was exactly what Hellman had in mind. Happily for McCarthy, the business ended in June 1984, when Hellman died on Martha's Vineyard.

McCarthy faded off the scene after the Hellman suit. Though she was writing and lecturing and "keeping up" as she had always done, her audience and her "clout" had diminished. She had made her strongest mark in the 1940s and 1950s—the frank scandals of *The Company She Keeps,* the vivid revelations of *Memories of a Catholic Girlhood,* the wide-ranging insights of the books on Florence and Venice. The uproar over *The Group* burned out fairly quickly. Her Vietnam pieces failed to attract much attention. By the 1980s, Mary McCarthy no longer "mattered" in the urgent way she once had. Reviews for her final collections were quiet and disappointing. *The New Yorker* editors misplaced her memoir of the marriage to Wilson and then declined to publish it.

McCarthy kept at it anyway, working as hard as ever in her last years. She had the solace of a good marriage, at last, to Jim West, a lovely apartment in Paris, and the grand house on Castine's Main Street that West had bought, on a tip from Robert Lowell, in 1967. Castine, and the deaths of so many of their common friends, brought Hardwick and McCarthy closer together. Hardwick had been summering in Castine since the 1950s, and she remained loyal to the serene, white-clapboard seaside town even after Lowell, who adored it and wrote many of his finest poems there, left her. After the divorce Hardwick ended up with the Castine property, which included a rambling old house on the town common and a barn on the shore where Lowell used to work (the property was actually in Hardwick's name even when they were married; Lowell's beloved cousin Harriet, who had originally owned it, had passed it down to Hardwick on the assumption that she was the more practical of the two). With Lowell gone, Hardwick decided to sell the house and use the proceeds to expand and remodel the barn. So now she had "her" Castine, and it was there that Lowell went to spend his final summer.

Hardwick had always had her differences with McCarthy, but she came to rely on her presence in Castine—the wonderful food, the flow of guests from all over the world, the picnics, the gossip. As survivors of the old crowd, they were often paired at awards ceremonies and literary banquets. "I was always being called upon to introduce her," Hardwick says today. "At her funeral I was tempted to say, 'This is my last introduction of Mary McCarthy.' " McCarthy's death followed a siege of illnesses—breast cancer, trouble with her heart, emphysema, arthritis affecting her spine. She had fought and recovered from each of these, but lung cancer overpowered her in October 1989. She died in New York Hospital, where Wilson had committed her for a nervous breakdown all those years ago and where their son had been born. McCarthy asked to be buried in Castine, in "the graveyard [that] shelves on the town" that Lowell wrote of in his haunting poem "Skunk Hour."

Diana Trilling had tangled memorably with both McCarthy and Hellman, and it must have pleased her to outlive them both—for at least she got the last word in. She died in October 1996 at the age of ninety-one. Diana's husband, Lionel, had died in 1975, and for her last twenty-one years she had lived alone in their Claremont Avenue apartment near Columbia University, writing, arguing, bearing the flame of her husband's reputation, reviewing her peers, and interpreting the past they had shared. She spoke of missing Lionel "hour by hour, minute by minute," and she never remarried.

Diana Trilling's greatest moment of fame, outside the confines of the *PR* world, came in 1981, when she published a book about Jean Harris, the headmistress of a posh girls' private school who was convicted of the murder of her lover, Herbert Tarnower, the so-called Scarsdale Diet doctor. *Mrs. Harris: The Death of the Scarsdale Diet Doctor* received spectacularly mixed reviews, with some critics praising Trilling as a shrewd, keen-eyed journalist while others raged against her huffy, snobbish, pretentious moralism. Trilling herself noted that feminism played a role in her initial interest in Jean Harris: like many other women, Trilling saw Harris as the victim of an arrogant, overbearing, sexually predatory male, a victim who finally summoned the will and courage to take revenge. But during the course of the trial, Trilling radically changed her mind, and in the end she concluded that Mrs. Harris existed on the same lowly moral and esthetic plane as the man she was convicted of killing and that neither of them was worthy of much sympathy or pity. Far from being a feminist heroine, Jean Harris was in Trilling's view a symptom of America's social and cultural decline.

Diana Trilling's memoir of her marriage, *The Beginning of the Journey,* published three years before her death, stirred up even fiercer debate, especially among survivors of the *PR* circle. In austere, unadorned prose, Trilling described what it felt like to be a woman and a wife in that pugnacious male world, how hard it was to break out of the role of "Lionel Trilling's wife" and establish her own voice and authority, how she and Lionel sorted out, often unconsciously or tacitly, the issues of gender roles, division of labor, and precedence in their marriage. "Actually, with my upbringing I had to be married to a man who was more successful than I," she writes at one point. "I should not have known how to manage if the scales had been tipped differently. . . . I was reared to curb my energies. If we can say that I was born with ten units of personal power, I never used more than five. What would have happened to my marriage if I had used all ten, I obviously cannot know. But I surmise that the marriage would not have endured as it did." Trilling deliberately went about exposing the darker side of herself, her marriage, and her husband in order to correct the common perception of Lionel Trilling as an urbane, elegant, controlled, rather detached intellectual—and for this she received many slaps. But far sharper attacks came from fellow intellectuals with whom she had settled old scores, picked old bones, or dished old dirt. Midge Decter, a former Trilling friend and member of the *PR* circle who had turned, like her husband, Norman Podhoretz, into an outspoken neoconservative, took Trilling to task for writing a "heavily gloomy book . . . almost thrilling in its obtuseness." Decter also detected a "lurking . . . contemporary feminist subtext" in which Diana arrogantly tried to muscle her husband aside and put herself forward as "the braver and more honest" of the pair.

There is no question that Mary McCarthy and Hannah Arendt would have hated the book for the same reason—as well as more personal reasons including the highly unflattering vignettes of them. The idea of Diana Trilling standing up and *speaking for* their generation was repugnant to her peers, for whatever reason or combination of reasons. But speak she did, with candor and clarity. She closed the book with a moving, unflinching elegy of the "strange difficult ungenerous unreliable unkind and not always honest people who created the world in which Lionel and I shared": "The New York intellectuals had their moment in history and it has passed. . . . They had no gods, no protectorates or sacred constituencies. They were a small, geographically concentrated group, but if they did nothing else, they kept the general culture of the country in balance. It is no longer in balance." None of them, living or dead, would disagree.

As it turned out, Hardwick's memorial at McCarthy's funeral was not her last introduction, for she rose to the task yet again when she wrote the foreword to the posthumous *Intellectual Memoirs* in 1991. Hardwick, whom McCarthy had criticized in a letter for her overindulgence in rhetorical flourishes ("too many organ-stops out and mounting cadences"), concludes her essay on a plain, quietly personal note:

> I would have liked Mary to live on and on, irreplaceable spirit and friend that she was; even though I must express some relief that her memoirs did not proceed to me and my life, to be looked at with her smiling precision and daunting determination on accuracy. She had her say, but I never knew anyone who gave so much pleasure to those around her. Her wit, great learning, her gardening, her blueberry pancakes, beautiful houses. None of that would be of more than passing interest if it were not that she worked as a master of the art of writing every day of her life. How it was done, I do not know.

It's fitting that Hardwick should have the last word, for she is the last of them, alive and well in her eighties, living, as she has done for nearly four decades now, on New York's West Sixty-seventh Street. Her life, judging by externals, has changed little. She still publishes occasional reviews and essays in *The New York Review of Books*, which still lists her on the masthead as "advisory editor." She never remarried. Hardwick's relief that Mary McCarthy's memoirs "did not proceed to me and my life" is characteristic—for she has never liked to see her life exposed, with precision and accuracy, in memoirs or biographies. But what a volume she could write if she were willing to "have her say."

"How it was done, I do not know," Hardwick concludes her farewell essay about McCarthy, a touch disingenuously perhaps. For Hardwick has always known far more than she was willing to say.

Notes

▨ FOR EACH chapter I have included a brief accounting of the sources I found most useful or relevant. I have footnoted only the most important, lengthy, or controversial interviews or quoted passages.

The bibliography on page 303 includes complete citations of all the books referred to below, as well as lists of the major works by each figure in this book.

INTRODUCTION

For background on the mores, politics, tribal rites, and peculiar preoccupations of this circle, I drew on Diana Trilling's *The Beginning of the Journey,* Mary McCarthy's *Intellectual Memoirs,* Alfred Kazin's *Starting Out in the Thirties* and *New York Jew,* William Barrett's *The Truants,* William Phillips's *A Partisan View,* Lionel Abel's *The Intellectual Follies,* Norman Podhoretz's *Ex-Friends,* Alan M. Wald's *The New York Intellectuals: The Rise and Decline of the Anti-Stalinist Left from the 1930s to the 1980s,* Terry A. Cooney's *The Rise of the New York Intellectuals,* and

Alexander Bloom's *Prodigal Sons: The New York Intellectuals and Their World*. Elizabeth Hardwick's collection *A View of My Own: Essays in Literature and Society* is also illuminating throughout.

Page

17   "Men writers write": Anthea Disney, "A Heaven Without God," *Sunday Observer,* August 5, 1979.

17   "Feminism had not emerged": Author interview with Arthur Schlesinger, Jr., New York, N.Y., November 7, 1997.

18   "Mary McCarthy led a life": Author telephone interview with Barbara Epstein, November 13, 1997.

18   "People with a real gift": Author interview with Elizabeth Hardwick, Castine, Maine, July 15, 1997.

18   "We didn't need feminists": Author interview with William Phillips, New York, N.Y., November 11, 1997.

18   "With women in that crowd": Author interview with Jason Epstein, New York, N.Y., November 13, 1995.

21   "In order for a genius": Dawn Powell, journals, published in *The New Yorker,* July 26 and July 3, 1995, p. 109.

23   As she boasts: Mary McCarthy, *Intellectual Memoirs* (New York: Harcourt Brace Jovanovich, 1992), p. 62.

26   "They crossed the line": Author interview with Diana Trilling, New York, N.Y., November 14, 1995.

29   In her brilliant: Jean Stafford, "Children Are Bored on Sunday," in *The Collected Stories of Jean Stafford* (Austin: University of Texas Press, 1993), pp. 374–375.

CHAPTER ONE: *Partisan Review* REBORN

In writing about the young Philip Rahv and the rebirth of *Partisan Review,* I relied on Mary McCarthy's memorial essay, "Philip Rahv 1908—1973," originally published in *The New York Times Book Review* on February 17, 1974, and reprinted in her *Occasional Prose;* Irving Howe's "Philip Rahv: A Memoir," published in *The American Scholar* in Autumn, 1979; Diana Trilling's *The Beginning of the Journey;* William Barrett's *The Truants;* and Alfred Kazin's *Starting Out in the Thirties.* I gained more intimate glimpses of Rahv and McCarthy from conversations with Lionel Abel, Elizabeth Hardwick, Jason Epstein, William Phillips, and Diana Trilling. Arthur Schlesinger, Jr. wrote a brief and vivid account of his friendship with Mary McCarthy, reprinted in *Twenty-four Ways of Looking at Mary McCarthy: The Writer and Her Work,* edited by Eve Stwertka and Margo Viscusi. McCarthy's *Memories of a Catholic Girlhood* provides a fascinating, if not altogether reliable, account of her childhood. Scenes from her college days and early career in New York also turn up in her novels *The Company She Keeps* and *The Group.*

For background, dates, factual information, and many useful details and insights about McCarthy, I turned to the three major biographies: Carol Brightman's *Writing Dangerously: Mary McCarthy and Her World,* Doris Grumbach's *The Company She Kept,* and Carol Gelderman's *Mary McCarthy: A Life.* Carol Brightman elaborated patiently on several points during a couple of phone conversations with me.

Page

40   "Mary McCarthy was": Quoted in Carol Brightman, *Writing Dangerously: Mary McCarthy and Her World* (San Diego: Harcourt Brace & Company, 1992), p. 150.

40   "We polarized each other": Mary McCarthy, *Intellectual Memoirs: New York 1936–1938* (San Diego: Harcourt Brace Jovanovich, 1992), pp. 68–69.

43   "It was getting": Ibid., pp. 62–63.

43   "In her fiction": Elizabeth Hardwick, "Mary McCarthy," in *A View of My Own: Essays in Literature and Society* (New York: Farrar, Straus and Cudahy, 1962), pp. 35–36.

44   "To enter a man's world": William Barrett, *The Truants: Adventures Among the Intellectuals* (Garden City, N.Y.: Anchor Press, 1982), p. 67.

44   "I remained, as the *Partisan Review*": Quoted in Carol Gelderman, *Mary McCarthy: A Life* (New York: St. Martin's Press, 1988), p. 81.

46   "In the actual conduct": Diana Trilling, *The Beginning of the Journey: The Marriage of Diana and Lionel Trilling* (New York: Harcourt Brace & Company, 1993), p. 21.

47   "[I]f she had felt safe": Mary McCarthy, "The Man in the Brooks Brothers Shirt," in *The Company She Keeps* (San Diego: Harcourt Brace & Company, 1970), pp. 111–112.

CHAPTER TWO: THE SOUTHERN BRANCH

For background on Allen Tate and Caroline Gordon, I used the following books: *Allen Tate: A Recollection* by Walter Sullivan, *Allen Tate: A Literary Biography* by Radcliffe Squires, *Memoirs and Opinions* by Allen Tate, *Close Connections* by Ann Waldron, *Caroline Gordon* by Veronica A. Makowsky, *The Years of Our Friendship* by William Doreski, and *Friendship and Sympathy* by Rosemary M. Magee. Ann Waldron also shared many insights and observations in the course of phone interviews. Robert Lowell's "Visiting the Tates," reprinted in his *Collected Prose,* provided many details about that famous summer at Benfolly. For accounts of the Fugitive and Agrarian movements, I found Paul K. Conkin's *The Southern Agrarians* and Alexander Karanikas's *Tillers of a Myth: Southern Agrarians as Social and Literary Critics* most helpful. Eileen Simpson provides memorable sketches of Tate and Gordon, as well as Robert Lowell and Jean Stafford, in her memoir *Poets in Their Youth,* and she furnished many more details and insights during our conversation in New York.

Robert Lowell and Jean Stafford have both been well served by biographers. Ian Hamilton's *Robert Lowell,* the first biography, is still invaluable; Paul Mariani adds a good deal of interesting new information in his *Lost Puritan: A Life of Robert Lowell. The Interior Castle* by Ann Hulbert is the best biography of Jean Stafford and offers a shrewd assessment of the Stafford-Lowell union. Both Hulbert and Mariani answered my questions during phone conversations. Stafford's college friends Paul and Dorothy Thompson furnished a useful introduction to their correspondence with Stafford housed in the archives of the University of Colorado. The most valuable details about Lowell and Stafford and their stormy courtship came from my interviews with their surviving friends: Frank Parker, Blair Clark, Cecile Starr, James Robert Hightower, and Robert Berueffy. Peter Davison includes sketches of the young Lowell and Stafford in his charming book *The Fading Smile.*

Page

57   Gordon fomented a bit: Quoted in Jeffrey Meyers, *Edmund Wilson: A Biography* (New York: Houghton Mifflin, 1995), p. 138.

CHAPTER THREE: SEVEN YEARS OF HELL

My information on the Wilson-McCarthy marriage came from the McCarthy biographies cited above, as well as *Edmund Wilson: A Biography* by Jeffrey Meyers and *Near the Magician* by Rosalind Wilson. McCarthy herself wrote repeatedly of the marriage in memoir and fiction, notably in her novel *A Charmed Life,* in the short stories "Ghostly Father, I Confess" and "The Weeds," and in her *Intellectual Memoirs.* Interviews and correspondence with Lewis Dabney, Reuel Wilson, Jason Epstein, Daniel Aaron, Mary Meigs, and Elizabeth Hardwick were extremely helpful.

For background on the politics of the day, I relied on *Literature at the Barricades: The American Writer in the 1930s,* edited by Ralph F. Bogardus and Fred Hobson; Daniel Aaron's *Writers on the Left;* Gregory D. Sumner's *Dwight Macdonald and the* politics *Circle;* and *Up from Communism* by John P. Diggins. Wilson's *To the Finland Station* conveys the sense of excitement that Marxist ideology generated at that time, as do the essays and editorials Philip Rahv wrote in these years, some of the best of which have been collected in *Essays on Literature and Politics, 1932–1972.*

Page

80   "As a child of the 1920s": Arthur Schlesinger Jr., "Remembrances of an Old Friend," in Eve Stwertka and Margo Viscusi, eds., *Twenty-four Ways of Looking at Mary McCarthy: The Writer and Her Work* (Westport, Conn.: Greenwood Press, 1996), p. 202.

80   "Life and people here": Letter from Edmund Wilson to Allen Tate, March 22, 1932, in Elena Wilson, ed., *Letters on Literature and Politics* (New York: Farrar, Straus and Giroux, 1977), p. 225.

83   "Under cover of this": James T. Farrell, "The End of a Literary Decade," in Ralph F. Bogardus and Fred Hobson, eds. *Literature at the Barricades: The American Writer in the 1930s* (University, Ala.: The University of Alabama Press, 1982), p. 208.

83   "In no other Western": Irving Howe, "The Thirties in Retrospect," in Bogardus and Hobson, p. 24.

85   "There was the class crime": Mary McCarthy, *The Company She Keeps,* pp. 260–261.

89   When he learned: Edmund Wilson to Allen Tate, quoted in Meyers, p. 139.

90   McCarthy laid it out: Gelderman, p. 91.

90   In her 1988 reconstruction: Brightman, p. 174.

92   His daughter Rosalind: Rosalind Wilson, *Near the Magician: A Memoir of My Father, Edmund Wilson* (New York: Grove Weidenfeld, 1989), pp. 81, 114.

92   Judith *(screaming):* Edmund Wilson, *The Little Blue Light: A Play*

in Three Acts (New York: Farrar, Straus 1950), p. 81.

92   Wilson scholar Lewis Dabney: Author telephone interview with Lewis Dabney, February 10, 1996.

93   "You oughtn't to be": Quoted in Brightman, p. 177.

CHAPTER FOUR: COUNTRY WIVES

Jean Stafford's voluminous, undated letters to James Robert Hightower, archived at the Jean Stafford Collection, Norlin Library, University of Colorado at Boulder, were a crucial source of information on the events leading up to her marriage to Lowell. Hightower himself, along with Blair Clark, Robert Berueffy, and Frank Parker, supplied me with many details. I drew on Ann Hulbert's *The Interior Castle* as well as telephone interviews and correspondence with Cecile Starr and Patrick Quinn for the early years of the Lowell-Stafford marriage. *My First Cousin Once Removed,* a memoir by Lowell's cousin Sarah Payne Stuart, recounts the reaction of Lowell's mother's family to the Stafford marriage. Eileen Simpson offers some memorable scenes from the marriage in her *Poets in Their Youth.* Stafford's fiction, especially *Boston Adventure, The Mountain Lion,* and "A Country Love Story," and the poems Lowell collected in *Land of Unlikeness* and *Lord Weary's Castle* also yield coded insights into their lives and the state of their marriage.

Page

117   "She had to start": Ian Hamilton, *Robert Lowell: A Biography* (New York: Random House, 1982), p. 80.

117   Blair Clark confirmed: Author interview with Blair Clark, New York City, July 26, 1996.

CHAPTER FIVE: THE WAR

For the discussion of Dwight Macdonald's opposition to the United States' involvement in World War II and his clash with the *PR* circle, I drew on Michael Wreszin's *A Rebel in Defense of Tradition: The Life and Politics of Dwight Macdonald* and *Dwight Macdonald and the politics Circle* by Gregory D. Sumner. Lionel Abel's *Intellectual Follies* and Alfred Kazin's *New York Jew* also contain illuminating passages on the attitudes and awareness of New York intellectuals in wartime.

William Alfred, Blair Clark, Frank Parker, Elizabeth Hardwick, and

Jonathan Raban offered their own insights into Robert Lowell's politics and fielded questions about his opposition to the war. For details about Lowell and Stafford's relationship during the war, I relied on Stafford's letters to Peter and Eleanor Taylor, archived with the Peter Taylor Papers at the Jean and Alexander Heard Library, Special Collections, Vanderbilt University.

Elisabeth Young-Bruehl's biography *Hannah Arendt: For Love of the World* provides an admirable introduction to her life and worth, and Young-Bruehl helped me clarify many points in the course of two telephone interviews. I also found *Hannah Arendt* by Derwent May useful in providing a brief overview of her career. Arendt's friend and literary executor Lotte Kohler and her friend Jerome Kohn also answered many questions during long conversations. Alfred Kazin wrote vividly of Arendt in several books, including *A Lifetime Burning in Every Moment, Writing Was Everything,* and *New York Jew.* William Phillips included a portrait of Arendt in his memoir *A Partisan View,* and William Barrett wrote of her briefly in his memoir *The Truants.* Kazin shared a few pithy comments about Arendt in a very brief telephone interview not long before his death. Diana Trilling, Lionel Abel, and William Phillips also spoke to me about Arendt during our interviews in New York.

I found Amos Elon's essay in *The New York Review of Books,* "The Case of Hannah Arendt" (November 6, 1997), extremely helpful in understanding Arendt as a writer and a woman of her time, and Claudia Roth Pierpont wrote insightfully of Arendt and McCarthy in her review of their correspondence in *The New Yorker* ("Hearts and Minds," March 20, 1995). Randall Jarrell's satirical novel *Pictures from an Institution* contains an amusing fictionalized portrait of Arendt and Blücher. And of course Mary McCarthy's eulogy, "Saying Good-by to Hannah," reprinted in *The New York Review of Books* on January 22, 1976, is wonderfully warm and revealing about Arendt in every way. Most illuminating of all in understanding Arendt as a woman and a friend was the correspondence between her and McCarthy, which Carol Brightman has collected and edited in the volume *Between Friends: The Correspondence of Hannah Arendt and Mary McCarthy 1949–1975.* Brightman's introduction is superb in its clarity and thoughtful appreciation of what these two women shared.

Page

150   "[A]lways wound up": Alfred Kazin, *A Lifetime Burning in Every*

Moment: From the Journals of Alfred Kazin (New York: Harper-Collins, 1996), p. 107.

154 "[T]his specialist": Alfred Kazin, *New York Jew* (New York: Alfred A. Knopf, 1978), pp. 195–196.

155 "After he left Berlin": Elisabeth Young-Bruehl, *Hannah Arendt: For Love of the World* (New Haven, Conn.: Yale University Press, 1982), pp. 135–136.

156 "[T]here was never": William Phillips, *A Partisan View* (New York: Stein and Day, 1983), p. 105.

157 "What luck": Kazin, *A Lifetime Burning,* pp. 106, 107, 109.

159 "They were vehemently": Kazin, *New York Jew,* p. 198.

CHAPTER SIX: DIVORCES

For the Wilson-McCarthy divorce, I relied on the biographies of Wilson and McCarthy cited above as well as conversations and correspondence with Margo Viscusi, Arthur Schlesinger, Jr., Michael Macdonald (whose unpublished essay "The Admirable Minotaur of Money Hill" was also illuminating), Reuel Wilson, and Lewis Dabney.

The best source of information about the Lowell-Stafford breakup is the harrowing letters Stafford wrote to Lowell and to Peter and Eleanor Taylor from Payne Whitney. The letters to Lowell are at Harvard's Houghton Library, and the letters to the Taylors are at the Jean and Alexander Heard Library, Special Collections, Vanderbilt University. Stafford's letters to Paul and Dorothy Thompson and to Cecile Starr, archived at the Jean Stafford Collection, Norlin Library of the University of Colorado, and Lowell's letters to Peter Taylor, archived at Vanderbilt, were also useful. Stafford's story "An Influx of Poets," published in *The New Yorker* on November 6, 1978, contains a hilarious semifictional account of the marriage and divorce. Eileen Simpson writes at length about the Lowells' final summer together in *Poets in Their Youth*. The biographies cited above contain much useful information. I also drew on interviews with Blair Clark, Frank Parker, Cecile Starr, Ann Hulbert, and Eileen Simpson.

Stafford's "A Country Love Story" and *The Mountain Lion* and Lowell's *Lord Weary's Castle, The Mills of the Kavanaughs,* and the poem "The Old Flame" are highly revealing of their creators' psyches during the period when their marriage broke up.

Ann Waldron's biography of Caroline Gordon and several conversations with her were my primary source of information on the Gordon-Tate divorce. I also drew on correspondence between the Tates and the Lowells: letters written to the Tates by Lowell and Stafford are archived at Princeton (the Gordon and Tate papers); letters written by Gordon and Tate to Lowell and Stafford are at the McFarlin Library, University of Oklahoma at Tulsa, and the Jean Stafford Collection at the University of Colorado.

Page

164 "Everybody had gone": Quoted in Brightman, p. 250.

165 "How many women had": Mary McCarthy, "The Weeds," in *Cast a Cold Eye* (San Diego: Harcourt Brace Jovanovich, 1978), pp. 10–11.

186 The divorce was slow: Blair Clark told me in the course of my July 26, 1996, interview with him that Lowell got the money from the sale of the Maine house in the divorce settlement, but I could find no other corroboration of this claim.

CHAPTER SEVEN: THE TRANQUILIZED FIFTIES: INSANITY AND LIBERALISM

For my portrait of Elizabeth Hardwick, I drew on an interview she granted me in Castine, Maine, in July 1997, as well as conversations with William Alfred, Frank Parker, Blair Clark, Jason Epstein, William Phillips, Lionel Abel, Paul Mariani, and Diana Trilling. Phillips wrote briefly of Hardwick in *A Partisan View,* and Hilton Als published a useful profile in *The New Yorker* ("A Singular Woman," July 13, 1998). I also used Hardwick's letters to Mary McCarthy (at Vassar College Library Special Collections) and McCarthy's letters to Hardwick (at the Harry Ransom Humanities Research Center at the University of Texas at Austin). Hardwick has deposited many papers at the Ransom Center, and I was able to read a number of published and unpublished interviews with her there as well as her valuable memo of corrections to Ian Hamilton's biography of Lowell. Her interview with Darryl Pinckney, published in *Paris Review,* Number 96, 1985, is especially candid. I also drew heavily on Hardwick's essays, collected in *A View of My Own, Seduction and Betrayal,* and *Bartleby in Manhattan,* and her novel *Sleepless Nights.*

My discussion of the emergence of liberal anticommunism is based on interviews with Diana Trilling and William Phillips, as well as essays and editorials by Philip Rahv published in *Essays on Literature and Politics, 1932–1972*. Of the many books about this chapter of our political and cultural history, I found Alan M. Wald's *The New York Intellectuals,* John P. Diggins's *Up from Communism,* Diana Trilling's *The Beginning of the Journey,* and Norman Podhoretz's *Ex-Friends* the most useful.

The biographies of Lowell cited above contain complete portraits of his manic episodes and repeated institutionalizations. I also found his letters to Elizabeth Bishop, archived at the Vassar College Library Special Collections, illuminating. Lowell's letters to Hardwick, at the Ransom Center, and his letters to Peter Taylor, at Vanderbilt, contain insights into the couple's extended stay in Europe in the early 1950s. Hardwick's letters to Mary McCarthy at Vassar and to her friend Susan Turner at the Ransom Center are extraordinarily candid.

For my discussion of Mary McCarthy in this chapter, I relied on the biographies cited above as well as essays by Arthur Schlesinger, Jr. and Stacey Lee Donohue published in *Twenty-four Ways of Looking at Mary McCarthy,* cited above. Interviews with Hardwick, Margo Viscusi, William Phillips, Lionel Abel, Carol Brightman, and Schlesinger supplied details.

Young-Bruehl's biography of Hannah Arendt, cited above, gives a useful portrait of the flowering of the McCarthy-Arendt friendship, as does Carol Brightman's introduction to *Between Friends,* the indispensable collection of their correspondence. I also drew on Kazin's *A Lifetime Burning in Every Moment.* Arendt's *The Origins of Totalitarianism* is the seminal work of this period of intellectual history.

Page

195   FBI agents appeared: Author interview with Elizabeth Hardwick, Castine, Maine, July 15, 1997.

198   As Alan M. Wald: Alan M. Wald, *The New York Intellectuals: The Rise and Decline of the Anti-Stalinist Left from the 1930s to the 1980s* (Chapel Hill: University of North Carolina Press, 1987), pp. 12, 168.

199   "Our prosperous, unique": Elizabeth Hardwick, 1961 postscript to "Riesman Considered" in *A View of My Own: Essays in Literature and Society* (New York: Farrar, Straus and Cudahy, 1962), p. 126.

201   She told an interviewer: Anthea Disney, "A Heaven Without God," in *The Sunday Observer* (London), August 5, 1979.

209   "this business of Cal's": Elizabeth Hardwick to Mary McCarthy,

April 3, 1961, Vassar College Special Collections.

210   She wrote to a friend: Elizabeth Hardwick to Susan Turner, July 7, 1954, Harry Ransom Humanities Research Center, University of Texas at Austin.

211   "Are women 'the equal' ": Elizabeth Hardwick, "The Subjection of Women," in *A View of My Own,* p. 176.

213   "Elizabeth has just finished": Robert Lowell to Peter Taylor, March 25, 1953, Vanderbilt University.

215   "I'm now convinced": Mary McCarthy to Elizabeth Hardwick, October 27, 1953, Harry Ransom Humanities Research Center, University of Texas at Austin.

218   "Into the charged": Alan Wald, *The New York Intellectuals: The Rise and Decline of the Anti-Stalinist Left from the 1930s to the 1980s* (Chapel Hill: University of North Carolina Press, 1987), p. 269.

219   "Heinrich liked women": Telephone interview with Lotte Kohler, March 23, 1998.

220   Trilling also claimed: Author interview with Diana Trilling, New York, N.Y., November 14, 1995.

221   "Diana had been writing": Alfred Kazin, *New York Jew,* pp. 45–46.

221   "Women in particular": Diana Trilling, *The Beginning of the Journey,* p. 351.

CHAPTER EIGHT: THE EARLY 1960S: FIRESTORMS

Paul Mariani's biography of Lowell provided background and details about the early days of the Lowell-Hardwick marriage and the couple's move to Boston. Peter Davison's *The Fading Smile* is an invaluable examination of the Boston poetry "scene" in the 1950s and early 1960s. Lowell's *Life Studies* and *For the Union Dead* were my primary guides to his psyche during this period.

Jason Epstein, Blair Clark, and Barbara Epstein provided details on the founding of *The New York Review of Books* during my interviews with them. I relied on Philip Nobile's *Intellectual Skywriting: Literary Politics and the New York Review of Books* for background.

Hannah Arendt's *Eichmann in Jerusalem* is still a highly controversial book and merits reconsideration. I drew on the McCarthy-Arendt correspondence in describing the furor that erupted over its publication and how Arendt reacted. Interviews with Lotte Kohler, Elisabeth Young-Bruehl, Diana Trilling, William Phillips, Lionel Abel, and Jerome Kohn shed new light. I found additional information in Lionel Abel's memoir *Intellectual Follies,* Norman Podhoretz's *Ex-Friends,* Amos Elon's essay "The Case of Hannah Arendt," and Alexander Bloom's *Prodigal Sons.*

For accounts of the Allen Ginsberg reading at Columbia, I relied on Diana Trilling's *The Beginning of the Journey,* a profile of Diana Trilling by Lis Harris published in *The New Yorker* on September 13, 1993, and David Lehman's *The Last Avant-Garde: The Making of the New York School of Poets. The Feminine Mystique* by Betty Friedan, published in 1963, makes very interesting reading in the company of *The Group* and *Eichmann in Jerusalem,* which appeared in the same year.

Page

230   "Every time the door opened": The details of this notorious cocktail party and the quotes from guests come from Peter Davison, *The Fading Smile,* pp. 275ff.

231   She laid waste impersonally: All the quotes come from Elizabeth Hardwick, "Boston," in *A View of My Own,* pp. 145, 150, 159.

235   But Mailer's review: Norman Mailer, "The Mary McCarthy Case," *The New York Review of Books,* October 17, 1963, p. 3.

236   "I think you have done": Robert Lowell to Mary McCarthy, August 7, 1963, Vassar College Special Collections.

237   She wrote McCarthy: Elizabeth Hardwick to Mary McCarthy, November 30, 1963, Vassar College Special Collections.

237   "Please give Elizabeth": Mary McCarthy to Robert Lowell, January 9, 1964, Houghton Library, Harvard University.

238   "If I am upset": *Between Friends,* pp. 155–156.

238   "I am afraid": Ibid., p. 156.

240   "Wherever Jews lived": Hannah Arendt, *Eichmann in Jerusalem: A Report on the Banality of Evil* (New York: Viking, 1963), pp. 111, 104.

241   McCarthy asserted, with some justification: Mary McCarthy, *Writing on the Wall* (New York: Harcourt, Brace & World, 1970), p. 55.

242   "That Eichmann:" Robert Lowell, letter to the editor, *The New York Times Book Review,* June 23, 1963, p. 5.

242   Arendt broke with the party: Arendt, *Eichmann in Jerusalem,* p. 9.

CHAPTER NINE: THE LATE 1960s: DISPERSAL

My material on Hannah Arendt's attitude toward the war in Vietnam and the radical New Left politics of the 1960s comes from the correspondence with McCarthy in *Between Friends* and from Young-Bruehl's biography, cited above.

Lowell's poetry collections of the late 1960s and 1970s—the various versions of *Notebook, For Lizzie and Harriet, History,* and *The Dolphin*—richly capture the spirit of the times as well as his own inner weather. Adrienne Rich's letters to Lowell and Hardwick, archived at Houghton Library and the Harry Ransom Humanities Research Center, offer a fascinating feminist perspective on the breakup of their marriage. Rich's *Diving into the Wreck* is a potent sign of the changing times.

Details about Lowell's final years come from interviews with Jonathan Raban, John Malcolm Brinnin, Helen Vendler, and Stanley Kunitz. Hardwick's correspondence with Mary McCarthy at Vassar also shed some light. I relied on Brightman's biography and Joan Mellen's *Hellman and Hammett* for details about McCarthy's final years and the lawsuit with Lillian Hellman.

Page

248   "Hannah asked me": Author telephone interview with Lotte Kohler, March 23, 1998.

255   "Negros demand": *Between Friends,* pp. 229–230.

255   "*all* utterances": *Between Friends,* pp. 236–237.

256   "One felt assaulted": Phillips, *A Partisan View,* pp. 252, 18.

257   You can hear the mood: Elizabeth Hardwick to Mary McCarthy, May 3, 1968, and February 9, 1970, Vassar College Library Special Collections.

258   "[W]hat is disclosed": *Between Friends,* p. 204.

261   "To me, his finding": *Between Friends,* p. 258.

262   "She was a wonderful": Author interview with Elizabeth Hardwick, Castine, Maine, July 15, 1997.

263   She now felt "more as men feel": Elizabeth Hardwick to Susan Turner, April 1, 1971, Harry Ransom Humanities Research Center, University of Texas at Austin.

263   "There is always something": Elizabeth Hardwick, *Seduction and Betrayal* (New York: Random House, 1974), pp. 79–80.

264   "In the case of artists": Ibid., p. 102.

264   "[S]lick persons create": Ibid., p. 99.

265   "I myself do not think": Ibid., p. 121.

265   Lowell's shrewdest insight: All quotes are from Robert Lowell,

"Sylvia Plath's *Ariel,*" reprinted in Robert Giroux, ed., *Robert Lowell: Collected Prose* (New York: Farrar, Straus and Giroux, 1987), pp. 122–125.

270   "The inner changes": Elizabeth Hardwick, "Domestic Manners," in *Bartleby in Manhattan* (New York: Random House, 1983), pp. 96–97.

276   "I must admit": *Between Friends,* p. 352.

276   "The task that had fallen": Mary McCarthy, "Saying Good-by to Hannah," *The New York Review of Books,* January 22, 1976, p. 8.

286   "Actually, with my upbringing": Diana Trilling, *The Beginning of the Journey,* p. 352.

287   "I would have liked": Elizabeth Hardwick, Foreword to *Intellectual Memoirs* by Mary McCarthy, pp. xxi–xxii

Bibliography

■ Major Works by the Principal Figures Discussed in the Text

Hannah Arendt
The Origins of Totalitarianism (New York: Harcourt, Brace & World, 1966; first published 1951).
Eichmann in Jerusalem: A Report on the Banality of Evil (New York: Viking, 1963).
Men in Dark Times (New York: Harcourt, Brace & World, 1968).
Rahel Varnhagen: The Life of a Jewish Woman, rev. ed. (New York: Harcourt Brace Jovanovich, 1974).
Between Friends: The Correspondence of Hannah Arendt and Mary McCarthy 1945–1975, ed. Carol Brightman (New York: Harcourt, Brace & Company, 1995).

Elizabeth Hardwick
The Ghostly Lover (New York: Harcourt Brace, 1945).

The Simple Truth (New York: Ecco Press, 1955).

A View of My Own: Essays in Literature and Society (New York: Farrar, Straus and Cudahy, 1962).

Seduction and Betrayal: Women and Literature (New York: Random House, 1974).

Sleepless Nights (New York: Random House, 1979).

Bartleby in Manhattan and Other Essays (New York: Random House, 1983).

ROBERT LOWELL

Land of Unlikeness (Cummington, Mass.: Cummington Press, 1943).

Life Studies and For the Union Dead (New York: The Noonday Press, 1964).

Notebook, 3rd ed., rev. and expanded (New York: Farrar, Straus & Giroux, 1970).

The Dolphin (New York: Farrar, Straus & Giroux, 1973).

History (New York: Farrar, Straus & Giroux, 1973).

For Lizzie and Harriet (New York: Farrar, Straus & Giroux, 1973).

Day by Day (New York: Farrar, Straus & Giroux, 1977).

Lord Weary's Castle and The Mills of the Kavanaughs (San Diego: A Harvest/HBJ Book, Harcourt Brace Jovanovich, 1979).

Collected Prose (New York: Farrar, Straus & Giroux, 1987).

MARY McCARTHY

The Company She Keeps (San Diego: Harcourt, Brace & Company, 1992; first published 1942).

The Oasis (New York: Random House, 1949).

Cast a Cold Eye (San Diego: Harcourt Brace Jovanovich, 1992; first published 1950).

The Groves of Academe (San Diego: Harcourt Brace Jovanovich, 1980; first published 1952).

A Charmed Life (New York: Harcourt, Brace and Company, 1955).

Memories of a Catholic Girlhood (New York: Harcourt Brace, 1957).

On the Contrary (New York: Farrar, Straus & Cudahy, 1961).

The Group (New York: Harcourt Brace & Company, 1963).

The Writing on the Wall and Other Literary Essays (New York: Harcourt, Brace & World, 1970).

Occasional Prose (New York: Harcourt Brace Jovanovich, 1985).

Intellectual Memoirs: New York 1936–1938 (San Diego: Harcourt

Brace Jovanovich, 1992).

PHILIP RAHV
Essays on Literature and Politics 1932–1972 (Boston: Houghton Mifflin, 1978).

JEAN STAFFORD
Boston Adventure (New York: Harcourt Brace Jovanovich, 1971).
The Mountain Lion (Austin: University of Texas Press, 1992).
The Collected Stories of Jean Stafford (Austin: University of Texas Press, 1993).

ALLEN TATE
The Fathers (Denver: Alan Swallow, 1960).
The Swimmers and Other Selected Poems (New York: Charles Scribner's Sons, 1970).
Memoirs and Opinions (Chicago: The Swallow Press, 1975).

DIANA TRILLING
The Beginning of the Journey: The Marriage of Diana and Lionel Trilling (New York: Harcourt Brace & Company, 1993).

EDMUND WILSON
Axel's Castle: A Study in the Imaginative Literature of 1870–1930 (New York: Scribner's, 1931).
The American Jitters: A Year of the Slump (New York: Scribner's, 1932).
To the Finland Station: A Study in the Writing and Acting of History (New York: Harcourt Brace, 1940).
The Wound and the Bow: Seven Studies in Literature (New York: Houghton Mifflin, 1941).
Memoirs of Hecate County (New York: Doubleday, 1946).
The Little Blue Light: A Play in Three Acts (New York: Farrar, Straus, 1950).
Letters on Literature and Politics, 1912–1972, edited by Elena Wilson (New York: Farrar, Straus & Giroux, 1977).
The Thirties: From Notebooks and Diaries of the Period, edited by Leon Edel (New York: Farrar, Straus & Giroux, 1980).
The Forties: From Notebooks and Diaries of the Period, ed. Leon Edel (New York: Farrar, Straus & Giroux, 1983).

■ BIOGRAPHIES AND CRITICAL STUDIES

HANNAH ARENDT
May, Derwent. *Hannah Arendt* (Harmondsworth, England: Penguin, 1986).

Young-Bruehl, Elisabeth. *Hannah Arendt: For Love of the World* (New Haven; Conn.: Yale University Press, 1982).

ROBERT LOWELL
Axelrod, Steven Gould. *Robert Lowell: Life and Art* (Princeton: Princeton University Press, 1978).

Axelrod, Steven Gould, and Helen Deese, eds. *Robert Lowell: Essays on the Poetry* (Cambridge, England: Cambridge University Press, 1986).

Hamilton, Ian. *Robert Lowell: A Biography* (New York: Random House, 1982).

Mariani, Paul. *Lost Puritan: A Life of Robert Lowell* (New York: Norton, 1994).

Meyers, Jeffrey. *Robert Lowell: Interviews and Memoirs* (Ann Arbor: University of Michigan Press, 1988).

CAROLINE GORDON
Makowsky, Veronica A. *Caroline Gordon* (New York: Oxford University Press, 1989).

Waldron, Ann. *Close Connections: Caroline Gordon and the Southern Renaissance* (New York: G. P. Putnam, 1987).

MARY MCCARTHY
Brightman, Carol. *Writing Dangerously: Mary McCarthy and Her World* (San Diego: Harcourt, Brace & Company, 1992).

Gelderman, Carol. *Mary McCarthy: A Life* (New York: St. Martin's Press, 1988).

Grumbach, Doris. *The Company She Kept* (New York: Coward-McCann, 1967).

Stwertka, Eve, and Margo Viscusi, eds. *Twenty-four Ways of Looking at Mary McCarthy: The Writer and Her Work* (Westport, Conn.: Greenwood Press, 1996).

JEAN STAFFORD
Hulbert, Ann. *The Interior Castle: The Art and Life of Jean Stafford*

(New York: Alfred A. Knopf, 1992).

ALLEN TATE

Doreski, William. *The Years of Our Friendship: Robert Lowell and Allen Tate* (Jackson: University Press of Mississippi, 1990).

Squires, Radcliffe. *Allen Tate: A Literary Biography* (New York: Pegasus, 1971).

Sullivan, Walter. *Allen Tate: A Recollection* (Baton Rouge: Louisiana State University, 1988).

EDMUND WILSON

Meyers, Jeffrey. *Edmund Wilson: A Biography* (Boston: Houghton Mifflin, 1995).

Wain, John. *An Edmund Wilson Celebration* (Oxford, England.: Phaidon Press, 1978).

Wilson, Rosalind. *Near the Magician: A Memoir of My Father* (New York: Grove, Weidenfeld, 1989).

MEMOIRS AND REMINISCENCES

Abel, Lionel. *The Intellectual Follies* (New York: Norton, 1984).

Barrett, William. *The Truants: Adventures Among the Intellectuals* (Garden City, N.Y.: Anchor Press, 1982).

Davison, Peter. *The Fading Smile* (New York: Alfred A. Knopf, 1994).

Kazin, Alfred. *A Lifetime Burning in Every Moment: From the Journals of Alfred Kazin* (New York: HarperCollins, 1996).

———. *New York Jew* (New York: Alfred A. Knopf, 1978).

———. *Starting Out in the Thirties* (Boston: Little, Brown, 1965).

———. *Writing Was Everything* (Cambridge, Mass., Harvard University Press, 1995).

Phillips, William. *A Partisan View: Five Decades of the Literary Life* (New York: Stein and Day, 1983).

Podhoretz, Norman. *Ex-Friends* (New York: The Free Press, 1999).

———. *Making It* (New York: Random House, 1967).

Simpson, Eileen. *Poets in Their Youth* (New York: Random House, 1982).

FUGITIVES AND AGRARIANS

Blotner, Joseph. *Robert Penn Warren: A Biography* (New York: Random House, 1997).

Conkin, Paul K. *The Southern Agrarians* (Knoxville: University of Tennessee Press, 1988).

Karanikas, Alexander. *Tillers of a Myth: Southern Agrarians as Social and Literary Critics* (Madison: University of Wisconsin Press, 1966).

Magee, Rosemary M., ed. *Friendship and Sympathy: Communities of Southern Women Writers* (Jackson: University Press of Mississippi, 1992).

THE NEW YORK INTELLECTUALS AND AMERICAN RADICAL POLITICS

Aaron, Daniel. *Writers on the Left: Episodes in American Literary Communism* (New York: Harcourt, Brace & World, 1961).

Bloom, Alexander. *Prodigal Sons: The New York Intellectuals and Their World* (New York: Oxford University Press, 1986).

Bogardus, Ralph R., and Fred Hobson, eds. *Literature at the Barricades: The American Writer in the 1930s* (University, Ala.: The University of Alabama Press, 1982).

Cooney, Terry A. *The Rise of the New York Intellectuals: Partisan Review and Its Circle* (Madison: University of Wisconsin Press, 1986).

Diggins, John P. *The American Left in the Twentieth Century* (New York: Harcourt Brace Jovanovich, 1973).

———. *Up from Communism* (New York: Harper & Row, 1975).

Jumonville, Neil. *Critical Crossings: The New York Intellectuals in Postwar America* (Berkeley: University of California Press, 1991).

Sumner, Gregory D. *Dwight Macdonald and the* politics *Circle* (Ithaca, N.Y.: Cornell University Press, 1996).

Wald, Alan M. *The New York Intellectuals: The Rise and Decline of the Anti-Stalinist Left from the 1930s to the 1980s* (Chapel Hill: University of North Carolina Press, 1987).

Wreszin, Michael. *A Rebel in Defense of Tradition: The Life and Politics of Dwight Macdonald* (New York: Basic Books, 1994).

Index